FOOD AND IDENTITY IN EARLY RABBINIC JUDAISM

Food often defines societies and even civilizations. Through particular commensality restrictions, groups form distinct identities: those with whom we eat ("Us") and those with whom we cannot eat ("Them"). This identity is enacted daily, turning the biological need to eat into a culturally significant activity. In this book, Jordan D. Rosenblum explores how food regulations and practices helped to construct the identity of early rabbinic Judaism. Bringing together the scholarship of rabbinics with that of food studies, this volume first examines the historical reality of food production and consumption in Roman-era Palestine. It then explores how early rabbinic food regulations created a distinct Jewish, male, and rabbinic identity. Rosenblum's work demonstrates how rabbinic food practices constructed an edible identity.

Jordan D. Rosenblum is Belzer Assistant Professor of Classical Judaism at the University of Wisconsin, Madison. He has contributed to the *Journal for the Study of Judaism*, *Jewish Quarterly Review*, and the *Journal of Jewish Studies*.

Food and Identity in Early Rabbinic Judaism

JORDAN D. ROSENBLUM
University of Wisconsin, Madison

CAMBRIDGE
UNIVERSITY PRESS

32 Avenue of the Americas, New York NY 10013-2473, USA

Cambridge University Press is part of the University of Cambridge.

It furthers the University's mission by disseminating knowledge in the pursuit of education, learning and research at the highest international levels of excellence.

www.cambridge.org
Information on this title: www.cambridge.org/9781107666436

© Jordan D. Rosenblum 2010

This publication is in copyright. Subject to statutory exception and to the provisions of relevant collective licensing agreements, no reproduction of any part may take place without the written permission of Cambridge University Press.

First published 2010
First paperback edition 2013

A catalogue record for this publication is available from the British Library

Library of Congress Cataloguing in Publication data

Rosenblum, Jordan, 1979–
Food and identity in early rabbinic Judaism / Jordan Rosenblum.
p. cm.
ISBN 978-0-521-19598-0 (hardback)
1. Jews – Dietary laws.   2. Jews – Food – History.   3. Jews – Identity.   4. Rabbinical literature – History and criticism.   I. Title.
BM710.R615   2010
296.7'309015 – dc22   2009047361

ISBN 978-0-521-19598-0 Hardback
ISBN 978-1-107-66643-6 Paperback

Cambridge University Press has no responsibility for the persistence or accuracy of URLs for external or third-party internet websites referred to in this publication, and does not guarantee that any content on such websites is, or will remain, accurate or appropriate.

For Valerie

Contents

Acknowledgments	page ix
Abbreviations	xiii
Introduction	1
"The Set Table": Organization and Structure	10
A Brief Introduction to the Tannaitic Corpus	13

1 Realia — 15
What Did They Eat? — 17
How Did They Obtain Their Food? — 22
How Did They Prepare Their Food? — 24
In What Manner Did They Eat Their Food? — 30
Realia: Conclusions — 33

2 Jewish Identity — 35
Pre-Tannaitic Evidence for Commensality Restrictions — 36
Food as Metonym/Food as Embodiment — 45
   The "Abominable Pig" — 48
   Manna — 58
   The Passover — 63
   The Laws of *Kashrut* — 68
   Food as Metonym/Food as Embodiment: Conclusions — 73
The Status of Food Correlates with the Status of Its Cook — 75
   Meat — 76
   Non-Meat Items — 81
   Conclusions — 89
Commensality as Idolatry — 91
Jewish Identity: Conclusions — 101

vii

3	**Jewish Male Identity**	103
	Preparing Food as (Re)Producing Male Identity	104
	Sharing the Kitchen with the *Ḥabēr* and the *'Am hā'Āreṣ*	117
	Preparing Food as (Re)Producing Male Identity:	
	Conclusions	120
	Women at the Tannaitic Table?	123
	"It Leads to Transgression": Commensality Among *Zābîm*	132
	Jewish Male Identity: Conclusions	135
4	**Jewish Male Rabbinic Identity**	138
	The Cuisine of the Rabbinic Jew	140
	Purity and Commensality	143
	Commensality between the *Ḥabēr* and the *'Am hā'Āreṣ*	146
	Purity and Commensality: Conclusions	153
	The Status of Food Correlates with the Status of Its Cook	154
	Reinterpreting Festival Observance	161
	Passover	162
	Sukkot	170
	The Sabbath	174
	Commensality and the Synagogue	178
	Jewish Male Rabbinic Identity: Conclusions	182
	Conclusion	185
Bibliography		193
Selected General Index		209
Index of Pre-Modern Sources		212
Selected Index of Modern Scholars		220

Acknowledgments

Like a good meal, scholarship is best when shared with others. Over the course of my time at various universities, I have been fortunate to enjoy the company of many people at both the seminar table and the dinner table. I am delighted to have the opportunity to thank several of them. To those whom space or memory limitations prevent me from acknowledging, I owe a home-cooked meal.

As this book began its life as a dissertation, I would first like to thank the members of my dissertation committee. My advisor, Michael Satlow, forced me to reconsider my assumptions and to probe deeper, often sending me back to the drawing board. What has emerged, I hope, is a much clearer argument that is a testament to his guidance. Ross Kraemer always made time for her "other Jordan." Sue Alcock offered me the encouragement I needed to endure the long process of getting the thoughts out of my head and onto paper.

Although I owe a debt of gratitude to many teachers, I would like to acknowledge three in particular. Bill Gilders and Saul Olyan are two mentors whom I am now proud to call friends. Seth Schwartz was instrumental in inspiring me to pursue both this profession and the topic of this book.

Several scholars have been generous with their time, especially Jonathan Brumberg-Kraus, David Kraemer, Susan Marks, Jon Schofer, and Susan Weingarten. David Freidenreich offered careful and insightful comments on an early draft of this manuscript. Our conversations have always pushed me to rethink, reformulate, and sharpen my ideas. Gregg Gardner served as a sounding board on both my work and my fantasy football team, and e-mailed me countless references.

Revisions of this manuscript were completed while enjoying the patronage of two world-class institutions. In the spring of 2009, I was a Starr Fellow at the Center for Jewish Studies at Harvard University. I thank the acting director, Bernard Septimus, and Shaye Cohen. The University of Wisconsin–Madison has offered, despite the winter temperatures, a warm environment in which to research and teach. In particular, I would like to thank Rachel Brenner, Michael Fox, Philip Hollander, Cynthia Miller, and Ron Troexel. Chris Dargis deserves mention for her help with various administrative matters. I am grateful to Kevin Mattison for his assistance in creating the index. I would also like to thank my students, who push me toward greater clarity in both my written and spoken words. I would be remiss if I did not acknowledge the help of my teaching assistants, Israel Haas, Chris Jones, and Jonathon Wiley, whose capable assistance allowed me to devote more time to research.

At Cambridge University Press, I would like to acknowledge the help of my editor, Beatrice Rehl, and her assistant, Amanda Smith.

Earlier versions of sections of Chapter 2 appeared in the following journals, whose editors I gratefully acknowledge for granting me permission to reprint them: "Kosher Olive Oil in Antiquity Reconsidered," *JSJ* 40/3 (2009): 356–365; "'Why Do You Refuse to Eat Pork?': Jews, Food, and Identity in Roman Palestine," *JQR* 100/1: 95–110; and "From Their Bread to Their Bed: Commensality, Intermarriage, and Idolatry in Tannaitic Literature," *JJS*: in press.

Eddie Ross and Michael Slater helped remind me that there is more to life than work. Daniel Ullucci and Steven Larson have been colleagues and friends, offering insightful, constructive, and occasionally humorous advice. Ross Wolfson and Stan Zipper have been my best friends since high school. We have shared many meals and memories, from late night trips to Long Island diners to pancakes in Atlanta and Rhode Island. Through it all, they have helped me to keep perspective. I am fortunate to have such friends.

Many family members have offered support. In particular, I would like to thank Aunt Elaine, Uncle Chuck (*z"l*), Uncle Rom, Aunt Debby, Avi, Bubbie (*z"l*), and Grandma Mina (*z"l*). Dad, Rose, and Michael have been supportive particularly in these last few years. Sarah Maine and Scott Sherratt have brightened many meals – both in Rhode Island and New York City. Ron and Eugenie Maine have opened their home and table to me. Ian Rosenblum deserves acknowledgment, if only for putting up with me as his younger brother. My mother and stepfather, Rona and Harold Blau, still worry that I do not eat enough. They have encouraged and supported me every step of the way.

    I dedicate this book to my wife, Valerie Maine. Val has, among many other things, helped me to translate French and Italian, listened to me perseverate about this project, cooked me amazing food, and provided timely support and comic relief. Whether strolling through the streets of Rome, Italy, or Snug Harbor, Rhode Island, Val is always both my literal and figurative compass. Thank you for constantly reminding me that meals are not only for the dead.

Abbreviations

AB	Anchor Bible
ABD	Anchor Bible Dictionary
ANRW	Aufstieg und Niedergang der römischen Welt
AJSR	*Association for Jewish Studies Review*
b.	*ben/bar* ("son" in Hebrew/Aramaic)
b.	Babylonian Talmud (*Bavli*)
BJS	Brown Judaic Studies
CD	*Damascus Document* (Cairo Genizah copy)
DJD	*Discoveries in the Judean Desert*
DSD	*Dead Sea Discoveries*
HTR	*Harvard Theological Review*
JBL	*Journal of Biblical Literature*
JESHO	*Journal of the Economic and Social History of the Orient*
JJS	*Journal of Jewish Studies*
JQR	*Jewish Quarterly Review*
JSJ	*Journal for the Study of Judaism in the Persian, Hellenistic, and Roman Periods*
JSP	*Journal for the Study of Pseudepigrapha*
JSQ	*Jewish Studies Quarterly*
LCL	Loeb Classical Library
m.	Mishnah
OTP	*Old Testament Pseudepigrapha*
PGM	*Papyri Graecae Magicae* (Greek Magical Papyri)
R.	Rabbi

SBL	*Society of Biblical Literature*
SBLDS	*Society of Biblical Literature Dissertation Series*
SJT	*Scottish Journal of Theology*
t.	Tosefta
y.	Jerusalem Talmud (*Yerushalmi*)

Introduction

On July 11, 1883, Hebrew Union College in Cincinnati, Ohio hosted a banquet to celebrate the ordination of the college's first class of Reform rabbis. The menu for this gourmet feast, later (in)famously known as the "*Terefah* [nonkosher] Banquet" and greatly mythologized, included four biblically forbidden foods (clams, crabs, shrimp, and frogs).[1] Over a series of elaborate courses, each accompanied with its own wine or spirit, the diners who partook of this feast – and those who stormed out – each made a statement about Reform Judaism's stance on the traditional Jewish dietary laws and, by extension, on its theology in general. The intra- and interdenominational consternation inspired, in part, by the "*Terefah* Banquet" eventually contributed to the bifurcation of American Judaism that we still see today.[2] More than simply consuming calories, it would appear that the "*Terefah* Banquet" was about staking a claim on a new Jewish identity.[3]

However, the use of a meal to create social distinctions and to enact and maintain distinct communities is far from a modern phenomenon, both

---

[1] A copy of the menu can be found in Jacob Rader Marcus, ed., *The Jew in the American World: A Source Book* (Detroit: Wayne State University Press, 1996), 240–241. On the myths surrounding this event, see Lance J. Sussman, "The Myth of the Trefa Banquet: American Culinary Culture and the Radicalization of Food Policy in American Reform Judaism," *American Jewish Archives Journal* 57/1–2 (2005): 29–52. As will be discussed in Chapter 2, the absence of pork from this menu is significant (see also Sussman, "Myth of the Trefa Banquet," 34–43).

[2] For a brief overview, see Marcus, *Jew in the American World*, 238–239; Sussman, "Myth of the Trefa Banquet," 43–44.

[3] Although the extent to which those who organized, hosted, dined, abstained, or departed from this banquet were, at that moment, intentionally or consciously engaging in making active identity statements is debated, it is clear that this is how the event was subsequently interpreted. See Sussman, "The Myth of the Trefa Banquet."

in Judaism and cross-culturally. The early rabbinic (tannaitic) corpus is replete with legislation concerning what and with whom one should or should not eat. The authors of these texts (singular: Tanna; plural: Tannaim) build on earlier precedents and introduce innovative practices regulating commensal interactions. In short, the food on one's plate serves as a social symbol (or sign) that communicates group association and disassociation.

This book examines how the tannaitic movement constructed identity through regulating culinary and commensal practices. Focusing on the extant literary corpus, redacted in circa third-century C.E. Palestine, I argue that the Tannaim both draw on earlier and contemporary Jewish and non-Jewish culinary and commensal customs and introduce innovations as part of an attempt to establish a discrete tannaitic identity. In these texts, the table is a locus for identity negotiation. Rules that regulate what, with whom, and how one eats – and how one prepares that food – are therefore understood to divide the world into a binary: those with whom "We" eat and those with whom "We" do not eat. Although commensality regulations are not the only manner in which the Tannaim attempt to establish their own unique identity (purity, for example, is another way), these rules are a key component of the larger identity formation process.

In addition to explaining a specific ancient data set, I develop a methodological framework for analyzing the interlocking dimensions of identity formation and commensality regulations that can be applied cross-culturally. As every recorded society that I am aware of has some form of food taboo (many for sound biological reasons),[4] the utility of refining such a heuristic model for cross-cultural and transhistorical studies is vast.

In particular, I seek to avoid three weaknesses that I detect in studies addressing the intersection between diet and identity in ancient Judaism.

---

[4] For example, evolutionary anthropologists Daniel M. T. Fessler and Carlos David Navarrete trace the origin of meat taboos specifically to "evolved psychological mechanisms and predispositions" developed to avoid biological harm to the human body. See "Meat Is Good to Taboo: Dietary Proscriptions as a Product of the Interaction of Psychological Mechanisms and Social Processes," *Journal of Cognition and Culture* 3/1 (2003): 1–40, 26. In addition to biological factors, anthropologist Marvin Harris argues that food taboos "can be explained by nutritional, ecological, or dollar-and-cents choices" (*Good to Eat: Riddles of Food and Culture* [Long Grove, IL: Waveland Press, 1998], 17).

First, piecemeal data from texts spanning a large timeframe and covering a wide swath of geographically and culturally diverse territory (for example, Palestine and Babylonia) are assumed to present one coherent and consistent picture.[5] This scrapbook approach represents the bulk of previous scholarship in the field of rabbinics in general.[6] However, the recent trend in the field has been toward greater sensitivity to this issue.[7] To address this concern, I limit my scope to tannaitic literature.[8] Further, whenever possible, I distinguish between commensality regulations with precedents in earlier (almost always Second Temple-period) extant evidence and those that appear to represent tannaitic innovations. This approach brings into relief the ways in which the Tannaim specifically manipulate culinary and commensal practices as part of their identity construction.

Second, by focusing only on culinary regulations (what one eats) and commensal regulations (how one eats) between Jew and non-Jew, or between rabbinic Jew and nonrabbinic Jew, previous studies fail to address a key component of boundary maintenance: that the proverbial "fence around the Torah"[9] – the rabbinic metaphor for a hedging policy of erring on the side of caution, to prevent violating biblical legislation – allows for the creation of laws and practices designed to keep both "Us" in and "Them" out. Scholarship that concentrates solely on regulations

---

[5] E.g., Sacha Stern, *Jewish Identity in Early Rabbinic Writings* (New York: Brill, 1994).

[6] This approach is not unique to the study of rabbinics. Classicists, for example, grapple with this same issue. As Mary Beard notes, with regard to scholarship on the Vestal virgins: "The ancient texts it considers are *excavated*, not *read*. The method is a familiar one: the Roman antiquarian literature is combed – a bit of Labeo (quoted by Aulus Gellius) is dug out here, some convenient lines of Festus on the Vestal hairdo deployed there, with plenty of snippets from Pliny the Elder and Valerius Maximus sprinkled on for good measure. The byways of Latin literature ransacked and minutely dismembered, all (as intended) making a very learned impression. But what is left out of the picture (what Ancient History, as a discipline, has consistently ignored) is the character, point and focus of the texts so expertly dissected: what were these writers writing *about* when they wrote about the Vestals? Who wrote about Vestals, to whom, and why?" ("Re-reading (Vestal) Virginity," in *Women in Antiquity: New Assessments*, ed. Richard Hawley and Barbara Levick, 166–177 [New York: Routledge, 1995], 171–172, emphasis in original).

[7] E.g., Michael L. Satlow, *Tasting the Dish: Rabbinic Rhetorics of Sexuality*, BJS 303 (Atlanta: Society of Biblical Literature, 1995); Alyssa M. Gray, *A Talmud in Exile: The Influence of Yerushalmi Avodah Zarah on the Formation of Bavli Avodah Zarah*, BJS 342 (Atlanta: Society of Biblical Literature, 2005).

[8] "Rabbinic literature," writ large, refers to both the tannaitic and amoraic corpora, as I discuss later in this chapter.

[9] E.g., *m. Avot* 1:1 (ed. Albeck 4:353).

either between rabbinic and nonrabbinic Jews[10] or between Jews and non-Jews[11] does not provide a complete picture. Here I am influenced by the work of Arjun Appadurai, who examines the role that the practice of writing cookbooks plays in creating a national cuisine – and hence, identity – in contemporary India. Appadurai notes:

What we see in these many ethnic and regional cookbooks is the growth of an anthology of naturally generated images of the ethnic Other, a kind of "ethnoethnicity," rooted in the details of regional recipes, but creating a set of generalized gastroethnic images of Bengalis, Tamils, and so forth. Such representations, *produced by both insiders and outsiders*, constitute reflections as well as continuing refinements of *the culinary conception of the Other* in contemporary India.[12]

To understand the identities constructed in cookbooks, a burgeoning topic in food studies, one must consider how these recipe collections construct the identity of both "Self" and "Other."[13] An important result of parsing the tannaitic data in this manner is that it highlights a key difference, namely that the boundaries that the Tannaim erect between

---

[10] For a recent example of this general approach to identity construction, although not in the domain of culinary and commensality regulations, see Daniel Boyarin, *Border Lines: The Partition of Judaeo-Christianity* (Philadelphia: University of Pennsylvania Press, 2004).

[11] E.g., David Moshe Freidenreich, Foreign Food: Restrictions on the Food of Members of Other Religions in Jewish, Christian, and Islamic Law (Ph.D. dissertation, Columbia University, 2006).

[12] "How to Make a National Cuisine: Cookbooks in Contemporary India," *Comparative Studies* 30/1 (1988): 3–24, 16, emphasis added. Further, I am particularly interested in Appadurai's suggestion that "[i]n the contemporary Indian situation, and to some degree generically, cookbooks appear to belong to the literature of exile, of nostalgia and loss" (p. 18). This conception makes apt the comparison between Indian cookbooks and rabbinic literature – which is written by a group of people who have experienced exile from, and the loss of sovereignty over, a land to which they feel theologically attached, as well as the destruction of their central cultic institution.

[13] The role that cookbooks play in Jewish identity formation in modernity has been the subject of several recent scholarly articles. For examples, see Nefissa Naguib, "The Fragile Tale of Egyptian Jewish Cuisine: Food Memoirs of Claudia Roden and Colette Rossant," *Food & Foodways* 14 (2006): 35–53; Alice Nakhimovsky, "You Are What They Ate: Russian Jews Reclaim Their Foodways," *Shofar: An Interdisciplinary JJS* 25/1 (2006): 63–77; Steve Siporin, "From Kashrut to Cucina Ebraica: The Recasting of Italian Jewish Foodways," *Journal of American Folklore* 107/424 (1994): 268–281. For a brief synthetic summary, including additional references, see Marion A. Kaplan, *The Making of the Jewish Middle Class: Women, Family, and Identity in Imperial Germany* (New York: Oxford University Press, 1991), 72–74. For a longer discussion, see Jenna Weissman Joselit, "Kitchen Judaism," in *The Wonders of America: Reinventing Jewish Culture, 1880–1950*, 171–218 (New York: Henry Holt, 2002).

themselves and nonrabbinic Jews are not necessarily the same as those built between themselves and non-Jews. With different guests, there is a different etiquette. Therefore, I examine both sets of regulations.

The third weakness is that much of scholarship on Jewish identity rarely theorizes the term itself.[14] As such, identity – which can be broadly defined, following Sacha Stern, as "the *perception and experience of a person's self* in its lived dimensions"[15] – is often used as a catch-all category in such a way as to have no clear meaning. For example, as Theodore R. Schatzki notes, "a person's identity embraces two analytically distinguishable and possibly divergent components: that person's meaning and that person's understanding of his or her meaning. The fact that identity possesses these two components opens the possibility of people's self-understandings diverging from the identities attributed to and foisted on them by or through others."[16] To overcome this confusion, I focus on tannaitic self-identity as a category of practice and not as an analytical category.[17]

Focusing on identity as a category of practice offers two advantages. First, because the tannaitic data are predominantly textual, one must be careful to avoid treating identity as being merely constituted by words or as being a purely discursive affair.[18] In this approach, rather than treating identities as linguistic phenomena, I follow Schatzki's suggestion that identities are "practice phenomena with linguistic aspects."[19] A prescription, for example, is not empty rhetoric, but rather is an attempt to craft a bundled set of social activities – a practice – that constructs, in part, a discrete identity. Understanding a practice to constitute a bundle of social activities allows me to combine both actions and words in my analysis of commensality regulations in the tannaitic corpus.[20]

[14] E.g., David Kraemer, *Jewish Eating and Identity Through the Ages* (New York: Routledge, 2007).
[15] *Jewish Identity*, xiv, emphasis in original.
[16] Theodore R. Schatzki, *The Site of the Social: A Philosophical Account of the Constitution of Social Life and Change* (University Park, PA: Pennsylvania State University Press, 2002), 47.
[17] Here I follow Rogers Brubaker and Frederick Cooper, "Beyond 'Identity'," *Theory and Society* 29 (2000): 1–47, especially pp. 4–6, 34.
[18] Schatzki, *Site of the Social*, 50–51.
[19] *Site of the Social*, 50; see also p. 77, in which Schatzki notes that practices are a "motley" of both "discursive and nondiscursive actions."
[20] In Schatzki's nomenclature: "doings" and "sayings." In general, see *Site of the Social*, 70–88. Schatzki ultimately defines a practice thus: "In sum, a practice is a temporally evolving, open-ended set of doings and sayings linked by practical understandings,

Second, practices establish social orders.[21] Because "[p]ractices are not just the context, but also the site where the meanings of arranged entities are instituted,"[22] understanding identity as a category of practice provides a glimpse at the blueprint for a society. For example, American *identity* is, at least in part, derived from one's participation in certain commensal practices, such as ingesting turkey, stuffing, cranberry sauce, and the like on the fourth Thursday of November (Thanksgiving); attending a barbecue, eating hot dogs, and watching fireworks on July 4 (Independence Day); consuming apple pie; and eating "peanuts and Cracker Jacks" at a baseball game, to name a few. To engage in these bundled sets of social activities is, in some sense, to perform an American identity. *Practices* are the means by which a given person or group of persons is plugged into a matrix of social relations. This observation offers a further avenue for crossing the theoretical chasm between text and social history. In short, *texts prescribe practices; practices index identity.*

By understanding identity to constitute a category of practice, I therefore argue that when tannaitic texts prescribe the consumption of or abstention from certain foods, for example, the texts themselves do not establish a distinct identity. In contrast, the prescriptions contained in a text are part of a tannaitic attempt to regulate practices, and those practices contextualize and establish the participant's identity for those people writing that text. Thus, the oft-stated principle that "you are what you eat" is understood to be a statement about identity insofar as it refers to the practice of eating as constituting an individual's identity.[23]

---

rules, teleoaffective structure, and general understandings" (*Site of the Social*, 87). My definition of a practice is also informed by another statement by Schatzki: "Practices are the bundled activities that one type of component of social orders performs" (*Site of the Social*, 71).

[21] See Schatzki, *Site of the Social*, 89–105.
[22] Schatzki, *Site of the Social*, 100.
[23] This saying apparently originates in a statement made by Jean Anthelme Brillat-Savarin: "Tell me what you eat, and I shall tell you what you are (*Dis-moi ce que tu manges, je te dirai ce que tu es*)" (*Physiologie du Goût: Première Édition Mise Ordre et Annotée avec une Lecture de Roland Barthes* [Paris: Hermann, 1975], 37; translation from *The Physiology of Taste, or, Meditations on Transcendental Gastronomy*, trans. M. F. K. Fisher [New York: Heritage Press, 1949], 1. I owe this reference to Hasia R. Diner, *Hungering for America: Italian, Irish, and Jewish Foodways in the Age of Migration* [Cambridge: Harvard University Press, 2001], 4). For similar proverbs, see the sources cited in Emiko Ohnuki-Tierney, *Rice as Self: Japanese Identities through Time* (Princeton, NJ: Princeton University Press, 1993), 3.

My usage of the term identity here contrasts with that of Sacha Stern, who describes rabbinic identity as "an all-embracing, ontological experience which covers all areas of one's existence."[24] The notion that identity is "all-embracing" is a rabbinic rhetorical strategy that Stern accepts too easily. Elsewhere, Stern explicitly refers to the role that practice plays in this identity, noting that "[i]n some contexts, it becomes more appropriate for us to refer to Jewish identity not as a passive 'experience' but rather as a *practice*."[25] In contrast, I argue throughout this study that culinary and commensally constructed tannaitic identity is *always* about practice. Identity is not a passive experience. Like the act of eating, it is an active social practice.

Further, the fact that the Tannaim utilize practices to construct a distinct identity is unsurprising. As Shaye Cohen has cogently argued, Jewish identity – which he labels "Jewishness" – emerges in the Hasmonean period (circa second to first century B.C.E.), when the term "Judean" took on a religious, rather than an ethnic, connotation.[26] From this time on, Jews in the Second Temple and Rabbinic periods emphasized their distinctiveness primarily via their practices, including circumcision and commensality regulations. Whereas to be a "Judean" meant that one was born into an ethnic lineage, starting in the second century B.C.E., to be a "Jew" meant to engage in specific practices. The who, what, when, where, and how of these practices, however, was up for debate.

Throughout, I occasionally use the term "edible identity" to refer to the complex of culturally significant activities surrounding the preparation and ingestion of food that allows diners to make an identity statement by the manner in which they partake of their dinner. Through commensality practices, individuals act out their self-conceptions as members of a group and their public identifications with a group to form distinct identities: namely, those with whom "We" can eat ("Us") and those with whom "We" cannot eat ("Them"). This identity is enacted daily, turning

---

[24] *Jewish Identity*, xxxiii. Because Stern considers both tannaitic and amoraic literature, his conclusions will sometimes require adjustment for use in this book.
[25] *Jewish Identity*, 79, emphasis in original.
[26] Shaye J. D. Cohen, *The Beginnings of Jewishness: Boundaries, Varieties, Uncertainties* (Berkeley and Los Angeles: University of California Press, 2000), 109–139, especially pp. 135–136. For a recent critique of this approach, see Steve Mason, "Jews, Judaeans, Judaizing, Judaism: Problems of Categorization in Ancient Judaism," *JSJ* 38 (2007): 457–512.

the biological need to ingest calories into a culturally significant activity.[27] Massimo Montanari, an Italian historian of food in the medieval period, reminds us of the cultural relativity of these practices: "Culinary identities were not inscribed in the heavens."[28] I use the term "edible identity" to refer to this matrix of interrelated practices, the range and depth of which form the core focus of this work.

On a final note, I often interact with the work of anthropologists. Underlying these theories is the assumption that meals (and their concomitant social rules) form a decipherable code or language. For example, discussing the "code" of a meal, Mary Douglas notes, "To sum up, the meaning of a meal is found in a system of repeated analogies. Each meal carries something of the meaning of the other meals; each meal is a structured social event which structures others in its own image."[29] Here, Douglas is influenced by the work of Roland Barthes, who observes that "[t]o eat is a behavior that develops beyond its own ends, replacing, summing up, and signaling other behaviors, and it is precisely for these reasons that it is a sign."[30] The theories of Douglas and Barthes, among others, have become the regnant scholarly view with regard to understanding how a meal operates culturally. In short, food is a system of signs – a code that can be decrypted.

Scholars have therefore worked to create a proverbial Rosetta Stone, seeking to translate the "language" of a meal. Montanari summarizes this approach well:

In all societies, eating habits and rituals are governed by conventions analogous to those that give meaning and stability to verbal languages themselves. This aggregate of conventions, which we shall call "grammar," informs the food system not as a simple *compilatio*n [sic] of products and foods,

---

[27] Food is not unique in this manner. As Mary Douglas notes: "Like sex, the taking of food has a social component, as well as a biological one" ("Deciphering a Meal," in *Food and Culture: A Reader*, ed. Carole Counihan and Penny van Esterik, 36–54 [New York: Routledge, 1997]).

[28] *Food Is Culture*, trans. Albert Sonnenfeld (New York: Columbia University Press, 2006), 137.

[29] "Deciphering a Meal," 44.

[30] "Toward a Psychosociology of Contemporary Food Consumption," in *Food and Culture: A Reader*, ed. Carole Counihan and Penny van Esterik, 20–27 (New York: Routledge, 1997). Douglas herself acknowledges her debt to Barthes ("Deciphering a Meal," 36).

assembled in more or less casual fashion, but rather as a structure, inside of which each component defines its meaning.

The lexicon on which this language is based obviously consists of the repertory of available animal and vegetable products, very much like the kind of morphemes (the basic units of meaning) on which are built words as well as the entire dictionary. Thus, it is a lexicon that redefines itself in the changing context of environmental, economic, social, and cultural circumstances.[31]

Thus, the "syntaxes ('menus'), and styles ('diets')"[32] of a culture allow the careful historian or anthropologist to act like a lexicographer.

Where I depart significantly from anthropologists of food, and the field of food studies in general, is in my data set. Too often, these scholars have turned their attention only to the food taboos contained in the Hebrew Bible.[33] The rabbinic corpus, however, is almost always ignored. Although they are interesting, I do not believe any of the anthropological originary claims for these food taboos (usually focused on the anomaly of the pig) – from Douglas's notion that pig is an animal "out of place" to Harris's economic and environmental causal argument – to be verifiable, as the data are too slender and their arguments are too often circular. Therefore, I prefer in my own work to look at a data set in which the absolute origins of the prohibition against pork, for example, are irrelevant. What matters for the Tannaim is that God instituted the ban in the Hebrew Bible. How they interpret, understand, and enact this regulation is verifiable.[34]

Even though I advocate a shift in focus, the theories that anthropologists have developed are useful for analyzing this different data set. Therefore, I adopt their approach in general throughout this book and attempt to translate the language of the meal, as constructed in tannaitic literature. I argue that the culinary and commensal regulations developed (and, in some cases, inherited) by the Tannaim are part of a larger process

---

[31] *Food Is Culture*, 99, emphasis in original.
[32] Barthes, "Toward a Psychosociology of Contemporary Food Consumption," 23.
[33] Most famously, see the many works of Mary Douglas: e.g., *Purity and Danger: An Analysis of the Concepts of Pollution and Taboo* (New York: Routledge, 1999 [1966]), 42–58; and her recent reevaluation in *Leviticus as Literature* (New York: Oxford University Press, 2000); also see Harris, *Good to Eat*, 67–87; and Jean Soler, "Biblical Reasons: The Dietary Rules of the Ancient Hebrews," in *Food: A Culinary History*, ed. Jean-Louis Flandrin and Massimo Montanari, 46–54 (New York: Penguin Books, 2000).
[34] See Chapter 2 for an in-depth discussion of the pig.

of identity formation. From the daily dinner table – a "domestic theatre where members of the family in turn play the roles of performers and audience"[35] – to the festival meal, commensality is a social performance that enacts and maintains particular identities.

"THE SET TABLE": ORGANIZATION AND STRUCTURE

Shaye Cohen observes, "Between Us and Them is a line, a boundary, drawn not in sand or stone but in the mind."[36] In this study, I examine the commensal practices that erect the tannaitic boundary in the mind. To do so, I begin by looking at the historical realia. In Chapter 1 ("Realia"), I discuss the daily and annual life cycles of commensality in Tannaitic-period Palestine. Drawing on textual and material evidence from both tannaitic and roughly contemporary (Greek, Roman, and Christian) sources, I briefly (re)construct the culinary and commensal world that tannaitic meal practices seek to regulate. Without knowing what this world might have looked like, it would be difficult to establish the difference between rabbinic fantasy and historical description.[37] I therefore ask four questions: What did they eat? How did they obtain their food? How did they prepare their food? In what manner did they eat their food? In answering these questions, we discover that, in general, most of the evidence for the historical realia of food production and consumption for Jews and non-Jews does not differ greatly. However, this is only on the macro level (i.e., in general structure and appearance); on the micro level, as we shall later see, there are important nuances and subtle distinctions. Although the body of this chapter is designed to be accessible to the reader, I include detailed footnotes for experts in the field, as this is the only examination of this material in regard to tannaitic literature in particular. Although this study primarily addresses

---

[35] Jeremy MacClancy, *Consuming Culture: Why You Eat What You Eat* (New York: Henry Holt, 1993), 98.
[36] *Beginnings of Jewishness*, 341.
[37] Miriam B. Peskowitz uses the term "fantasy" as a critical term for the study of rabbinic literature. See *Spinning Fantasies: Rabbis, Gender, and History* (Berkeley and Los Angeles: University of California Press, 1997), 60–62, and *passim*. This term helps to caution against the following scholarly tendency to uncritically accept a text's rhetoric: "The vivid details of tailors, peddlers, and millstone grinders lend the passage a sense of accuracy and practicality. Reading it, I can almost hear the hustling chatter of artisans and customers at the marketplace. But this is a seduction" (*Spinning Fantasies*, 62).

the cultural meanings of these practices, it is nevertheless important to survey briefly what we know about what and how people ate in ancient Palestine.

Chapter 2 ("Jewish Identity") begins my examination of the role that meal practices play in the construction of a distinct tannaitic identity. Focusing on the binary Jew/non-Jew, I explore the various discursive and nondiscursive practices that separate a Jew and a non-Jew at the table (*com–mensally*). Tannaitic commensal practices bring this boundary in the mind to life through three specific techniques. First, certain culinary items are understood to be metonymic (the "sole" food of Us/Them) and to embody those who ingest them (the "soul" food of Us/Them). Jews are understood to eat certain foods and to have a unique foodway that, via ingestion, embodies them as Jews. Second, the status of the food produced is directly correlated with the status of its cook. As a result of this correlation, the Tannaim develop what I label the "chef/sous-chef principle." According to this principle, only food produced by a Jewish "chef" is valid for tannaitic ingestion. Food prepared by a non-Jewish "chef," even if in accordance with all other rabbinic precepts, is nonkosher simply because it was prepared by a non-Jew. However, a non-Jew may assist a Jew in the cooking process (as the "sous-chef"), as long as a Jew functions as the "chef." As we shall see, the purpose of distinguishing these roles in the tannaitic corpus seems to be to subordinate and control the actions of non-Jews, while still allowing for shared cooking. Third, a connection is established among commensality, intermarriage, and idolatry. This innovative association allows the Tannaim to stigmatize, if not yet ban outright, commensal encounters between Jews and non-Jews. Once again, the issue is not the *kashrut* of the food so much as whether or not the social situation itself is kosher. Throughout this chapter, we will see that tannaitic food practices help to construct an identity that is separate but that does not completely separate Jews and non-Jews. Economic, and even social, interactions are allowed, although they are increasingly limited.

Chapter 3 ("Jewish Male Identity"), as its title implies, builds on the observations in the previous chapter by exploring the manner in which tannaitic commensal practices enact and maintain a *specifically male* Jewish identity. It has become the regnant scholarly view that the normative rabbinic identity is gendered as male. The tannaitic evidence discussed in this chapter – which includes texts both prescribing women's actions while cooking and regulating their presence at the tannaitic table – accords with this view. Further, the rhetorical function of women (as a hypothetical legal variable rather than as a historical entity) comes into greater clarity when, for example, examining texts that speak of women cooking only with other Jewish women and not professionally. As we shall see, this observation also has ramifications for understanding tannaitic purity discourse. Throughout, I will argue that, in the tannaitic corpus, women's actions are of interest only insofar as they affect men's practice. Although women often appear in the discursive site that is the tannaitic kitchen, they function as sous-chefs. Men, even if not physically present, are always the chefs in the tannaitic kitchen. Finally, although women are found in the tannaitic kitchen, their presence at the tannaitic table is called into question. Given their focus on male practice, it should not be surprising that the Tannaim do not provide a clear account of the extent of women's presence (or absence) at the tannaitic table. In surveying these data, I will argue that the – albeit ambiguous and incomplete – evidence suggests that women's presence at the ideal (if not the real) tannaitic table is, at best, problematic.

Chapter 4 ("Jewish Male Rabbinic Identity") completes the picture by turning attention to the rabbinic identity inscribed by tannaitic commensal practices. Whereas Chapters 2 and 3 looked at non-Jews and women, this chapter addresses a thornier subject (from the tannaitic perspective): nonrabbinic Jews. Nonrabbinic Jews sit between the poles in the Us/Them polarity. Although they are legally Jewish, they do not follow Jewish law, as interpreted and promulgated by the Tannaim. Unlike non-Jews, nonrabbinic Jews are not monolithic; rather, they are painted with a fine brush in tannaitic literature. Even though they may have Jewish mothers and even be circumcised, nonrabbinic Jews are depicted as participating in a variety of unrabbinic actions (e.g., eating forbidden foods). In this chapter, I focus on four tannaitic food practices that construct, in part, a rabbinic identity. First, the Tannaim develop a distinctly rabbinic Jewish cuisine. Rabbinic Jews are understood to adhere to a unique foodway that distinguishes them from nonrabbinic Jews. It is this conception that underlies, for example, the innovative tannaitic prohibition of consuming meat and cheese together. Second, the Tannaim expand purity laws vis-à-vis food and consumption. In doing so, as was the case in Chapter 2, *mutatis mutandis*, the Tannaim prescribe practices that establish a separate identity that nevertheless does not completely separate rabbinic from nonrabbinic Jews. Third, once again, the Tannaim correlate the status of food and the status of its cook. This correlation indicates that there is a predictable analogy between tannaitic food regulations and desired social relations, suggesting that the latter generates the former. Fourth, the Tannaim reinterpret festival rules to exclude nonrabbinic Jews from the "proper" observance of these festivals. Passover, Sukkot, and Sabbath observance now requires – according to tannaitic fiat – specific commensal practices. Failure to adhere to these new regulations, at least for the Tannaim, is tantamount to failure to observe the festivals at all.

A BRIEF INTRODUCTION TO THE TANNAITIC CORPUS

The primary source for this book is the tannaitic corpus. Redacted in circa-third-century C.E. Palestine, the literary canon of the Tannaim consists of several documents.[38] The Mishnah, traditionally considered the first rabbinic document, is thought to have been compiled circa 200 C.E. Arranged according to topic, the Mishnah is part law code and part record of various debates. The exact purpose of the Mishnah remains a matter of scholarly debate.[39] Shortly thereafter, a collection of roughly similar – though often more expansive – traditions was redacted, known as Tosefta ("The Addition" in Aramaic).[40] Further, the Tannaim are also credited

---

[38] For a general discussion of tannaitic texts, including the issues involved with dating them, see H. L. Strack and Günter Stemberger, *Introduction to the Talmud and Midrash*, trans. and ed. Markus Bockmuehl (Minneapolis: Fortress Press, 1996), 108–163, 247–275. Unless otherwise noted, all translations from Hebrew will be my own.

[39] To offer two examples: the Mishnah is a philosophy (e.g., Jacob Neusner, *Judaism: The Evidence of the Mishnah*, BJS 129, Second Edition [Atlanta: Scholars Press, 1988]) or a rabbinic textbook (e.g., Abraham Goldberg, "The Mishnah – A Study Book of Halakha," in *The Literature of the Sages: Part 1: Oral Tora, Halakha, Mishna, Tosefta, External Tractates*, ed. Shmuel Safrai, 211–251 [Philadelphia: Fortress Press, 1987]).

[40] With regard to the relationship in general between Mishnah and Tosefta, I adopt Shamma Friedman's approach. Friedman argues against the traditional *a priori* assumption that the Mishnah predates Tosefta and that Tosefta (as its name in Aramaic implies) is "the addition" that comments on the earlier Mishnah. Rather, following Friedman, each pericope is judged on its own merits, as sometimes Tosefta appears to comment on an earlier version of a mishnaic tradition than is preserved in the extant corpus of the Mishnah. For example, see Shamma Yehudah Friedman, "Mishnah and Tosefta Parallels (1): Shabbat 16:1," *Tarbiz* 62 (1993): 313–338 (Hebrew).

On a style note, I depart from a scholarly convention and do not use the definite article ("the") before Tosefta (or Mekilta or Sifra), because the "a" (= *aleph*) on the end of the word denotes the definite article in Aramaic. As such, I believe that Tosefta

with the creation and compilation of a series of verse-by-verse exegetical commentaries on four of the five books of the Torah (Pentateuch). Often referred to by the Hebrew term for rabbinic biblical interpretation (*midrash;* plural: *midrashim*), these commentaries are *Mekilta d'Rabbi Ishmael* and *Mekilta d'Rabbi Shimon bar Yohai* (both on Exodus), *Sifra* (on Leviticus), *Sifre Numbers*, and *Sifre Deuteronomy*. Finally, there are reputed tannaitic traditions found in later rabbinic documents, known as *bāraitôt* (hereafter *baraitot*; singular: *bāraitā'*, hereafter *baraita*). Because these traditions are not found *in situ* – that is, within the tannaitic corpus itself – I assess the historical veracity of each relevant *baraita* on a case-by-case basis.

Immediately following the Tannaim are a group of rabbis who voluminously expand on the tannaitic corpus. Living in both Palestine and Babylonia, these rabbis, known as the Amoraim, created the Palestinian and Babylonian Talmuds, as well as several *midrash* collections.[41] Although a consideration of their work is beyond the purview of this book, occasional reference will be made to their corpus, particularly when it clarifies a tannaitic text.

and the like should follow the same grammar conventions in English as does *hoi polloi* (= "*the* people"), which also omits the definite article in its proper English usage.

[41] For a general discussion of these works, see Strack and Stemberger, *Introduction to the Talmud*, 164–232, 276–359.

1

∾

Realia

Food is central to our sense of identity. The way any given human group eats helps it assert its diversity, hierarchy and organization, and at the same time, both its oneness and the otherness of whoever eats differently. Food is also central to individual identity, in that any given human individual is constructed, biologically, psychologically and socially by the food he/she choses [*sic*] to incorporate.[1]

Human beings are omnivores. Unable to survive on a single species of plant or animal, we must turn to a cornucopia of fruits, vegetables, and protein sources to acquire all the nutrients necessary for survival. In this search for protein, carbohydrates, vitamins, and minerals, human beings look for variety; at the same time, they attempt to avoid danger. For example, although a dish might taste better (and be more nutritious) with a variety of mushrooms, this benefit must be weighed against the potential that one of those mushrooms could be poisonous. This phenomenon is often referred to as either the "omnivore's paradox" or, more famously, "the omnivore's dilemma."[2]

In the ancient Mediterranean (and, in fact, in all places and time periods prior to the invention of modern refrigeration and transportation), human beings relied on the food sources that were either available in

---

[1] Claude Fischler, "Food, Self and Identity," *Social Science Information* 27/2 (1988): 275–292, 275.
[2] The classic discussion is Paul Rozin, "The Selection of Foods by Rats, Humans and Other Animals," *Advances in the Study of Behavior*, ed. J. S. Rosenblatt, R. A. Hinde, E. Shaw, and C. Beer, 6 (1976): 21–76. See also Fischler, "Food, Self and Identity," 277–279; and the modern journalistic effort of Michael Pollan, *The Omnivore's Dilemma: A Natural History of Four Meals* (New York: Penguin Press, 2006).

their immediate environment or that preserved well enough to travel.[3] Although this study is focused primarily on tannaitic discourse on culinary and commensal regulations, it is important to contextualize this prescriptive rhetoric within its historical milieu. To do so, I consider both Jewish and non-Jewish evidence for the diet and manner of food consumption of the inhabitants of Roman-period Palestine. Tannaitic literature does not provide enough information by itself, so one must also turn to contemporary non-Jewish literary and material evidence to draw a fuller picture.[4] When this evidence contrasts with tannaitic literature, I discuss the possible meanings and ramifications of these differences. For example, when pork is deployed as a metonymic food – a symbol of "Self" and "Other" – in both Jewish and non-Jewish texts, does this literary image accord with the other extant data about Jewish and Gentile diets in the ancient Mediterranean?

This chapter asks four main questions, each of which constitutes a separate subsection. First, what did they eat? Of what did the diet of Jews and non-Jews in Roman-period Palestine consist? Second, how did they obtain their food? What was purchased in the market? By and from whom? Third, how did they prepare their food? What food technology and processes did they employ? Fourth, in what manner did they eat their food? What were their meal customs?

In answering each of these questions, I provide a general overview of the culinary and commensal world in which the Tannaim produced their literary corpus. I do not, however, attempt an exhaustive survey of the historical realia of food production, distribution, and consumption of Roman-period Palestine – which would be a book in and of itself.[5]

---

[3] For a popular history of food transportation, see Sarah Murray, *Moveable Feasts: From Ancient Rome to the 21st Century, the Incredible Journeys of the Food We Eat* (New York: St. Martin's Press, 2008).

[4] In contrast to other studies, however, I do not use amoraic data to complete this picture. Too often, later rabbinic evidence is relied on uncritically to explain the realia of earlier rabbinic documents.

[5] The classic point of entry for rabbinics scholars to this field is Samuel Krauss, *Talmudische Archäologie*, 3 vols. (Leipzig: Buchhandlung Gustav Fock, 1910), 1:78–126; 2:214–247. A useful English language survey is Gildas Hamel, *Poverty and Charity in Roman Palestine, First Three Centuries C.E.* (Berkeley and Los Angeles: University of California Press, 1990), 8–56. Hamel's primary use of Palestinian sources makes him the best resource for inquiry on this subject. Further work on this topic, however, is a desideratum, as Hamel's survey contains many errors (see the critique by Seth Schwartz, "Review of Gildas Hamel, *Poverty and Charity in Roman Palestine, First Three Centuries C.E.*,"

WHAT DID THEY EAT?

Bread, a staple food in both the ancient and modern Mediterranean, constituted 50 percent of the caloric intake for Jews and Gentiles in Roman-period Palestine.[6] *m. Hallah* 1:1 mentions five grains that can be used to make bread: wheat, barley, rice wheat, two-row barley, and spelt wheat.[7] Grains are also ingested in a variety of other forms, including raw or roasted cereals,[8] porridges and gruels,[9] and sweet dessert-like delicacies.[10]

Even though bread and grains accounted for more than half of a person's daily caloric intake, one cannot live on bread alone. Although the wealthy could afford the foodstuffs necessary for a truly varied diet, the poor (i.e., the majority of the population) subsisted on a much

---

AJSR 17/2 [1992]: 293–296). For a popular overview of Jewish foodways in antiquity, see John Cooper, *Eat and Be Satisfied: A Social History of Jewish Food* (Northvale, NJ: Jason Aronson, 1993), 37–78. Although Cooper provides an accessible survey, he treats rabbinic sources uncritically and combines tannaitic and amoraic, as well as Palestinian and Babylonian, data.

[6] Magen Broshi, "The Diet of Palestine in the Roman Period: Introductory Notes," in *Bread, Wine, Walls and Scrolls*, 121–143 (New York: Sheffield Academic Press, 2001), 121; Shimon Dar, "Food and Archaeology in Romano-Byzantine Palestine," in *Food in Antiquity*, ed. John Wilkins, David Harvey, and Mike Dobson, 326–335 (Exeter, UK: University of Exeter Press, 1996), 329. Both scholars derive this statistic from analyzing the list of provisions that one must provide for a wife maintained by a third party mentioned in *m. Ketubbot* 5:8–9 (ed. Albeck 3:106–107). For a discussion of bread in the ancient Mediterranean in general, see Andrew Dalby, *Food in the Ancient World from A to Z* (New York: Routledge, 2003), 58–61; Hamel, *Poverty and Charity*, 11–15; on the modern period, see Hélène Balfet, "Bread in Some Regions of the Mediterranean Area: A Contribution to the Studies on Eating Habits," in *Gastronomy: The Anthropology of Food and Food Habits*, ed. Margaret L. Arnott, 305–314 (Chicago: Mouton Publishers, 1975). On the concept of a "staple" food in anthropological studies, see Emiko Ohnuki-Tierney, *Rice as Self: Japanese Identities through Time* (Princeton, NJ: Princeton University Press, 1993), 4, 30.

[7] *m. Hallah* 1:1 (ed. Albeck 1:275; = *Mekilta d'Rabbi Ishmael Bo* 8 [ed. Horowitz 26, 29]). My translation of these terms follows the suggestions of botanist Jehuda Feliks ("Five Species," in *Encyclopaedia Judaica*, second printing, 16 vols., 6:1331–1332 [Jerusalem: Encyclopaedia Judaica, 1973]). For a list and discussion of the different types of bread referenced in rabbinic literature, see Krauss, *Talmudische Archäologie*, 1:102–106.

[8] E.g., *m. Terumot* 5:1–3 (ed. Albeck 1:192–193). In fact, the food that Jesus' disciples eat (controversially) on the Sabbath is plucked raw grain (Mark 2:23; Luke 6:1; Matthew 12:1).

[9] E.g., *m. Makhshirin* 6:2 (ed. Albeck 6:430–431). For further references and a discussion, see Hamel, *Poverty and Charity*, 12.

[10] E.g., *m. Hallah* 1:4, 6 (ed. Albeck 1:276, 276–277; cp. *t. Hallah* 1:2 [ed. Lieberman 1:275]); *t. Berakhot* 5:12 (ed. Lieberman 1:27).

simpler regimen.[11] The tannaitic *locus classicus* for a poor person's diet is *t. Pe'ah* 4:8,[12] which discusses the amount of food necessary to provide to an indigent traveler. According to this text, one is given bread to eat if passing through by day,[13] to which oil and legumes are added if the traveler stays the night. If the person remains for the Sabbath, the community must provide "food for three meals, [namely] oil, legumes, fish, and a vegetable."

This text serves as an excellent exemplar of the other components of the diet of those who both authored and lived in the time and location depicted in the tannaitic corpus. First, oil (specifically, olive oil) and, to a lesser extent, other fruits complemented the daily diet of bread. Tannaitic literature mentions several different types of olives, which are consumed raw, preserved, and as oil (often as an accompaniment to bread).[14] Olives, along with grapes – used primarily for wine, which, served mixed with water, seems to have been the main beverage – represent a significant portion of both the agricultural crop and the daily diet.[15] In addition,

---

[11] For a detailed comparison between the diets of the wealthy and the poor, see Hamel, *Poverty and Charity*, 31–52. In general, see Peter Garnsey, *Famine and Food Supply in the Graeco–Roman World: Responses to Risk and Crisis* (New York: Cambridge University Press, 1988); and *Food and Society in Classical Antiquity* (New York: Cambridge University Press, 1999), especially pp. 43–61.

[12] *t. Pe'ah* 4:8 (ed. Lieberman 1:57; = *m. Pe'ah* 8:7 [ed. Albeck 1:65]). For a comparison between these mishnaic and toseftan passages, see Gregg Elliot Gardner, Giving to the Poor in Early Rabbinic Judaism (Ph.D. dissertation, Princeton University, 2009), 62–65.

[13] The text lists this minimum amount as "[worth] a *pundyôn*, [made from wheat that costs at least] one *sela'* for four *sĕ'în*." According to Hamel, this is the "equivalent of 1/12 *denarius* worth of bread per day, when the 'market price' of grain was at 1 *se'ah* for 1 *denarius*. A poor person was therefore supposed to receive two loaves of bread, enough for two meals" (*Poverty and Charity*, 39). Further, Ze'ev Safrai concludes, "A *seah* of wheat... is 6.3 kilograms. Thus, the Mishnah is describing a loaf that weighed 0.525 kilograms" (*The Economy of Roman Palestine* [New York: Routledge, 1994], 105). I have followed here the translation suggested by Roger Brooks (*Support for the Poor in the Mishnaic Law: Tractate Peah*, BJS 43 [Chico, CA: Scholars Press, 1983], 146).

[14] E.g., *m. Pe'ah* 7:1 (ed. Albeck 1:59); *m. Terumot* 1:9; 2:6 (ed. Albeck 1:181–182; 184); *m. Bikkurim* 1:3 (ed. Albeck 1:311–312, which mentions that olives used for oil are not the choicest ones).

[15] Olives and grapes as consumed whole and in liquid state (oil, wine): *m. Terumot* 1:9 (ed. Albeck 1:181–182). I discuss the production of both olive oil and wine in the "How Did They Prepare Their Food?" section of this chapter. For references to the agricultural bounty of olives and grapes in Roman Palestine, see Safrai, *Economy of Roman Palestine*, 108, 118–136. According to Dar, "every person consumed twenty kilos of olive oil per year as food, and an additional quantity for cosmetics and for illumination" ("Food and

people consumed a variety of other fruits, including figs, dates, carob, pomegranates, caperbush berries, *ethrogs* (citrons), melons, and plums.[16] In general, these fruits were eaten in various forms, including "fresh, pressed into cakes for storage and later consumption, or boiled to make honey – a sweet and thick jam."[17]

Second, legumes were an important part of the daily diet in Roman-period Palestine. Although eaten by members of every class of society, legumes are often called the "poor man's meat."[18] Beans, lentils, chickpeas, vetch, and other legumes were consumed raw and cooked (in the form of gruel, pancakes, bread, and the like) and, fortunately, were both rich in protein and easy to store. For those who could rarely afford meat, legumes provided much of the necessary protein essential for bodily function.

Third, the Sabbath day – a festive occasion – brings with it the inclusion of a vegetable into the diet. Although *t. Pe'ah* 4:8 refers to provisions for an indigent traveler, it does not necessarily reflect the daily cuisine of others. In general, it seems that vegetables – whether grown oneself, by proxy, purchased, bartered for, or foraged for – were a fairly

---

Archaeology," 331). On mixing wine, see, e.g., *m. Bava Metzi'a* 3:27 (ed. Lieberman 5:80); *t. Bava Metzi'a* 3:26 (ed. Lieberman 5:79–80); *Sifra Shemini parasha* 1 (ed. Weiss 56a, which both prescribes mixing wine and states the amount necessary to become drunk); cp. 2 Maccabees 15:39. In later rabbinic sources, Markham J. Geller detects a pattern of preference for wine in Palestinian sources and beer in Babylonian sources ("Diet and Regimen in the Babylonian Talmud," in *Food and Identity in the Ancient World*, ed. Cristiano Grottanelli and Lucio Milano, 217–242 [Padova: S.A.R.G.O.N. Editrice e Libreria], 237–240). On wine in Ancient Palestine in general (including support for Geller's findings), see Magen Broshi, "Wine in Ancient Palestine: Introductory Notes," in *Bread, Wine, Walls and Scrolls*, 144–172 (New York: Sheffield Academic Press, 2001).

[16] On fruit in rabbinic literature, see Dar, "Food and Archaeology," 331–332; Hamel, *Poverty and Charity*, 9–10 (from which the above list is primarily drawn, although he classifies carob as a legume [p. 16]); Krauss, *Talmudische Archäologie*, 1:113–115; Safrai, *Economy of Roman Palestine*, 118–144.

[17] Hamel, *Poverty and Charity*, 9.

[18] For example, see Garnsey, *Food and Society*, 15; Hamel, *Poverty and Charity*, 15 n. 62. On legumes in general, see Dar, "Food and Archaeology," 330–331; Garnsey, *Food and Society*, 15; Hamel, *Poverty and Charity*, 15–17; Krauss, *Talmudische Archäologie*, 1:115–116; Safrai, *Economy of Roman Palestine*, 145–146. In Daniel 1:12–16, Daniel requests a simple diet of legumes and water to prove a point when refraining from eating the non-Judean king's food. In *b. Ketubbot* 67b, legumes are associated with the diet of the poor, whereas meat is associated with the diet of the wealthy.

common component of the daily diet.[19] Vegetables were consumed raw, dried, steamed, preserved, cooked, or roasted.[20] The list of vegetables that composed some part of their diet is quite large, including, but not limited to onions, garlic, leeks, squashes, cabbages, radishes, parsnips, beets, gourds, cucumbers, artichokes, mushrooms, and lettuce.[21]

Fourth, fish and animal proteins were a component of the diet of the inhabitants of Roman-period Palestine.[22] Obviously, the quality, quantity, and frequency of animal protein consumption depended on one's economic resources.[23] Nevertheless, a variety of animal protein – including cows, oxen, lambs, goats, asses, deer, gazelles, chickens, fish, grasshoppers, and locusts – found its way into the diet of both Jews and

---

[19] On vegetables in general, see Dar, "Food and Archaeology," 330–331; Hamel, *Poverty and Charity*, 17–18; Krauss, *Talmudische Archäologie*, 1:116–118; Safrai, *Economy of Roman Palestine*, 144–145. For an interdisciplinary examination of foraging for wild plants in times of famine, see Rebecca Huss-Ashmore and Susan L. Johnston, "Wild Plants as Famine Foods: Food Choice Under Conditions of Scarcity," in *Food Preferences and Taste: Continuity and Change*, ed. Helen Macbeth, 83–100 (Providence, RI: Berghahn Books, 1997).

[20] Hamel, *Poverty and Charity*, 17.

[21] I draw this list primarily from Hamel, *Poverty and Charity*, 17–18. There are a few *baraitot* that caution against the ingestion of certain vegetables (and other foods) on medical grounds (e.g., *b. Pesahim* 42a; *b. Eruvin* 29b). For a discussion, including references to Greek medical literature, see Geller, "Diet and Regimen," 224–230.

[22] In fact, according to Justin Lev-Tov, the most profound impact of Roman foodways on those of Palestinian inhabitants was in significantly increasing the amount of fish and fish sauce in their diet ("'Upon What Meat Doth This Our Caesar Feed...?': A Dietary Perspective on Hellenistic and Roman Influence in Palestine," in *Zeichen aus Text und Stein: Studien auf dem Weg zu einer Archaeologie des Neuen Testaments*, ed. S. Alkier and J. Zangenberg, 420–446 [Tübingen, Germany: Francke, 2003], 16–20). I was able to track down only an online version of this article, so it is to this online version that the second set of page numbers refers. Available online at www.as.ua.edu/rel/pdf/rel346levtov.pdf.

[23] Meat was a prized resource in both Jewish (for example, see the *baraita* on *b. Ketubbot* 67b; *m. Hullin* 5:3 [ed. Albeck 5:131–132, which discusses slaughtering meat for holiday consumption]; Hamel, *Poverty and Charity*, 25–29) and non-Jewish (see Garnsey, *Food and Society*, 122–127) sources from antiquity. For cross-cultural comparisons, see Marvin Harris, *Good to Eat: Riddles of Food and Culture* (Long Grove, IL: Waveland Press, 1998), 19–46. However, Lev-Tov argues that archaeological evidence suggests that meat consumption in antiquity is underestimated, pointing to the often overlooked fact that the zooarchaeological record for Roman-period Palestine contains far more animal bones with obvious human butchering mark patterning than the wealthy elite alone could eat ("'Upon What Meat,'" 8–10; see also Dar, "Food and Archaeology," 332–333). This point is well taken, as further work on assessing the historical veracity of the oft-repeated truism of meat as a scarce commodity – particularly by systematically assessing the faunal remains that are often ignored in archaeological excavations of Roman-period Palestine – is a desideratum.

non-Jews in antiquity (particularly on festivals).[24] To this list, one should also add two biblically prohibited domesticated quadrupeds: the camel and the pig. In particular, the pig presents an interesting test case (as we shall see in Chapter 2), as both literary and zooarchaeological evidence possibly suggests that Jews refrained from ingesting its flesh, although it appears to have been the most common categorically nonkosher meat ingested by non-Jews (and some Jews?) in the ancient Mediterranean.[25] It is important to keep in mind, however, that, despite the general trend in scholarship, one should refrain from assuming a priori that all Jews in antiquity adhered to every biblical dietary prohibition.[26] Further, animal protein was also ingested in the form of eggs and in a variety of milk products, including cheese, butter, *leben*, and milk.[27]

---

[24] On animal protein in general, see Dar, "Food and Archaeology," 332–333; Hamel, *Poverty and Charity*, 19–21 (from which I primarily draw this list); Krauss, *Talmudische Archäologie*, 1:108–113; Safrai, *Economy of Roman Palestine*, 163–182 (on the economics of fishing, grazing, and raising animals for food). On the problems associated with locusts (some of which are biblically proscribed), see Hamel, *Poverty and Charity*, 19. Animal products are prepared and cooked in a variety of different ways, some of which will be discussed in the "How Did They Prepare Their Food?" section of this chapter. For further discussions of these cooking processes, see the sources cited earlier in this note.

[25] Billy Grantham suggests that the average Roman dietary allotment of meat in ancient Sepphoris (Palestine) consisted of 20 percent pig, with the remaining sources (cow, chicken, goat, and sheep) being kosher animals (A Zooarchaeological Model for the Study of Ethnic Complexity at Sepphoris [Ph.D. dissertation, Northwestern University, 1996], 104, fig. 8). For additional information on the prevalence of pork in antiquity, see David Kraemer, *Jewish Eating and Identity Through the Ages* (New York: Routledge, 2007), 32–33. On the raising of pigs in Roman-period Palestine, see Safrai, *Economy of Roman Palestine*, 172–173.

[26] The extent to which Jews in antiquity adhered to biblical dietary prohibitions is rarely discussed in any serious or systematic fashion. For example, the fact that pig, camel, hyrax (*šāpān*), and catfish bones are found in Palestine (albeit in small numbers), if ever noted, is usually ignored, minimized, or associated with neighboring non-Jews. Although Lev-Tov rightly critiques this approach, his short article is only the first step in the necessary process of the reevaluation and recovery of this often neglected evidence ("'Upon What Meat,'" 10–13).

[27] See Hamel, *Poverty and Charity*, 20–21; Krauss, *Talmudische Archäologie*, 1:124–126 (on eggs); 2:134–137 (on milk and milk products). Although eggs appear only once in the New Testament (Luke 11:12), they are more common in tannaitic literature (e.g., *m. Eduyyot* 2:4 [ed. Albeck 4:289, which describes a kind of vegetable omelet]; *t. Terumot* 9:5 [ed. Lieberman 1:156, which appears as a *baraita* on *b. Hullin* 64b]; *t. Zavim* 2:5 [ed. Zuckermandel 677]). Although Josephus claims that, owing to the excellent grass in the area, the cattle in Judea yield more milk than do cattle in other districts, it seems that Palestinian Jews, much like their Roman contemporaries, did not drink much cow's milk, let alone milk itself. When they did require milk, it was obtained mainly from a

Finally, the diet was rounded out by a variety of other foods, including water,[28] nuts,[29] spices,[30] honey,[31] and salt.[32] Although not every person would have had access to this cornucopia of food items, this brief survey provides an overview of the possible food choices in the spatial and temporal location in which tannaitic literature was composed and redacted.[33]

HOW DID THEY OBTAIN THEIR FOOD?

The primary means of obtaining a variety of food items seems to have been the widespread and economically important markets that occurred on both permanent and periodic bases throughout Palestine and, in fact, in the entire Roman Empire.[34] Any and all of the food items mentioned in the previous section were available for purchase or barter at these markets. Both men and women went to the market, although rabbinic literature evidences a discomfort with women doing so. Further, as will be discussed throughout this study, the Tannaim in general either did not interfere with economic exchange in the market (for example, by prescribing a blanket prohibition against all economic activities between Jews and

---

sheep or a goat. See Josephus, *Jewish War*, 3:50; Joan M. Frayn, *Subsistence Farming in Roman Italy* (London: Centaur Press, 1979), 41.

[28] See Hamel, *Poverty and Charity*, 21–22.

[29] E.g., *m. Pe'ah* 4:1 (ed. Albeck 1:49).

[30] On spices, see Hamel, *Poverty and Charity*, 21; Krauss, *Talmudische Archäologie*, 1:118–119; Safrai, *Economy of Roman Palestine*, 146–147.

[31] On honey, see Safrai, *Economy of Roman Palestine*, 182–184.

[32] On salt, see Hamel, *Poverty and Charity*, 21; Krauss, *Talmudische Archäologie*, 1:119; Safrai, *Economy of Roman Palestine*, 185–187 (on salt production).

[33] For a discussion of the different diets of those living in ancient Palestine, based on both class and occupation, see Hamel, *Poverty and Charity*, 22–43. For a survey of available food choices in antiquity that is oriented toward scholars of early Christianity, see Andrew McGowan, *Ascetic Eucharists: Food and Drink in Early Christian Ritual Meals* (Oxford: Clarendon Press, 1999), 35–45.

[34] On markets in Tannaitic-period Palestine, see especially Ben-Zion Rosenfeld and Joseph Menirav, *Markets and Marketing in Roman Palestine*, trans. Chava Cassel (Boston: Brill, 2005); also see L. de Light, *Fairs and Markets in the Roman Empire: Economic and Social Aspects of Periodic Trade in a Pre-Industrial Society* (Amsterdam: J. C. Gieben, 1993), 70–73, 128; Hayim Lapin, *Early Rabbinic Civil Law and the Social History of Roman Galilee: A Study of Mishnah Tractate* Baba' Meṣi'a', BJS 307 (Atlanta: Scholars Press, 1995), 134–147; Safrai, *Economy of Roman Palestine*, 222–321. On Roman markets in general, see de Light, *Fairs and Markets*. Although there are differences in the food resources to which an inhabitant of a city or a village had access, I have tried my best in this section (and, indeed, in this chapter as a whole) to describe the variety of possibilities available to a resident of Roman-period Palestine in general. For the specific differences between resources available in towns and cities during this time, please consult the sources cited earlier in this note.

non-Jews), or they created accommodations that allowed rabbinic Jews to engage in commerce with non-Jews and nonrabbinic Jews.[35]

In addition to markets, one could acquire cooked food from a hostel or inn, which served travelers and, in Palestine in particular, pilgrims.[36] Although inns served prepared foods, some tannaitic texts suggest that travelers occasionally provided their own food to be cooked by the proprietor.[37]

People also procured both raw and prepared food items through informal systems of borrowing and bartering with friends and neighbors. These informal arrangements were often gendered, as they are usually described in tannaitic literature as occurring between the wife of one rabbinic Jew and the wife of another (predominantly) nonrabbinic Jew. As such, I comment further on them in Chapter 3.

One could also engage in agriculture, hunt, and/or gather. Although tannaitic literature prescribes various tithing and agricultural production practices, the impact of these pronouncements is uncertain, though most likely minimal. Subsistence production was common, but there is no indication that tannaitic prescriptions were widely followed.[38] Likewise, although the Tannaim frowned on hunting, they did not ban it outright, but only on the Sabbath and festivals.[39] Although the Tannaim

---

[35] This view accords with the evaluation of Rosenfeld and Menirav, *Markets and Marketing*, 177–179. Although the Tannaim do attempt to regulate economic interactions between Jews and non-Jews on occasion, these rules do not prevent such activities from occurring completely, only under certain conditions and in specific circumstances. For an example of perhaps the most far-reaching of this legislation, see *m. Avodah Zarah* 1:1–3 (ed. Albeck 4:325–326; *t. Avodah Zarah* 1:1–18 [ed. Zuckermandel 460–461]), which limits the economic interactions between Jews and non-Jews on the days surrounding "the festivals of Gentiles."

[36] For the extant textual and material evidence, see Rosenfeld and Menirav, *Markets and Marketing*, 223–226; Ben-Zion Rosenfeld, "Innkeeping in Jewish Society in Roman Palestine," *JESHO* 41/2 (1998): 133–158.

[37] See *m. Demai* 3:5 (ed. Albeck 1:79); *t. Demai* 4:32 (ed. Lieberman 1:84), discussed in Chapter 3.

[38] On agricultural production of food in general, see Safrai, *Economy of Roman Palestine*, 104–161, 219–221. Even though some of these laws are biblically based, the interpretation of these regulations varied among different Jewish communities in antiquity. Although tannaitic tithing prescriptions appear throughout the corpus, tractate *Pe'ah* provides a sustained discussion of these regulations (ed. Albeck 1:41–66; ed. Lieberman 1:41–61). For an interesting recent reassessment of tractate *Pe'ah*, see Gardner, Giving to the Poor.

[39] E.g., *m. Shabbat* 1:6 (ed. Albeck 2:19); *m. Betzah* 3:1–2 (ed. Albeck 2:294). For a discussion, see Hamel, *Poverty and Charity*, 20; also see Krauss, *Talmudische Archäologie*, 2:143–145. On fishing, see Krauss, *Talmudische Archäologie*, 2:145–146; Hamel, *Poverty and Charity*, 20; Safrai, *Economy of Roman Palestine*, 163–164.

did not discuss the issue of hunting much, it would seem that – given their innovative slaughtering practices, discussed in Chapters 2 and 4 – hunting a wild animal would not allow for the controlled environment and comparative precision encountered when slaughtering a domesticated animal.

Finally, whereas the bounty provided by gathering of available foodstuffs depended on where one resided (as well as on the season, weather patterns, and other factors), the officially endorsed, although not necessarily adhered-to, agricultural policy of the Tannaim was explicitly intended (based on biblical precepts) to aid indigent members of society in finding available food to gather.[40]

HOW DID THEY PREPARE THEIR FOOD?

As mentioned in the first section on diet, Jews and non-Jews in the ancient Mediterranean ate a variety of foods prepared in a variety of ways, including (but in no way limited to) raw, cooked, steamed, boiled, baked, preserved, and pickled. Because this chapter is not intended to provide exhaustive details about the historical realia of food production and consumption in the Tannaitic period, I focus here on the three culinary items that represent the so-called Mediterranean triad: grains, oil, and wine.[41] Further, because bread constituted half the caloric intake in the average daily diet, I offer more specific details about this process in particular.

The staple food of bread reached the tannaitic table in Roman-period Palestine in one of two ways: (1) it was purchased from a professional baker; or (2) it was made by a woman (usually, a wife) in or around the home. This conclusion, drawn from the texts themselves, leads to an interesting gender binary, as professional bakers are understood in both

---

[40] For example, see the various regulations found in *m. Pe'ah* (ed. Albeck 1:41–66). On the biblical basis for these laws, see Leviticus 19:9–19; 23:22; Deuteronomy 14:28–29; 24:19–22. In general, see Gardner, Giving to the Poor.

[41] On the Mediterranean triad in antiquity, see Garnsey, *Food and Society*, 13–17. The "Mediterranean diet" has been trumpeted as part of a healthy lifestyle over the past few decades. For a brief history of this phenomenon, see John Dickie, *Delizia!: The Epic History of the Italians and Their Food* (London: Hodder & Stoughton, 2007), 302–305. I discuss the Mediterranean triad further in Chapter 2.

Jewish and contemporary non-Jewish sources to be men.[42] However, tannaitic sources and the contemporary material culture indicate that most bread was made in or near the home by women.[43] For this reason, I focus here on the historical realia that underlies tannaitic discourse about women baking bread.

Making bread required a significant investment of time, labor, and money. Further, in antiquity[44] preparing food was a process that often involved the sharing of supplies and labor among the (almost always female) domestic cooks. As Cynthia M. Baker notes in regard to Tannaitic-period Palestine:

[O]vens, grindstones, and other everyday food-preparation tools might be shared by any number of people – within or outside a single dwelling – and require a fair degree of coming and going, giving and taking. We might imagine such arrangements in places where we find, for example, grinding mills that are not the small mortars or slabs used for more limited quantities of dry goods, but are larger installations that represent communal or commercial enterprise. These larger grinding mills (found at many sites) likely saw shared use, perhaps joint ownership, by a number of living groups.[45]

The fact that tannaitic literature contains literary fossils of such culinary and commensal interactions, as we shall see in Chapter 3, is therefore unsurprising.

[42] Garnsey, *Food and Society*, 110; Susan Weingarten, "'Magiros,' 'Nahtom' and Women at Home: Cooks in the Talmud," *JJS* 59/2 (2005): 285–297. I discuss the gender issues associated with tannaitic bread production in Chapter 3.
[43] See Rosenfeld and Menirav, *Markets and Marketing*, 95.
[44] And, one could argue, in cross-cultural history perhaps up until the popularization of the fast food industry and microwave meals (particularly in America) starting in the 1950s and 1960s. On the fast food industry, see Eric Schlosser, *Fast Food Nation: The Dark Side of the All-American Meal* (Boston: Houghton Mifflin, 2001). To offer two illustrative statistics: (1) one in three American children eats fast food for at least one meal a day; and (2) 19 percent of American meals are consumed in a motor vehicle (Pollan, *Omnivore's Dilemma*, 109, 110). On the effects of the microwave on food preparation and commensality in American culture, see MacClancy, *Consuming Culture*, 100, 215. Reacting to this trend, Carlo Petrini founded the "Slow Food" movement in Italy in 1986. The Slow Food movement draws on, and sometimes idealizes, traditional foodways. For a synopsis of its views, see Simona Malatesta, Sarah Weiner, and Winnie Yang, *The Slow Food Companion* (Bra, Italy: Centro Stampa srl, 2006).
[45] Cynthia M. Baker, *Rebuilding the House of Israel: Architectures of Gender in Jewish Antiquity* (Stanford, CA: Stanford University Press, 2002), 39. The sharing of ovens among Palestinian households (often in the courtyard) is also noted by Yizhar Hirschfeld (*The Palestinian Dwelling in the Roman–Byzantine Period* [Jerusalem: Israel Exploration Society, 1995], 140, 274).

The process of making bread in the Tannaitic period is as follows.[46] First, one must grind grain into flour in a mill.[47] Second, one must sift the flour.[48] Third, one must add water,[49] leaven,[50] salt,[51] and, if desired, spices

---

[46] A brief tannaitic summary of the entire process appears in *t. Berakhot* 6:2 (ed. Lieberman 1:33). For a synthetic, and less technical, overview of this process (which combines both Palestinian and Babylonian data), see Cooper, *Eat and Be Satisfied*, 37–42.

[47] The use of a mill/millstone (*rēḥayim*) is mentioned in regard to professional bakers (e.g., *m. Bava Batra* 2:3 [ed. Albeck 4:120–121]) and wives (e.g., *m. Ketubbot* 5:5 [ed. Albeck 3:105]; *m. Shevi'it* 5:9 [ed. Albeck 1:153–154]; *t. Ketubbot* 7:4 [ed. Lieberman 3:79]), as well as professional millers, that is, those who own a large mill and charge a fee for its use (e.g., *m. Demai* 3:4 [ed. Albeck 1:78–79]; implied in *t. Bava Qamma* 10:9 [ed. Lieberman 5:51–52]). On milling in rabbinic literature, see Krauss, *Talmudische Archäologie*, 1:93–97; Saul Lieberman, "[Grain] Mills and Those Who Work Them," *Tarbiz* 50 (1980–1981), 128–135 (Hebrew); and in the Roman world in general, see K. D. White, "Cereals, Bread and Milling in the Roman World," in *Food and Antiquity*, ed. John Wilkins, David Harvey, and Mike Dobson, 38–43 (Exeter, UK: University of Exeter Press, 1996), 40–41. According to Dar, the climate of Palestine prevents flour from being kept for a long period of time, thus necessitating grinding it on a daily basis ("Food and Archaeology," 330). In fact, according to *t. Niddah* 6:9 (ed. Zuckermandel 648), girls who grow up in villages develop larger breasts earlier than girls who are raised in the city because of the fact that, in a village, a girl must "work the grindstone" (and, by implication, in the city, a girl purchases flour or bread from a baker and, thus, does not develop in quite the same manner). Although *t. Pisha* 2:1 (ed. Lieberman 2:144–145) mentions the existence of bakers in villages, Rosenfeld and Menirav claim that "it can be assumed that this was a less common phenomenon than in urban settlements" (*Markets and Marketing*, 98). Prior to this process, grain was stored in the domestic space, often in clay silos. For a discussion of the relevant archaeological remains from Palestinian dwellings, see Hirschfeld, *Palestinian Dwelling*, 135–137.

[48] The use of a sieve/sifter (*nāpāh* or *kĕbārāh*) is also mentioned in regard to both professional bakers (e.g., *m. Kelim* 15:3, 4 [ed. Albeck 6:69–70]) and wives (e.g., *m. Shevi'it* 5:9 [ed. Albeck 1:153–154]). For a brief discussion of rabbinic references to this process, see Krauss, *Talmudische Archäologie*, 1:97–99. The sieve can also be used for other cooking purposes. For example, see Cato, *On Agriculture*, 76, which directs one to pass cheese through a flour sieve as part of a recipe for *placenta* (a type of cheesecake used in certain rituals). This step has quite an effect on the bread produced. As Weingarten notes, "There were different sizes of sieves, which let coarser or finer flour through. The quality of the bread thus depended not only on the raw material – wheat, barley or other grain – but on the fineness or coarseness of the flour produced" ("'Magiros,'" 292). See also Dar, "Food and Archaeology," 329–330.

[49] E.g., *m. Hallah* 3:1 (ed. Albeck 1:281; = *Sifre Numbers* 110 [ed. Horowitz 114]); *m. Betzah* 5:4 (ed. Albeck 2:300; = *t. Yom Tov* 4:6 [ed. Lieberman 2:302]) and implied in *m. Teharot* 4:10 (ed. Albeck 6:312–313).

[50] On leaven in bread in rabbinic literature, see Dar, "Food and Archaeology," 330; Krauss, *Talmudische Archäologie*, 1:99–100; and, in the ancient Mediterranean in general, see Dalby, *Food in the Ancient World*, 59; White, "Cereals, Bread and Milling," 41. Obviously, as discussed in n. 55, the use of leaven in bread presents a problem for the observance of Passover – of which the celebration includes a biblically mandated avoidance of leavened food items.

[51] E.g., *m. Betzah* 5:4 (ed. Albeck 2:300; = *t. Yom Tov* 4:6 [ed. Lieberman 2:302]).

or flavorings[52] to the flour to make dough. Fourth, one must knead the ingredients together to combine them and to attain the proper consistency (necessary for even baking and often dependent on one's personal preference).[53] Fifth, biblically and tannaitically ordained law requires one to separate out a portion of the dough as an offering to God.[54] Sixth, one must allow the dough to "rest" (i.e., to rise), permitting the yeast to ferment, expanding the size of the dough, and making it easier to roll.[55]

---

[52] Spices and flavors added to bread mentioned in tannaitic literature include wine, oil, and various liquids (*Mekhilta d'Rabbi Ishmael Bo* 10 [ed. Horowitz 35]), as well as the generic label of spices (*tablin*) in *m. Betzah* 5:4 (ed. Albeck 2:300; = *t. Yom Tov* 4:6 [ed. Lieberman 2:302]).

[53] On kneading dough, see e.g., *m. Pesahim* 3:4 (ed. Albeck 2:150; cp. *t. Pisha* 3:8 [ed. Lieberman 2:153] and *Mekhilta d'Rabbi Shimon b. Yohai* at Exodus 12:17 [ed. Epstein and Melamed 22]); *m. Menahot* 5:2 (ed. Albeck 5:74); *m. Tevul Yom* 4:2, 3 (ed. Albeck 6:467); *t. Bava Metzi'a* 8:7 (ed. Lieberman 5:104); *t. Ahilot* 5:11 (ed. Zuckermandel 602–603). The process of kneading dough requires water (e.g., *t. Pisha* 3:5, 7 [ed. Lieberman 2:151–152]) and occurs in a kneading trough (*'ărēbāh*; e.g., *m. Tevul Yom* 4:3 [ed. Albeck 6:467]; *m. Ohalot* 5:4 [ed. Albeck 6:139–140]; *m. Teharot* 8:8 [ed. Albeck 6:326–327]). On kneading and kneading troughs in rabbinic literature, see Krauss, *Talmudische Archäologie*, 1:100–101.

[54] On this regulation in the Hebrew Bible, see Numbers 15:18–20. This rule is often discussed in tannaitic literature; e.g., *m. Hallah* 1:1 and *passim* (ed. Albeck 1:275, 275–288; cp. *t. Hallah* [ed. Lieberman 1:275–282]); *m. Pesahim* 3:3 (ed. Albeck 2:150); *m. Niddah* 10:7 (ed. Albeck 6:406–407, which permits a woman to separate the dough offering even while menstruating); *m. Tevul Yom* 4:2, 3 (ed. Albeck 6:467); *Sifre Numbers* 110 (ed. Horowitz 113–116, extensively quoting *m. Hallah*). According to *m. Hallah* 2:7 (ed. Albeck 1:280), the necessary amount of dough to separate is one-twenty-fourth of the batch for domestic use and one-forty-eighth for professional bakers (and also for nonprofessional female bakers who intend to sell surplus dough in the market, a practice that Weingarten suggests is rare ["'Magiros,'" 293]). Originally, this offering was baked and given to the priests. Following the destruction of the Second Temple, the rabbis maintained that this offering must continue. Consequently, the separated piece of dough is burned in the oven as a symbolic offering to God. On the modern Jewish practice of separating a portion of dough, see Maggie Glezer, *A Blessing of Bread: The Many Rich Traditions of Jewish Bread Baking Around the World* (New York: Artisan, 2004), 317–323.

[55] Obviously, this step is minimized on Passover. In fact, in *Mekhilta d'Rabbi Ishmael Bo* 10 (ed. Horowitz 32–33; cp. *m. Pesahim* 3:4 [ed. Albeck 2:150; cp. *t. Pisha* 3:8 (ed. Lieberman 2:153) and *Mekhilta d'Rabbi Shimon b. Yohai* at Exodus 12:17 (ed. Epstein and Melamed 22)]), one is instructed to watch over dough on Passover and to punch it down with cold water on one's hands. This step disrupts the process of fermentation from properly occurring, which is why bakers even today suggest that it be avoided (Glezer, *Blessing of Bread*, 47). Even though open cells and an uneven texture result from punching dough down, this is necessary to ensure that unleavened bread is served on Passover.

Seventh, one must roll out[56] and shape[57] the fermented dough. Finally, the dough is baked in an oven and becomes, through the transformative cultural (and, of course, physical) process of preparation and the application of fire, bread.[58]

But bread is not consumed alone. Most often, the accompaniment for bread was olives – either whole (fresh, preserved, sliced) or, more commonly, in the form of olive oil.[59] The majority of olive crops were pressed to produce olive oil. In antiquity, as today, most olive oil was made in an olive press, and the first cold press was (and still is) most prized.[60] Pressing olive oil involved three steps: (1) crushing the olives;

---

[56] On rolling, see e.g., *m. Menahot* 5:2 (ed. Albeck 5:74); *m. Hallah* 3:1 (ed. Albeck 1:281; = *t. Hallah* 1:11 [ed. Lieberman 1:277]; *Sifre Numbers* 110 [ed. Horowitz 114]). Rolling, of course, requires a rolling pin (e.g., *m. Kelim* 15:2 [ed. Albeck 6:69]). It is perhaps because of the common association between women and rolling dough that a woman is to be examined for the plague (*nega'*) "like she rolls dough" (*m. Nega'im* 2:4 [ed. Albeck 6:205]).

[57] According to Krauss, dough is shaped either by hand or in a mold (*Talmudische Archäologie*, 1:101). As is also often the case today, dough shaped by hand implies domestically produced bread, whereas bread made in a mold (and thus, uniform and even) implies that it is the product of a professional baker (Rosenfeld and Menirav, *Markets and Marketing*, 95).

[58] On baking dough into bread, see e.g., *m. Ketubbot* 7:6 (ed. Albeck 3:112); *m. Eduyyot* 3:10 (ed. Albeck 4:296); *t. Bava Metzi'a* 8:7 (ed. Lieberman 5:104); *t. Yom Tov* 2:5 (ed. Lieberman 2:287). Because bakers have larger and hotter ovens, women sometimes prepare the dough themselves and then give the dough to a baker to bake for a small fee (e.g., *m. Hallah* 1:7 [ed. Albeck 1:277]). This practice also results from the fact that crowding and lack of space in some environments require one to pay for use of a baker's oven, much like the usage of a professional miller's millstone (for archaeological references, see Weingarten, "'Magiros,'" 293). Baking bread, as is the case with most culinary items in antiquity, employs one of two techniques: "first, baking directly in the hot ashes or fire, and second, baking in an enclosed heated container" (Anthony Cubberley, "Bread-Baking in Ancient Italy: *Clibanus* and *Sub Testu* in the Roman World: Further Thoughts," in *Food and Antiquity*, ed. John Wilkins, David Harvey, and Mike Dobson, 55–68 [Exeter, UK: University of Exeter Press, 1996], 56). On baking bread in rabbinic literature in general, see Krauss, *Talmudische Archäologie*, 1:101–102. For archaeological data on ovens in Palestinian dwellings, see Hirschfeld, *Palestinian Dwelling*, 140–141.

[59] In fact, the legal measurement for what constitutes an act of eating is often considered an amount of food that equals an olive's bulk (*kazayit*). This yardstick is found throughout tannaitic corpus (e.g., *t. Berakhot* 5:28 [ed. Lieberman 1:30]; *Sifra Emor pereq* 4 [ed. Weiss 97a]; *Mekilta d'Rabbi Shimon b. Yohai* at Exodus 12:4 [ed. Epstein and Melamed 10]). On eating bread with olives, see, for example, *t. Eduyyot* 2:2 (ed. Zuckermandel 457).

[60] See *m. Menahot* 8:4–5 (ed. Albeck 5:84–85; = *Sifra Emor parasha* 13 [ed. Weiss 103a–b]). An olive oil press is described in *m. Bava Batra* 4:5 (ed. Albeck 4:131) as consisting of a reservoir or vat for collecting the liquid (*yām*); a press-beam to crush the olives

(2) collecting the olive mash in baskets, which were piled on top of one another and pressed; and (3) separating the olive oil from the "black watery lees."[61] Because olive trees produce a sufficient crop usually only every other year, people needed to store a surplus of oil. Luckily, olive oil preserves well.[62]

Wine is the third member of the Mediterranean triad.[63] To paraphrase Psalm 104:15, wine gladdens the heart of humankind.[64] The production of wine first required grapes, which were (and remain to this day) difficult to grow because of the vine's sensitivity to environmental factors, including soil and weather.[65] After the grapes were grown and collected, wine production involved three main steps: (1) the grapes were trodden on a treading floor and the resulting liquid collected in a vat; (2) the remaining grape skins were pressed out (this step is optional); and (3) the juice was allowed to ferment into wine.[66] The longer the juice was allowed to

---

(*mamāl*); supporting posts for the pressing-beam (*bĕtûlôt*); pressing boards (*'ăkîrîn*); a wheel (*galgal*); and a beam that moves via the wheel (*qôrāh*). The component parts of the olive press are explained in detail by Rafael Frankel, "Presses for Oil and Wine in the Southern Levant in the Byzantine Period," *Dumbarton Oaks Papers* 51 (1997): 73–84; Krauss, *Talmudische Archäologie*, 2:217–226. Olive presses came in a variety of sizes, both large and small (e.g., *m. Shevi'it* 8:6 [ed. Albeck 1:161]). For references to archaeological discoveries of olive presses in Palestine, see Dar, "Food and Archaeology," 331; Rosenfeld and Menirav, *Markets and Marketing*, 223, 227 (who discuss the close proximity and association between synagogue and olive press remains). On the price of olive oil in Roman Palestine, see Safrai, *Economy of Roman Palestine*, 125–126.

[61] Frankel, "Presses for Oil and Wine," 74.

[62] For references on olive oil storage, see Hamish Forbes and Lin Foxhall, "Ethnoarchaeology and Storage in the Ancient Mediterranean: Beyond Risk and Survival," in *Food and Antiquity*, ed. John Wilkins, David Harvey, and Mike Dobson, 69–86 (Exeter, UK: University of Exeter Press, 1996), 74–75. According to Hamel, "[a]n olive tree in full production could give from 8 to 10 liters of oil per year" (*Poverty and Charity*, 10; see also Broshi, "Diet of Palestine," 127; Safrai, *Economy of Roman Palestine*, 123–125, 127).

[63] Wine was the beverage of choice in Palestine, whereas beer was the preferred drink in Egypt (and, as noted earlier, in Babylonia). Broshi aptly summarizes this difference: "Someone once said: behold the power of geography. Had Jesus been born in Egypt rather than in Palestine, the Christian ritual would use beer instead of wine (in the sacrament of the Eucharist) to this very day" ("Wine in Ancient Palestine," 145).

[64] This verse is cited on *t. Pisha* 10:4 (ed. Lieberman 2:196), which connects festival joy with imbibing wine.

[65] Krauss, *Talmudische Archäologie*, 2:227–232; Safrai, *Economy of Roman Palestine*, 128. Grape horticulture is mentioned in *m. Menahot* 8:6 (ed. Albeck 5:85).

[66] Frankel, "Presses for Oil and Wine," 74; see also Krauss, *Talmudische Archäologie*, 2:233–236. For tannaitic references to wine production, see e.g., *m. Avodah Zarah* 4:8–9 (ed. Albeck 4:338–339); *t. Avodah Zarah* 7:1, 3–5 (ed. Zuckermandel 471); *m. Shevi'it* 8:6 (ed. Albeck 1:161; = *t. Shevi'it* 6:28 [ed. Lieberman 1:194]).

ferment, the better the quality of the wine. As is the case in modern times, the Tannaim (and other classical authors) preferred old to new wine.[67]

Because of the economic and time constraints involved in grinding grain into flour and pressing olives into oil and grapes into wine, these acts were often undertaken by professional bakers and olive/wine pressers.[68] Sometimes the professional producers would sell their own goods. Otherwise a merchant (*tagār*) would purchase finished goods from these professionals and, acting as an intermediary, sell them to the public.[69] Although these food preparation processes occurred in some homes, wine and oil in particular were much more commonly acquired from a second or third party, rather than produced by an individual for personal consumption.

IN WHAT MANNER DID THEY EAT THEIR FOOD?

All the extant evidence suggests that, on the macro level (i.e., in general structure and appearance), tannaitic meals followed the typical patterns encountered throughout the ancient Mediterranean. Even though no tannaitic text of which I am aware offers information concerning the number of meals consumed on a daily basis, it seems reasonable to presume that the Roman meal structure would have been in place: a small breakfast eaten a few hours into the day, a small lunch around noon, and a larger dinner at the end of the day. However, those with limited resources were often able to afford only at most two meals a day.[70] More elaborate meals, usually dinners, appear to be quite similar

---

[67] E.g., *Sifra Behar pereq* 7 (ed. Weiss 109b). For a discussion, see Broshi, "Wine in Ancient Palestine," 151; Garnsey, *Food and Society*, 118–119. Although old wine is preferred, "[m]uch of the wine was probably light and did not keep very long" (Hamel, *Poverty and Charity*, 22).

[68] As noted earlier, obtaining bread from a professional baker appears to have been much more common in urban than in rural environments.

[69] E.g., *m. Bava Metzi'a* 4:11–12 (ed. Albeck 4:82–83). On the *tagār*, see Rosenfeld and Menirav, *Markets and Marketing*, 124–126, especially p. 125.

[70] For references and discussion about Roman daily meals, see Pedar William Foss, Kitchens and Dining Rooms at Pompeii: The Spatial and Social Relationship of Cooking to Eating in the Roman Household (Ph.D. dissertation, University of Michigan, 1994), 27–30. Safrai's suggestion that Jews in ancient Palestine ate two daily meals might reflect the perspective of the poor, although he provides no sources, rabbinic or otherwise, to support this claim (*Economy of Roman Palestine*, 105). Safrai does note that a third

to extant depictions of contemporaneous Roman and Greek banquets.[71] To offer the most commonly cited example, *t. Berakhot* 4:8 states:

What is the order of a meal [at a banquet]? Guests enter, and they are seated on benches and on chairs until [all the guests] are gathered [and seated]. [After] all of them are gathered, [and the servants] have given them [water] for their hands, every [guest] washes one hand.[72] When [the attendants] have mixed for them the cup [of wine], each one recites the benediction [over wine] for himself.[73] [When] they have brought before them appetizers,[74] each one recites the benediction [over them] himself. [When] they have arisen [from the benches and/or chairs] and reclined [for the second course of the meal] and [the attendants] have [again] given them [water] for their hands, even though [each person] has [already] washed one hand, he [now] washes both hands. When [the attendants] have mixed for them the cup [of wine], even though [each person] has [already] recited a benediction over the first [cup], he recites the benediction over the second [cup, as well].[75] [When] they have

---

meal is added on the Sabbath (also see Josephus, *The Life*, 279). I discuss the Sabbath further in Chapter 4.

[71] For references and a brief description, see Dennis E. Smith, *From Symposium to Eucharist: The Banquet in the Early Christian World* (Minneapolis: Fortress Press, 2003), 27–38, 145–147. For a more in-depth survey of the extant evidence, see Katherine M. D. Dunbabin, *The Roman Banquet: Images of Conviviality* (New York: Cambridge University Press, 2003).

[72] If one leaves the meal to urinate or to meet a friend, he must wash his hand(s) before returning. For these laws, see *t. Berakhot* 4:11 (ed. Lieberman 1:20). My usage of masculine pronouns here is intentional. I discuss the issues associated with women and tannaitic commensality in detail in Chapter 3.

[73] On reciting blessings over food both before and after a communal meal, see *m. Berakhot* 6:6; 7:1–5 (ed. Albeck 1:25, 26–28).

[74] Determining which portion went to which guest may have been decided by lots, as *m. Shabbat* 23:2 (ed. Albeck 2:70) implies.

[75] Perhaps the requirement for reciting benedictions again is due to the slight differences, according to *m. Berakhot* 6:6 (ed. Albeck 1:25), between reciting a benediction while sitting (each person recites separately) and while reclining (one person recites for everyone). In regard to the relationship between these two passages, Smith offers two possible reasons for this liturgical difference: (1) "This text [*m. Berakhot* 6:6] appears to be giving a legal definition to a social convention. The social convention is that a group reclining around a table together becomes a table community. The text indicates that the symbolism of table fellowship is especially carried by the setting in which they recline together rather than sit"; and (2) the cups of wine before and after the meal serve different functions. "Served during the meal, wine is evidently considered only an accompaniment. But the cup that is mixed at the end of the meal, and thus at the beginning of the symposium, is traditionally a ceremonial cup.... [T]he ceremonial cup carries the symbolism of a unified table community; thus the benediction over the cup should be said on behalf of all" (*From Symposium to Eucharist*, 146). On the various meanings of dining postures in the Roman period, see Matthew B. Roller,

brought before them desserts,[76] even though [each person] has [already] recited a benediction over the first [appetizers], he recites the benediction over the second [ones, as well], and one [person] recites a benediction for all of them. One who arrives after three [courses of] appetizers [have been served], is not allowed to enter [and participate in the meal].[77]

Although some of the micro details may be different (e.g., reciting the benediction over the appetizers), the banquet customs described herein would not seem too foreign to a non-Jew living at this time in the ancient Mediterranean.

Further, tannaitic literature records the occurrence of several festive meals. Some of these meals have Greek and Roman parallels (e.g., wedding[78] and funeral[79] banquets) and some do not (e.g., Sabbath and

---

Dining Posture in Ancient Rome: Bodies, Values, and Status (Princeton, NJ: Princeton University Press, 2006).

[76] The same word is used to describe a minor dish consumed before and after the meal (*parprā'ôt*).

[77] *t. Berakhot* 4:8 (ed. Lieberman 1:20). For other examples of tannaitic meal etiquette, see *t. Berakhot* 4:10 (ed. Lieberman 1:20); *t. Berakhot* 6:2 (ed. Lieberman 1:34).

[78] There are two types of wedding-related meals mentioned in tannaitic literature: betrothal meals and wedding banquets. On betrothal meals, see *m. Pesahim* 3:7 (ed. Albeck 2:151; = *t. Pisha* 3:12 [ed. Lieberman 2:154]); *m. Ketubbot* 1:5 (ed. Albeck 3:90); *m. Bava Batra* 9:5 (ed. Albeck 4:149); *t. Megillah* 3:14–15 (ed. Lieberman 2:356–357). The betrothal meal apparently involved the recitation of a "groom's blessing." On this blessing (the text of which actually appears for the first time in *b. Ketubbot* 7b–8a), see Michael L. Satlow, *Jewish Marriage in Antiquity* (Princeton, NJ: Princeton University Press, 2001), 63–65, 164. On the wedding banquet (often called a *mišteh*), see *m. Hallah* 2:7 (ed. Albeck 1:280; = *Sifre Numbers* 110 [ed. Horowitz 115]); *m. Nega'im* 3:2 (ed. Albeck 6:206; = *Sifra Tazria pereq* 5; *Mesora parasha* 5 [ed. Weiss 63b, 73a]); *Sifra Behuqotai pereq* 5 (ed. Weiss 111b); *t. Shabbat* 7:9 (ed. Lieberman 2:26); *t. Baba Metzi'a* 8:28 (ed. Lieberman 5:109). For additional references, see Satlow, *Jewish Marriage*, 339–340 n. 107. An inscription from the synagogue at Ḥorbat Susiya (southern Palestine) mentions a rabbi making a donation vow at the wedding feast (*mišteh*) of his son. This mosaic inscription, which is roughly contemporary to the Tannaitic period, provides extra-rabbinic evidence for both this event and this terminology. On this inscription, see Joseph Naveh, *On Stone and Mosaic: The Aramaic and Hebrew Inscriptions from Ancient Synagogues* (Jerusalem: Karta, 1978 [Hebrew]), no. 75 (pp. 115–116); Satlow, *Jewish Marriage*, 179–180. For nonrabbinic evidence for the wedding banquet, see John 2:1–5; Tobit 7–10; *Joseph and Aseneth*, 21:6; Josephus, *Jewish Antiquities*, 5:289.

[79] E.g., *m. Sanhedrin* 2:3 (ed. Albeck 4:174) and *t. Sanhedrin* 4:2 (ed. Zuckermandel 420), which both discuss the case of a king in mourning; *Sifra Qedoshim pereq* 6 (ed. Weiss 90a), which states that one sentenced to death by the court is not entitled to a funeral meal; *t. Mo'ed* 2:17 (ed. Lieberman 2:372–374), which refers to the death of a sage; and *m. Mo'ed Qatan* 3:7 (ed. Albeck 2:383), which contains the most extensive discussion

Sukkot meals).[80] These texts often reflect, like their Greek and Roman contemporaries, a socially and economically elite (and male) perspective.[81]

Finally, although respectable women did not seem to participate in banquets in the Greek custom, the Roman banquet custom reflects an increasing allowance over time of female attendance and participation.[82] The extent to which Roman custom influenced the Tannaim is difficult to ascertain, because tannaitic literature is often silent or ambiguous on this matter, as we shall see in Chapter 3.

REALIA: CONCLUSIONS

In sum, the tannaitic evidence for the diet, means of obtaining food, processes for food preparation, and the cadence of ingestion (on both daily and special occasions) does not seem to differ greatly on the macro level from that of their non-Jewish neighbors and contemporaries. Where it does differ, as we shall see over the course of the next three chapters, is on the micro level – for it is here that the Tannaim innovate and manipulate

---

of the practices at a nonunique (i.e., king or person on death row) funeral banquet. A Greek papyrus from the second half of the first century B.C.E. may refer to a burial association meeting at a *proseuche* (a "place of prayer" in Greek). For this text, see Victor A. Tcherikover, Alexander Fuks, and Menahem Stern, *Corpus Papyrorum Judaicarum*, 3 vols. (Cambridge, MA: Harvard University Press, 1957–1964), 1, no. 138 (pp. 252–254). However, "in view of the condition of our document and the scanty comparative material [in contemporary Jewish texts], it is safer to suspend judgement" (M. Stern, *Corpus Papyrorum Judaicarum*, 1:253). Lee I. Levine seems to interpret this datum in a more positive manner (*The Ancient Synagogue: The First Thousand Years* [New Haven, CT: Yale University Press, 2000], 129). For a brief description of the Greek and Roman funeral meal, see Smith, *From Symposium to Eucharist*, 40–42.

[80] I discuss these meals further in Chapter 4.

[81] On the elite perspective of rabbinic texts, see Catherine Hezser, *Jewish Literacy in Roman Palestine* (Tübingen, Germany: Mohr Siebeck, 2001); and Lapin, *Early Rabbinic Civil Law*; and for a contrasting view, see Lee I. Levine, *The Rabbinic Class of Roman Palestine in Late Antiquity* (New York: Jewish Theological Seminary, 1989), 69–71. For a textual example, see *Mekilta d'Rabbi Ishmael Yitro Amalek* 1 (ed. Horowitz 195–196), which assumes both that a banquet requires servants to bring out the food and that the status of those serving the food is inferior to that of those consuming the food.

[82] For a discussion, see Kathleen E. Corley, *Private Women, Public Meals: Social Conflict in the Synoptic Tradition* (Peabody, MA: Hendrickson, 1993), 24–66; Roller, *Dining Posture*, 96–156; Smith, *From Symposium to Eucharist*, 42–44.

food practices to construct a distinctly Jewish, male, and rabbinic identity. Having thus provided an orientation in terms of the historical realia of food production and consumption in ancient Palestine, we can now turn to an analysis of the tannaitic discourse on culinary and commensal regulations.

2

Jewish Identity

> In a village in Hesse the peasants enjoyed a stewlike bean soup (probably a form of Schalet). When questioned about what they were eating, they would laugh and say, "Today, I'm a Jew."[1]

Tannaitic culinary and commensal regulations prescribe social practices that enact and maintain a distinct Jewish identity. Non-Jews are understood to eat different foods in a different manner, resulting in different bodies.

The Tannaim build their Jewish identity via three food practices. First, they understand the ingestion of certain foods to be symbolic, or metonymic, of Self/Other. Concomitantly, a person is embodied by the consumption of – or abstinence from – metonymic food items. As we shall see, this phenomenon is not unique to tannaitic Judaism. One recent example of embodiment through ingestion is the renaming of "French fries" as "freedom fries" in the U.S. House of Representatives' cafeteria from 2003 through 2006. In this instance, differing views on policy toward Iraq led to a desire among some U.S. Representatives to rename a food item, lest by ingesting "French" food, one would become, in some way, "French." Tannaitic texts reflect this same notion, wherein consuming – or abstaining from – certain metonymic foodstuffs is understood to be an act of embodiment; it is a practice that creates an "Us" and a "Them."

---

[1] Marion A. Kaplan, *The Making of the Jewish Middle Class: Women, Family, and Identity in Imperial Germany* (New York: Oxford University Press, 1991), 73. Shaye J. D. Cohen also uses this quote as an epigraph (*The Beginnings of Jewishness: Boundaries, Varieties, Uncertainties* [Berkeley and Los Angeles: University of California Press, 2000], 140). *Schalet* (the German form of *cholent*) is a dish associated with Jews and the Sabbath. On this dish, see Kaplan, *Making of the Jewish Middle Class*, 72–73.

Second, the status of a food is correlated to the status of its preparer. The status and practices of the cook in the tannaitic kitchen therefore become vital for establishing and preserving the identity of the person eating his or her meal.

Third, commensality between Jews and non-Jews is understood as potentially "idolatrous" or as the first step down the slippery slope to "idolatry."[2] Stigmatizing this social practice indicates that, according to the Tannaim, even if the food is kosher, the practice of sharing it with a non-Jew is not.

This chapter explores these three tannaitic practices. Throughout, I seek to answer the question of how these practices construct Jewish identity. To do so, I must first discuss the pre-tannaitic evidence for separation at the table between Jew and non-Jew.

PRE-TANNAITIC EVIDENCE FOR COMMENSALITY RESTRICTIONS

Starting in the Hellenistic period, Jewish literary sources begin to show evidence of "unprecedented restrictions regarding food prepared by or eaten with gentiles."[3] The appearance at this time of these social and legal innovations is not coincidental. In the broader historical context, as noted in the Introduction, these commensal regulations are part of a larger process of identity formation. Discussing this overarching trend, Shaye Cohen states:

> ... in the century following the Hasmonean rebellion [167–142 B.C.E.] two new meanings of "Judeans" [*Ioudaioi*] emerge: Judeans are all of those, of

---

[2] The terms "idolatrous" and "idolatry" are polemical terms that should not be accepted as static and natural categories. For a general discussion, with particular emphasis on "idolatry" in texts of the Hebrew Bible, see Nathaniel B. Levtow, *Images of Others: Iconic Politics in Ancient Israel*, Biblical and Judaic Studies, Vol. 11 (Winona Lake, IN, Eisenbrauns, 2008), especially pp. 1–18. When I use these terms, I am referring to a tannaitic polemical category of practice. Although I do not place them in quotes every time, the caveats pointed out by Levtow always inform my usage of these terms. For a longer discussion of the application of Levtow's critiques to tannaitic texts, see Jordan D. Rosenblum, "From Their Bread to Their Bed: Commensality, Intermarriage, and Idolatry in Tannaitic Literature," *JJS*: in press.

[3] David Moshe Freidenreich, Foreign Food: Restrictions on the Food of Members of Other Religions in Jewish, Christian, and Islamic Law (Ph.D. dissertation, Columbia University, 2006), 82–83.

whatever ethnic or geographic origins, who worship the God whose temple is in Jerusalem (a religious definition), or who have become citizens of the state established by the Judeans (a political definition). In contrast with ethnic identity, religious and political identities are mutable: gentiles can abandon their false gods and accept the true God, and non-Judeans can become citizens of the Judean state. Thus, with the emergence of these new definitions in the second century B.C.E., the metaphoric boundary separating Judeans from non-Judeans became more and more permeable. *Outsiders could become insiders.*[4]

With the bifurcation of the term "Judean," translating "Judeans" (*Ioudaioi*) as "Jews," as referring to a religion and not an ethnicity, becomes an historically accurate nomenclature.

Coinciding with this shift in the boundaries of identity is the understanding that new "dangers" exist. Dining together is not an issue in the Hebrew Bible, except in the book of Daniel (discussed in the next paragraph), which is – not coincidentally – a Hellenistic-period text. For example, although the biblical books of Ezra and Nehemiah contain several invectives against intermarriage, they lack any commensality prohibitions.[5] However, the fact that the person sitting across from "you" can now become "you" leads to the creation of new social mores. Put simply, sharing a table is less fraught when, to rephrase Cohen, outsiders cannot become insiders.

This shift in view toward sharing the food and/or table of non-Jews is encountered in the late biblical book of Daniel. Daniel refuses to "defile himself" by eating the food provided by the Gentile King Nebuchadnezzar.[6] John Collins understands Daniel's refusal as an extension of the Israelite system of purity laws, which were "a symbolic means

---

[4] *Beginnings of Jewishness*, 109–110, emphasis added. For a recent critique of this approach, see Steve Mason, "Jews, Judaeans, Judaizing, Judaism: Problems of Categorization in Ancient Judaism," *JSJ* 38 (2007): 457–512.

[5] For a discussion, see Freidenreich, Foreign Food, 55–56.

[6] Daniel 1:5–16. On the date of Daniel, see John J. Collins, *Daniel: A Commentary on the Book of Daniel*, Hermeneia (Minneapolis: Fortress Press, 1993), 24–38; Louis F. Hartman and Alexander A. Di Lella, *The Book of Daniel: A New Translation with Introduction and Commentary*, AB, vol. 23 (New York: Doubleday, 1978), 29–42. Although the redacted version of Daniel dates to the first years of the Hasmonean Revolt, Collins dates the first chapter to the third century B.C.E. (*Daniel*, 36). If this dating is correct, then this trend is evidenced starting in texts that predate the Hasmonean Revolt. Regardless, these opening salvos explode in number in the period immediately following the revolt, as noted by Cohen.

of setting the people apart. The need for such symbols was more acute in the context of the Exile. Refusal of the king's food was not a refusal of political allegiance but a declaration of separate identity and an affirmation of the unconquered dignity of the exiles."[7] Freidenreich offers another anthropological theory for this passage:

Applying the insights of Claude Lévi-Strauss, one can further argue that Daniel's concerns specifically over prepared food stems from the fact that the act of food preparation ("cooking") by a gentile transforms a "raw" natural object into an embodiment of gentile culture best not ingested by a Jew who wishes to maintain a distinct cultural identity. After all, Daniel is happy to receive vegetables and water from gentiles.[8]

Both Collins and Freidenreich use anthropological literature to establish the fact that Daniel's refusal to partake of Nebuchadnezzar's food is a practice-based statement of identity. As the book of Daniel does not explicitly state that the ingredients per se are an issue, it seems that the fact that the food is presumably prepared by non-Jewish cooks for a non-Jewish king is Daniel's concern.[9]

The refusal by a Jew to eat the food and/or eat at the table of a non-Jewish authority figure (e.g., a political, military, or religious ruler) becomes a trope in Hasmonean-period texts. Interestingly, these sources do not reference culinary items explicitly prohibited by the Hebrew Bible. In the Greek version of Esther, for example, Esther exclaims, "Your maidservant has not dined at Haman's table, nor have I extolled a royal feast

---

[7] *Daniel*, 146. Collins references here Mary Douglas's classic study (*Purity and Danger: An Analysis of the Concepts of Pollution and Taboo* [New York: Routledge, 1999 (1966)], 42–58). Although Collins' understanding about the connection between commensality and impurity may be correct for the book of Daniel, this association in the context of meals shared between Jews and non-Jews does not appear in the tannaitic corpus, as I discuss later.

[8] Foreign Food, 69. Daniel accepts only water and vegetables from the king in Daniel 1:12–16. Similarly, a diet of vegetables is consumed by "the weak," according to Paul, in Romans 14:3. On the context of this pericope within the larger structure of the letter, see Stanley K. Stowers, *A Rereading of Romans: Justice, Jews, and Gentiles* (New Haven: Yale University Press, 1994), 320–323. Bread, vegetables, and water is also the diet of the Christian protagonists in the second-century C.E. text *The Acts of Paul and Thecla* 25. The absence of meat in these texts is perhaps not inconsequential for another reason, as meat is not consumed in the Garden of Eden. According to Genesis 9:3–4, humans are not allowed eat meat until after the Flood.

[9] Similarly, see Freidenreich, Foreign Food, 67.

nor drunk the wine of libations."[10] In the book of Judith, Judith brings her own food and refuses to use the silver dinnerware, eat the food, and drink the wine of the non-Jewish general Holofernes.[11] Even though she ultimately dines at Holofernes' table, she consumes her own food.[12] In *Joseph and Aseneth*, Joseph eats the Egyptian priest Pentephres' food, but at a separate table;[13] it is only after Joseph and Aseneth wed, following Aseneth's "conversion" experience, that Joseph engages in commensality with his "in-laws."[14]

Whereas sources such as Tobit note the avoidance of "the food of the gentiles,"[15] two Jewish texts from the Hasmonean period severely problematize commensality between Jews and non-Jews: *Jubilees* and the *Letter of Aristeas*. Throughout, I use the term "problematize" to refer to the fact that, even though certain texts do not contain a de jure requirement of separation at meals from Gentiles, they seem to buttress and innovate practices that affect a de facto separation at meals. Therefore, meals that were once acceptable are now socially problematic – if not always legally

---

[10] Addition to Esther C 28. Translation by Carey A. Moore, *Daniel, Esther and Jeremiah: The Additions: A New Translation with Introduction and Commentary*, AB, vol. 44 (New York: Doubleday, 1977), 209, with a slight alteration. On the date of Greek Esther, see Elias J. Bickerman, "The Colophon of the Greek Book of Esther," *JBL* 63 (1944): 339–362; John J. Collins, *Between Athens and Jerusalem: Jewish Identity in the Hellenistic Diaspora*, Second Edition (Grand Rapids, MI: Eerdmans, 2000), 110–111; Moore, *Daniel, Esther and Jeremiah*, 250–252.

[11] Judith 10:5; 12:1–4. On the date of Judith, see Carey A. Moore, *Judith: A New Translation with Introduction and Commentary*, AB, vol. 40 (New York: Doubleday, 1985), 67–70.

[12] Judith 12:17–20.

[13] *Joseph and Aseneth* 7:1. All citations from *Joseph and Aseneth* follow the version translated and commented on by Christoph Burchard, "Joseph and Aseneth," in *OTP*, ed. James H. Charlesworth, 2:177–247, 2 vols. (New York: Doubleday, 1985). On the date of *Joseph and Aseneth*, see Burchard, "Joseph and Aseneth," 187–188; Ross Shepard Kraemer, *When Aseneth Met Joseph: A Late Antique Tale of the Biblical Patriarch and His Egyptian Wife, Reconsidered* (New York: Oxford University Press, 1998), 225–244. For the textual issues, as well as a critical text, of *Joseph and Aseneth*, see Christoph Burchard, *Joseph und Aseneth: Kritisch Herausgegeben* (Boston: Brill, 2003).

[14] Not coincidentally, during her "conversion" experience, Aseneth throws her previously acceptable food out the window (*Joseph and Aseneth* 10:13). R. Kraemer argues against the traditional view of Aseneth having a transformative experience that we would label a conversion; rather, she suggests that this pericope could be read as conforming to the norms of an adjuration text (*When Aseneth Met Joseph*, 89–109). Joseph's commensality with his in-laws is implied in *Joseph and Aseneth* 20:8; 21:8.

[15] Tobit 1:10–13. On the date of Tobit, see Carey A. Moore, *Tobit: A New Translation with Introduction and Commentary*, AB, vol. 40a (New York: Doubleday, 1996), 15–17.

transgressive – for Jews to attend. In *Jubilees*, Abraham's blessing for Jacob includes the following injunction:

And you, also, my son, Jacob, remember my words, and keep the commandments of Abraham, your father. Separate yourself from the gentiles, *and do not eat with them*, and do not perform deeds like theirs. Because their deeds are defiled, and all of their ways are contaminated, and despicable, and abominable.[16]

Although Abraham does not supply an explicit rationale, his words in *Jubilees* directly connect social separation in general to social separation at the table.[17] This direct connection appears in an even further explicit fashion in the *Letter of Aristeas*, which states:

In his wisdom the legislator [i.e., Moses], in a comprehensive survey of each particular part, and being endowed by God for the knowledge of universal truths, *surrounded us with unbroken palisades and iron walls to prevent our mixing with any of the other peoples in any matter*, being thus kept pure in body and soul, preserved from false beliefs, and worshipping the only God omnipotent over all creation.... *So to prevent our being perverted by contact with others or by mixing with bad influences, he hedged us in on all sides with strict observances connected with meat and drink* and touch and hearing and sight, after the manner of the Law.[18]

[16] *Jubilees* 22:16. Translation by O. S. Wintermute, "Jubilees," in *OTP*, ed. James H. Charlesworth, 2:35–142, 2 vols. (New York: Doubleday, 1985), 98, emphasis added. On the date of *Jubilees*, see Wintermute, "Jubilees," 43–44. Freidenreich suggests that "[t]his foreign food restriction may be inspired by *Exod*. 34:15–16, which also regards shared sacrificial meals as leading to intermarriage and idolatry" (Foreign Food, 73). Although Freidenreich may be correct, the allusion is, at best, faint.

[17] Although Abraham comments on the "defiled" nature of "their deeds" and the "contaminated, and despicable, and abominable" nature of "their ways," these seem to refer to his previous statement about performing "deeds like theirs." In regard to the statement "and do not eat with them," Wintermute reasonably suggests that "[t]he implication is that the food prepared by the gentiles would not be prepared in accord with Jewish laws of purity" ("Jubilees," 98 n. d.). Even if Wintermute's understanding is correct, this connection is tacit and not explicit. Abraham's comment simply reads as an apodictic statement. In fact, purity concerns do not seem to underlie tannaitic commensality regulations between Jews and non-Jews. For a concise overview, see Christine E. Hayes, *Gentile Impurities and Jewish Identities: Intermarriage and Conversion from the Bible to the Talmud* (New York: Oxford University Press, 2002), 139–142.

[18] *Letter of Aristeas*, 139, 142, emphasis added. All translations of the *Letter of Aristeas* by R. J. H. Shutt, "Letter of Aristeas," in *OTP*, ed. James H. Charlesworth, 2:7–34, 2 vols. (New York: Doubleday, 1985). On the date of the *Letter of Aristeas*, see Shutt, "Letter of Aristeas," 8–9.

These comments dovetail on earlier remarks in the *Letter of Aristeas* attributed to the High Priest Eleazar. When explaining to a delegation of Greeks sent by the king of Egypt the rationale behind "their legislation concerning meats and drink and beasts considered to be unclean," Eleazar is reported to state:

You observe ... the important matter raised by modes of life and relationships, inasmuch as through bad relationships men become perverted, and are miserable their whole long life; if, however, they mix with wise and prudent companions, they rise above ignorance and achieve progress in life.[19]

Biblical food laws, therefore, prevent "bad influences" and encourage "progress in life." If this is so, then choosing the people who surround the table is as important as choosing the food placed on the table. Although not a de jure commensality restriction, the rhetoric of the *Letter of Aristeas* amounts to a de facto separation at the table between Jews and non-Jews. In sum, both *Jubilees* and the *Letter of Aristeas* "illustrate how, while such boundary markers have important social consequences, their textual function for the creation of an image of internal identity is no less significant."[20]

The *Letter of Aristeas*, however, among other texts, does not necessarily preclude *all* commensality between Jews and non-Jews. In fact, the letter describes a shared banquet between the translators of the Septuagint and the Egyptian king, wherein all food is prepared "in compliance with your habits" (*parestai kathēkontōs*) and over which a Judean priest makes a blessing.[21] Apparently, these provisions allow for commensality that accords with the previously stated views of Eleazar (and of the author of

---

[19] *Letter of Aristeas*, 128, 130. The *Letter of Aristeas* also points out that the biblical laws regarding permissible domesticated quadrupeds provide for prudent culinary decisions that encourage progress in life (see 150–155, discussed later in this chapter).

[20] Judith M. Lieu, *Christian Identity in the Jewish and Graeco–Roman World* (New York: Oxford University Press, 2004), 111.

[21] *Letter of Aristeas*, 181–202. For a discussion of the absence of purity concerns from this banquet scene, see Hayes, *Gentile Impurities*, 140; Freidenreich, *Foreign Food*, 87.

According to Philo, there is a yearly feast on the island of Pharos (in Alexandria) commemorating the completion of the Septuagint, at which "not only Jews but multitudes of others" attend and participate (*De Vita Mosis*, 2:41). I note this here because the *Letter of Aristeas* purports to describe the events surrounding the Greek translation of the Hebrew Bible, the Septuagint, and the feast described in the *Letter of Aristeas*, 181–202 celebrates the arrival of the Septuagint in Alexandria.

the *Letter of Aristeas*). 3 Maccabees makes a similar allowance.[22] Although this book states that "[b]y reverencing God and conducting themselves according to his Law, [the Jews] kept themselves apart in matters of food, and for this reason they appeared hateful to some," these same Jews later partake in a feast supplied by the king.[23] In 3 Maccabees, therefore, "'[k]eeping apart in the matter of food,' it would seem, does not require refraining from eating food provided by gentiles or attending gentile feasts."[24] Further, Josephus reports that the Tobiads ate and drank without problem at the table of the Ptolemies.[25] Perhaps the observance of biblical food laws was enough, at this time, to prevent the perceived ills of these commensal encounters.

A key question remains after this survey of the Second Temple period evidence: Do these texts reflect a common practice of separation at meals between Jews and non-Jews? The sources cited thus far indicate that, as Magnus Z. Zetterholm concludes:

As for table-fellowship between Jews and Gentiles, we have seen that it did exist and was perfectly possible, given the right circumstances, which must have depended on the specific individual's degree of halakhic [legal] observance. This may have varied for different groups and probably even geographically. We have noted that some groups may have considered all

---

[22] For a brief comparison of these two texts in general, see John M. G. Barclay, *Jews in the Mediterranean Diaspora: From Alexander to Trajan (323 BCE–117 CE)* (Berkeley and Los Angeles: University of California Press, 1996), 201–203.

[23] 3 Maccabees 3:4; 6:30–40. Translation by H. Anderson, "3 Maccabees," in *OTP*, ed. James H. Charlesworth, 2:509–529; 2 vols. (New York: Doubleday, 1985), 520. On the date of 3 Maccabees, see Anderson, "3 Maccabees," 510–512; Barclay, *Jews in the Mediterranean Diaspora*, 203; Collins, *Between Athens and Jerusalem*, 124–126.

[24] Freidenreich, *Foreign Food*, 89.

[25] *Jewish Antiquities*, 12:160–236 in general, with shared meals specifically mentioned in 173–174; 186–189; 210–213. Although commensality between different groups of Judeans/Jews was also sometimes avoided (as will be discussed further in Chapter 4), in *Jewish Antiquities*, 13:289 (cp. *b. Qiddushin* 66a), Josephus reports that the Pharisees ate at the table of the Hasmonean King Hyrcanus. However, the Pharisees' food boundaries were less strict than those of other contemporary Jewish groups (see Albert I. Baumgarten, *The Flourishing of Jewish Sects in the Maccabean Era: An Interpretation* [New York: Brill, 1997], 97). For this reason, both Baumgarten and Saldarini label the Pharisees a "reformist" sect. See Baumgarten, *Flourishing of Jewish Sects*, 13, 97; Anthony J. Saldarini, *Pharisees, Scribes and Sadducees in Palestinian Society: A Sociological Approach*, Second Edition (Grand Rapids, MI: William B. Eerdmans, 2001), 286–287. On the historical veracity of *Jewish Antiquities*, 13:289, see the concise summary in Saldarini, *Pharisees, Scribes and Sadducees*, 86 n. 17.

table-fellowship with Gentiles abominable while other groups had a more open attitude.[26]

Even though table-fellowship between Jews and non-Jews is clearly emerging as an issue, these most likely prescriptive sources suggest that this was not an insurmountable barrier for all Jews in the Hasmonean period. This is not to say, however, that some Jews did not consider commensality with other, nonsectarian Jews – let alone with non-Jews – to be completely verboten. Most notably, the Essenes and the Qumran sect both required one to be an initiate in their group to engage in commensality with other members.[27] In contrast to the extreme social separation at the meals of the Essenes and the Qumran sect, the "unbroken palisades and iron walls" described in the *Letter of Aristeas* are permeable enough, under certain circumstances, to allow for the Jewish Septuagint translators and the Egyptian king to presumably share a meal.

The Judean/Jewish social practice of connecting "[w]hat meats a man should abstain from, and what he may enjoy; with what person he should associate"[28] does not go unnoticed by Greek and Roman authors. Thus, in the first century B.C.E., Diodorus Siculus notes that, since the time of

---

[26] *The Formation of Christianity in Antioch: A Social-Scientific Approach to the Separation Between Judaism and Christianity* (New York: Routledge Press, 2005), 155. Zetterholm surveys the evidence from pp. 149–155. See also Cohen, *Beginnings of Jewishness*, 54. Freidenreich argues for the existence of geographical differences (Foreign Food, 93–95).

[27] Even though many scholars consider the Essenes and the Qumran sect to comprise the same group, I am not convinced. For a discussion, see Todd S. Beall, "Essenes," in *Encyclopedia of the Dead Sea Scrolls*, ed. Lawrence H. Schiffman and James C. VanderKam, 1:262–269, 2 vols. (New York: Oxford University Press, 2000), 265–267. For concise summaries of the commensality regulations of these two groups, see Baumgarten, *Flourishing of Jewish Sects*, 93–96; Freidenreich, Foreign Food, 77–81. Contrast, for example, Paul's rebuke in Galatians 2:11–21 of Peter's refusal to dine with Gentiles (see also Acts 10:28). On this text in general, see E. P. Sanders, "Jewish Association with Gentiles and Galatians 2:11–14," in *The Conversation Continues: Studies in Paul & John in Honor of J. Louis Martyn*, ed. Robert T. Fortna and Beverly R. Gaventa, 170–188 (Nashville, TN: Abingdon Press, 1990); Zetterholm, *Formation of Christianity*, 129–164. On the usage of the verb "to judaize" in this text, see Cohen, *Beginnings of Jewishness*, 182. For a general survey of commensality concerns in the New Testament, see Freidenreich, Foreign Food, 96–122.

[28] Josephus, *Contra Apion*, 2:174 (cp. *Jewish Antiquities*, 4:137–139). In 2:173–174, Josephus discusses how Mosaic law combines both precept and practice. As Barclay notes: "Josephus, proud that the law covers every department of life, links the distinction between acceptable and unacceptable food with the distinction between acceptable and unacceptable company" (*Jews in the Mediterranean Diaspora*, 437; similarly, see Baumgarten, *Flourishing of Jewish Sects*, 92).

Moses, "the Jews had made their hatred of mankind into a tradition, and on this account had introduced utterly outlandish laws: *not to share a table with anyone of another nation*, nor to show them any good will at all."[29] Further support for this interpretation of Jewish practice in the second century C.E. can be found in Tacitus. Commenting on how "toward every other people they [i.e., Jews] feel only hate and enmity," Tacitus' first supporting statement declares: "They sit apart at meals."[30] In the third century C.E., Philostratus continues this trope with his observation that:

For the Jews have long been in revolt not only against the Romans but against humanity; and a race that has made its own a life apart and irreconcilable, *that cannot share with the rest of mankind in the pleasures of the table* nor join in their libations or prayers or sacrifices, are separated from ourselves by a greater gulf than divides us from Susa of Bactra of the more distant Indies.[31]

Non-Jewish witnesses, therefore, buttress the testimony of Jewish ones, cumulatively suggesting the fact that both prior to and during the Tannaitic period, Jewish separatism at meals was a somewhat common practice.[32]

Even as Jews may "sit apart at meals" (either at separate tables or at separate meals), it is important to remember that the extant Second Temple-period evidence also contains accommodations for commensality between Jews and non-Jews. Thus, even in the texts that suggest separation at the table, the expectation is not necessarily of a complete social separation – a trend that continues in the tannaitic corpus, as we shall see later. *Therefore, the table itself is understood as a locus for identity negotiation.*[33] Accommodations are just that – adjustments, leniencies,

---

[29] *Bibliotheca Historica*, 34/35.1.2, emphasis added. I have altered Walton's translation in the LCL edition slightly to render the text more precisely. My alterations follow the suggestions offered by Freidenreich (Foreign Food, 83). Unless otherwise noted, all Greek and Latin texts and translations are from the corresponding LCL edition.

[30] *Historiae*, 5.5.1, 2 (*Separati epulis*). In addition to this statement, Tacitus suggests several other Jewish practices that serve to separate Jews from non-Jews (e.g., circumcision [*Historiae*, 5.5.2; see Cohen, *Beginnings of Jewishness*, 43–44]).

[31] *Vita Apollonii*, 5:33, emphasis added. There are several other Greek and Roman non-food references to the general social separation of Jews from non-Jews (e.g., Hecataeus, *Aegyptiaca*, apud: Diodorus Siculus, *Bibliotheca Historica*, 40.3.4; Josephus, *Contra Apion*, 2:148, 258).

[32] Barclay arrives at the same conclusion (*Jews in the Mediterranean Diaspora*, 437).

[33] Similarly, see Barclay, *Jews in the Mediterranean Diaspora*, 437; Baumgarten, *Flourishing of Jewish Sects*, 92; Cohen, *Beginnings of Jewishness*, 54.

and legal fictions that preserve one's identity while allowing for social interaction with one classed as the "Other." Although these texts should not be read as offering data on the precise nature of Jewish commensality restrictions, they do offer our first indication that (at least some) Jews are concerned about with whom they eat.[34] In solidifying "Jewish ethnic identity on a daily basis,"[35] commensality regulations are part of a larger process of Jewish identity construction that starts roughly in the Hasmonean period.

Tannaitic literature greatly expands on this emerging notion that the table is a locus for identity negotiation. However, although commensality with non-Jews becomes increasingly problematized, tannaitic culinary and commensal regulations – much like the Second Temple-period evidence surveyed thus far – also contain accommodations that allow for social interactions between Jews and non-Jews. The rest of this chapter is devoted to exploring this development. Throughout, it would seem that, in the ideal tannaitic world, Tacitus' observation would hold true: "[T]hey sit apart at meals."

FOOD AS METONYM/FOOD AS EMBODIMENT

Anthropologists have long noted the connection between the practice of eating certain food items and ascribed identity.[36] Concomitant with this notion that certain foods serve as a metonym for "Us" is the conception that eating metonymic food is a practice of embodiment. By the term *embodiment*, I mean to suggest that tannaitic food regulations create both individual and communal bodies (i.e., identities).[37] What is on the plate and the manner in which one consumes that food is a kind of "social digestion": breaking down and reassembling the building blocks of society. My understanding of the concept of embodiment is shaped by

---

[34] Similarly, see Freidenreich, Foreign Food, 84.
[35] Barclay, *Jews in the Mediterranean Diaspora*, 437.
[36] A classic and concise articulation of this view can be found in Claude Fischler, "Food, Self and Identity," *Social Science Information* 27/2 (1988): 275–292, 279–282. For an empirical psychological study of the "you are what you eat" principle, see Carol Nemeroff and Paul Rozin, "'You Are What You Eat': Applying the Demand-Free 'Impressions' Technique to an Unacknowledged Belief," *Ethos* 17/1 (1989): 50–69.
[37] Fischler refers to this same concept as "incorporation" ("Food, Self and Identity," 279–282).

Pierre Bourdieu's usage of this term with regard to the socially relative concept of "taste":

Taste, a class culture turned into nature, that is, *embodied*, helps to shape the class body. It is an incorporated principle of classification which governs all forms of incorporation, choosing and modifying everything that the body ingests and digests and assimilates, physiologically and psychologically.[38]

Tannaitic literature similarly contains a concept of embodiment, wherein food is "physiologically and psychologically" incorporated into the individual and collective body. This process of physical and social digestion is an integral component of tannaitic identity construction. To quote anthropologist Emiko Ohnuki-Tierney, "The beauty and purity of *we* are *embodied doubly in the body of the people and in the food that represents them*, and, conversely, the undesirable qualities of the other are embodied in *their* foods and foodway."[39] In short, you are what you eat.

I group the concepts of metonymy and embodiment together because they are related. Summarizing the intersection between these two principles, Ohnuki-Tierney notes:

The power of food as a symbol of self-identity derives from the particular nature of the symbolic process involved. An important food as a metaphor of a social group involves two interlocking dimensions. First, each member of the social group consumes the food,[40] which becomes part of his or her

---

[38] *Distinction: A Social Critique of the Judgment of Taste*, trans. Richard Nice (Cambridge: Harvard University Press, 2002), 190, emphasis in original. Emiko Ohnuki-Tierney uses a portion of this same quote (*Rice as Self: Japanese Identities through Time* [Princeton, NJ: Princeton University Press, 1993], 115).

[39] *Rice as Self*, 131, emphasis in original. Throughout, I adopt Frederick J. Simoons' concise definition of "foodways": "the modes of feeling, thinking, and behaving about food that are common to a cultural group" (*Eat Not This Flesh: Food Avoidances in the Old World* [Madison and Milwaukee: University of Wisconsin Press, 1967], 3). I employ this term with the understanding that "[f]oodways include food as material items and symbols of identity, and the history of a group's ways with food goes far beyond an exploration of cooking and consumption. It amounts to a journey to the heart of its collective world" (Hasia R. Diner, *Hungering for America: Italian, Irish, and Jewish Foodways in the Age of Migration* [Cambridge, MA: Harvard University Press, 2001], 9–10). Further, Ohnuki-Tierney is not the only scholar who notices this connection in Japan. See Anne Allison, "Japanese Mothers and Obentōs: The Lunch Box as Ideological State Apparatus," in *Food and Culture: A Reader*, ed. Carole Counihan and Penny van Esterik, 296–314 (New York: Routledge, 1997).

[40] To which I would add "or does *not* consume the food," as collective identity can also be formed through communal abstinence from ingesting a particular item or class of items. I have made this argument previously, with regard to the Jewish abstention from pork, as depicted in Roman and rabbinic sources. See Jordan D. Rosenblum, "'Why

body. The important food becomes *embodied* in each individual. It operates as a *metonym* for being part of the self. Second, the food is consumed by individual members of the social group who eat the food together.[41]

The practice of eating metonymic food is therefore perceived to have social and ontological ramifications for both individual and group identity.

Tannaitic literature builds on precedents and contains innovative practices that emphasize the connection between diet and identity. For example, one text equates Jews with "garlic eaters." *m. Nedarim* 3:10 notes that, if one vows not to derive benefit "from garlic eaters, he is forbidden [to derive benefit] from Jews and from Samaritans."[42] The term "garlic eaters" therefore functions as a metonym for Jews and Samaritans, according to this text. However, this metonym is not invoked elsewhere and there is no other evidence to suggest that Jews or Samaritans necessarily incorporated significantly more garlic into their diet than their non-Jewish Mediterranean contemporaries.[43]

In this section, I focus on two categories of foods: (1) foods "They" eat and from which "We" abstain (e.g., pig); and (2) foods "We" eat and from which "They" abstain (e.g., manna, the Passover sacrifice, and the practice of *kashrut* in general). The comparative discussions in these texts form what François Hartog labels "the rhetoric of otherness." Commenting on the role that comparison plays in this rhetoric, Hartog states:

It is a net the narrator throws into the waters of otherness. The size of the mesh and the design of the net determine the type and quality of the catch. And hauling in the net is a way of bringing what is "other" into proximity

---

Do You Refuse to Eat Pork?': Jews, Food, and Identity in Roman Palestine," *JQR* 100/1: 95–110. I return to this point later in this chapter.

[41] *Rice as Self*, 129–130, original emphasis.

[42] *m. Nedarim* 3:10 (ed. Albeck 3:156). According to *m. Nedarim* 8:6 (ed. Albeck 3:173), garlic is a Sabbath treat. However, other texts treat garlic as if it is a more common ingredient (e.g., *m. Tevul Yom* 2:3 [ed. Albeck 6:462], in which oil and garlic are used to flavor porridge). The connection between Jews and garlic persists, becoming part of an early modern German polemic against Jews. See Maria Diemling, "'As the Jews Like to Eat Garlick': Garlic in Christian-Jewish Polemical Discourse in Early Modern Germany," in *Food and Judaism: Studies in Jewish Civilization 15*, ed. Leonard J. Greenspoon, Ronald A. Simkins, and Gerald Shapiro, 215–234 (Omaha, NE: Creighton University Press, 2004). I discuss the association between Jews and Samaritans in Chapter 4.

[43] Gildas Hamel also questions the unique association between garlic and a Jewish diet (*Poverty and Charity in Roman Palestine, First Three Centuries C.E.* [Berkeley and Los Angeles: University of California Press, 1990], 17).

with what is the "same." Comparison thus has a place in the rhetoric of otherness, operating there as a procedure of translation.[44]

Casting their proverbial net into the "waters of otherness," the Tannaim emphasize the metonymy of certain foods. For each category, I discuss a specific culinary item (or items) that exemplifies how the practices of consumption and abstinence play a part in tannaitic identity formation.

The "Abominable Pig"

The "abominable pig"[45] offers a unique datum with regard to Jewish food regulations and practice in antiquity. Perhaps no other culinary item has received more attention from antiquity through modernity. In particular, modern anthropologists have fixated on this split-hoofed nonruminant in an attempt to understand the origin of biblical food prohibitions.[46]

Modern scholars, however, are not the first to attempt a logical explanation for this food taboo. For example, Philo offers (in typical fashion) an allegorical interpretation of the underlying principles behind this biblical proscription in general:

> [Moses] adds a general method for proving and testing the ten kinds [of pure domesticated quadrupeds], based on two signs, the parted hoof and the chewing of the cud. Any kind which lacks both or one of these is unclean [Leviticus 11:3; Deuteronomy 14:6–8]. Now both these two are symbols to teacher and learner of the method best suited for acquiring knowledge, the method by which the better is distinguished from the worse, and thus confusion is avoided. For just as a cud-chewing animal after biting through the food keeps it at rest in the gullet, again after a bit draws it up and masticates it and then passes it on to the belly, so the pupil after receiving from the teacher through his ears the principles and lore of wisdom prolongs the process of learning, as he cannot at once apprehend and grasp them securely, till by

---

[44] *The Mirror of Herodotus: The Representation of the Other in the Writing of History*, trans. Janet Lloyd (Berkeley and Los Angeles: University of California Press, 1988), 225.

[45] I take this phrase from a Marvin Harris chapter title (*Good to Eat: Riddles of Food and Culture* [Long Grove, IL: Waveland Press, 1998], 67–87).

[46] Most famously, see the work of Mary Douglas (e.g., *Purity and Danger: An Analysis of the Concepts of Pollution and Taboo* [New York: Routledge, 1999 (1966)], 42–58; and her recent reevaluation in *Leviticus as Literature* [New York: Oxford University Press, 2000]); Harris, *Good to Eat*, 67–87; Jean Soler, "Biblical Reasons: The Dietary Rules of the Ancient Hebrews," in *Food: A Culinary History*, ed. Jean-Louis Flandrin and Massimo Montanari, 46–54 (New York: Penguin Books, 2000).

using memory to call up each thing that he has heard by constant exercises which act as the cement of conceptions, he stamps a firm impression of them on his soul. But the firm apprehension of conceptions is clearly useless unless we discriminate and distinguish them so that we can choose what we should choose and avoid the contrary, and this distinguishing is symbolized by the parted hoof. For the way of life is twofold, one branch leading to vice, the other to virtue and we must turn away from the one and never forsake the other.[47]

According to Philo, the pig (and other similar animals) lacks the physiological apparatus to ruminate – literally and figuratively. For him, therefore, Mosaic law ensures that "rational" man eats only animals whose own eating process is itself a symbol of "proper" reasoning. Philo is not alone in this interpretation, as the *Letter of Aristeas* offers a similar interpretation about the connection between the rumination that occurs in an animal's cud and the rumination that occurs in the mind of the person who ingests that animal.[48] As Martin S. Jaffee notes, "The point, one supposes, is that you are what you eat. Consumption of hoof-parting cud-chewers encourages the ability to distinguish between right and wrong, just as it will enhance the memory, the central faculty in the mastery of wisdom."[49] The biblical food taboos are therefore understood to serve as reminder to Jews not only about how to eat, but also about how to think.

There is much to be learned about identity construction in antiquity from looking at both Jewish (rabbinic and nonrabbinic) and non-Jewish texts about pig abstention and/or consumption from pre-tannaitic and contemporary sources.[50] Biblically mandated,[51] the Jewish abstention from pig stood out to both Jewish and non-Jewish audiences from at least the second century B.C.E. on as a noticeable anomaly. For this reason, this single menu item provides an excellent test case for the role that food practices play in identity construction. As we shall see, both

---

[47] *De Specialibus Legibus*, 4:106–108.
[48] *Letter of Aristeas*, 153–155 (in general, see 142–155).
[49] *Early Judaism: Religious Worlds of the First Judaic Millennium*, Second Edition (Bethesda: University Press of Maryland, 2006), 129.
[50] On the rich amoraic material on the pig, see Rosenblum, "'Why Do You Refuse....'", 102–110.
[51] E.g., Leviticus 11:7; Deuteronomy 14:8. For a discussion with additional references, see Jacob Milgrom, *Leviticus 1–16: A New Translation with Introduction and Commentary*, AB, vol. 3 (New York: Doubleday, 1991), 649–653.

Judean/Jewish and Gentile sources equate the ingestion of, or abstention from, pork as indicative of one's identity.

One finds the connection between ingesting pork and ingesting otherness at least as far back as Third Isaiah (circa late sixth to mid-fifth century B.C.E.).[52] Describing the actions of those Israelites who act like the "Other," Isaiah 65:4 reports that they "eat the flesh of swine, with broth of unclean things in their bowls."[53] Further, the consumption of pig (Isaiah 66:17), as well as the manipulation of its blood (Isaiah 66:3), are associated with idolatrous cultic practices. To act like the "Other" is to eat like the "Other"; and to eat like the "Other" is to eat pork.[54] In short, pork is the ultimate metonym for the "culinary Other" in Israelite/Jewish literature long before the Tannaitic period.[55]

Several texts from the Second Temple period equate the ingestion of pork with the submission to foreign domination. For example, as recorded in 2 Maccabees 6:18–7:42, when presented by Antiochus IV with the option of either eating pork or being tortured and killed, both the scribe Eleazar and a family of eight (seven brothers and a mother) choose death.[56] 4 Maccabees elaborates extensively on these two tales, devoting almost the entirety of its text to them.[57] Antiochus' alleged decree calling

---

[52] On the dates for Third Isaiah, see Joseph Blenkinsopp, *Isaiah 56–66: A New Translation with Introduction and Commentary*, AB, vol. 19b (New York: Doubleday, 2003), 42–54.

[53] I emend the text based on the *qĕrê*. For a text critical discussion, see Blenkinsopp, *Isaiah 56–66*, 267 n. g.

[54] On the role that pig plays in the religious rituals of other groups in Palestine and Ancient West Asia, see Roland de Vaux, "Les Sacrifices de Porcs en Palestine et dans l'Ancien Orient," in *Bible et Orient*, 499–516 (Paris: Les Éditions du Cerf, 1967).

[55] I owe the felicitous phrase "culinary Other" to Arjun Appadurai ("How to Make a National Cuisine: Cookbooks in Contemporary India," *Comparative Studies* 30/1 [1988]: 3–24, 9).

[56] For a commentary on these verses, see Jonathan A. Goldstein, *II Maccabees: A New Translation with Introduction and Commentary*, AB, vol. 41a (New York: Doubleday, 1983), 282–288, 291–317; Daniel R. Schwartz, *The Second Book of Maccabees: Introduction, Hebrew Translation, and Commentary* (Jerusalem: Yad Ben-Zvi Press, 2004 [Hebrew]), 159–176. Idolatry is also an issue in these texts, although apparently "the factor of idolatry is introduced awkwardly as an afterthought" (Goldstein, *II Maccabees*, 283; see also Freidenreich, Foreign Food, 61–64). On the concept of martyrdom in 2 and 4 Maccabees, see Jan Willem van Henten, *The Maccabean Martyrs as Saviours of the Jewish People: A Study of 2 and 4 Maccabees* (New York: Brill, 1997) and in ancient Judaism and early Christianity in general, see Daniel Boyarin, *Dying for God: Martyrdom and the Making of Christianity and Judaism* (Stanford, CA: Stanford University Press, 1999); for reference to the books of Maccabees, see pp. 94–96, 115–118.

[57] See 4 Maccabees 5–18. On the date of 4 Maccabees, see H. Anderson, "4 Maccabees," in *OTP*, ed. James H. Charlesworth, 2:531–564; 2 vols. (New York: Doubleday, 1985),

for daily pig sacrifice on newly established altars throughout the region is presumably another instance of forcing Jews to ingest pork, as animal slaughter inevitably leads to individual or communal consumption of the sacrificial victim.[58] Philo reports that, during a pogrom in Alexandria in 38 C.E., mobs captured Jewish women and forced them to eat pork.[59] Those who ingest the pig meat – thus symbolically submitting to Flaccus (and, by extension, to Rome, as Flaccus is the Roman prefect of Egypt) via an act of ingesting the metonymic food of the "Other" – are let go; those who follow the example of their ancestors in 2 and 4 Maccabees are tortured.[60]

Regardless of the veracity of these accounts, the underlying assumption is that compelling Jews to ingest pork directly equates with compelling Jews to ingest Otherness.[61] Even though these various Jewish authors might embellish (or invent) historical facts, the very fact that they consider the forced consumption of pork to be a practice that affects Jewish identity highlights that the principle of "you are what you (do and do not) eat" is in operation in these texts. However, as David Kraemer correctly reminds us, it is unclear from these sources whether pork was actually abhorred by Jews significantly more than other nonkosher animals – such as, for example, the camel – or whether pork was simply the most common nonkosher meat that a Jew in Roman-period Palestine would encounter and, as such, was the most obvious (and hence,

---

533–534. Lieu points out that 4 Maccabees sidesteps impurity when discussing this act of "defiled eating" (*Christian Identity*, 111). For a reading of how gender operates in 4 Maccabees, see Stephen D. Moore and Janice Capel Anderson, "Taking It Like a Man: Masculinity in 4 Maccabees," *JBL* 117/2 (1998), 249–273.

[58] 1 Maccabees 1:44–50; Josephus, *Jewish Antiquities*, 12:253–256; 13:243 (cp. Diodorus Siculus, *Bibliotheca Historica*, XXXIV–XXXV, 1:3–4).

[59] *In Flaccum*, 95–96. On this pogrom, see Erich S. Gruen, *Diaspora: Jews Amidst Greeks and Romans* (Cambridge, MA: Harvard University Press, 2002), 54–83. Although the term "pogrom" is anachronistic, it captures the mood and actions of the event, as described by Philo. It is most likely for this reason that Gruen himself uses this term to describe the events in Alexandria (*Diaspora*, 54).

[60] The gendered component of this series of texts as a whole deserves further attention. However, it is beyond the scope of this book.

[61] In a perhaps coincidental note, the tenth legion of the Roman army (the Legio X Fretensis), nicknamed "the boar," participated in the Roman military response to the Great Revolt (for example, see Josephus, *Jewish War*, 5:269–270 [which discusses the legion's military prowess]; 6:237–243 [which notes that the commander of this legion took part in talks about the fate of the Temple]). I thank Tessa Rajak for bringing this to my attention.

over time, metonymic) food from the vantage point of both Jews and non-Jews.[62]

Logically, because Jews do not eat pork, Jews do not sacrifice pig. In the ancient Mediterranean world, the connection between altar table and kitchen table was inseparable.[63] Therefore, the absence of pig from the sacrificial altar attracted further attention from non-Jews in antiquity. Even though Jews are not the only ancient people to classify pig as ineligible for sacrifice,[64] this peculiar sacrificial, and thus culinary, behavior is especially identified with the Jews, even in the Greek Magical Papyri.[65] This observation, coupled with those made earlier in regard to forced ingestion of pork, explains why Antiochus IV reportedly offers on the Temple altar, and mandates that Jews offer on their own altars, swine as a sacrifice.[66] According to Peter Schäfer (here commenting on the passage from Diodorus):

---

[62] *Jewish Eating and Identity Through the Ages* (New York: Routledge, 2007), 31.

[63] See Stanley K. Stowers, "Greeks Who Sacrifice and Those Who Do Not: Toward an Anthropology of Greek Religion," in *The Social World of the First Christians: Essays in Honor of Wayne A. Meeks*, ed. L. Michael White and O. Larry Yarbrough, 293–333 (Minneapolis: Fortress Press, 1995); Daniel Ullucci, The End of Animal Sacrifice (Ph.D. dissertation, Brown University, 2008).

[64] For example, several ancient authors are aware of a similar pork taboo (sacrifice or ingestion) among Egyptians (Herodotus, *History*, 2:47; Josephus, *Contra Apion*, 2:137–142; Arrianus [citing Epictetus], *Dissertationes*, I:22:4; Sextus Empiricus, *Hypotyposes*, 334:222; Celsus Philosophus, *The True Doctrine* [as quoted in Origen, *Contra Celsum*, 5:41 (ed. Chadwick, 297)]), as well as Phoenicians (Porphyry, *De Abstinentia*, I:14 [ed. Clark 37]) and Syrians (the sixth-century fragment from Damascius, *Vita Isidori*, 227 [ed. M. Stern 2:675–677]).

[65] This is particularly true in later Greek and Latin texts, according to Cristiano Grottanelli ("Avoiding Pork: Egyptians and Jews in Greek and Latin Texts," in *Food and Identity in the Ancient World*, ed. Cristiano Grottanelli and Lucio Milano, 59–93 [Padova: S.A.R.G.O.N. Editrice e Libreria], 81). For the reference in the Greek Magical Papyri (PGM), see PGM IV:3007–3086, intended for people possessed by daimons, which includes the instructions not to eat pork alongside the fact that the charm is Hebraic in origin. However, it should be noted that the Greek Magical Papyri also contain knowledge of a pork taboo in Egyptian culture (see PGM I:105).

[66] 1 Maccabees 1:47; Josephus, *Jewish Antiquities*, 12:253–256; 13:243; cp. Diodorus Siculus, *Bibliotheca Historica*, XXXIV–XXXV, 1:3–4. I phrase this sentence in the hypothetical (i.e., "reportedly") in an attempt to sidestep the question of historiography. As I have stated above, whether these events actually happened (as reported, or at all), the resonance of the symbol of pork vis-à-vis edible identity endures. For a discussion of the historiography of this passage, as well as Josephus' sources for this story, see Peter Schäfer, *Judeophobia: Attitudes Toward the Jews in the Ancient World* (Cambridge, MA: Harvard University Press, 1997), 66–68. In addition, on the problems associated with determining Diodorus' sources (also mentioned by Schäfer), see M. Stern, *Greek and Latin Authors on Jews and Judaism*, 3 vols. (Jerusalem: Israel Academy of Sciences and Humanities), 1:142–144, 168.

The most radical way to annihilate these *nomima* [i.e., perceived Jewish misanthropy and xenophobic laws] would be to do exactly what the Jews most abhor: to sacrifice sows and to eat their flesh. The sacrifice of a pig in the Temple and the eating of pork are seen here as the most extreme perversion of the Jewish religion in order to exterminate once and for all their *misanthrōpia*. The prohibition against eating pork is the embodiment of *misanthrōpia*; once the Jews eat pork, they have given up their *misoxena nomima* [xenophobic laws] and will become like any other nation.[67]

Through an act of ingestion of this metonymic food, a Jew loses his or her distinct identity.[68] Antiochus IV seemingly anticipates modern social anthropology in his laws and actions – at least, rhetorically – manipulating food practices in an attempt to effect change in the identity of Jews in antiquity.

Another interesting avenue for exploration is the series of "porcine *topoi*" (in the felicitous wording of Grottanelli) that one encounters in Greek and Roman literature. Commenting on these *topoi*, Grottanelli notes:

[A]n ancient and consistent series of porcine *topoi*... was used by Greek and Romans to answer the difficult question: "What is the identity of the Jews?" by answering the apparently more specific, and thus seemingly easier question: "Why do Jews avoid eating pork?"[69]

Therefore, whereas pork is the metonymic food for the "Other" in Jewish sources, the abstention from pork marks the "Other" in several Roman-period texts. Schäfer divides the extant comments of Greek and Roman authors on this peculiar culinary abstention into two main categories: (1) texts that make "casual reference" to, or offer an "ethnographic explanation" for, this Jewish practice; and (2) the Latin satirists.[70] Schäfer's first

---

[67] *Judeophobia*, 67.
[68] I use gender-neutral language here due to the appearance of women – even if only as a literary foil – in some of these accounts. As I note above, an examination of the role that gender plays in these passages is a desideratum.
[69] "Avoiding Pork," 82.
[70] Schäfer classifies remarks by Apion, Epictetus, Sextus Empiricus, Julian, Damascius, Plutarch, Tacitus, and Porphyry as belonging to the first category (*Judeophobia*, 69–77). Petronius, Juvenal, and Macrobius are assigned to the second category (*Judeophobia*, 77–81). Schäfer's work on this subject is much more careful in teasing out trends than is Louis H. Feldman's, which conflates all this material (*Jew and Gentile in the Ancient World* [Princeton, NJ: Princeton University Press, 1993], 167–170).

category encompasses a wide variety of texts and authors, which offer a generally neutral evaluation of the Jewish pork taboo. He notes:

To sum up, most authors providing an ethnographic explanation for the Jews' abstinence from pork refer to the antiquity of this custom. This is in itself a favorable argument in the eyes of a pagan author. Except for Tacitus they all express open sympathy with the Jewish determination not to transgress the law and to follow their ancient customs (*ta patria nomima*), contrasting it with the carelessness and irreligiosity of their own or other peoples. Plutarch even goes so far as to find it consistent if the Jews revered the pig because it taught them how to cultivate the soil.[71]

These casual references and ethnographic comments evidence the fact that non-Jews were aware of a somewhat distinctive Jewish food taboo.

Although this category of texts indicates an awareness of Jewish food practices, it is in the work of Roman satirists that this observation receives the most attention. From Petronius' comment about Jews worshipping a "pig-god,"[72] to Juvenal's contention that, in Palestine, "a long established clemency suffers pigs to attain old age,"[73] to the significantly later Macrobius' preservation of a quip of Augustus, that he would "rather be Herod's pig than Herod's son,"[74] Schäfer concludes that comments about Jewish abstinence from pork are more prominent in Roman texts than in Greek ones and that, although most of these are neutral or simply ethnographic in tone, the Roman satirists – particularly Petronius and Juvenal – "use the motif of the pig with an anti-Jewish bias."[75] In short,

---

[71] *Judeophobia*, 77. The Tacitus reference is to *Historiae*, 5:4:1–2 and the Plutarch reference is to *Quaestiones Convivales*, 4:5:2. For Schäfer's comments on both these pericopae, see *Judeophobia*, 72–75. Compare Schäfer's views with those of E. P. Sanders, who notes that "Jews and Gentiles disagreed about a lot of things: about pork, but not about whether or not dietary laws were appropriate" (*Judaism: Practice and Belief, 63 BCE–66 CE* [Philadelphia: Trinity Press, 1994], 230).

[72] *Fragmenta*, no. 37.

[73] *Saturae*, 6:160.

[74] *Saturnalia*, 2:4:11 (ed. M. Stern S2:665), which dates to the fifth century C.E.

[75] *Judeophobia*, 193, 81. See also Gruen, who states: "In general, then, the Jews' exclusion of pork from their diet provoked perplexity, much misinformation, and a lot of amused disdain" (*Diaspora*, 51). Feldman agrees with this general principle, claiming that Latin has more terms that refer to the pig than to any other single animal and comparing the Jewish abstention from pork to a modern English citizen's abstention from roast beef, as some British people believe "that patriotism and roast beef are somehow connected" (*Jew and Gentile*, 167). Although Feldman's assertion about the connection between the English and roast beef is supported by Fischler's observation that "Roastbeefs" is a

the Latin satirists bring into relief two main points: (1) the absence of pig from the Jewish table is assumed knowledge on the part of several authors (and their audience, as the satirists' ability to mock this behavior depends on the audience's ability to get the joke); and (2) this peculiar culinary practice is considered to be an identifiable marker of "Jew" and "Roman."[76]

When the Roman emperor Gaius reportedly asks Philo, "Why do you refuse to eat pork?" his comment is met with laughter by those present. Despite the ambassador's rational answer, the fact that Gaius' question is considered humorous underscores the role that the practices of pork ingestion and abstention play in Jewish and Roman identity in these texts;[77] here, the categories of "Self" and "Other" revolve around one's

slang term to refer to the British ("Food, Self and Identity," 280), I am unsure of the empirical basis for Feldman's claim that Latin has more words for swine than for any other animal.

[76] The assumption of pig as quintessentially Roman led Varro to comment, in a context unrelated to Jews: "Who of our people [i.e., Romans] cultivates a farm without keeping swine?" (*On Agriculture*, 2:4:3). Peter Garnsey interprets Varro's comment as suggesting that this practice is ubiquitous among Romans (*Food and Society in Classical Antiquity* [New York: Cambridge University Press, 1999], 17). This assumption is buttressed by zooarchaeological evidence, which indicates that "in the Hellenistic/Roman period pork consumption was high in urban settings, an archaeological observation in keeping with the prominence of pigs and pork in the writings of the classical authors" (Brian Hesse and Paula Wapnish, "Can Pig Remains Be Used for Ethnic Diagnosis in the Ancient Near East?," in *The Archaeology of Israel: Constructing the Past, Interpreting the Present*, ed. Neil Asher Silberman and David Small, 238–270 [Sheffield, UK: Sheffield Academic Press, 1997], 250). For a detailed discussion of the methodology behind using pig bones to establish regional ethnicity, see Billy Grantham, A Zooarchaeological Model for the Study of Ethnic Complexity at Sepphoris (Ph.D. dissertation, Northwestern University, 1996). A trenchant, although not fatal, critique of these scholars' theoretical models for interpreting zooarchaeological remains is offered by Justin Lev-Tov, "'Upon What Meat Doth This Our Caesar Feed...?': A Dietary Perspective on Hellenistic and Roman Influence in Palestine," in *Zeichen aus Text und Stein: Studien auf dem Weg zu einer Archaeologie des Neuen Testaments*, ed. S. Alkier and J. Zangenberg, 420–446 (Tübingen, Germany: Francke, 2003). In contrast to the Roman evidence, according to *m. Bava Qamma* 7:7 (ed. Albeck 4:39), Jews are forbidden to even raise pigs anywhere (i.e., this law does not apply just to the land of Israel). Amoraic literature offers an "historical" interpretation of this prohibition (*b. Bava Qamma* 82b; *y. Ta'anit* 4:5, 68c).

[77] *Legatio ad Gaium*, 361–363. Philo further notes that the ensuing laughter annoys some of the emperor's servants, who consider it indecorous behavior before the emperor. For Philo's philosophical defense of the pork taboo in Mosaic law, see *De Specialibus Legibus*, 4:101, 106–108 (discussed previously). Again, the veracity of Philo's claim is irrelevant; either way, the fact remains that Philo's audience presumably understands why Gaius' court would laugh at this question. Humor – in the form of irony – perhaps

56 FOOD AND IDENTITY IN EARLY RABBINIC JUDAISM

dietary relationship to pork.[78] Although the same culinary item is the topic of discussion, the significance of ingestion or abstention is a matter of perspective.

By the Tannaitic period, it seems clear that pork served as a symbol of identity. This is an instance in which ancient rhetoric accords with the archaeological evidence, as pork seems to have been the most common categorically nonkosher meat consumed in Roman Palestine.[79] As knowledge of the Jewish practice of abstaining from eating this common meat grew, "pork could grow into a symbol – it could be viewed more and more prominently as the food of the other."[80] For this reason, non-Jewish mockery of this practice continued. According to *Sifra Aharei pereq* 13, for example, the "nations of the world" – which this text points out are idolaters – mock the Jewish prohibition against eating pork.[81] The differing food practices of Jews and non-Jews, and how they relate to identity, are explicit in *Mekilta d'Rabbi Ishmael Mishpatim Nezikin* 18: "You may not say to him [i.e., the resident outsider (*gēr*), here understood as a convert]: 'Last night you worshiped Bel [and] bowed [to] Nebo.[82]

---

also plays a part in Mark 5:1–20 (= Matthew 8:28–34; Luke 8:26–39), when Jesus casts unclean spirits out of a man and into a herd of swine (unclean beasts!). On this interpretation, see Joel Marcus, *Mark 1–8: A New Translation with Introduction and Commentary*, AB, vol. 27 (New York: Doubleday, 2000), 347. Marcus also comments on the sexualized nature of this account (pp. 345, 350, 352) and on the political nature of the pig – with a brief reference to the Legio X (pp. 351–352).

[78] In fact, the pig is symbolic of Rome in later rabbinic literature. For references, see Rosenblum, "'Why do you refuse . . . '"; Sacha Stern, *Jewish Identity in Early Rabbinic Writings* (New York: Brill, 1994), 57. I have not found a tannaitic source that contains this association. Many scholars claim that a connection between Esau (and, by extension, Rome) and the pig appears as early as 1 Enoch 89:12 (e.g., the brief mention in Louis Ginzberg, *The Legends of the Jews*, 7 vols. [Philadelphia: Jewish Publication Society, 1979], 5:294 n. 162; and the much longer discussion in David Bryan, *Cosmos, Chaos and the Kosher Mentality* [Sheffield, UK: Sheffield Academic Press, 1995], 115–118). Needless to say, further work on this subject is a desideratum.

[79] See Chapter 1 for references.

[80] D. Kraemer, *Jewish Eating*, 33.

[81] *Sifra Aharei pereq* 13 (ed. Weiss 86a). For a discussion, see D. Kraemer, *Jewish Eating*, 32.

[82] *Mekilta d'Rabbi Ishmael Mishpatim Nezikin* 18 (ed. Horowitz 311). Bel and Nebo are both Babylonian deities (see Joseph Blenkinsopp, *Isaiah 40–55: A New Translation with Introduction and Commentary*, AB, vol. 19a [New York: Doubleday, 2000], 265–268). The word *q-w-r-s*, however, presents a difficulty. Jacob Neusner renders this word as referring to one of three deities: "you worshiped Bel, Kores, and Nebo" (*The Mekhilta According to Rabbi Ishmael: An Analytical Translation*, 2 vols., BJS 148 and 154 [Atlanta: Society of Biblical Literature, 1988], 2:210). Jacob Z. Lauterbach, perhaps influencing

Behold, there is [still] pig-meat[83] between your teeth! And now, you speak words against me!'" The convert used to eat the food of the "Other" – for which pig is a metonym;[84] now he speaks "words against" a rabbinic Jew, most likely suggesting a debate over "words" of Torah.[85] His former identity both literally and figuratively still remains between his teeth.

Although tannaitic literature only occasionally alludes to the pig in the midst of discussions about Jewish identity, these references do not

---

Neusner, translates the phrase similarly, commenting that "The word קורס (Isa. 46.1) seems to have been understood by the *Mekhilta* as the name of an idol" (*Mekhilta De'Rabbi Ishmael: A Critical Edition, Based on the Manuscripts and Early Editions, with an English Translation, Introduction, and Notes,* 2 vols. [Philadelphia: Jewish Publication Society, 2004], 2:451 n. 1). If Lauterbach and Neusner are correct, then perhaps *Mekilta* understands Qores to be the deity Kairos (personified Opportunity), from the Greek word *kairós*, meaning "proper time or season" (on this etymology, see Marcus Jastrow, *A Dictionary of the Targumim, the Talmud Babli and Yerushalmi, and the Midrashic Literature* [New York: Judaica Press, 1996], 1369 s.v. *qêrās*; H. G. Liddell and R. Scott, *An Intermediate Greek-English Lexicon,* Seventh Edition [New York: American Book Company, 1995], 392 s.v. *kairós*; on this deity, see Herbert Jennings Rose and Karim W. Arafat, "Kairos," in *The Oxford Classical Dictionary,* Third Edition, ed. Simon Hornblower and Anthony Spawforth, 806 [New York: Oxford University Press, 1996]). In contrast, I suggest that this list is a corruption of Isaiah 46:1 (as noted, but not translated accordingly, by Lauterbach), which states: "Bel is cowering, Nebo is bowed" (*kāraʿ bēl qōrēs nĕbô*). Thus, *Mekilta* quotes Isaiah 46:1, substituting the biblical verb for "cowering/bowed" (*kāraʿ*) with the much more common verb "worshipped" (*ʿôbēd*). The participle *ʿôbēd* here follows the Masoretic text's participial form *qōrēs*, unlike the perfect form of *kāraʿ* in the Hebrew Bible. Therefore, my understanding accords well with the context, word order, and grammar of this passage. In addition, this reading is supported in some variant manuscripts of this tradition in *Gerim* 4:1 (ed. Kanevski 31; contrast ed. Simon 61a), a later minor tractate of the Talmud, in which *ʿôbēd* appears but *kāraʿ* is absent; thus, only the Babylonian deities Bel and Nebo are referenced. Rather than positing the presence of a third deity, my reading directly follows the wording of the underlying base text. Further, this reference perhaps indicates more of a rhetorical and theoretical exchange with biblical motifs than a reflection of contemporary Palestinian realia, a trend that Peter Schäfer detects in *y. Avodah Zarah* ("Jews and Gentiles in Yerushalmi Tractate Avodah Zarah," in *The Talmud Yerushalmi and Graeco–Roman Culture,* ed. Peter Schäfer, 335–352 [Tübingen, Germany: Mohr Siebeck, 2002].

[83] For clarity in English, I follow the variant that supplies the adjective "meat" (*bāśār*).
[84] This is not uncommon in rabbinic literature. As S. Stern notes, "[r]eferences to pork can be considered, in many such cases, as metonymic for forbidden food in general" (*Jewish Identity,* 56). As we shall see in Chapter 4, a Jew who eats pork is considered an apostate (*t. Horayot* 1:5 [ed. Zuckermandel 474]) and the bread of a Samaritan is compared to pig-meat (*m. Sheviʿit* 8:10 [ed. Albeck 1:162]).
[85] I base my interpretation on both context and on the content of variants noted by Hoffman. Further, see the intriguing interpretation of Saul Lieberman, who suggests that in the convert's voice can be heard the braying of the pig, brought back to life (*Tosefta Ki-fshuṭah: A Comprehensive Commentary on the Tosefta,* 10 vols., Second Augmented Edition [New York: Jewish Theological Seminary, 1992 (Hebrew)], 9:185).

distinguish themselves as unique compared with the testimony of prior and contemporary Jewish and non-Jewish witnesses. However, the porcine *topoi* – drawn here almost exclusively from non-tannaitic sources – are a reminder that, whether examining the tannaitic or cross-cultural corpora, one needs to look at both ingestion and abstention to fully understand how food practices establish identities within a given community.[86] I now turn to focus on foods that "We" eat and from which "They" abstain.

Manna

Claude Fischler notes that "[w]ithin the same culture a group often defines the neighbouring group as '...-eaters.'"[87] The inverse of this statement is also true: groups define "Self" as "...-eaters." A modern Jewish example of this phenomenon is clearly encountered in the food critic Mimi Sheraton's book on the history of the bialy, *The Bialy Eaters*. As Sheraton notes, Jews from Bialystok, Poland both referred to themselves and were referred to by non-Jews as "*Bialystoker kuchen fressers*, prodigious eaters (*fressers*) of those oniony bread buns [*Bialystoker kuchen*, or bialys]."[88] Having discussed the identities constructed through the practice of consuming or abstaining from pork, I focus now on the foods that, in tannaitic literature, "We" eat. Before proceeding to real foodstuffs, however, it is worth dwelling for a moment on tannaitic theoretical discussions about manna. For, as we shall see, tannaitic sources themselves define rabbinic Jews as "manna eaters."

Manna, the heaven-provided sustenance for the post-Exodus Israelites wandering in the desert, is the subject of much debate.[89] Because the period during which one had physical access to this food item had long

---

[86] On the pig and Jewish/non-Jewish identity in the Middle Ages, see Claudine Fabre-Vassas, *The Singular Beast: Jews, Christians and the Pig*, trans. Carol Volk (New York: Columbia University Press, 1997). On the role that pig has played in legislation of the modern state of Israel, see Daphne Barak-Erez, *Outlawed Pigs: Law, Religion, and Culture in Israel* (Madison: University of Wisconsin Press, 2007).

[87] "Food, Self and Identity," 280.

[88] *The Bialy Eaters: The Story of a Bread and a Lost World* (New York: Broadway Books, 2000), 5.

[89] For example, several texts attempt to ascertain its taste. Numbers 11:7–9 makes a brief reference to this, which is expanded in the tannaitic corpus (e.g., *Mekilta d'Rabbi Ishmael Beshelah Vayassa* 5 [ed. Horowitz 170–171]; *Sifre Numbers* 87 [ed. Horowitz 86–87]). On manna in the Hebrew Bible in general, see, e.g., Exodus 16:4–5.

since ended, these tannaitic discussions are, obviously, theoretical. Talking about something in theory, however, is an attempt to translate that mythical entity into the reality of one's cultural milieu. Despite the fact that manna had long since disappeared from the Israelite menu, the Tannaim (at least metaphorically) still drew on the practice of eating it in their construction of Jewish identity. For the Tannaim, the Israelites' ingestion of manna generations ago was retroactively interpreted as a practice of acquiring and, quite literally, embodying Torah knowledge.

The understanding of manna as imparting Torah knowledge as well as caloric value to the Israelites who ingested it is not unique to tannaitic Judaism. Philo, for example, makes this association in several texts. *De Fuga et Inventione*, 137–139, nicely summarizes Philo's allegorical interpretation of manna as edible heavenly wisdom:

When they sought what it is that nourished the soul (for, as Moses says, "they knew not what it was" [Exodus 16:15]), they became learners and found it to be a saying of God, that is the Divine Word [*logon theion*], from which all kinds of instruction and wisdom flow in perpetual stream. This is the heavenly nourishment, and it is indicated as such in the sacred records, when the First Cause in his own person says, "Lo, it is I that am raining upon you bread out of the heaven" [Exodus 16:4]; for in every deed God drops from above the ethereal wisdom upon minds which are by nature apt and take delight in Contemplation; and they see it and taste it and are filled with pleasure, being fully aware of what they feel, but wholly ignorant of the cause which produced the feeling. So they inquire "What is this" [Exodus 16:15] which has a nature making it sweeter than honey and whiter than snow [Exodus 16:31]? And they will be taught by the seer that "This is the bread, which the Lord hath given them to eat" [Exodus 16:15]. Tell me, then, of what kind the bread is. "This saying," he says, "which the Lord ordained" [Exodus 16:16]. This Divine ordinance fills the soul that has vision alike with light and sweetness, flashing forth the radiancy of truth, and with the honied grace of persuasion imparting sweetness to those who hunger and thirst after nobility of character.[90]

Seeking nourishment for the soul, the Israelites were led to manna, which Philo understands as an allegory for the Divine Word (*Logos*). Philo's allegorical interpretation here is similar to his explanatory rationale for

---

[90] See also *Legum Allegoriae III*, 175–176; *De Mutatione Nominum*, 258–260. I have slightly emended the translation here because of a typographical error in the LCL text.

the biblical legislation regarding domesticated quadrupeds in *De Specialibus Legibus*, 4:106–108, discussed in the section on the "Abominable Pig." In both instances, Philo argues that the Israelite diet is literally an embodiment of its overall philosophy. Commenting on Philo's allegorical approach toward manna, Andrea Lieber notes:

> Israel's capacity for divine vision is linked to a consumption of "soul food" – the acquisition of esoteric knowledge that nourishes the mind the way food nourishes the body. *Mannah* has a mediating quality in Philo – the food mediates between the angelic/cognitive realm and the human realm of the senses. *Mannah* is identified with both Logos and Torah, and even with Moses himself in some cases.[91]

The connection between manna and *Logos*/Torah, therefore, is by no means a tannaitic innovation. However, the Tannaim further the notion that manna is the "soul food" of Israel.

Building on these precedents, the Tannaim focus on a simple concept that becomes a guiding principle in this context: God provided manna to the same community to whom he would later provide the Torah. Therefore, according to tannaitic logic, Israel (on both the individual and communal level) is *embodied* in manna. One who was ineligible to receive the manna is also ineligible to receive the Torah. Without "manna in the mouth," one cannot have "Torah in the Mouth."[92]

This concept appears twice in *Mekilta d'Rabbi Ishmael*. Although the context for each passage differs, both include a tradition attributed to R. Shimon bar Yohai. Although this attribution is parsed differently in each textual environment, together they present a unified conception of edible identity: ancestral access to manna provides access to Torah,

---

[91] "I Set a Table before You: The Jewish Eschatological Character of Aseneth's Conversion Meal," *JSP* 14/1 (2004): 63–77, 72. Also see Peder Borgen, *Bread from Heaven: An Exegetical Study of the Concept of Manna in the Gospel of John and the Writings of Philo* (Leiden, the Netherlands: Brill, 1965), 111–115. On the identification of Moses with manna, see Geza Vermes, "'He is the Bread': Targum Neofiti Exodus 16:15," in *Post-Biblical Jewish Studies*, 139–146 (Leiden, the Netherlands: Brill, 1975). On the role that manna plays in the New Testament (for example, in John 6:58), see Bruce J. Malina, *The Palestinian Manna Tradition* (Leiden, the Netherlands: Brill, 1968), 94–106.

[92] Here I use Martin S. Jaffee's felicitous translation of the term for Oral Law (*tôrāh šebĕ'al peh*). According to Jaffee, the Tannaim "developed the essential outlines of their conceptions of Torah in Script [i.e., the Written Torah, or Hebrew Bible] and Torah in the Mouth [i.e., rabbinic traditions]" (*Torah in the Mouth: Writing and Oral Tradition in Palestinian Judaism 200 BCE–400 CE* [New York: Oxford University Press, 2001], 67).

the study of which is the sine qua non of male rabbinic identity.[93] In neither instance does *Mekilta d'Rabbi Ishmael* address how the convert fits into this ancestral theory. One might assume that the convert would be treated as a native-born Jew, as is explicit in the discussion about a convert's access to the Passover in *Mekilta d'Rabbi Ishmael Bo* 15,[94] mentioned in the next section. However, this logic is never explicitly stated, so it remains conjecture.

In the first passage, *Mekilta* comments on a possible interpretation of Exodus 13:17: "Now when Pharaoh let the people go, God did not lead them by way of the land of the Philistines, although it was near(er); for God said, 'Lest the people repent when they see war and return to Egypt.'" After offering several interpretations of Exodus 13:17, *Mekilta* states:

Another interpretation: All the more so should not the Holy-One-Blessed-be-He have brought them on the straight(er) road to the land of Israel instead of the way of the wilderness?[95] The Holy-One-Blessed-be-He says [i.e., hypothetically reasons]: "If I should bring the Israelites into the Land right now, each person would immediately take possession of a field or a vineyard, and they would neglect Torah. Rather, I will take them into the wilderness (for) forty years, *that they might eat manna and drink well-water*[96] *[so that] Torah will be absorbed [niblelet] into their bodies.*" On account of this, R. Shimon b. Yohai would say: "The Torah is only handed over for interpretation to manna eaters, and like them are heave-offering eaters."[97]

According to this text, God purposely led Israel on a long and circuitous journey through the wilderness to prevent the neglect of Torah. Manna eaters have ingested their identity and as such are not only eligible for,

---

[93] I return to this connection between Torah study and Jewish male identity in Chapter 3.
[94] *Mekilta d'Rabbi Ishmael Bo* 15 (ed. Horowitz 56; = *Sifre Numbers* 71 [ed. Horowitz 67]).
[95] On the "way of the wilderness," see Exodus 13:18.
[96] The belief that "well water" (i.e., the fresh water sources in the desert provided to the Israelites by God) imparts knowledge is not unknown in other Jewish texts. For example, the Dead Sea Scrolls reflect this understanding. When commenting on Numbers 21:18 ("the well that the princes dug and the nobles of the people excavated, with a ruler..."), the *Damascus Document* succinctly states, "The 'well' is the Torah" (CD VI:3–4). Numbers 21:16–20 are the base verses from which the idea that God also constantly provides well water for the Israelites in the desert originates. This concept appears elsewhere (e.g., Pseudo–Philo 10:7; I Corinthians 10:4).
[97] *Mekilta d'Rabbi Ishmael Beshelah Vayehi* 1 (ed. Horowitz 76; cp. *Mekilta d'Rabbi Shimon b. Yohai* at Exodus 13:17 [ed. Epstein and Melamed 45]), emphasis added. I discuss the meaning of the phrase "heave-offering eaters" immediately below.

but also apparently gastronomically predisposed toward, Torah study.[98] Manna seemingly has all the essential vitamins and nutrients for Torah exegesis. After it is "absorbed into their bodies," manna *ontologically changes the manna eaters.* In this case, the notion of eating practices embodying tannaitic identity seems to be both figurative and literal.[99]

This assumed connection between manna eaters and interpreters of Torah is also found in another passage in *Mekilta*. During a series of comments that understand manna as a heaven-provided food for which the Israelites did not have to work, *Mekilta* states:

On account of this, R. Shimon b. Yohai would say: "The Torah is only handed over for interpretation to manna eaters." How so? If one sits [in order to study] and interprets [Torah], and did not know from where he would eat and drink, or from where he would clothe and cover himself – lo, "the Torah is only handed over for interpretation to manna eaters, and equivalent to them are heave-offering eaters."[100]

Just as "heave-offering eaters" are entitled to free food via access to priestly provisions, so too are the Torah-interpreting "manna eaters."[101] This text further clarifies the second part of R. Shimon b. Yohai's statement, that manna eaters are equivalent to heave-offering eaters. The logic of this pericope seems to be that the interpreters of Torah ("manna eaters") have inherited the role of the priests and, as such, this entitles them to the priestly rations.[102] Whether one spends all day inside the Temple

---

[98] Contrast John 6:41–59, in which Jews who recognize Jesus (who is identified with manna) and eat his flesh/bread (i.e., manna) are granted eternal life.

[99] For a similar interpretation of this text, see Joel Hecker, *Mystical Bodies, Mystical Meals: Eating and Embodiment in Medieval Kabbalah* (Detroit, MI: Wayne State University Press, 2005), 42–43.

[100] *Mekilta d'Rabbi Ishmael Beshelah Vayassa* 2 (ed. Horowitz 161; = *Mekilta d'Rabbi Shimon b. Yohai* at Exodus 16:4 [ed. Epstein and Melamed 107]).

[101] Similarly, see W. David Nelson, *Mekhilta de-Rabbi Shimon bar Yohai* (Philadelphia: Jewish Publication Society, 2006), 80 n. 5.

[102] Women would thus fit into the nascent rabbinic system similarly to how they fit into the biblical priestly system (as understood by the rabbis). Here (and elsewhere, as I will show in more depth in Chapter 3), the work of Nancy Jay on gender and sacrificial systems proves useful (*Throughout Your Generations Forever: Sacrifice, Religion, and Paternity* [Chicago: University of Chicago Press, 1992]). I am not the first to notice the applicability of Jay's theories to rabbinic literature. For example, see Jonathan Brumberg-Kraus, "Meat Eating and Jewish Identity: Ritualization of the Priestly 'Torah of Beast and Fowl' (Lev 11:46) in Rabbinic Judaism and Medieval Kabbalah," *AJSR* 24/2 (1999): 227–262, 234, 259–260.

or inside the study house, he is equivalent with regard to the priestly rations.

Although the connection between manna (and well water) and Torah is clearly not a tannaitic innovation, the Tannaim further develop their theoretical discussion about manna into a broader notion of the embodiment of metonymic food. Non-Jews are tacitly denied access to Torah because of their prior ineligibility to be "manna eaters." In at least one text, the difference between Jew and non-Jew created by the former's ingestion of manna appears to be ontological, as well as metaphorical. In this respect, the Tannaim understand manna to have functioned in a roughly analogous manner to that in which Christians have come to view the Eucharist: namely, as an act of ingestion that results in embodiment.[103] Further, "manna eaters" are now equated with "heave-offering eaters," making an analogy between rabbis and priests. By ingesting the metonymic and embodying food that is manna, it would seem that the Tannaim understand themselves to have gained priestly authority. In sum, tannaitic views on manna reify an ontological difference that was present, but inchoate, in Philo's allegorical interpretations on this subject. Thus, serving as another metonym for a rabbinic Jew, the "manna eater" consumes more than just calories: his act of ingestion is retroactively understood to be a practice that affects identity construction.

The Passover

Another example of a Jewish metonymic food is the Passover sacrifice (hereafter referred to as "the Passover"). Before looking at the tannaitic

---

[103] The notion that the Eucharist represents the body and blood of Jesus Christ may be present in the New Testament in texts such as John 6. Whereas John 6 discusses mainly the eternal life granted via ingesting Jesus' body and blood, John 6:56 comes close to clearly articulating an ontological change in the ingestor's body, claiming that Jesus will abide in the body of those who eat his flesh and blood. Later Christian writers greatly expand this concept, developing a significantly broader notion of embodiment and ontological change in those who ingest the Eucharist. For a collection of these sources, see Daniel J. Sheerin, *The Eucharist* (Wilmington, DE: Michael Glazier, 1986). Two Christian texts that articulate this notion that conform to the timeframe of the present study are Justin Martyr, *First Apology*, 66 and Clement of Alexandria, *Paedagogus*, 2.19.3. The connection among the Eucharist, embodiment, and ontological change plays an important role in the lives of Christian women in the Middle Ages. For a discussion, see Caroline Walker Bynum, *Holy Feast and Holy Fast: The Religious Significance of Food to Medieval Women* (Berkeley and Los Angeles: University of California Press, 1988).

texts on this issue, one must first understand the biblical prohibitions against non-Israelite consumption of the Passover, which is knowledge assumed in this corpus. According to Exodus 12:43–49:

Yhwh said to Moses and Aaron: "This is the law of the Passover: no (non-resident) alien[104] may eat of it. But any slave a man has acquired for money: [after] you circumcise him, then he may eat.[105] In one house it shall be eaten; you shall not take any of the flesh outside of the house; and as for the bones, you shall not break any of them.[106] The entire community of Israel shall offer it. If a resident outsider who resides with you intends to make a Passover to Yhwh, every male belonging to him shall be circumcised, and then he may approach to make it; he shall then be as the native of the land. But no uncircumcised male may eat of it. There shall be *one law* for the native and for the resident outsider who resides in your midst."[107]

This biblical legislation both prevents the foreigner from ingesting the Passover and provides a process – circumcision – by which a male slave or a resident outsider may eat thereof.[108]

---

[104] Here I employ Saul M. Olyan's translation of *ben-nēkār* (*Rites and Rank: Hierarchy in the Biblical Representations of Cult* [Princeton, NJ: Princeton University Press, 2000], 67). Although I focus on the convert in this chapter, access to the Passover is denied (in the midst of exegesis on this verse) to both the Jewish *mešûmād* ("apostate") and the non-Jew in *Mekilta d'Rabbi Ishmael Bo* 15 (ed. Horowitz 53). Contrast *Mekilta d'Rabbi Shimon b. Yohai* at Exodus 12:43 (ed. Epstein and Melamed 35), which discusses only the Jewish *mešûmād*. Both traditions appear in the Targumim (Aramaic translations of the Hebrew Bible) at Exodus 12:43 (for a discussion, see Bernard Grossfeld, *The Targum Onqelos to Exodus: Translated, with Apparatus and Notes*, Vol. 7 [Wilmington, DE: Michael Glazier, 1988], 34–35 n. 23). The apostate, while not quite a non-Jew, is equated with one, as he is prevented from eating the metonymic food of Israel. I comment further on the issue of the Jewish "apostate" in Chapter 4.

[105] For the tannaitic understanding of the circumcised slave's access to the Passover, see *Mekilta d'Rabbi Ishmael Bo* 15 (ed. Horowitz 53).

[106] Here I render the Hebrew collective singular as an English plural for the sake of better comprehension. The fact that the Passover must be consumed in "one house" is discussed further in Chapters 3 and 4.

[107] Emphasis added. According to Olyan, this pericope is one example that indicates that "some Holiness texts insist on equal cultic and quasi-cultic obligations and privileges for the circumcised resident outsider" (*Rites and Rank*, 74; see also pp. 70, 169 n. 161).

[108] For information about biblical circumcision, see Robert G. Hall, "Circumcision," in *ABD*, ed. David Noel Freedman, 1:1025–1031, 6 vols. (New York: Doubleday, 1992). For the role that circumcision plays in the rabbinic conversion ceremony, see Cohen, *Beginnings of Jewishness*, 198–238. In a later work, Cohen explores the gender implications of why only men were circumcised (*Why Aren't Jewish Women Circumcised?: Gender and Covenant in Judaism* [Berkeley and Los Angeles: University of California Press, 2005]; cf. Howard Eilberg-Schwartz, *The Savage in Judaism: An Anthropology of*

Exegesis of this biblically ordained principle provides an opportunity in tannaitic texts to establish the identity status of the convert through a food regulation (regardless of the fact that this discussion, from the tannaitic perspective, is an entirely "scholastic"[109] exercise, as no sacrifice can occur after the destruction of the Second Temple). Because the Passover is a metonymic food – it can be eaten only by "Us" – the moment that the Passover is ingested, one is *embodied* as part of Israel. Because tannaitic literature does not always appear to be entirely consistent on whether converts are included in biblical commandments incumbent on Israel, extrapolations from concepts such as the Passover allow for a "hermeneutical moment," wherein a general principle can be established.[110] Like the rite of circumcision that precedes it, participation in the Passover is therefore an outward manifestation of the convert's new identity. Despite the fact that he continues to be labeled as a "convert," the convert is legally considered to be one of "Us." Rather than questioning whether a convert can eat the Passover, the Tannaim ask: (1) Is there a waiting period after one converts before he may partake of the Passover? and (2) If so, for how long?

The first attempts at articulating this principle are reputed to be found in an argument between the Houses of Shammai and Hillel, two rabbinic schools that often debated one another. This discussion first appears in

---

Israelite Religion and Ancient Judaism [Bloomington and Indianapolis: Indiana University Press, 1990], 141–176). Although nothing precludes Jewish women from eating the Passover, the fact that circumcision is a primary indicator for access to this food certainly suggests that the biblical author(s) (and, following this lead, the Tannaim as well) are interested here in discussing male Jewish identity.

[109] On the term "scholastic," see Shaye J. D. Cohen, who states: "The Mishnah constructs legal categories, which often appear to be theoretical and abstruse, and then discusses, usually in great detail, the precise definitions and limits of those categories. It creates lists of analogous legal phenomena, and then proceeds to define and analyze every item on the list. It posits legal principles, and devotes much attention to those objects, cases, or times, which seem to be subject to more that one principle at once, or perhaps to none of the principles at all. These modes of thinking and writing, which can be characterized as *scholastic*, are endemic to the Mishnah, from one end to the other, and are not found in any pre–mishnaic Jewish document. Here we have come not to a source of mishnaic law but to the distinctive contribution of its creators" ("The Judean Legal Tradition and the *Halakhah* of the Mishnah," in *The Cambridge Companion to the Talmud and Rabbinic Literature*, ed. Charlotte Elisheva Fonrobert and Martin S. Jaffee, 121–143 [New York: Cambridge University Press, 2007], 134–135, emphasis in original). Although Cohen comments here on the beginning of this trend in the Mishnah, the scholastic approach permeates the subsequent rabbinic corpus.

[110] See S. Stern, *Jewish Identity*, 90–91.

m. Pesahim 8:8, which is quoted, clarified, and expanded on in *t. Pisha* 7:13–14:[111]

R. Yosi b. R. Yehudah says... "But an uncircumcised male on behalf of whom the blood [of the Passover] is tossed,[112] and who afterwards was circumcised: behold, he does not eat [the meat from the Passover]; and, he is obligated to observe the second Passover."[113]

R. Lazar b. R. Sadoq says: "The House of Shammai and the House of Hillel agree concerning an uncircumcised [Jewish] male who receives sprinkling and then eats [the Passover]. Concerning what did they differ? Concerning the uncircumcised Gentile. For, *the House of Shammai says: 'He immerses and eats his Passover in the evening.' But the House of Hillel says: 'He who separates [himself] from [his] foreskin is like one who separates [himself] from the grave.'*"[114]

According to Tosefta, the houses agree that an uncircumcised Jew may undergo circumcision and then immediately eat the Passover. The issue at hand, however, is how the convert's identity status changes after he undergoes circumcision.[115] For, just as is the case with circumcision, eating the Passover is a practice that marks Jewish identity. The logic of Tosefta appears to be that the uncircumcised Jew is always eligible, once he meets the one condition set forth in Exodus 12:48: "But no

---

[111] *m. Pesahim* 8:8 (ed. Albeck 2:171); *t. Pisha* 7:13–14 (ed. Lieberman 2:181–182). "Pisha" (meaning "the Passover") is the Aramaic title given to the toseftan tractate corresponding to *m. Pesahim*.

[112] For a discussion and analysis of blood manipulation in the Hebrew Bible, see William K. Gilders, *Blood Ritual in the Hebrew Bible: Meaning and Power* (Baltimore: Johns Hopkins University Press, 2004).

[113] On the second Passover, see Numbers 9:1–12.

[114] The words in italics also appear in *m. Pesahim* 8:8 (ed. Albeck 2:171; = *m. Eduyyot* 5:2 [ed. Albeck 4:305]), which states in full: "A convert who converted on the eve of Passover [i.e., the fourteenth day of the month of Nisan] – the House of Shammai says: 'He immerses and eats his Passover in the evening.' But the House of Hillel says: 'He who separates [himself] from [his] foreskin is like one who separates [himself] from the grave.'" On the purity issues associated with this pericope, see Hayes, *Gentile Impurities*, 116–122.

[115] It is this framing that clarifies the ambiguous final clause in *m. Pesahim* 8:8. Tosefta's narrative framing of the Mishnaic tradition suggests a reading of this clause wherein, as Hayes notes, "[t]he Gentile's uncircumcision at the time of the sacrifice of the Paschal offering renders him ineligible for the entire observance. It is not permitted to sacrifice on his behalf in anticipation of his conversion" (*Gentile Impurities*, 121, where Hayes cites as further support the *baraitot* found on *y. Pesahim* 8:8, 36b). For an extended discussion, see Christine Hayes, "Do Converts to Judaism Require Purification?: M. Pes. 8:8 – An Interpretative Crux Solved," *JSQ* 9 (2002): 327–352.

uncircumcised male may eat of it"; the uncircumcised Gentile's access to the Passover after he is circumcised is not as clear.[116]

Another text bears directly on the previous passage. According to Rabbi,[117] a convert who converts between the two Passovers is required to make the second Passover; R. Natan disagrees, on the basis that the convert was not a Jew at the time of the first Passover. These opinions accord with the previous views espoused by the two houses. The resolution to this dispute is finally found in *Mekilta d'Rabbi Ishmael Bo* 15:[118]

"If a resident outsider who resides with you makes a Passover to Yhwh..." [Exodus 12:48]. Might I infer that as soon as one converts, he can make a Passover immediately? Scripture therefore says: "he shall then be as the native of the land" [Exodus 12:48]. [This teaches that] just as the native [offers a Passover] on the fourteenth [day of the month of Nisan], the convert also [offers a Passover] on the fourteenth [of Nisan]. R. Shimon ben Eliezer says: "Behold, [regarding] one who converts between the two Passovers: I might infer that he should make the second Passover. Scripture therefore says: 'he shall then be as the native of the land.' [This teaches that] just as the native of the land makes the second [Passover] only when he did not make the first [Passover], so too [in the case of] the convert: whoever did not make the first [Passover, *but was eligible at the time to do so*], should make the second [Passover]."

In this text, the variables are clearly laid out. A circumcised[119] convert is directly equated with a "native of the land" and, as such, all the Passover

---

[116] Further, see *t. Pisha* 8:4 (ed. Lieberman 2:184), which states: "'A convert [*gēr*] who converts between the two Passovers is required to make the second Passover,' the words of Rabbi. R. Natan says, 'He does not need to make the second Passover, since he was not already obligated at [the time of] the first [Passover].'" In rabbinic literature, the term *gēr* often refers to a convert, as is the case in this pericope. This connection is made explicit, for example, in *Mekilta d'Rabbi Shimon b. Yohai* at Exodus 12:49 (ed. Epstein and Melamed 37). For a list of (and discussion about) those ineligible for the first Passover but required to offer the second Passover, see *t. Pisha* 7:11–8:1 (ed. Lieberman 2:179–183).

[117] All attributions to "Rabbi" are traditionally understood as referring to Rabbi Judah I (Yehudah ha-Nasi = Judah the Patriarch/Prince), a patriarch and the reputed redactor of the Mishnah. See H. L. Strack and Günter Stemberger, *Introduction to the Talmud and Midrash*, trans. and ed. Markus Bockmuehl (Minneapolis: Fortress Press, 1996), 81.

[118] *Mekilta d'Rabbi Ishmael Bo* 15 (ed. Horowitz 56; = *Sifre Numbers* 71 [ed. Horowitz 67]).

[119] The importance of the fact that a man – even if he is Jewish – must be circumcised to have access to the Passover is accented throughout *Mekilta d'Rabbi Ishmael Bo* 15 (ed. Horowitz 52–57).

consumption regulations apply equally to him. Until this process is complete, however, he cannot partake in the Passover. Thus, access to food marked as distinctly Jewish – the Passover – indicates the identity status of a person. A non-Jew cannot eat the metonymic food of Israel; a circumcised convert, however, is *embodied* in Israel through his consumption of this archetypical Jewish food. Both the acts of circumcision and of ingesting the Passover are therefore seen as effecting physical alteration, as practices of embodiment into the corporate body of Israel.

Throughout this section, I have argued that tannaitic texts that discuss a convert's access to the Passover engage in a debate over *when* a convert may ingest the sacrificial offering, not *whether* a convert may do so.[120] Following the Hebrew Bible, these texts presume the eating of the Passover to be metonymic for Jewish identity. By further presuming a convert's access to this metonymic food, the Tannaim use food practices as yet another way to signal the incorporation of a convert into the body of Israel.

The Laws of Kashrut

Do the laws of *kashrut* apply to non-Jews? Tannaitic literature asks this question several times and comes to the same negative conclusion. The tannaitic questioning of whether the statutes of *kashrut* apply to non-Jews is important in that it establishes kosher food as the required diet and foodway specifically of the Jew. Not surprisingly, to eat kosher is therefore understood as a culinary and commensal practice of Jewish identity formation.

According to Leviticus 17:15–16:

Any person [*nepeš*] who eats carrion[121] or *ṭerēfāh*,[122](See footnote on next page) whether he is a native or a resident outsider [*gēr*], shall wash his clothes, bathe in water and remain unclean until evening; then he shall be clean. But

---

[120] In fact, a convert must offer a sacrifice to enter the covenant (*Mekilta d'Rabbi Shimon b. Yohai* at Exodus 12:48 [ed. Epstein and Melamed 37]). A comparable discussion about a convert's access to animal sacrifice, though in a non-Passover context, is found on *t. Sheqalim* 3:20–21 (ed. Lieberman 2:217–218).

[121] In the corpus of the Hebrew Bible, carrion (*nevēlāh*) refers to an animal that has suffered a natural death, rather than being slaughtered or killed by another animal, and is specifically prohibited (see Milgrom, *Leviticus 1–16*, 653–654). For example, see Deuteronomy 14:21, which states: "You shall not eat anything that dies a natural death

if he does not wash [his clothes] or his body he does not bathe, then he shall bear his guilt.

The Tannaim seek to understand the precise meaning of the word "person" (*nepeš*, literally "soul"). Does this seemingly all-encompassing term include non-Jews as well, or is *kashrut* a distinctly Jewish foodway? In typical rabbinic fashion, *Sifra* parses the verse to include and to exclude categories of people:

"Any person." Might one suppose [that this] also [refers to] the Gentile? Scripture therefore says: "a convert" [*gēr*][123] [but not the Gentile]. If [it applies to the] convert, might one suppose that [it applies] also to the resident outsider [*gēr tôšāb*]? Scripture therefore says: "a native." Just as a native is a member of the covenant, so too is the convert a member of the covenant.[124]

[*nevēlāh*]; you may give it to the resident outsider [*gēr*] who [resides] within your gates to eat or you may sell it to a foreigner. For you are a holy people unto Yhwh, your God." My translation of the Hebrew term *gēr* as "resident outsider," instead of the regnant translation of "resident alien," follows the suggestion of Olyan (*Rites and Rank*, 7, 68–69). However, in other biblical texts (usually attributed to the Priestly [P] source), carrion is prohibited only to Israelite priests (e.g., Leviticus 11:40; 17:15–16; Ezekiel 44:31). In rabbinic literature, carrion is usually understood more specifically as any animal that has not been slaughtered according to rabbinic procedure (e.g., *m. Hullin* 2:4 [ed. Albeck 5:119–120]). According to *m. Shevi'it* 7:3 (ed. Albeck 1:157; cp. *t. Shevi'it* 5:8 [ed. Lieberman 1:187]), Jews are forbidden from any business transaction that involves carrion.

[122] (*See Footnote citation 122 on page 68*) *Ṭerēfāh* refers to meat that comes from an animal killed by another animal and is not the product of human slaughter. Biblically prohibited, this class of meat is often paired with carrion (e.g., Leviticus 7:24; 22:8; see also 17:15–16, with the caveat mentioned in the immediately preceding note in regard to carrion in this text). However, in contrast to carrion, tannaitic law permits a Jew to derive economic benefit from this meat (*t. Shabbat* 7:20 [ed. Lieberman 2:28]). Although this term still maintains this connection with animals, it also develops another technical meaning in the rabbinic corpus: *ṭerēfāh* is the meat from an animal that received a rabbinically proper slaughter, but was invalidated in some other manner. See *m. Hullin* 2:4 (ed. Albeck 5:119–120); *t. Hullin* 2:9 (ed. Zuckermandel 502). In modern times, *ṭerēfāh* is used less technically to refer to any nonkosher food, even if that foodstuff is not subject to rabbinic rules regulating slaughter (e.g., lobster).

[123] As I have already noted, rabbinic literature uses the term *gēr* to refer to converts. It seems to me that the text here understands the term "resident outsider" in the Hebrew Bible to refer to the convert, hence the distinction is about to be made between the *gēr* and the *gēr tôšāb*. Contrast Neusner's translation: "sojourner" (*Sifra: An Analytical Translation*, 3 vols., BJS 138, 139, and 140 [Atlanta: Society of Biblical Literature, 1988], 3:67).

[124] *Sifra Aharei pereq* 12:1 (ed. Weiss 84b). In Weiss' edition, *pereq* 12 is mislabeled as *pereq* 11. As such, this pericope is the second *pereq* 11 on 84b.

Sifra understands the phrase "any person" to be limited to the categories of the convert and the native-born. Therefore, the prohibitions against eating carrion or *ṭerēfāh* apply only to Jews (native-born and converted). In sum, a Jew is commanded to eat in a manner that differs from that of a non-Jew.

Another text from *Sifra* is even more explicit about the fact that non-Jews are not included in Jewish dietary proscriptions. The base text for this passage is Leviticus 7:22–27, which states:

And Yhwh spoke to Moses, saying: "Speak to the Israelite people as follows: 'All fat from the ox or the sheep you shall not eat. And as for the fat from carrion or the fat from *ṭerēfāh*, it may be put to any use, but you must not eat it. If anyone eats the suet of an animal from which a food gift is presented to Yhwh,[125] then the person who eats it shall be cut off from his kin. And all blood, of either bird or of animal, you shall not eat in your settlements. Any person who eats blood shall be cut off from his kin.'"

In typical Leviticus fashion, this passage includes several specific prohibitions against the consumption of both suet and blood. Yet again, *Sifra* asks the question of whether these regulations also apply to non-Jews:

"Israelite people" are prohibited from [eating] fat, but Gentiles are not prohibited from [eating] fat. But is not [the opposite of that proposition] a matter of logic? Just as [in the matter of not cutting off the] limb from a living being, [on account of] which one is not liable to extirpation, is forbidden for the children of Noah as for the children of Israel,[126] [the prohibition against eating] fat, [on account of] which one is not liable to extirpation, is it not logical that it [i.e., Scripture] [should also] forbid the children of Noah as for the children of Israel? Scripture therefore says, "The Israelite people." The

---

[125] This translation follows Milgrom, *Leviticus 1–16*, 380.

[126] The Noahide Laws are a set of universal laws that the rabbis consider incumbent on all of humanity. The Tannaim articulate this concept in *t. Avodah Zarah* 8:4–8:8 (ed. Zuckermandel 473–474), a list that explicitly prohibits both Gentile and Jew from consuming a limb cut off from a living beast (8:6). See also *t. Demai* 2:24 (ed. Lieberman 1:72). The tradition that Gentiles should follow a general code that is incumbent on all of humanity, and that includes some form of food regulations, is also attested in Acts 15:19–20 (see Smith, *From Symposium to Eucharist*, 166). On the Noahide laws in general, see David Novak, *The Image of the Non-Jew in Judaism: An Historical and Constructive Study of the Noahide Laws*, Toronto Studies in Theology 14 (New York: Edwin Mellen Press, 1983). Interestingly, Tosefta understands this principle as applying only to clean (i.e., kosher) animals (*t. Hullin* 7:9 [ed. Zuckermandel 509]). See my discussion later in this chapter.

children of Israel[127] are prohibited from [eating] fat, but Gentiles[128] are not prohibited from [eating] the fat. I know only [that the prohibition applies to] the children of Israel. From where do I derive that it includes converts and emancipated slaves? Scripture therefore says, "If anyone eats (the) fat [of the animals from which offerings may be made to Yhwh, *then the person who eats it shall be cut off from his kin*]."[129]

Again, *Sifra* parses a verse from Leviticus in such a way as to exclude Gentiles and to include native-born Israelites/Jews, converts, and emancipated slaves among the "Israelite people" – the very people on whom, according to the Tannaim, the biblical dietary laws are incumbent. Although the Tannaim consider the Noahide law of not consuming the limb from a living being to be applicable to all humanity, this is seen only as a generic taboo that distinguishes a civilized person from an animal. All humans are required to act in accordance with the tannaitic definition of generic human behavior; however, not all humans are required to eat in accordance with every tannaitic food regulation. Rather, *kashrut* is a distinctly Jewish foodway.

Whereas the texts from *Sifra* focus on the diner, a cluster of texts from *m.* and *t. Hullin* focus on the dinner. The question is whether specific rules that apply to pure (i.e., kosher) animals also apply to impure (i.e., nonkosher) ones. According to *t. Hullin* 7:8:[130]

[The prohibition against ingesting the sinew of the hip][131] applies to a pure [animal] and not to an impure [animal]. R. Yehudah says: "Also to an impure [animal], because the prohibition thereof came before the giving of the Torah." They said to R. Yehudah: "It does not say [in Genesis 32:33], 'Therefore, the children of Jacob, Reuben and Shimon will not eat the sinew of the thigh,' but 'the children of Israel' – those who stood before Mount

---

[127] Although *Sifra* employs the same terminology as the Hebrew Bible, I differentiate between the two of them ("Israelite people" for the Hebrew Bible and "children of Israel" for *Sifra*) both for the sake of clarity and for parallel structure with the common translation of the other category mentioned in *Sifra* ("the children of Noah").

[128] Literally "worshippers of the stars," i.e., idolaters.

[129] *Sav pereq* 15 *parasha* 10:1 (ed. Weiss 38b), emphasis added. This pericope is an excellent example of *Sifra*'s concept of the fallibility of logic without the guidance of Scripture (in general, see Neusner, *Sifra*, 1:46–51 and *passim*).

[130] *t. Hullin* 7:8 (ed. Zuckermandel 509). Here, Tosefta comments on *m. Hullin* 7:6 (ed. Albeck 5:137).

[131] For the biblical origin of this practice, see Genesis 32:23–33.

Sinai. So why does he [i.e., Moses] write it there [in the time of Jacob]? To tell you on account of what it is prohibited."[132]

Using a clever (though circular) reading of Genesis, the anonymous Sages overrule R. Yehudah and claim that the biblical prohibition of the sinew of the hip applies only to kosher meat. Apparently, non-Jews are free to eat the sinew of both pure and impure animals. Once again, the laws of *kashrut* serve as a distinctly Jewish foodway.

Tannaitic discussions that restrict the applicability of the kosher laws to Jews are part of a larger trend of solipsism that Sacha Stern detects in rabbinic literature. Stern defines solipsism as an experience "where the other is considered by the self to be non-existent."[133] Stern notes that in rabbinic literature in general, solipsism results in non-Jews' exclusion from most of the commandments and, thus, from the practices that construct Jewish identity.[134] Because of culinary distinctions, the act of eating is a different practice for Jews and non-Jews, which results in the formation of separate identities. The fact that one must consume calories on a daily basis for survival makes culinary distinctions an important and extremely effective practice by which an individual or group can signal social inclusion and exclusion. Furthermore, one could suggest that limiting the laws of *kashrut* to Jews marks Jews as physically different from non-Jews. This distinctly Jewish foodway – which eschews pork and once included manna and the Passover – embodies both the individual Jew and Israel (i.e., the collective entity that constitutes the communal body of all Jews).[135]

One final example of this concept is encountered in two tannaitic texts that contrast the diet of a convert before and after conversion. We have already seen *Mekilta d'Rabbi Ishmael Mishpatim Nezikin* 18, which cautions against disparaging a recent convert who is debating Torah

---

[132] *t. Hullin* 7:9 (ed. Zuckermandel 509), the immediately preceding text, contains a similar discussion with regard to the prohibition against cutting off the limb of a living animal (i.e., it applies only to a pure beast). Because citing this text in full would be repetitive, I simply note it as one more piece of corroborating evidence. On the status of the biblical commandments prior to their revelation at Sinai, see Gary A. Anderson, "The Status of the Torah before Sinai: The Retelling of the Bible in the Damascus Covenant and the Book of Jubilees," *DSD* 1/1 (1994): 1–29.

[133] *Jewish Identity*, 200.

[134] *Jewish Identity*, 204.

[135] On the notion of "Israel" as a "single, homogenous entity," see S. Stern, *Jewish Identity*, 12–13 and *passim*.

while still having pig-meat between his teeth. A second example of this trope can be found on *t. Bava Metzi'a* 3:25, which states, "[If] one saw a convert who came to study Torah, he should not say to him [i.e., the convert]: 'Look who is coming to study Torah – the one who ate carrion, *ṭerēfāh*, abominations, and creeping things!'"¹³⁶ Alhough in both texts the convert engages in debate over words of Torah – the quintessential male rabbinic activity¹³⁷ – his previous foodway, and hence his identity, is embodied in the food that still remains between his teeth.

Food as Metonym/Food as Embodiment: Conclusions

Tannaitic literature offers the rough outline of a distinct Jewish foodway that will expand voluminously over time.¹³⁸ Through the intersecting notions of the metonymy and embodiment of food, the Tannaim innovate and augment food practices as part of a larger process of identity formation. It seems clear from *Sifre Deuteronomy* 354 that the Tannaim are aware of the ramifications of this emerging Jewish foodway:

> [The other nations] would then go up to Jerusalem and observe Israel [i.e., the people of Israel] – who worshipped only one God and ate only one food; whereas, amongst the nations, the god of one [nation] was not the god of another, and the food of one [nation] was not the food of another. [Thus,] they would say: "There is no better nation to cling to than this."¹³⁹

Through both theological and culinary monotheism – worshiping one God and eating one food commanded by the one God – Israel creates

---

¹³⁶ *t. Bava Metzi'a* 3:25 (ed. Lieberman 5:79). *m. Bava Metzi'a* 4:10 (ed. Albeck 4: 82) simply states, "If he was a child of converts, one may not say to him: 'Remember the deeds of your ancestors!'" In a later text, *Avot d'Rabbi Natan* A16:13–17 (ed. Schechter 63), R. Akiba rejects two beautiful Gentile women sent to seduce him on the grounds that they smelled of nonkosher food.

¹³⁷ This activity also serves to construct the "male" identity in rabbinic literature. See Michael L. Satlow, "'Try to be a Man': The Rabbinic Construction of Masculinity," *HTR* 89/1 (1996): 19–40.

¹³⁸ In general, see D. Kraemer, *Jewish Eating*, which discusses this expansion with particular attention to the diachronically increasing regulations mandating the separation between milk and meat.

¹³⁹ *Sifre Deuteronomy* 354 (ed. Finkelstein 416). There is a parallel version to this story (which lacks any mention of "one food") in a later text (*Genesis Rabba* 355 [ed. Theodor and Albeck 3:1263]). Also compare the Midianite maidens' comments, recorded by Josephus, that, "your food is of a peculiar sort and your drink is distinct from that of other men" and that Jews eat "strange meats" (*Jewish Antiquities*, 4:137, 139).

an identity that, according to this pericope, its neighbors envy.[140] Here I disagree with Stern, who interprets *Sifre Deuteronomy* 354 in the following manner: "In this passage, the distinctiveness of Israel from the nations lies in their unparalleled *unity*, rather than in their dietary laws."[141] Although I agree with Stern that this passage focuses on Israel's "unparalleled *unity*," I believe that this "unparalleled *unity*" is enacted and maintained *through* its dietary laws.

Although monotheism is an oft-discussed identifier of Israel, monophagy receives comparatively little attention. What does it mean to eat "one food"? What does the "one food" consist of? I understand the "one food" of Israel to consist of the network of culinary and commensal practices discussed in this section that differentiate "Jewish" food from "non-Jewish" food; it is a foodway that affects both dinner and diner.

The manner in which modern Japanese culture uses rice provides an analog to the tannaitic data on metonymic foods and foodways. As Ohnuki-Tierney suggests, "Amid a flood of Western foods, contemporary Japanese continue to reaffirm their collective self by constructing their own foodway."[142] In Japan, rice is marked as the dietary staple of the "Self," whereas meat is considered the staple of the "Other." This belief is reflected in a statement by Den Fujita, the man who brought McDonald's to Japan, touting the ontological advantages of a McDonald's diet for the Japanese people. Although a diet of rice forged the modern Japanese body, "'[i]f we eat McDonald's hamburgers and potatoes for a thousand years,' Fujita once promised his countrymen, 'we will become taller, our skin will become white, and our hair will be blonde.'"[143] The metonymic food of America (McDonald's hamburgers and French fries) is understood as embodying, and thus physically altering. Fujita's words provide a modern analog for the claim in *Sifre Deuteronomy* 354 that other nations might envy an identity created by ingesting "one food." Of course, the Tannaim and the Japanese are not unique in this matter, as one could offer any

---

[140] Non-Jews' envy of Israel is a trope detected in rabbinic literature by Stern (see *Jewish Identity*, 50, where he provides only amoraic evidence as support).
[141] *Jewish Identity*, 78 n. 212, original emphasis.
[142] *Rice as Self*, 108.
[143] Eric Schlosser, *Fast Food Nation: The Dark Side of the All-American Meal* (Boston: Houghton Mifflin, 2001), 231.

number of examples.[144] Therefore, the tannaitic data are understood as one more instance of a culture using food practices and foodways in the discourse of "Self" and "Other." From the pages of Leviticus to domestic rice patties in Japan, "*to eat* was a powerful verb."[145]

THE STATUS OF FOOD CORRELATES WITH THE STATUS OF ITS COOK

Turning from the table to the tannaitic kitchen, we encounter a series of food preparation practices that affect the status of the food and, thus, the identity of the person who consumes that food. These practices, some of which have Second Temple-period precedents but the majority of which are tannaitic innovations, can be divided roughly into two categories: (1) regulations pertaining to animal slaughter; and (2) regulations pertaining to non-meat items. In each category, the operative notion is that the food that people prepare is an extension of themselves.

Throughout this section, I argue that the Tannaim use a rhetoric of analogy in their construction of "Self" and "Other." For an analogy to work, the second term (i.e., that to which an object or category is compared) must belong to the shared knowledge of both the author and the audience.[146] Tannaitic literature continually makes analogies between

---

[144] E.g., Diner, *Hungering for America* (Italian, Irish, and Jewish); Appadurai, "How to Make a National Cuisine" (Indian); in general, see several of the essays in the collection edited by Jean-Louis Flandrin and Massimo Montanari, *Food: A Culinary History from Antiquity to the Present*, trans. Albert Sonnenfeld (New York: Penguin Books, 1999). To offer one modern manifestation of this phenomenon from the area in which the majority of this present study was composed, a journalist has recently argued that Dunkin' Donuts represents a specific class and identity status for New Englanders as compared with the Seattle-based Starbucks chain. According to Mike Miliard, in New England culture Dunkin' Donuts represents working-class people born and bred in New England, whereas Starbucks is perceived to represent upper-class foreigners. Thus, he labels the Dunkin' Donuts chain's products "identity donuts" ("Thinkin' About Dunkin': How One Little Post-War Doughnut Shop Became Synonymous with Boston's Identity," *The Providence Phoenix* 20/10 [March 9–15, 2007], 6–9). The newspaper's cover page offers a more suitable (for my purposes) title for Miliard's article: "Choosing Our Religion: New England's Coffee Cult."

[145] Bynum, *Holy Feast*, 3, original emphasis. Although Bynum's work is concerned with medieval Christian women, many of her comments about the power of the metaphor of ingestion are applicable in other contexts, as well.

[146] Hartog, *Mirror of Herodotus*, 225. See also Bourdieu, *Distinction*, 53.

one entity and another. Each analogical act is an act of identity construction, because to speak of the "Other" is really to speak of the "Self." The Us/Them polarity therefore constitutes an "indestructible framework" for a given narrative.[147] In the texts discussed in this section, the Tannaim make an analogy between the status of the food and the status of the preparer, whereby the identity of the preparer – "the one responsible for the act of cultural transformation" – affects the status of that which is prepared.[148] Thus, this rhetoric indicates that there is a predictable analogy between food regulations and desired social relations, suggesting that the latter generates the former.

Meat

Meat is the single most cross-culturally tabooed food item.[149] In the felicitous wording of Fessler and Navarrete, "meat is good to taboo." As such, the utilization of this culinary category for the development of a principle of social boundary formation makes sense on both empirical and theoretical grounds. In fact, even the removal of a meat taboo can serve to establish boundaries, as Paul's apparent repeal in I Corinthians 10:23–30 of meat taboos, except for that which is explicitly known to be sacrificed to idols, marks Christians as different from Jews via their relationship to nonkosher meat. Paul acquiesces to the alteration of meat taboos to allow for increased commensality with non-Christians, thus

---

[147] Hartog, *Mirror of Herodotus*, 368.
[148] Freidenreich, Foreign Food, 160. Freidenreich, like myself, is here influenced by the work of Lévi-Strauss. For a cross-cultural and cross-historical survey that also follows Lévi-Strauss, see Massimo Montanari, who argues that "[s]uch a connotation accompanies food all along the pathway that leads it to the mouth of a man" (*Food is Culture*, trans. Albert Sonnenfeld [New York: Columbia University Press, 2006], xi). However, as Freidenreich correctly observes, "It is worth noting that concerns regarding impurity play no role in the Rabbinic prohibition of foreign food" (Foreign Food, 157). For discussions of impurity in ancient Judaism see Olyan, *Rites and Rank*, 38–62 (biblical); Jonathan Klawans, *Impurity and Sin in Ancient Judaism* (New York: Oxford University Press, 2000); Hayes, *Gentile Impurities*. On impurity and food in Jewish Hellenistic sources, see Aharon Oppenheimer, *The 'Am ha-Aretz: A Study in the Social History of the Jewish People in the Hellenistic–Roman Period*. trans. Israel L. Levine (Leiden, the Netherlands: Brill, 1977), 57–66. I discuss issues of purity in more depth in Chapter 3.
[149] See Daniel M. T. Fessler and Carlos David Navarrete, who offer an "evolutionary psychological explanation" for the special prevalence of meat in taboos, based on an "evolved predisposition" toward meat taboos ("Meat Is Good to Taboo: Dietary Proscriptions as a Product of the Interaction of Psychological Mechanisms and Social Processes," *Journal of Cognition and Culture* 3/1 [2003]: 1–40).

reconfiguring the borders of the nascent Christian community beginning with the borders of their tables.[150] Further, the act of slaughter marks the moment at which the cooking process begins and, thus, according to Claude Lévi-Strauss, the cultural moment when culture (cooked food) begins to exert its influence on nature (raw food).[151] Thus, this is both an obvious and a vital moment in which to insert an identity-based food prohibition.

Hebrew Bible texts never regulate who may participate in non-cultic slaughter. The only slaughter-related prohibition found therein is the prohibition against the ingestion of animal blood, which must be poured out prior to eating the meat.[152] The Tannaim, on the other hand, regulate who may and may not effect "proper" animal slaughter. Turning to the most logical point of departure – the mishnaic tractate devoted to nonconsecrated animal slaughter (*ḥûllîn*)[153] – one encounters an example of this principle literally from its opening words:

All may slaughter, and their slaughter is valid, except for a deaf-mute, a mentally disabled person, or a minor,[154] lest they ruin [the meat] in their

---

[150] See also Romans 14, where Paul seems to advocate vegetarianism in such commensal encounters. On Paul's notoriously difficult discussion of the "weak" and the "strong," see Smith, *From Symposium to Eucharist*, 182–184, 209–211.

[151] E.g., Claude Lévi-Strauss, *The Raw and the Cooked: Introduction to a Science of Mythology*, trans. John and Doreen Weightman (New York: Harper and Row, 1975); "The Culinary Triangle," in *Food and Culture: A Reader*, ed. Carole Counihan and Penny van Esterik, 28–35 (New York: Routledge, 1997). For a critique of Lévi-Strauss's work, see Jack Goody, *Cooking, Cuisine and Class: A Study in Comparative Sociology* (Cambridge: Cambridge University Press, 1996), 17–29. Although anthropologists have debated Lévi-Strauss' theories, I find his general observations useful. However, I do not wish to argue that Lévi-Strauss's binary categorization explains the entire workings of a given culture because, as Goody correctly indicates, this approach "may neglect those important aspects of that culture which are linked with social or individual differences" (*Cooking, Cuisine and Class*, 28). Also, see Montanari, who uses the Japanese culinary specialty sushi, for example, to problematize a rigid reading of Lévi-Strauss's raw/cooked binary (*Food Is Culture*, 29–33). Although sushi does involve some cooking (i.e., rice), the real culturally transformative act is one of raw preparation. Interestingly, my colleague Juliette Rogers has pointed out to me that Lévi-Strauss' theory appears to inform the language employed in support of the "raw food movement," which argues that uncooked food is more natural and healthy.

[152] See Leviticus 17:10–14; Deuteronomy 12:15–27; 15:23. On pouring out a slaughtered animal's blood, see *m. Hullin* 2:9 (ed. Albeck 5:121–122).

[153] Valid consecrated animal slaughter (*zĕbāḥîm*), which receives its own mishnaic tractate, can be performed only by a valid priest.

[154] On slaughter by a minor, contrast *t. Hullin* 1:3 (ed. Zuckermandel 500); *t. Hagigah* 1:2 (ed. Lieberman 2:375).

act of slaughtering. But all of these [i.e., the deaf-mute, the mentally disabled person, and the minor] who slaughter while others observe them, their slaughter is valid. *An animal slaughtered by a Gentile*[155] *is carrion, and it imparts impurity through carrying [it].* One who slaughters at night, and so too a blind person who slaughters, his slaughter is valid. One who slaughters on the Sabbath or on Yom Kippur, even though he becomes liable for death [for performing an act forbidden on these days], his slaughter is valid.[156]

Among a list of potentially problematic butchers, the redactor seemingly inserts an anomalous passage about the status of an animal slaughtered by a Gentile into an earlier tradition. In fact, reading this line as a later insertion makes sense, as the passage reads cleanly – and more uniformly – without the line "An animal slaughtered by a Gentile is carrion, and it imparts impurity through carrying [it]."[157] Whether or not this clause is a later insertion, the tannaitic innovation that an animal slaughtered by a non-Jew is not fit for Jewish consumption *simply because it is slaughtered by a non-Jew* is introduced without justification and, so it would seem, without controversy.[158]

Another important innovation found in this text is that slaughter by a Gentile is considered carrion. Carrion (*nevēlāh*) is a technical term for an animal that has died a natural death. Therefore, not only is the slaughter of a Gentile forbidden for Jewish consumption, but "it is legally

---

[155] Literally, "the animal slaughter of a Gentile."
[156] *m. Hullin* 1:1 (ed. Albeck 5:115), emphasis added.
[157] It should be noted, however, that this phrase is present in the two extant Mishnah manuscripts of this pericope (Kaufman A 50 381 and Parma 3173 128R), as well as in manuscripts of the Babylonian Talmud (Munich 95; Vatican Ebr. 120–121 and 122); there is no tractate *Hullin* in the Palestinian Talmud.
[158] As Freidenreich states, "The redactor of the Mishnah, however, has chosen not to articulate the rationale that underlies this preparer-based restriction.... By redactional sleights-of-hand, he incorporates these restrictions into his legal collection without drawing attention to the fact that they are based on rationales foreign to the Torah" (Foreign Food, 166–167). This redactional prestidigitation is similar to Pierre Bourdieu's concept of misrecognition, in which a power relationship is intentionally glossed over (for example, the art dealer's ability to "consecrate" one painting as valuable art and another as an invaluable drawing). This concept appears throughout Bourdieu's corpus (e.g., *Language and Symbolic Power*, ed. John B. Thompson, trans. Gino Raymond and Matthew Adamson [Cambridge, MA: Harvard University Press, 1991], 169–170; *The Field of Cultural Production: Essays on Art and Literature*, ed. Randal Johnson [New York: Columbia University Press, 1993], 81).

equivalent to no slaughter at all."[159] This principle can also be found in *t. Hullin* 1:1:

> All [Jews] are fit to slaughter [an animal], even a Samaritan, even an uncircumcised [Jew], even a Jewish apostate. An animal slaughtered by a heretic [*mîn*] is [regarded as an act of] idolatry.[160] An animal slaughtered by a Gentile – behold, this is invalid. And an animal slaughtered by an ape – behold, this is invalid. As it is said: "*you* may slaughter . . . and *you* may eat."[161] *You* may not [eat] that which a Gentile has slaughtered; *you* may not eat that which an ape has slaughtered; *you* may not eat that which is slaughtered by its own action.[162]

In order for slaughter to be tannaitically valid for Jewish ingestion, the butcher must be a Jew. Butchery – a cultural practice that separates

---

[159] Freidenreich, *Foreign Food*, 162. Slaughter by a Gentile is also possibly equated with carrion in *m. Hullin* 8:5 (ed. Albeck 5:139), which prohibits both categories of meat in the same clause.

In rabbinic literature, carrion also develops a more specific meaning: an animal that is not slaughtered according to rabbinic procedure (e.g., *m. Hullin* 2:4 [ed. Albeck 5:119–120]). If this more specific understanding is in operation in this text, then the actions of the Gentile are not animalistic; they are equivalent to nothing because the Gentile's slaughter is invalid for the simple fact that a Gentile is a priori incapable of tannaitically valid animal slaughter. However, as I argue below, I believe that the connection between a Gentile and an animal is here both intentional and important for interpreting tannaitic foodways. I thank David Brodsky, Ben Elton, and Seth Kunin for helping me to sharpen my thinking on this issue.

[160] See also *t. Hullin* 2:20 (ed. Zuckermandel 503). Elsewhere, scriptural support for this principle is adduced from Exodus 34:15: "'You must not cut a covenant with the inhabitants of the land, for they will whore after their gods and sacrifice to their gods [and invite you and you will eat of their sacrifices]' [Exodus 34:15]. Because [Scripture] warned not to eat their slaughter, you learn that their slaughter is prohibited. On account of this, they [i.e., the Sages in *m. Hullin* 1:1] said: "An animal slaughtered by a Gentile is carrion, and it imparts impurity through carrying [it]" (*Mekilta d'Rabbi Shimon b. Yohai* at Exodus 34:15 [ed. Hoffman 163]). This comment is not present in Epstein and Melamed's critical edition – the standard scholarly version of *Mekilta d'Rabbi Shimon b. Yohai*. It is found, however, in Hoffman's (usually roughly similar) text. For a brief summary of the differences between these two, and other, editions of *Mekilta d'Rabbi Shimon b. Yohai*, see Nelson, *Mekhilta de-Rabbi Shimon bar Yohai*, xiii–xvii.

[161] This is a partial quotation from Deuteronomy 12:21, which states, in regard to valid animal slaughter and meat consumption, "If the place where Yhwh your God has chosen to establish His name is far from you, *you may slaughter* from the cattle or the sheep that Yhwh gives you, as I have commanded you; and *you may eat* to your heart's content in your gates" (emphasis added).

[162] *t. Hullin* 1:1 (ed. Zuckermandel 500). Emphasis added. I discuss the categories of apostate, heretic, and Samaritan in Chapter 4.

humans from animals – is now marked by the Tannaim as a distinctly Jewish practice. Gentile slaughter is (pejoratively, it would seem) equated with slaughter by an ape. This is another instance in which Stern's notion of solipsism applies. Unlike the heretic, whose slaughter is recognized as actually occurring (and hence is pejoratively branded as idolatrous), the Gentile's slaughter is likened to the action of an animal; it is a natural, not human, act.[163]

In an attempt to establish the minimum Jewish involvement in order for slaughter to be deemed a "valid" act of butchery, *t. Hullin* 1:2–3 states:

A Jew who slaughtered and a Gentile finished the slaughter – his act of slaughter is invalid. [If] he slaughtered in it two or the greater part of two [organs of the throat], his slaughter is valid. A Gentile who slaughtered and a Jew finished the slaughter – his act of slaughter is valid. [If] he [i.e., the Gentile] slaughtered something in it that does not render it *ṭerēfāh*, and a Jew came and completed [the act of slaughter], it is permitted for eating.[164]

A Jew and a Gentile who were holding a knife and slaughtering, even if [the hand of] one was above and [the hand of] the other was below, their slaughter is valid. Similarly, a blind person who knows [how] to slaughter – his slaughter is valid; a minor who knows [how] to slaughter, his slaughter is valid.

According to Tosefta, as long as the one who severs most of the trachea and the esophagus (i.e., the two organs of the throat) is a Jew, the act of slaughter results in meat valid for Jewish consumption.[165] Even if a Jew and a Gentile hold a knife and slaughter an animal concurrently – certainly more a pedagogical than a practical example[166] – the meat is valid; it is classified as having been slaughtered by a Jew.

[163] S. Stern, *Jewish Identity*, 202. Further, as Freidenreich notes, "The reference to an animal 'which is slaughtered by its own action,' a strange phrase found nowhere else in Rabbinic literature, reflects the author's effort to incorporate a reference to carrion into the literary structure of his interpretation of the Biblical verse. The message is that animal slaughter performed by a non-Jew, even if the act of slaughter conforms to all the dictates of Rabbinic law, is prohibited simply because it was performed by a non-Jew. Slaughter by a gentile is legally equivalent to no slaughter at all, so an animal slaughtered by a gentile is equivalent to carrion, whose consumption (but not benefit) is prohibited according to *Deuteronomy*" (Foreign Food, 162).
[164] *t. Hullin* 1:2–3 (ed. Zuckermandel 500). Compare *t. Ahilot* 2:1 (ed. Zuckermandel 598).
[165] This reading accords with Freidenreich's views (Foreign Food, 165).
[166] Here I paraphrase Freidenreich's wording (Foreign Food, 165). Earlier, Freidenreich also notes that "the utility of such a case in clarifying legal nuances comes at the expense of the probability that it will actually occur" (Foreign Food, 164).

Putting aside the *dramatis personae* for a moment, the procedure itself by which the animal is slaughtered does not necessarily distinguish between Jew and non-Jew, as a study of the butchery patterns in ancient Sepphoris by Grantham has only suggested a possible Jewish preference for procuring meat from professional butchers, rather than butchering the animals themselves. There were no other significant differences in butchery patterns.[167] Thus, it is not about the butchery itself as much as it is about the butcher being a Jew.

In sum, as long as a Jew is considered by the Tannaim to be the head butcher, then the meat is valid; the Gentile's support role (as we shall soon see) does not necessarily invalidate food. If a Jew is not involved, however, then the meat is deemed to be equivalent to an animal that died from natural causes – carrion – and is thus prohibited for Jewish consumption. While allowing for shared cooking, often an economic necessity, the Tannaim still account for the social ramifications of this leniency. By making an analogy between the one who slaughters and that which is slaughtered, therefore, the Tannaim introduce a food prohibition that regulates desired social relations at the same time that it regulates animal slaughter.

Non-Meat Items

The tannaitic problematization of food based on the status of its preparer is not isolated to meat. I focus in this section on the so-called Mediterranean triad of wine, bread, and olive oil.[168] In tannaitic literature, the status of all these dietary staples is directly correlated to the status of their preparer.

Wine is an extremely problematic beverage from a tannaitic standpoint. As the only intoxicant suitable for idolatrous libation, the Tannaim are concerned that, at any moment, a non-Jew will overtly or covertly offer a portion of wine to a deity.[169] For this reason, tannaitic literature contains a series of prohibitions against wine and wine-related

---

[167] Zooarchaeological Model, 152–165.
[168] On the Mediterranean triad, see Chapter 1.
[169] Greek and Roman sources also attest to the fact that fermented grape wine is the only suitable intoxicant for offering a libation to a deity. For a brief discussion with references, see H. H. J. Brouwer, *Bona Dea: The Sources and a Description of the Cult* (New York: Brill, 1989), 334.

products.¹⁷⁰ For example, *m. Avodah Zarah* 5:5 discusses the rules for the permissibility of wine when a Jew shares a table with a Gentile:

[If a Jew] was eating with [a Gentile] at the [same] table, and [the Jew] leaves a bottle [of wine] on the table and a bottle on the side-table and left [the Gentile alone]¹⁷¹ and went out – what is on the table is prohibited [for Jewish consumption] and what is on the side-table is permitted. But if he said to him: "Mix for yourself and drink" – even that which is on the side-table is prohibited. [Wine in] open jugs is prohibited; [wine in jugs that are] sealed [are prohibited if the Gentile was alone for enough time] to open it and reseal it, and for the seal to dry.¹⁷²

On the surface, this passage allows for commensality between Jews and Gentiles, as long as a Jew "properly" guards his wine. Almost comically, however, this text assumes (as does rabbinic literature in general) that, if left alone, a Gentile cannot fight the urge to libate any wine in sight – even to the point of boring a hole in a wine jug and then sealing it up.

Most commentators focus correctly on the fact that this passage, and those like it, is indicative of a rhetoric of accommodation, whereby the Tannaim misrecognize certain activities to allow for economic and social interaction between Jews and non-Jews. To do so, the Tannaim make a distinction between a Gentile engaged in business and social activities and a Gentile engaged in idolatrous practice.¹⁷³ Even though this is true,

---

¹⁷⁰ E.g., *m. Avodah Zarah* 2; 4:8–5:11 (ed. Albeck 4:328–332; 338–344); *t. Avodah Zarah* 4:8–10, 12; 7; 8 [ed. Zuckermandel 466–468; 471–474). Paul also problematizes imbibing libated wine and partaking in an idolatrous sacrificial banquet (I Corinthians 10:20–22). On Paul's view of food offered to idols in 1 Corinthians, see Freidenreich, Foreign Food, 99–105.

¹⁷¹ The subject of the third-person masculine pronominal subject is ambiguous in this context. I have followed Albeck's suggested interpretation, that it refers to the Gentile (and thus is equivalent to "him"). It could also refer to the wine (thus meaning "it"), as Jacob Neusner understands the word (*The Mishnah: A New Translation* [New Haven: Yale University Press, 1988], 671).

¹⁷² *m. Avodah Zarah* 5:5 (ed. Albeck 4:341–342). This same time-based prohibition principle appears earlier in this chapter in the Mishnah (*m. Avodah Zarah* 5:3 [ed. Albeck 4:341]). According to Gary G. Porton, this is one of 346 passages in the Mishnah and Tosefta that contain anonymous statements about Gentiles. For a list, see Gary G. Porton, *Goyim: Gentiles and Israelites in Mishnah-Tosefta*, BJS 155 (Atlanta: Society of Biblical Literature, 1988), 115–116 n. 10.

¹⁷³ As Porton argues, in general, "The writers of the Mishnah-Tosefta were able to distinguish between the gentile as farmer, merchant, borrower, lender, and the like, and the *gentile as idolater* who was also a farmer, merchant, borrower, lender, and the like. The distinction was important, for only when the gentile was overtly engaged in, or was presumed to be engaged in, the worship of his idol was he considered to be an

the fact remains that wine is the drink *par excellence* in the ancient Mediterranean world. Therefore, both the avoidance of Gentile wine and the fear of Gentile wine practices stigmatize commensal interactions.[174] In regard to this beverage, assumed Gentile practice constructs an identity for those who do and do not imbibe this wine. It would seem that, at least for the Tannaim, were a Jew to drink Gentile wine, this action would be tantamount to idolatry. And, as we shall see later in this chapter, the assumed connection between commensality with non-Jews and idolatry is used by the Tannaim to justify an ever-increasing distance from one another at the table.

Bread, the second component of the Mediterranean triad, presents a different problem to the Tannaim. Even though the fear of idolatrous ritual is not attached to bread as it is with wine, the Tannaim still problematize Gentile bread. In doing so, the Tannaim introduce a concept that I label the "chef/sous-chef principle." According to this principle, the Tannaim differentiate between the transformative work of the "chef" – the type of kitchen activity that requires a Jew to either play the "lead" (as defined by the Tannaim) or a supervisory role – and the work of the "sous-chef" – the type of kitchen activity, often preparatory, that does not require a Jew, so long as certain other conditions are met (e.g., *kashrut*). The main purpose of distinguishing these roles in the tannaitic corpus seems to be to subordinate and control the

---

idolater whom Israelites had to avoid. Therefore, those *sugyot* [passages] which seek *to prevent* the Israelite from interacting with gentiles do so when they perceive this interaction, not as normal social or economic intercourse, but as being part of the gentiles' religious activities" (*Goyim*, 243, emphasis in original). For a similar view, see Yaron Z. Eliav, "Viewing the Sculptural Environment: Shaping the Second Commandment," in *The Talmud Yerushalmi and Graeco-Roman Culture*, ed. Peter Schäfer, Vol. 3, 411–433 (Tübingen, Germany: Mohr Siebeck, 2002); Freidenreich, Foreign Food, 150; Seth Schwartz, *Imperialism and Jewish Society 200 B.C.E.–640 C.E.* (Princeton, NJ: Princeton University Press, 2001), 164–165; Peter J. Tomson, *Paul and the Jewish Law: Halakha in the Letters of the Apostle to the Gentiles* (Minneapolis: Fortress Press, 1990), 231–232.

[174] This prohibition is extended in later texts for explicitly commensal reasons, to preclude drinking non-wine intoxicants (i.e., alcoholic beverages that are not suitable for idolatrous rituals) with non-Jews, lest it lead to intermarriage (e.g., *b. Avodah Zarah* 31b). Notably, in neither instance do the rabbis prohibit the consumption of all wine or non-wine intoxicants (e.g., beer), which might have been an easier solution. Rather, in seeking to permit but limit the consumption of these culturally important beverages, the rabbis once again indicate their desire to create accommodations for navigating and interacting with their surrounding, non-Jewish, environment.

actions of non-Jews, while still allowing for shared cooking. We have already encountered a form of this principle in the preceding section, in regard to animal slaughter. Although the act of cooking is not involved in butchery, this concept – that a Jew must play the primary role of the "chef" – also applies to tannaitic animal slaughter regulations. As is the case in modern restaurants, these divisions often seem semantic, as the work of the chef sometimes looks quite similar to the work of the sous-chef (both literally and figuratively). The differences between the "chef" and the "sous-chef" are thus more about ascribing different status in the kitchen than about describing different work in the kitchen. I therefore intend these terms to function as a second-order heuristic aid; they are not intended to function as rigid categories in a structuralist model.

In general, it is forbidden to consume, but not to derive benefit from, the bread of Gentiles – that is, bread baked by a non-Jewish "chef."[175] One text goes so far as to equate foreign bread with pork.[176] Yet if a Jew plays the role of a "chef," then the bread is not considered by the Tannaim to be "Gentile" bread. For example, according to *t. Avodah Zarah* 4:11:[177]

A loaf of bread that a Gentile baked without Jewish supervision, and cheese that a Gentile curdled without Jewish supervision, [both] are prohibited. [But] a loaf of bread that a Jew baked, even though the Gentile kneaded [the dough], and cheese that a Jew curdled, even though the Gentile works it[178] – behold, this is permitted.

---

[175] *m. Avodah Zarah* 2:6 (ed. Albeck 4:331). For a discussion of this text, see Zvi Aryeh Steinfeld, "Concerning the Prohibition Against Gentile Bread," *Proceedings of the Ninth World Congress of Jewish Studies* 3 (1985): 31–35 (Hebrew). Also see *t. Shevi'it* 5:9 (ed. Lieberman 1:187). The concept of "deriving benefit from" is a common rabbinic legal category. While certain items are forbidden for ingestion or use by a Jew, it is sometimes permissible to derive benefit from them (to sell, trade, or use them in some specific way). Thus, with regard to Gentile bread, for example, a Jew may not consume it, but may sell it to a non-Jew, thereby deriving benefit from the bread of a Gentile.

[176] *m. Shevi'it* 8:10 (ed. Albeck 1:162). I discuss this text in Chapter 4.

[177] *t. Avodah Zarah* 4:11 (ed. Zuckermandel 467).

[178] My colleague Daniel Ullucci has suggested to me that this might refer to "collecting the curd and shaping it into cheese. This also produces a nice chiastic structure: gentile kneads, Jew bakes, Jew curdles, gentile works" (personal communication; December 17, 2006).

In this text, which addresses the production of both bread and cheese, the fact that a Jew and a non-Jew share the same kitchen does not *necessarily* invalidate these culinary items for Jewish consumption. Although the scenario in which a non-Jew prepares bread and cheese alone is considered immediately to render these products prohibited for Jewish consumption, the shared kitchen receives further deliberation. As long as a Jew physically acts as the "chef" – baking the dough and curdling the cheese – then the bread and cheese produced in a shared kitchen are permitted for Jewish consumption.[179] In accordance with a recurring trend, this leniency allows for the economic necessity of shared food production, as discussed in Chapter 1.

Bakers of bread impart not only flavor, but also status vis-à-vis the tannaitic community through their work in the kitchen. This logic further underlies the tannaitic principle that, when in a town occupied by both Jews and non-Jews,

[if] one found bread in it [i.e., in the town], [the bread's status] follows after the majority of the bakers. And if it was bread [made out] of pure flour, [its status] follows the majority of those who eat bread [made out] of pure flour. R. Yehudah says: "If it was bread [made out] of coarse meal, [its status] follows the majority of those who eat bread [made out] of coarse meal."[180]

---

[179] See also *m. Hallah* 3:5 (ed. Albeck 1:282), which states: "[If] a Gentile who gave [flour] to a [male] Jew to make dough for him, [the dough] is exempt from dough offering. [If the Gentile] gave it to him as a gift – [if it was given] before he rolled [the dough], it is obligated [to be separated for a dough offering]; but [if the Gentile gave him the dough] after he rolled [it], it is exempt. One who prepares dough [in partnership] with a Gentile – if [the amount of dough] belonging to the Jew does not comprise the [necessary minimum] volume [subject to] dough offering, it is exempt from dough offering." This text refers to three different scenarios. First, a non-Jew gives dough to a Jew to bake for him. In this capacity, the Jew provides either a personal favor or a professional service for a non-Jew. Second, a non-Jew may give dough to a Jew as a gift. Third, a Jew and a non-Jew may form a baking partnership (again, either personal or professional) and prepare and bake dough together. The issue at hand here is assuring the separation of the dough offering. Thus, the shared kitchen does not present a problem in this text, as long as the Jew plays the role of the "chef."

[180] *m. Makhshirin* 2:8 (ed. Albeck 6:420). This principle also applies to meat (*m. Makhshirin* 2:9 [ed. Albeck 6:420]; *t. Makhshirin* 1:8 [ed. Zuckermandel 674]) and chicken (*t. Hullin* 2:6 [ed. Zuckermandel 502]). The tannaitic "finders keepers" principle in general is articulated in *m. Bava Metzi'a* 2:1 (ed. Albeck 4:68–69), which specifically mentions bakers' loaves, among other food items.

Bread found in these mixed environments follows the presumed identity status of the majority of the people likely to have transformed the bread from its raw ingredients into its cooked form – from nature to culture.[181] Implied in this statement is that bread baked by a Jew is permitted, whereas bread baked by a non-Jew is prohibited.

At issue in these texts is the identity of the preparer and not the ingredients themselves. A non-Jewish "chef" bakes prohibited bread, no matter what his recipe contains. However, the participation of a Gentile in the cooking process is mitigated by considering him to be a "sous-chef" – that is, by stressing his subordinate status in the cooking process.[182] Yet again, a tannaitic commensality regulation establishes a set of practices that affect identity formation, while allowing for economic conditions that might require a shared kitchen.

Usually served as an accoutrement into which to dip bread, olive oil is the third culinary item in the Mediterranean triad.[183] In contrast to wine and bread, however, the Tannaim take a more lenient stance on olive oil than their predecessors, as several Second Temple-period sources attest to the fact that Jews considered the use of Gentile olive oil legally transgressive.[184] The Mishnah initially reflects this understanding, although it is immediately modified by an editorial insertion. According to *m. Avodah Zarah* 2:6: "These things belonging to Gentiles are forbidden, but it is not prohibited to derive benefit [from them]: milk

---

[181] See the story about Rabban Gamaliel on *t. Pisha* 2:15 (ed. Lieberman 2:146–147), which concludes by stating the principle that, to establish the status of a food found in a road, "they follow the majority of those who travel the roads." The principle that the religion of the majority of a town's residents is used to determine status is found in a nonfood context on *m. Ketubbot* 1:10 (ed. Albeck 3:92).

[182] I thank one of the anonymous reviewers for helping me to sharpen my thinking on this point.

[183] D. Kraemer argues that the fact that olive oil is a dip for bread, and hence secondary to bread, explains why there is not a special rabbinic blessing just for oil, although there is one for bread (*Jewish Eating*, 79–80). *b. Berakhot* 35b discusses the precedence of bread over oil in regard to reciting blessings over food.

[184] E.g., Josephus, *The Life*, 74; *Jewish War*, 2:591; *Jewish Antiquities*, 12:120. For references and discussion, see Martin Goodman, "Kosher Olive Oil in Antiquity," in *A Tribute to Geza Vermes: Essays on Jewish and Christian Literature and History*, ed. Philip R. Davies and Richard T. White, 227–245 (Sheffield, UK: Sheffield Academic Press, 1990); Barclay, *Jews in the Mediterranean Diaspora*, 256–257; Sidney B. Hoenig, "Oil and Pagan Defilement," *JQR* 61/1 (1970): 63–75. An expanded version of this section appeared in Jordan D. Rosenblum, "Kosher Olive Oil in Antiquity Reconsidered," *JSJ* 40/3 (2009): 356–365.

that a Gentile milked without Jewish supervision, and their bread and their oil – Rabbi[185] and his court permitted [their] oil."[186]

In this text, an apparently widespread Jewish food regulation is first endorsed and then reversed. If this is the case, then one must account for the change in the status of Gentile olive oil. Goodman proceeds to argue that this insertion results from Rabbi's inability to find a valid, legal basis for this apparently long-standing prohibition of Gentile olive oil; he thus reversed it.[187] Yet, the Tannaim see no need to justify their much more innovative ban on Gentile bread.

How then do we resolve this inconsistency? To start, I turn to a discussion about another food item: cheese. *m. Avodah Zarah* 2:5 provides an interesting, and complicated, analog:[188]

R. Yehudah said: "R. Yishmael asked [the following question] to R. Yehoshua when they were walking along the road: He said to him, 'For what reason did they prohibit [the consumption of] Gentile cheese?' He replied, 'Because they curdle it with rennet of carrion.' [R. Yishmael] said to him: 'But is not the rennet of the burnt offering subject to a more stringent restriction than the rennet of carrion, and yet, they said: "A priest who is not squeamish may suck it out raw"'? (But they did not concur with him, but rather said: 'One may not derive benefit, but one [who does] is not [obligated with

---

[185] The Babylonian Talmud suggests that, in this instance, "Rabbi" refers to Rabbi Judah I's grandson, Rabbi Judah Nesiah (*b. Avodah Zarah* 37a). On this identification issue, Goodman notes: "Since the Mishnah was compiled by R. Judah I, the lack of editing to incorporate the words into the surrounding texts fits well into the tradition that the reform took place two generations after his time. However, both Talmuds also referred the reform [*sic*] at other places to R. Judah I. Perhaps in the case of a controversial decision which elicited opposition (as the *gemara* attests...), both patriarchs felt impelled to issue decrees, just as Roman emperors sometimes reissued laws when they were not widely observed" ("Kosher Olive Oil," 232). For the purposes of my argument, I do not need to take a stance on this issue. However, I find Goodman's suggestion intriguing.

[186] *m. Avodah Zarah* 2:6 (ed. Albeck 4:331). The parallel toseftan text adds little, stating, "Rabbi Judah and his court permitted the oil of Gentiles by a vote" (*t. Avodah Zarah* 4:11 [ed. Zuckermandel 467]). Both Talmuds contain discussions about Rabbi's regulatory reversal. For references and commentary, see Goodman, "Kosher Olive Oil," 232–243; Freidenreich, Foreign Food, 185–88; Zvi Aryeh Steinfeld, "Concerning the Prohibition Against Gentile Oil," *Tarbiz* 49 (1980): 264–277 (Hebrew).

[187] Like most scholars, I read Rabbi's comment as an editorial insertion. Similarly, see Goodman, "Kosher Olive Oil," 231–232; David Rosenthal, *Mishnah Avodah Zarah: Critical Edition Plus Introduction*, 2 vols. (Jerusalem: Hebrew University, 1981 [Hebrew]), 1:167. For Goodman's argument about the rationale behind Rabbi's reversal, see "Kosher Olive Oil," 241–243.

[188] *m. Avodah Zarah* 2:5 (ed. Albeck 4:330–331).

regard to transgressing the] laws of sacrilege.') [R. Yehoshua] returned [to R. Yishmael's initial question] and said to him: 'Because they curdle it with the rennet of calves sacrificed to idols.' [R. Yishmael] said to him: 'If so, why did they not prohibit it [i.e., Gentile cheese] with a [prohibition against deriving] benefit?'[189] [R. Yehoshua] changed the subject. He said to him: 'Yishmael, my brother, how do you read [this following verse from Song of Songs 1:2]: "For your [masculine] love is better than wine" or "For your [feminine] love is better [than wine]"'? He said to him: 'For your [feminine] love is better [than wine].' [R. Yehoshua] said to him: 'The matter is not so. For behold, its neighbor [Song of Songs 1:3] teaches concerning it: "Your [masculine] ointments have a pleasing aroma."'"

Like Song of Songs 1:3, this passage is the neighbor to our text – the mishnah in which Rabbi permits Gentile olive oil. Here, R. Yehoshua attempts to explain to R. Yishmael why the consumption of Gentile cheese is prohibited. R. Yishmael easily parries every suggestion offered by R. Yehoshua and, thus, unable to justify this preparer-based prohibition, R. Yehoshua changes the subject.[190] All of R. Yehoshua's unsustainable explanations rely on ingredient-based prohibitions, namely carrion and the products of idolatry. As R. Yishmael points out, these prohibitions represent inconsistencies in the early rabbinic culinary regulations. Yet, although these inconsistencies are tacitly acknowledged, they are not overturned.

What clarity does this example provide? In this case, the justificatory rationale is deemed insufficient. However, the prohibition against consuming Gentile cheese here is not repealed. We have already seen that cheese fits within the chef/sous-chef principle, so the topic at hand here appears to be cheese prepared without a Jewish chef present or participating. One possibility for this exception is that olive oil is a dietary staple, whereas cheese is not.[191] There is therefore a greater need for leniency

---

[189] R. Yishmael correctly notes that tannaitic law allows Jews to derive benefit from the cheese of non-Jews (e.g., *t. Shevi'it* 5:9 [ed. Lieberman 1:187]).

[190] Similarly, see Freidenreich, Foreign Food, 171. Interestingly, *t. Parah* 10:3 (ed. Zuckermandel 638–639) attests to another conversation between these two rabbis in which R. Yehoshua changes the subject using a text-critical discussion of Song of Songs 1:2.

[191] Although a common rabbinic problem with cheese is that it is made with rennet (a curdling enzyme often derived, especially in the ancient world, from the stomach of an animal), this issue is brushed aside by R. Yishmael in our text. It thus seems that rennet is not the concern here. For this reason, as I discuss below, I pursue another avenue of explanation. On the tannaitic prohibition of rennet, see *m. Hullin* 8:5 (ed. Albeck

in regard to olive oil than there is for cheese. Further, unlike wine, olive oil did not make the Tannaim fret about idolatry.[192] Thus, it would seem that a complete ban on Gentile oil did not appear to be a necessity. And, compared with bread (and cheese), olive oil is more expensive to produce. In addition to the cost and production issues associated with olive oil discussed in Chapter 1, there is evidence for economic monopolies on olive oil.[193] The fact that one might have little choice but to purchase olive oil from a select group of sources at an inflated price seems a viable reason for this policy of accommodation. Although some sources of olive oil could be Jewish homes or Jewish vendors (who sometimes operated storefronts located in or around synagogues),[194] one could not always count on this. In the case of olive oil, then, the Tannaim balance the desire for a food deemed to be a dietary staple against the desire to construct a distinct identity via food practices.[195]

Conclusions

Writing about how the rabbis could have navigated their contemporary urban world, Seth Schwartz states:

So the rabbis, who needed to take the Pentateuchal horror of paganism very seriously in formulating their own views, also needed to develop a mechanism to allow them to live in the cities and to participate in some [of] the the [sic] cities' public activities, pagan though they were. This mechanism, I would like to argue, was an act of misprision, of misinterpretation, whereby

---

5:139). For a discussion of rennet in rabbinic literature, see Freidenreich, *Foreign Food*, 167–172.

[192] This statement also applies to other food items (e.g., fish). Because fish is unsuitable for Greek or Roman sacrifice, the fear of idolatry is not attached to it, unlike in the case of meat. To summarize the tannaitic view on fish, Jews can consume fish prepared by a non-Jew as long as it is a recognizably kosher fish. For example, a Jew can eat unminced fish and brine with fish floating in it (*m. Avodah Zarah* 2:7 [ed. Albeck 4:331]). On the prohibition of eating minced fish or brine without fish floating in it, see *m. Avodah Zarah* 2:6 (ed. Albeck 4:331). For a discussion, see Freidenreich, *Foreign Food*, 155.

[193] On monopolies, see Ben-Zion Rosenfeld and Joseph Menirav, *Markets and Marketing in Roman Palestine*, trans. Chava Cassel (Boston: Brill, 2005), 110–116.

[194] Olive oil presses are found near at least four Palestinian synagogues (see Rosenfeld and Menirav, *Markets and Marketing*, 227–229).

[195] Underlying this argument is an assumption about economic factors affecting *halakhah*. For a discussion, see Rosenblum, "Kosher Olive Oil," especially pp. 360–364. On the concept of a "staple" food in anthropological studies, see Ohnuki-Tierney, *Rice as Self*, 4, 30.

the rabbis defined pagan religiosity as consisting exclusively of cultic activity, affirmed, and even extended the biblical prohibitions of it, but in so doing declared the noncultic, but still religious, aspects of urban culture acceptable.... What I argue, though, is that the rabbis' misprision, whether they knew it or not, allowed them to live and work in the cities, the very places where they could most easily accumulate wealth, social ties, and influence.[196]

Rabbinic literature is therefore understood to reflect the development of a rhetoric of accommodation. Yet, this "misprision" (or, in the language of Bourdieu, "misrecognition") did not prevent the rabbis from using food practices to forge an identity that made Jews and Gentiles distinct. However, as was the case with the Second Temple-period data discussed earlier in this chapter, this identity did not require Jews to live completely apart from Gentiles, perhaps owing to economic necessities. In fact, several food regulations that control the extent to which a Gentile and a Jew can work together (e.g., animal slaughter, baking bread) assume that Jews and Gentiles interact on an economic, if not also a social, level.

The tannaitic data on food regulations provide an opportunity to understand how one can construct an identity that is separate but does not fully separate. Unlike the Qumran sect, whose food rules are part of an identity system intended to reify a social segregation, tannaitic literature reflects a conception of edible identity that defines itself within the context of its greater environment.[197] To do so, tannaitic literature contains allowances for shared butchery and cooking. These commensal practices allow Jews and non-Jews to interact, while still ensuring that the transformative act of cooking is also an act of identity formation and maintenance. This explains, for example, why a Jew and a non-Jew may slaughter together, although only a Jew is considered capable of the human act of animal slaughter. The Tannaim therefore walk a fine line, making both analogies between Gentiles and animals in regard to animal

[196] *Imperialism*, 164–165. For a similar view, see Yaron Z. Eliav, "Viewing the Sculptural Environment"; Porton, *Goyim*, 243.

[197] Similarly, see Eliav, "Viewing the Sculptural Environment," 433. Although Eliav's article addresses the Palestinian rabbinic interaction with the "sculptural environment," his findings accord with mine. I would argue that the rabbinic views toward idolatry are also part of the larger construction of a distinct rabbinic identity, in which food plays an important – but not exclusive – role. On the Qumran sect, see Baumgarten, who argues that their "food regulations were employed as a means of sharply marking off their sect from others" (*Flourishing of Jewish Sects*, 95).

slaughter and allowances for interactions with Gentiles in the tannaitic kitchen.

COMMENSALITY AS IDOLATRY[198]

Interacting with Gentiles in the kitchen is one thing; attending their wedding banquets (and, as we shall see, marrying their daughters) is quite another. In Hebrew Bible texts, commensality between Israelites and non-Israelites at a wedding banquet does not appear to cause a serious issue. To prove this claim, one need look no further than the lengthy discussion of the riddles Samson tells to the Philistine guests at his seven-day wedding banquet, recounted in Judges 14. Starting in the Second Temple period, however, intermarriage increasingly becomes an issue in Jewish texts, culminating in several prohibitions found in the Babylonian Talmud.[199] For the Tannaim, a Gentile wedding banquet is the type of commensal interaction that they wish to avoid. Because marriage affirms and reaffirms social relations and order, the meal that celebrates this occasion is clearly laden with meaning.[200] To share this particular table is to plug oneself into a network of social relationships of which tannaitic texts appear, at best, wary.

This phenomenon is encountered in *t. Avodah Zarah* 4:6, which states:

R. Shimon ben Elazar says: "Jews [literally: Israelites] outside of the Land [of Israel] are idolaters."[201] How so? A non-Jew makes a [wedding] banquet for

---

[198] An earlier version of this section appeared as Rosenblum, "From Their Bread."
[199] See Cohen, *Beginnings of Jewishness*, 241–262.
[200] As Michael L. Satlow notes: "Why marry? Hellenistic Jewish writers and Palestinian rabbis offer reasons remarkably close to those articulated by the Stoics: it is a man's duty to marry in order to create a household, an essential goal of which is the reproduction of children. Together, these households comprise a 'natural' social order, one that is in accordance with the divine plan" (*Jewish Marriage in Antiquity* [Princeton, NJ: Princeton University Press, 2001], 39).
[201] Some manuscripts read "worship idols in purity." This formulation also appears in R. Shimon ben Elazar's statement in *Avot d'Rabbi Natan* A26:6 (ed. Schechter 82) and in *b. Avodah Zarah* 8a (where some manuscripts attribute the saying to R. Ishmael; for references, see Zvi Aryeh Steinfeld, "On the Prohibition of Eating with a Gentile," *Sidra: A Journal for the Study of Rabbinic Literature* 5 [1988]: 131–148 [Hebrew], 131 n. 1). Christine Elizabeth Hayes suggests the following implication of this extra word: "the term should be taken literally – 'in purity,' that is, without being levitically defiled by the idol.... R. Shimon b. Elazar wants to say that even if one strives to preserve levitical purity and observe the dietary laws, if he is present at an idolatrous feast it is as if he has eaten of the most abominable and impure items there – the sacrifices to the idols"

his son[202] and goes and invites all of the Jews who live in his town. Even if they eat and drink [only] their own [food and wine] and their own servant stands and serves them, they are idolaters, as it is said: "And he will invite you and you will eat from his sacrifice" [Exodus 34:15].[203]

Despite the fact that the food is clearly kosher, the banquet at which it is consumed is not. The concern here is commensal in nature, and not culinary – it is about *with whom* you eat, and not *what* you eat.

Discussing this pericope, Christine Hayes notes that R. Shimon ben Elazar's statement should be understood as a moral, and not legal, pronouncement.[204] Hayes' point is well-founded, as numerous tannaitic texts attest to the fact that commensality between Jews and Gentiles still occurs, even as it is increasingly marginalized.[205] Even if R. Shimon ben

(*Between the Babylonian and Palestinian Talmuds: Accounting for Halakhic Difference in Selected Sugyot from Tractate Avodah Zarah* [New York: Oxford University Press, 1997], 161). Hayes' understanding suggests that, even in these manuscript variants, purity itself does not play a part in tannaitic commensality regulations between Jews and non-Jews.

[202] *t. Avodah Zarah* 4:6 (ed. Zuckermandel 466). In some manuscripts of the Babylonian version of *m. Avodah Zarah* 1:3 (ed. Albeck 4:325–326), the case of a "non-Jew who makes a [wedding] banquet for his son" is included in a list of regulated private feast days in which economic and social interaction with Gentiles is prohibited. However, the omission of this phrase "from the entire Palestinian branch of the Mishnah manuscripts, and its jarring interruption of the mishnah's style in the Babylonian branch, indicate that it is not original to the text of the mishnah but added to the Babylonian version at some point in the text's transmission history" (Hayes, *Between*, 155–156). Rosenthal attributes this tradition to a *baraita* found on *b. Avodah Zarah* 14a (*Mishnah Avodah Zarah*, 1:58–59).

[203] A *baraita* on *b. Sanhedrin* 104b attributes to R. Shimon ben Elazar the view that the Israelites were exiled because King Hezekiah allowed non-Israelites to eat at his table. Of course, this reading retrojects a later concern back into biblical times. For a rather positivistic attempt to read these texts together for social history, see Steinfeld, "Eating with a Gentile," 135–136.

[204] *Between*, 160, in which Hayes also suggests that R. Shimon ben Elazar's comment functions as a riddle "designed to pique the curiosity of its hearers." Elsewhere, Hayes also refers to this as a "brain teaser" (*Between*, 243 n. 14). Similarly, see Freidenreich, Foreign Food, 173–174, who suggests that R. Shimon ben Elazar's statement be taken "with a grain of salt" (p. 173). Tomson seems to take R. Shimon ben Elazar's statement more seriously, although he contrasts it with an opinion attributed to R. Shimon ben Elazar's reputed teacher R. Meir in *Pesiqta d'Rav Kahana* 6 (ed. Mandelbaum 115), suggesting that these texts "represent two divergent views on relations with gentiles within the same pious tradition" (*Paul*, 234).

[205] For a roughly contemporary analog in Christian texts, see Canon 7 of the Council of Ancyra, a council that convened in Asia Minor in 314 C.E. This canon punishes Christians who attend a pagan feast, even if they bring and consume their own food. The problematization of commensality between Jews and non-Jews as exemplified in

Elazar's statement does not carry the weight of law for other Tannaim, its implicit moral judgment against commensality with non-Jews is part of the emerging tannaitic discourse of table-based identity construction. In sum, a meal that was once acceptable is now socially problematic – if not necessarily legally transgressive – for tannaitic Jews to attend.

This accords with Stern's observation that in rabbinic literature in general, all non-Jews are considered idolaters; as such, it seems reasonable to conclude that idolatry and non-Jewishness are coterminous.[206] To eat with a non-Jew is therefore to encounter, and to some extent engage in, idolatry. Therefore, the food itself is insufficient to mark one as a Jew; because the perceived ramifications of commensality with Gentiles are so severe, one must not even attend the event, as doing so constitutes a social practice that threatens one's Jewish identity. It is for this reason that R. Shimon ben Elazar morally stigmatizes a social event that was previously permissible to attend. In short, now even if the food is kosher, the banquet itself is nonkosher.[207]

The fact that R. Shimon ben Elazar uses a wedding banquet as an example of an intrinsically nonkosher meal is quite telling. As previously noted, marriage affirms and reaffirms social relations and order. Yet, intermarriage is not consistently prohibited in texts of the Hebrew Bible.[208] Tannaitic literature occasionally expresses discomfort with this practice, but these texts are, as in the case of the wedding banquet described in *t. Avodah Zarah* 4:6, implicit moral judgments, if not yet outright unconditional bans. In this case, by problematizing the diner instead of just the dinner, these regulations create practices that control social interactions. One can no longer engage in indiscriminate table-fellowship.

The problematization of sharing a table and sharing a bed is found in a few tannaitic texts that, using a "slippery slope" argument, connect commensality between Jews and non-Jews with intermarriage. Tacit

---

the wedding banquet is a subject explored in later rabbinic texts (e.g., *Avot d'Rabbi Natan* A26:6 [ed. Schechter 82]; *b. Avodah Zarah* 8a). On these, and other relevant, texts, see Freidenreich, Foreign Food, 192–194; Hayes, *Between*, 160–170; Steinfeld, "Eating with a Gentile"; Stern, *Jewish Identity*, 151–152.

[206] Stern, *Jewish Identity*, 196.

[207] Although *t. Avodah Zarah* 4:6 specifically refers to diaspora Jews, I concur with Freidenreich's interpretation that "the logic of this assertion applies equally with the Land of Israel, where a Jew might also receive a wedding invitation from a gentile neighbor or choose to attend such a celebration" (Foreign Food, 174).

[208] See Olyan, *Rites and Rank*, 81–90.

within such statements is a condemnation of two practices with which the Tannaim disagree. A good example of this trend can be found in *Mekilta d'Rabbi Shimon b. Yohai*. Commenting on Exodus 34:17, which proscribes making molten gods, the following statement appears:

Thus, if one eats of their sacrifices, he will marry from amongst their daughters, and they will lead him astray and he will worship idols.[209]

The connection between "eating of their sacrifices" – a phrase that refers to both the meat itself and the sacrificial banquet at which that meat is ingested – and taking "their daughters" as wives is understood in *Mekilta d'Rabbi Shimon b. Yohai* as the rationale behind Exodus 34:17's prohibition of molten gods.

To better understand this exegetical move, it is worth taking a moment to review Exodus 34:15–17:

Lest you make a covenant with the inhabitants of the land and they will whore after their gods and sacrifice to their gods and he will invite you and you will eat from his sacrifice. And you will take [wives] from amongst their daughters for your sons, their daughters will whore after their gods and will make your sons whore after their gods. As for molten gods, you shall not make them for yourselves.

This text should seem familiar, as *t. Avodah Zarah* 4:6 uses part of it as a proof-text. The concern here is against covenant-making with the Canaanites and ingesting sacrifices to other deities.[210] Whereas *t. Avodah Zarah* 4:6 uses Exodus 34:15 to indicate that willingly attending such a commensal interaction is akin to participating in the idolatrous sacrifice itself,[211] *Mekilta d'Rabbi Shimon b. Yohai* at Exodus 34:17 cleverly reweaves the fabric of Exodus 34:15–17 into a tapestry that explicitly connects commensality between Jews and non-Jews with intermarriage, and both these activities with idolatry. Reading Exodus 34:15–17 as a conditional statement, *Mekilta d'Rabbi Shimon b. Yohai* at Exodus 34:17 breaks

---

[209] *Mekilta d'Rabbi Shimon b. Yohai* at Exodus 34:17 (ed. Epstein and Melamed 222).

[210] This text also presumes that women are corruptors of men, leading men to whore after other gods – a clearly gendered terminology for idolatry. Although a discussion of the gendered aspects of this text in its biblical context lies beyond the purview of this book, it is important to note for our current purposes that this gendered terminology influences tannaitic literature, as we shall see again later.

[211] See Hayes, *Between*, 161.

these biblical verses into two segments: a protasis ("if one eats of their sacrifices") and an apodosis ("he will marry from amongst their daughters, and they will lead him astray and he will worship idols"). This "if/then" formulation logically suggests that separation at the table enacts and maintains a separate social identity – that of "Us" (the monotheists) and "Them" (the idolaters). This is part of a larger trend in rabbinic literature, detected by Stern, in which "separateness or disassociation constitutes a form of social control, designed to protect the integrity of Israel as a distinctive social group."[212] The borders of the collective whole of Israel in this context, therefore, are understood to begin at the borders of the table.

The connection between intermarriage and commensality with Gentiles is further found in *Sifre Numbers* 131. In the midst of an expansion on the account in Numbers 25:1–3 about how Moabite women seduced Israelite men, enticing them to worship Ba'al Pe'or, the text states:[213]

She [i.e., a Moabite woman] would say to him [i.e., an Israelite man]: "Would you like to drink [some] wine?"[214] He would drink and the wine would burn within him and he would say: "Listen to me [i.e., have intercourse with me]!" She would take out an image of Pe'or from under her bra and say to him: "Rabbi, is it your desire that I listen to you? [If so, then] bow to this!"[215]

The fact that Ba'al Pe'or is a biblical – *not contemporary* – deity does not seem to deter the Tannaim from making their larger point:[216] namely,

---

[212] *Jewish Identity*, 170. Stern goes on to write: "Intermarriage, in particular, may be perceived as related to *avoda zara*, but it is equally considered a threat to Jewish identity; as we have seen, its prohibition implies a passionate commitment to preserving the integrity of Israel" (p. 170).

[213] Psalm 106:28 understands the sacrificial feast depicted in Numbers 25:1–3 as being a ritual associated with a funerary cult. On Josephus' interpretation and narrative expansion of this biblical text, see *Jewish Antiquities*, 4:126–151, especially 137–140; W. C. van Unnik, "Josephus' Account of the Story of Israel's Sin with Alien Women in the Country of Midian (Num. 25:1ff)," in *Travels in the World of the Old Testament: Studies Presented to Professor M. A. Beek on the Occasion of his 65th Birthday*, ed. M. S. H. G. Heerma van Voss, Ph. H. J. Houwink ten Cate, and N. A. van Uchelen, 241–261 (Assen, the Netherlands: Van Gorcum, 1974).

[214] *Sifre Numbers* 131 (ed. Horowitz 171). This sentence is prefaced in *Sifre Numbers* by a comment that "the wine of non-Jews was not yet forbidden to Israel."

[215] For amoraic parallels to this tale, see Michael L. Satlow, *Tasting the Dish: Rabbinic Rhetorics of Sexuality*, BJS 303 (Atlanta: Society of Biblical Literature, 1995), 149–150.

[216] See Schwartz, *Imperialism*, 166. Contrast the positivistic interpretation of this text offered by Ephraim E. Urbach, "The Rabbinical Laws of Idolatry in the Second and Third Centuries in the Light of Archaeological and Historical Facts," in *Collected*

that sharing wine with Gentile women leads to an attempted seduction of Israelite men into idolatrous worship. On the one hand, this text is simply about the prohibition of Gentile wine on the grounds of idolatry. However, the sexualized nature of this interaction can be read to suggest that any commensal encounter with a non-Jewish woman might result in an inappropriate (from the tannaitic standpoint) social relationship.[217]

Commenting on idolatry in general in rabbinic literature, Sacha Stern notes, "*Avoda zara* [literally "foreign worship," hence idolatry] is...a defining *metaphor* of non-Jewishness, or even its embodiment. This is why in the context of intermarriage the avoidance of *avoda zara* and of non-Jewishness are virtually undistinguishable."[218] Tannaitic texts that connect table-fellowship between Jews and non-Jews with idolatry via seduction by non-Jewish/Israelite women contribute to the blurring of the boundaries of which Stern speaks. The not-so-tacit question in these texts appears to be: If idolatry is the binary opposite of Jewishness, then how can a Jewish man share a table with a non-Jewish woman who could tempt him into such a practice? Sharing a table is therefore understood as the first step toward sharing a bed and, consequently, the first step down the slippery slope that leads to the embodiment of non-Jewishness: idolatry.[219] The Amoraim later make this association even

---

Writings in Jewish Studies, ed. Robert Brody and Moshe D. Herr, 151–193 (Jerusalem: Magnes Press, 1999), 181–182. For a brief critique of Urbach's approach in this article in general, see Schwartz, *Imperialism*, 172. This is part of a general trend in rabbinic literature when discussing idolatry to interact with the world of the Hebrew Bible rather than with its own contemporary environment. Thus, this text, like many others, should be read as "a discourse with texts, to be sure texts filtered through everyday life and experience, hence through the 'cultural space' in which they lived, but this cultural space has left surprisingly little imprint" on the document (Schäfer, "Jews and Gentiles," 351; in general, see pp. 346–352). Schäfer's comments refer specifically to the Palestinian Talmud, but they also apply to tannaitic literature.

[217] This observation accords with Michael L. Satlow's argument that Palestinian rabbinic literature in general contains a stereotype that, "[s]exually speaking, women are trouble" ("Fictional Women: A Study in Stereotypes," in *The Talmud Yerushalmi and Graeco–Roman Culture*, ed. Peter Schäfer, 225–243, Vol. 3 [Tübingen, Germany: Mohr Siebeck, 2002], 235).

[218] *Jewish Identity*, 196–197, emphasis in original. The usage of "foreign worship" for a metaphor for "foreigners" is both obvious and apt.

[219] This discomfort is not unique to tannaitic literature, as anthropologists have noted a cross-cultural connection between conjugal and commensal relations. In the words of

more concrete by providing an explicit rationale for certain rabbinically ordained food prohibitions: "because of intermarriage."[220] By problematizing commensality with non-Jews, the Tannaim seek to reinforce Jewish identity. With whom you eat is therefore seen as a practice that makes an active identity statement in the present, as well as an accurate predictor of one's identity in the future. Sitting apart at meals, to paraphrase Tacitus' observation about Jewish behavior,[221] is perceived in tannaitic literature to be a reliable method of preserving a distinct Jewish identity.

Even though tannaitic texts marginalize commensality with Gentiles, they still provide evidence for the possibility of such social interactions. As we have seen several times already, the Tannaim introduce tensions and restrictions in regard to commensal encounters that are often unprecedented. Yet, these "fences around the table" (to play on a rabbinic idiom)[222] – like the "unbroken palisades and iron walls" in the *Letter of Aristeas* – are not impenetrable. Thus, these texts appear to employ what Satlow refers to as "persuasive rhetorics." As this term implies, persuasive rhetorics promote normative practices without necessarily appealing to legal justifications.[223] Applying this concept, *mutatis mutandis*, to the topic at hand helps to explain the tannaitic texts that problematize, but stop short of legally prohibiting, commensality with Gentiles.[224] In these texts, the shared table is the first step down a slippery slope that leads to idolatry. As such, commensality with non-Jews is a social situation best avoided.

Ohnuki-Tierney, "Commensality and sexual union are the fibers that weave human relationships into a tapestry of culturally meaningful patterns" (*Rice as Self*, 119). The fact that these fibers intersect at the table should not be surprising; we have continuously seen that the table is a locus for identity negotiation. Further, the table is also a locus for establishing power, as Bynum persuasively argues in regard to medieval Christian women (*Holy Feast*).

[220] *b. Avodah Zarah* 31b and 35b (also see 36b).
[221] *Historiae*, 5.5.2.
[222] E.g., *m. Avot* 1:1 (ed. Albeck 4:353).
[223] See Satlow, *Tasting the Dish*, 8. Satlow also defines "legal rhetorics" as "rabbinic discussions of the law, their attempts to define transgressions, categorize them, and establish issues of liability" (*Tasting the Dish*, 8).
[224] Legal prohibitions do appear, however, in amoraic literature. An historical analog can be found in Canon 50 from the early-fourth-century Council of Elvira, which prohibits Christians from engaging in commensality with Jews. On the role that food regulations play in the Council of Elvira, see Freidenreich, Foreign Food, 135–141.

I would thus argue that the Tannaim are concerned with both foreign worship and foreigners.[225] Tannaitic (and, especially, later amoraic) literature piggybacks rhetorics of persuasion against commensality with non-Jews on legal rhetorics prohibiting idolatry.[226] This principle also applies to R. Shimon ben Elazar's moral condemnation of the non-Jewish wedding banquet in *t. Avodah Zarah* 4:6. Costuming persuasive rhetoric in the guise of a legal rhetoric – an act of misrecognition – allows the Tannaim to stigmatize commensality with Gentiles. By expanding laws about idolatry, drawing on assumptions about sexuality, and employing the "slippery slope" principle, the Tannaim marginalize commensality with non-Jews and begin to prescribe social practices that result in separation at meals. With whom one eats becomes an even stronger statement of identity in tannaitic literature than in previous Judean and Jewish sources, as the fault line between "Us" and "Them" is ever increasingly located down the center of the table.

When discussing the connections between commensality and idolatry, one must consider another tannaitic practice that establishes a distinctly Jewish identity through regulating commensal interactions with non-Jews: the institution of specific "table talk." I define the term "table talk" rather broadly as constituting all regulated formulae (e.g., blessings, meal prayers), structures (e.g., the Passover *haggadah*), topics (e.g., Torah), and genres (e.g., philosophical symposia) that prescribe words spoken around the table in a commensal setting. Table talk is a common feature in descriptions of Greek and Roman dining scenes.[227] Because the food on a Jew's plate is often quite similar to that of a non-Jew in antiquity – usually consisting of the Mediterranean triad – then the style and content of table talk may be the only distinguishing feature of many "Jewish" meals.[228] Tannaitic table talk provides interesting data for the discussion of commensality regulations. On the one hand, as we have already seen, several texts introduce laws and practices that seemingly

---

[225] Contra Freidenreich, who argues that the Tannaim are not concerned with foreigners as much as they are concerned with foreign worship (Foreign Food, 150). I believe that both trouble them, as one inevitably leads to the other.

[226] This fits a general trend in rabbinic literature, summarized by Stern, *Jewish Identity*, 195–198.

[227] On the topics and customs of symposium table conversations in Greek and Roman sources, see Smith, *From Symposium to Eucharist*, 50–64.

[228] See D. Kraemer, *Jewish Eating*, 73.

prevent this social intercourse. On the other hand, other texts suggest that commensality with Gentiles can occur. Further, even texts that do assume that Jews and non-Jews can share a table often use persuasive rhetorics that stigmatize these social interactions.

Texts that possibly suggest that commensality with non-Jews can occur discuss the role that non-Jews can or cannot play in the recitation of food blessings. For example, we learn that non-Jews do not count toward the prayer quorum necessary to recite grace after meals[229] and that a Jew may respond "amen" to the blessing in the name of God offered by a non-Jew.[230] One could read these texts as descriptive and conclude that the Tannaim recognize the presence of non-Jews at the meal and are seeking to determine to what extent non-Jews can participate in tannaitically ordained table talk; one could argue that these texts are prescriptive and that the Tannaim seek to use table talk to marginalize or exclude non-Jews from the tannaitic table; finally, one could suggest some combination of these two opinions, or even another similar theory (for example, they are simply scholastic in nature). Although I prefer to read these texts as prescriptive, regardless of what stance one takes, by addressing the case of non-Jews, these texts explicitly mark them as "Other." As we shall also see in Chapters 3 and 4, tannaitic literature often focuses on those who are not "Us" – women, slaves, children, and nonrabbinic Jews. In doing so, the Tannaim use the "Other" to define the "Self."[231] Therefore, even if these data point toward the inclusion of non-Jews at the tannaitic

---

[229] *m. Berakhot* 7:1 (ed. Albeck 1:26). On the literary structure and parallelism of this mishnah, see Tzvee Zahavy, *The Mishnaic Law of Blessings and Prayers: Tractate Berakhot*, BJS 88 (Atlanta: Scholars Press, 1987), 101. Some scholars speculate that a document at Qumran (4Q434) resembles the rabbinic formula for the version of grace after meals recited in the house of a mourner (e.g., Moshe Weinfeld, "Grace After Meals in Qumran," *JBL* 111/3 [1992]: 427–440; Moshe Weinfeld and David Rolph Seely, "4Q434. 4QBarkhi Nafshi," In *Qumran Cave 4. XX, Poetical and Liturgical Texts, Part 2*, DJD 29, 267–286 [Oxford: Clarendon Press, 1999]). If this interpretation is correct – and it seems more like conjecture than substantiated fact – then there is a pre-tannaitic precedent for this liturgical formula.

[230] *t. Berakhot* 5:21 (ed. Lieberman 1:28). This is a general statement in Tosefta and does not apply solely to blessings over food. However, its context *in situ* in the midst of a discussion of food-based blessings suggests its applicability to the subject at hand.

[231] As S. Stern observes, this type of rhetorical move "suggests a dialectical relationship of self and other where the other serves no other purpose, and has no other *raison d'être*, but to define and enhance the essence of self" (*Jewish Identity*, 46).

table, non-Jews are not perceived as full participants in table talk, a key commensal practice that marks tannaitic identity.

Non-Jewish participation in tannaitic commensality is especially problematized in *m. Avot* 3:3:

> R. Shimon said: "[If] three [men][232] have eaten on one table and they did not speak words of Torah, it is as if they had eaten of the sacrifices to dead [idols], as it is said: 'For all tables are filled with vomit and filth without God.'[233] But three [men] who ate on one table and spoke words of Torah, it is as if they had eaten from the tables of God Blessed-Be-He, as it is said: 'And he said to me: "This is the table that is before Yhwh."'"[234]

Torah-based table talk is one of the social practices that mark the difference between an idolatrous sacrifice and a "proper" sacrifice to Yhwh. *m. Avot* 3:3 contains the common tannaitic connection between the table of the Jewish home and the table (i.e., the altar) of the Jewish Temple. Without proper table talk, the meal devolves into idolatry. Although I may be reading too much into this text, which is the only tannaitic reference that explicitly draws this connection, this conclusion does not seem far off base, especially in light of some of the texts that we have already discussed.

If indeed meals devoid of Torah-based table talk are equated with idolatrous sacrifices,[235] then sharing a table with one unversed in Torah

---

[232] I supply a masculine subject here because I believe this text to assume that these diners are men, and not women. I discuss gender issues in Chapter 3. The number three is not insignificant, as it is the required quorum for reciting grace after meals (e.g., *m. Berakhot* 7:1 [ed. Albeck 1:26]).

[233] *m. Avot* 3:3 (ed. Albeck 4:363–364). This is a clever rereading of Isaiah 28:8. In the biblical verse, the final words are "without a [clean] place." However, the word for "place" (*māqōm*) is a common rabbinic term for God. Through decontextualization and anachronism, the rabbinic author crafts a "proof-text" without changing a single word.

[234] Ezekiel 41:22. *m. Avot* 3:2 (ed. Albeck 4:363) also mentions the importance of two who sit together discussing "words of Torah," but does not explicitly set the proverbial scene at a dining table. Medieval Kabbalists draw on *m. Avot* 3:3 to establish a range of table-based practices. For a discussion, see Hecker, *Mystical Bodies*, 108–109, 117–121, 160–162.

[235] Similarly, see Jonathan Brumberg-Kraus, "Meals as Midrash: A Survey of Ancient Meals in Jewish Studies Scholarship," in *Food and Judaism: Studies in Jewish Civilization 15*, ed. Leonard J. Greenspoon, Ronald A. Simkins, and Gerald Shapiro, 297–317 (Omaha, NE: Creighton University Press, 2004), 303. For later Jewish interpretations of *m. Avot* 3:3, see Brumberg-Kraus, "Meals as Midrash," 306–307.

is tantamount to idolatry. We have previously encountered texts that distance non-Jews from Torah knowledge in our earlier discussion of manna.[236] Reading these sources in concert suggests that, owing to the absence of manna from their diet in the time of the Exodus, non-Jews have no access to Torah and, hence, are incapable of "proper" table talk.[237] In this case, two tannaitic culinary and commensal practices combine to form Jewish identity: ingesting metonymic (and embodying) food, and "proper" table talk.

Tannaitic legal and persuasive rhetorics suggest a growing concern regarding commensality with Gentiles. Non-Jews are marked as the "Other" through both legal discussions about their ability to participate in meal-based liturgy and persuasive rhetorics that employ the slippery-slope argument in regard to commensality with Gentiles and idolatry, and discussions that concern their inability to participate in Torah-based (and hence, nonidolatrous) discourse. As the table is an important locus of identity negotiation, eating with those who can both fully participate and are knowledgeable in tannaitic table talk allows Jews to secure their Jewish identity. In short, commensality with Gentiles has become a practice best avoided by Jews.

JEWISH IDENTITY: CONCLUSIONS

Commensality regulations are practices, bundled sets of doings and sayings, that index membership in communal bodies, essentially dividing the world into two distinct categories: those with whom one eats, and those with whom one does not eat. The Tannaim deploy a variety of strategies to turn the biological necessity of ingesting calories into a cultural act of identity negotiation.

In this chapter, we have seen how the Tannaim perceive preparing and eating food to be an act of social, and sometimes ontological, identity construction for a Jew in three specific ways. First, by understanding certain foods (i.e., pig, manna, the Passover, and *kashrut* practices in general) as metonymic and embodying, the Tannaim construct a network

---

[236] For other examples, see Stern, *Jewish Identity*, 210–214.
[237] The Torah-based table talk of Jews is contrasted with the lascivious table talk of non-Jews in later rabbinic texts (e.g., *Esther Rabba* 3:13; *b. Megillah* 12b).

of culinary and commensal practices that constitute a distinctly Jewish foodway. Second, by correlating the status of that which is prepared (i.e., meat and the Mediterranean triad) with the status of its preparer, the Tannaim make a predictable analogy between food regulations and desired social relations. Third, by connecting commensality between Jews and non-Jews (i.e., via intermarriage and table talk) with idolatry, the Tannaim use legal and persuasive rhetorics, as well as the slippery-slope argument, to problematize social relations with those whom they do not wish Jews to interact. Throughout, tannaitic culinary and commensal regulations include accommodations allowing for controlled interactions with non-Jews. Yet even though Jews and Gentiles are not completely separated, commensal interactions become increasingly more difficult, as the meal becomes increasingly laden with social practices that construct Jewishness.

3

Jewish Male Identity

Women [in World War II America] were not considered full citizens worthy of the blessings of liberty; instead, they were designated as the keepers of a more communally minded, classically republican notion of civic virtue.... [W]omen's real and most important battlefield was the kitchen. There women could – and should – fight the war and prove their patriotism by cooking and serving the right kinds of foods in the right kinds of ways. Every meal served was a political act.[1]

Another "Other" that tannaitic commensal practices establish in part is the category of women.[2] A woman is not the "normative" Tanna, who is in general, "a male, property owning, rabbi or rabbinic disciple."[3]

---

[1] Amy Bentley, *Eating for Victory: Food Rationing and the Politics of Domesticity* (Urbana and Chicago: University of Illinois Press, 1998), 4, 31.

[2] In general, see Ross S. Kraemer, "The Other as Woman: An Aspect of Polemic among Pagans, Jews, and Christians in the Greco-Roman World," in *The Other in Jewish Thought and History: Constructions of Jewish Culture and Identity*, ed. Laurence J. Silberstein and Robert L. Cohn, 121–144 (New York: New York University Press, 1994); Miriam Peskowitz, "Spinning Tales: On Reading Gender and Otherness in Tannaitic Texts," in *The Other in Jewish Thought and History: Constructions of Jewish Culture and Identity*, ed. Laurence J. Silberstein and Robert L. Cohn, 91–120 (New York: New York University Press, 1994); Miriam B. Peskowitz, *Spinning Fantasies: Rabbis, Gender, and History* (Berkeley and Los Angeles: University of California Press, 1997). For a clear textual example of the phenomenon of man as the presumed "Self" in tannaitic literature, see *Mekilta d'Rabbi Shimon b. Yohai* at Exodus 12:22 (ed. Epstein and Melamed 26), in which the second person plural pronoun ("you") in the Hebrew Bible is assumed to refer to men, but must be explained on a case-by-case basis to refer to "Others" (which explicitly includes women here).

[3] Michael L. Satlow, "Fictional Women: A Study in Stereotypes," in *The Talmud Yerushalmi and Graeco–Roman Culture*, ed. Peter Schäfer, 225–243, Vol. 3 (Tübingen, Germany: Mohr Siebeck, 2002), 225. On the economic assumptions of the Mishnah, see Hayim Lapin, *Early Rabbinic Civil Law and the Social History of Roman Galilee: A Study of Mishnah Tractate* Baba' Meṣi'a', BJS 307 (Atlanta: Scholars Press, 1995), 119–235.

As the actions and participants surrounding the tannaitic table become increasingly regulated, this observation comes into greater focus.

In this chapter, I divide the tannaitic data into two groups: (1) texts pertaining to women preparing food and (2) texts pertaining to women at the table. Each group illustrates differently how tannaitic commensality practices enact and maintain a distinct Jewish male identity. From texts legislating the preparation of food by women, we encounter the literary role that women play in the tannaitic corpus. In these pericopae, women are often not "real" women; they are literary foils, serving a discursive purpose.[4] As characters in a drama, they are introduced only to elucidate the social and legal effects of certain culinary and commensal practices on tannaitic men. From texts legislating the presence of women at the table, we discover an emerging set of regulations that mark women as "Them" and men as "Us." In both instances, we encounter numerous culinary and commensal practices that are unprecedented in earlier sources.

PREPARING FOOD AS (RE)PRODUCING MALE IDENTITY

Throughout our discussion thus far, women have rarely appeared. As men are the normative gender in rabbinic literature in general, the paucity of texts discussing women is not entirely surprising. However, women do appear quite often in one culinary and commensal context: food preparation. Although men occasionally appear in this context (usually involving animal butchery, professional cooking, or interactions with non-Jews, as we have seen in Chapter 2), tannaitic literature usually depicts the activities involved in domestic food preparation as the domain of women. To look into the kitchen is therefore to glimpse into the literary (and, to some extent, historical) world of women.[5]

---

[4] Of course, this statement also applies to any other non–normative person depicted in rabbinic literature. As Satlow further notes, "When the rabbis discuss any other character [besides a 'normative' rabbi], we must ask to what degree they are reporting a 'real' incident, and to what degree they are creating a fantasy, a projection that serves some ulterior motive of self-definition" ("Fictional Women," 226; in general, see pp. 225–227). We have already encountered this notion in Chapter 2. For example, the entire conception of a "culinary Other" rests on the notion that the foodway of the "Other" is embodying, therefore creating a stereotypical, literary, and fictive characterization of a non-Jew.

[5] I leave aside the issue of commerce (i.e., selling prepared foods to a third party, usually occurring in a market). Even though the subject of women buying and selling in the

This division creates a tension, however. If a man is *what* he eats, for example, how can he rely on an "Other" – a woman – to prepare his food? This tension is not unique to tannaitic literature, as historically food is perhaps the only resource over which women consistently exercise control, in terms of both its preparation and storage.[6] If power is defined as "resource control,"[7] then ceding the kitchen to women provides them with a powerful tool with which to harness social power.[8] To counteract or

marketplace is interesting, I generally ignore issues of commerce throughout this study, as they require a separate book of their own (e.g., the laws regulating whether or not a culinary item is permissible for Jewish ingestion and Jewish economic benefit are often different). I offer here one concrete example to summarize the relevant issues. *m. Hallah* 2:7 (ed. Albeck 1:280) specifies the size of the dough offering for nonprofessional female bakers who intend to sell surplus dough in the market as one-forty-eighth of the batch. Commenting on this pericope, Susan Weingarten notes: "This does not seem to have been common practice, however, and the rabbis generally disapproved of women going to the market" ("'Magiros,' 'Nahtom' and Women at Home: Cooks in the Talmud," *JJS* 59/2 [2005]: 285–297, 293). Rabbinic disapproval of women going into the market is certainly evidenced in tannaitic literature. However, as Cynthia M. Baker points out, this disapproval indicates a discourse about women's bodies and the desire for men to control them; it is not evidence of the absence of women from the market (*Rebuilding the House of Israel: Architectures of Gender in Jewish Antiquity* [Stanford, CA: Stanford University Press, 2002], 77–112). "Reading the corners and niches of rabbinic writing," tannaitic literature contains ample evidence that women participated in commerce far more often than one would assume based on reading the texts with the grain (Peskowitz, *Spinning Fantasies*, 64). Even though a post-tannaitic text can claim that "[i]t is the way of a woman to dwell in her home, and it is the way of a man to go out to the market" (*Genesis Rabba* 21:9 [ed. Theodor and Albeck 1:160–161]), such a statement does not necessarily accord with contemporary social reality.

[6] See Peter Garnsey, *Food and Society in Classical Antiquity* (New York: Cambridge University Press, 1999), 109. Also see Caroline Walker Bynum, who, when discussing the ways in which medieval Christian women manipulated food to gain individual and social control, notes, "Because food preparation was woman's sphere, food asceticism and food distribution were for women obvious modes of imitating the vulnerability and generosity of Christ.... Food-related behavior was central to women socially and religiously not only because food was a resource women controlled but also because by means of food women controlled themselves and their world" (*Holy Feast and Holy Fast: The Religious Significance of Food to Medieval Women* [Berkeley and Los Angeles: University of California Press, 1988], 193).

[7] As Garnsey defines it in regard to Greek texts on food and gender (*Food and Society*, 109).

[8] For other examples, see Anne Allison, "Japanese Mothers and Obentōs: The Lunch Box as Ideological State Apparatus," in *Food and Culture: A Reader*, ed. Carole Counihan and Penny van Esterik, 296–314 (New York: Routledge, 1997), 310; Bynum, *Holy Feast*. The social power afforded via food in general is reflected in several English idioms. As James N. Davidson notes, "Eating is a potent metaphor in all societies. We have our 'Fat-cats' controlling banks and utilities, our 'gravy-trains' packed with politicians, and we still argue over 'slices of the cake'" (*Courtesans and Fishcakes: The Consuming Passions of Classical Athens* [London: Harper Collins, 1997], 283). Further, "the phrase

minimize the power of resource control theoretically available to women, the Tannaim institute a variety of legal prescriptions. In following these tannaitic enactments, women become sous-chefs, whether male, rabbinic chefs are in the kitchen, or like modern-day "executive chefs," supervise from afar.

Methodologically, my argument here is based on a key assumption: namely, I read the tannaitic authors as *ascribing* to women specific experiences, rather than *describing* them. Thus, I understand the actions of women in tannaitic literature to be, more often than not, idealizations – what Peskowitz labels rabbinic "fantasy" – as opposed to historical events.[9] This reading presents a common challenge for historians. As Sacha Stern notes, "Reconstructing women's experiences on the sole basis of men's interpretations of them is a task which could be dismissed as self-defeating. It is possible, however, to unravel what our sources *thought* women experienced."[10] The actions of women in tannaitic literature, therefore, provide us with more information about the male authors than about the purported female subjects. Satlow argues that this is a trope in Palestinian rabbinic literature in general, stating that "*rabbinic stereotypes of women reveal rabbinic understandings of, and anxieties about, their own masculinity.*"[11] I therefore read the tannaitic evidence about women and food preparation for evidence about male identity; combing the tannaitic corpus for descriptive information regarding women is often akin to searching for the red herring in a mystery novel.

More than just "Other," women play a specific rhetorical role in rabbinic literature. As Satlow notes:

When a woman appears in a rabbinic story, her appearance as a woman is almost never incidental; her character is not interchangeable with a male one.... That

---

'to eat humble pie' implies being forced to take a position lower than one has assumed" (Jack Goody, *Cooking, Cuisine and Class: A Study in Comparative Sociology* [Cambridge: Cambridge University Press, 1996], 141).

[9] See *Spinning Fantasies*, 62 and *passim*.
[10] *Jewish Identity*, 241, emphasis in original. This stance is not unique, as many studies of gender in rabbinic literature arrive at a similar conclusion. Among the many examples, see Charlotte Elisheva Fonrobert, *Menstrual Purity: Rabbinic and Christian Reconstructions of Biblical Gender* (Stanford, CA: Stanford University Press, 2000), 211–212; Satlow, "Fictional Women," 227.
[11] "Fictional Women," 241, emphasis in original.

is, the appearance of women in these stories functions as a kind of flare for the reader. The presence of a woman alerts the reader that something will be different about this case or story, and signals her or him to break out an appropriate set of interpretive tools.[12]

Reading early rabbinic texts in this light, then, assumes that the appearance of women is a hermeneutical marker – indicative of a different scenario.[13] Women present a different *halakhic* case in these texts because they themselves are not "the encoded implicit reader" (i.e., the normative audience).[14]

In tannaitic texts about women and food preparation, *women's actions are of interest only insofar as they affect men's practice.*[15] As we shall see,

---

[12] "Fictional Women," 226, 232, emphasis in original. Satlow's observations are especially apt for this study because his article specifically addresses Palestinian rabbinic literature.

[13] On the concept of hermeneutical markedness, see Azzan Yadin, *Scripture as Logos: Rabbi Ishmael and the Origins of Midrash* (Philadelphia: University of Pennsylvania Press, 2004), 48–79.

[14] On the application of this literary theory term to ancient texts, see Stanley K. Stowers, *A Rereading of Romans: Justice, Jews, and Gentiles* (New Haven, CT: Yale University Press, 1994), 21–22.

[15] In many ways, this statement is generalizable to the entire corpus of rabbinic literature.
 Using Pierre Bourdieu's notions of habitus and hexis, Sacha Stern argues that the rabbinic concept of *ṣnî'ût* (modesty, self-concealment) allows women to belong to the collective body of Israel, an identity that is established and reified via social practices from which women are often excluded in rabbinic literature. According to Stern, women's identity in rabbinic literature "is grounded not in a distinct *praxis*, as with men's commandments, but rather in a *habitus* or *hexis*, which we have identified as *tzeniut*" (*Jewish Identity in Early Rabbinic Writings* [New York: Brill, 1994], 247, emphasis in original; on the notions of habitus and hexis, see Pierre Bourdieu, *Outline of a Theory of Practice*, trans. Richard Nice [New York: Cambridge University Press, 1998 (1977)], 72–95). Even though Stern's argument works for his specific example, I do not accept it for the case at hand. I offer as evidence the three points that Stern himself uses to correlate *ṣnî'ût* with habitus/hexis. Like Bourdieu's notion of habitus, *ṣnî'ût* is (1) a system of dispositions rather than a rigid *halakhic* ruling, (2) "'a system of *durable and transposable* dispositions,' which can affect the widest variety of experiences," (3) an embodied habitus, or hexis, "which is to say, 'a pattern of postures ... charged with a host of social meanings and values" (*Jewish Identity*, 235–236; quoting Bourdieu, *Outline of a Theory*, 72, 87, emphasis in original). In contrast, tannaitic discourse on women and food preparation is about the actions that women must take to ensure the food-based identity of men. It is not an abstract set of transferable dispositions as much as a specific set of guidelines for women to follow to assist in male practice. To concretize my argument, I offer one specific example. Stern argues that the habitus of *ṣnî'ût* is implied in *m. Ketubbot* 7:6 (ed. Albeck 3:112, discussed further in this chapter) by the category "law of the Jews (or Jewess)." However, the rules of untithed food and separating dough offering, in explicit reference to the actions of women, are discussed under the separate category of "the law of Moses" *in that very text*. Therefore, Stern's notion of *ṣnî'ût* as the habitus that incorporates women into the body of Israel does

the tannaitic glimpse into the kitchen is only to ensure that women are preparing food (most often bread) in the tannaitically prescribed manner. Male identity requires, in part, a tannaitically proper diet. Women, in the role of domestic food preparers, must comply with tannaitic food regulations. If they do not, they undermine the entire system.[16] Of course, this observation is not unique to food preparation, as analogs are found elsewhere in the rabbinic corpus (e.g., menstrual purity).[17] However, the data gleaned from glimpses into the tannaitic kitchen are particularly illustrative of this phenomenon.

In tannaitic literature, as in many ancient and modern cultures, women are depicted as playing the prominent role in domestic food preparation.[18] For example, the presumption that women must engage

---

not apply to the discussion at hand. Instead, as I discuss further below, I read these texts as focusing on male practice and identity and understand the presence of women as discursively necessary to establish the role that women's actions play in maintaining tannaitic male identity.

[16] An interesting example can be found in *m. Teharot* 7:9 (ed. Albeck 6:323–324; cp. *t. Teharot* 8:16 [ed. Zuckermandel 669]). While discussing the case of a woman who leaves a pot of heave-offering alone on a fire and returns to find another woman raking the coals underneath the pot, R. Elazar ben Pila declares that "women are gluttonous." Hence, they are suspected of having tasted the food, making it impure. As Tal Ilan points out, this text implies that, unlike women, men are *not* gluttonous (*Jewish Women in Greco-Roman Palestine: An Inquiry into Image and Status* [Tübingen, Germany: Mohr Siebeck, 1995], 124). Women's gluttony, which affects the status of the food, is perceived here as directly affecting male Tannaim. Because men (except for beggars, a specific exception mentioned in this text) can control themselves, they do not threaten the status of their own food. Women, however, represent a threat and must conform to tannaitically prescribed actions to aid the male Tannaim in their "proper" practice.

[17] As Fonrobert notes, "[T]he whole system only works if women play along and accept the [rabbinic] authority to define. The woman is the one who has to make the decision to seek the rabbi's advice and submit herself to his expert authority, the woman is the one who has to observe her own blood-flow, and the woman is the one who has to regard a stain as problematic or indicative of something" (*Menstrual Purity*, 117–118). In Bourdieu's nomenclature, one might refer to this phenomenon as the "opposition between the *centrifugal*, male orientation and the *centripetal*, female orientation, which . . . is the true principle of the organization of domestic space" (*Outline of a Theory*, 92, emphasis in original). This nomenclature is adopted by Stern (*Jewish Identity*, 132–135, 237).

[18] Professional cooking is a different story. I treat this subject in Chapter 1 and later on, specifically in regard to the relationship between bread baked at home by a female and bread baked professionally by a male baker. However, I do not wish to claim that baking bread is solely "women's work," a criticism that Peskowitz offers of many scholars who view "the category of 'women' and 'worker' [as] conceptually incompatible" (*Spinning Fantasies*, 63; in general, see pp. 61–66).

in the transformative cultural act of cooking is explicit in *m. Ketubbot* 5:5:

These are the labors that a wife performs for her husband: she grinds [grain to make flour], and she bakes [bread],[19] and she launders [clothes]; she cooks, and she nurses her child; she makes the bed, and she works in wool.[20]

Much like the biblical "woman of valor," who rises early to give food to her household, the tannaitic wife is expected (either directly or indirectly) to prepare her husband's food.[21] I argue that these literary contexts reflect

---

[19] In fact, according to tannaitic law, if a wife does not properly tithe food or separate out the dough offering while making bread, she can be divorced without receiving her *kĕtûbbā* (marriage settlement; see *m. Ketubbot* 7:6 [ed. Albeck 3:112], discussed later in this chapter). Once again, this text assumes the primary role that women play in household food preparation. For a brief summary of the tannaitic *kĕtûbbā* payment, see Michael L. Satlow, *Jewish Marriage in Antiquity* (Princeton, NJ: Princeton University Press, 2001), 202, in which he concisely defines the term as "a delayed endowment pledge from the groom." On the broader history of the *kĕtûbbā* payment, see Michael L. Satlow, "Reconsidering the Rabbinic Ketubbah Payment," in *The Jewish Family in Antiquity*, ed. Shaye J. D. Cohen, 133–151, BJS 289 (Atlanta: Scholars Press, 1993).

[20] *m. Ketubbot* 5:5 (ed. Albeck 3:105). *m. Ketubbot* 5:5 continues to discuss how a woman who brings slaves along with her when she marries is relieved of certain duties, because the slaves can perform her "necessary" chores in her stead. I omit this part of the text because it is merely redundant vis-à-vis my main point: namely, that women are expected to engage in domestic food preparation. For a discussion of the rest of this pericope, see Peskowitz, *Spinning Fantasies*, 97–101; Judith Romney Wegner, *Chattel or Person?: The Status of Women in the Mishnah* (New York: Oxford University Press, 1988), 76–77; Weingarten, "'Magiros,'" 291–292.

[21] Proverbs 31:15. The concomitant presumption of expertise in matters of the kitchen perhaps underlies why a woman's ruling vis-à-vis impurity and an oven is accepted over a man's in *t. Kelim Bava Qamma* 4:17 (ed. Zuckermandel 573–574). In texts that discuss the situation in which a man gives food to a female innkeeper (*m. Demai* 3:5 [ed. Albeck 1:79]; *t. Demai* 4:32 [ed. Lieberman 1:84]), mother-in-law (*m. Demai* 3:6 [ed. Albeck 1:79]), or a female neighbor (*t. Demai* 4:31 [ed. Lieberman 1:84]), the topic worthy of note is the possibility of the woman substituting improperly tithed food for the man's properly tithed food. The assumption that a woman would "naturally" prepare the food for a man is tacit. For a discussion of these pericopae, see Richard S. Sarason, *A History of the Mishnaic Law of Agriculture: A Study of Tractate Demai* (Leiden, the Netherlands: Brill, 1979), 147–149. These texts are part of a trend in rabbinic literature: a kitchen scene with a woman busy at work is invoked to discuss the further application of a law. For examples from the tannaitic corpus, see *m. Teharot* 2:1 (ed. Albeck 6:303–304), in which a woman is pickling vegetables in a pot in the midst of a discussion of purity; *m. Makhshirin* 5:11 (ed. Albeck 6:430), in which a woman with pure hands is stirring an impure cooking pot. The fact that these two cases involve purity concerns is significant. As I argue in this chapter, women are described in food preparation contexts interacting only with other rabbinic or nonrabbinic Jews and not with non-Jews. Purity concerns do not appear in culinary and commensal interactions between Jews and non-Jews.

both the historical reality of women as primary domestic cooks (discussed in Chapter 1) and the discursive reality of women playing the role of food preparers in the tannaitic system of edible identity.

The tannaitic data on women sharing the proverbial kitchen can be divided into two types of encounters: (1) sharing cooking utensils and ingredients and (2) cooking together.[22] The issue at hand in these encounters is almost always the purity status of the food involved. The importance of purity in these texts highlights two important observations. First, the actions of women in the kitchen appear insofar as they are germane to the construction of male identity; second, women are almost always depicted as cooking with other rabbinic or nonrabbinic Jewish women, and not with non-Jewish women.

The first observation is not surprising, as we have already encountered several texts that support this claim. The second point, however, requires further elaboration. Tannaitic discussions of women interacting with other women during the food preparation process almost always implicitly or explicitly assume that all the women in the kitchen are Jews – rabbinic or otherwise. As I argue in Chapter 4, purity concerns do not appear in tannaitic identity construction with regard to commensality and non-Jews. On the other hand, purity concerns are explicitly negotiated in culinary and commensal interactions between rabbinic and nonrabbinic Jews.[23] Thus, the nature of theoretical discussions about purity perhaps explains the reason that women are almost always depicted in tannaitic literature as cooking solely with other rabbinic or nonrabbinic Jews.

The question remains, however, as to whether this is the social reality for tannaitic women. Even though tannaitic women are, for example, depicted as sharing garments with non-Jewish women,[24] they are never – to my knowledge – depicted sharing a sieve, a rolling pin, or any other

---

[22] For example, sharing baking supplies: *m. Shevi'it* 5:9 (ed. Albeck 1:153–154); *t. Ketubbot* 7:4 (ed. Lieberman 3:79); sharing baking ingredients: *m. Betzah* 5:4 (ed. Albeck 2:300); *t. Yom Tov* 4:6 (ed. Lieberman 2:301–302); and preparing and baking bread together: *m. Shevi'it* 5:9 (ed. Albeck 1:153–154); *m. Hallah* 4:1 (ed. Albeck 1:284). As I discuss later in this chapter, the fact that all these examples refer to the supplies, ingredients, and process involved with making bread is not coincidental, as this is the food item that women are most often mentioned preparing in tannaitic literature.

[23] Though this does not necessarily bar them from interacting. For example, according to *t. Yevamot* 1:11 (ed. Lieberman 3:3), even the differences between the Houses of Hillel and Shammai did not prevent them from preparing food requiring purity together.

[24] *m. Niddah* 9:3 (ed. Albeck 6:400).

cooking utensil. In fact, the only cooking interaction between a Jewish and a non-Jewish woman that I have encountered appears in a *baraita* on *b. Avodah Zarah* 38a–b. This *baraita* describes a situation in which a woman leaves a female idolater alone to stir a pot while she goes out. However, the extent to which one can extrapolate from this datum is uncertain for two reasons. First of all, this is a single statement that is part of a literary parallel structure, as it immediately follows a similar case in which a man leaves a male idolater alone to turn meat over a flame while he is away. This rhetorical structure suggests at least the possibility that this is a scholastic and not an actual case. Second, the fact that this statement is found in a *baraita* and not *in situ* in a tannaitic text suggests at least the possibility that this is a later statement. Although the word "late" is sometimes applied by scholars to excuse inconvenient data, the possibility that this statement postdates the tannaitic corpus must be considered.[25] For these reasons, I view this text as akin to a statistical outlier. The sum of the tannaitic data suggests that women interacted in the kitchen only with rabbinic or nonrabbinic Jewish women.[26] The possibility that the *baraita* on *b. Avodah Zarah* 38a–b contains an historical kernel leads me, however, to qualify the previous statement throughout this chapter.

Although this qualification is intended for scholarly caution, I believe the tannaitic evidence points to the fact that the events described in these texts are the products of scholastic discussion and are part of a discursive attempt to regulate social interaction and to test nascent tannaitic law. Arising out of considerations for purity, the Tannaim turned to the necessary social reality of food preparation both to illustrate their point and to further regulate their ideal (if not also real) society. Women did cook with other women. However, the extent to which rabbinic women

---

[25] To properly ascertain whether this statement postdates the tannaitic corpus, one would need to survey the relevant amoraic texts on this issue to see whether this remark conforms to the amoraic data. Unfortunately, such a survey is well beyond the purview of this book, which considers only tannaitic literature. Continuing my analysis into the amoraic corpus is a desideratum.

[26] My approach here is similar to Shaye Cohen's treatment of the series of *baraitot* about the *'am hā'āreṣ*, found on *b. Pesahim* 49b. Cohen dates these *baraitot* to the post-tannaitic period, based on the fact that the views expressed therein do not accord with the rest of the tannaitic data. See Shaye J. D. Cohen, "The Place of the Rabbi in Jewish Society of the Second Century," in *The Galilee in Late Antiquity*, ed. Lee I. Levine, 157–173 (New York: Jewish Theological Seminary, 1992), 166–167, 173.

cooked with nonrabbinic women or that Jewish women cooked with non-Jewish women cannot be reconstructed from these texts. What can be (re)constructed, on the other hand, is male tannaitic discourse on female food preparation and purity, and how those actions affect male practice.

The female food preparation process most often referenced in tannaitic literature is that of baking bread. This is not surprising, as bread, a staple food in both the ancient and modern Mediterranean, constitutes 50 percent of the caloric intake for Jews in Roman-period Palestine.[27] Further, the fact that the process of baking bread requires the separation of an additional dough offering makes bread an excellent *halakhic* example for issues involving purity and tithes in a shared kitchen. Thus, discussion of bread can serve as a case study of the scholastic discourse of the Tannaim.

As discussed in Chapter 1, literary and material evidence indicates that the majority of bread consumed in Roman-period Palestine was prepared both in or around the home and by women.[28] This conclusion leads to an interesting gender binary, as professional bakers are understood in both Jewish and contemporary non-Jewish sources to be men.[29] Further, texts about professional bakers – which represent only a handful of those

[27] See Chapter 1 for references and discussion.
[28] Ben-Zion Rosenfeld and Joseph Menirav, *Markets and Marketing in Roman Palestine*, trans. Chava Cassel (Boston: Brill, 2005), 95. To offer one example from a nonbaking context, *m. Shabbat* 23:1 (ed. Albeck 2:69) discusses the case in which a man borrows wine or oil from his male neighbor and a woman borrows bread from her female neighbor (both assumed by the text to be rabbinic Jews) on the Sabbath. In the midst of a pericope concerned with borrowing food vis-à-vis the Sabbath laws, we encounter yet another instance in which a woman is presumed to provide the bread for her household. There are scant references to nonprofessional men being involved in the production of bread (e.g., *m. Hallah* 2:7 [ed. Albeck 1:280]). *Mekhilta d'Rabbi Ishmael Bo* 10 (ed. Horowitz 35) further genders this activity by assigning the role of kneading dough to the wife and the role of heating the oven (i.e., the "real" cooking) to the husband. I suggest that the heating of the oven signifies "real" cooking here based on a comparison of this pericope to, for example, *t. Avodah Zarah* 4:11 (ed. Zuckermandel 467, discussed in Chapter 2), in which a loaf of bread kneaded by a Gentile is permissible as long as a Jew himself bakes the bread. Thus, the chef/sous-chef principle is once again in operation. Whereas the Jewish male remains the "chef," in this case the "sous-chef" is a Jewish woman, not a non-Jewish male. As I mentioned earlier in this chapter, rabbinic regulations result in women becoming sous-chefs in the tannaitic kitchen, whether or not a male is present. I thank one of the anonymous reviewers for pushing me to further use this concept throughout this chapter.
[29] Garnsey, *Food and Society*, 110; Weingarten, "'Magiros.'" This assumption appears (either tacitly or explicitly) in several tannaitic texts: e.g., *m. Hallah* 1:7; 2:7 (ed. Albeck 1:277, 280). Goody observes that this trend is, to some extent, a cross-cultural one,

mentioning the production of bread – do not evidence the tensions encountered in those discussing domestic baking by women. This lack of tension is almost certainly due to the fact that professional bakers are presumed to be male and, as such, the potentially problematic scenarios brought about by women do not apply to them. For these reasons, I focus here on tannaitic discourse about women baking bread.[30]

The main tension in tannaitic texts about women and the bread-making process is that the actions of women directly affect male practice. For example, a wife who serves her husband improperly tithed food or does not separate out the dough offering while making bread undermines her husband's practice-based identity. It is perhaps for this reason that *m. Shabbat* 2:6[31] lists failure to separate the dough as one of the three reasons that women die in childbirth and that *m. Ketubbot* 7:6 allows such a wife to be divorced without receiving her *kĕtûbbā* payment.[32] One way of reading these statements is that they are thinly veiled threats. Rather than simply trusting women to adhere to this system, these texts warn of future bodily and economic harm for those who do not comply and play the role of the dutiful sous-chef.[33] However, if this reading is correct, it

---

noting that "the difference between high and low [cooking] tended to be one between male and female" (*Cooking, Cuisine and Class*, 193).

[30] It should be noted, however, that male professional bakers must follow many of the same rules that apply to female domestic bakers.

[31] *m. Shabbat* 2:6 (ed. Albeck 2:23). For references to parallels in amoraic literature, see Stern, *Jewish Identity*, 238 n. 247.

[32] *m. Ketubbot* 7:6 (ed. Albeck 3:112). Compare *m. Gittin* 9:10 (ed. Albeck 3:304), which allows a man to divorce a wife if she "spoiled his dish" (most likely by burning it, although there is also a sexual connotation here, as *Sifre Deuteronomy* 235 [ed. Finkelstein 267–268] interprets this phrase to imply marital infidelity). The metaphorical connection between a bad wife and a bad cook – that they are one and the same – appears in several amoraic texts (e.g., *Genesis Rabba* 17:3 [ed. Theodor and Albeck 1:152–154]; *b. Yevamot* 63a). Further, there is a strongly gendered component to the dough-offering regulations in tannaitic literature. In addition to the repercussions for failure to make this offering, a few texts suggest that some women are more than forgetful: they knowingly avoid giving the dough offering. This understanding perhaps underlies *m. Ketubbot* 9:4 (ed. Albeck 3:119–120), in which R. Eliezer rules that a man may impose an oath on his wife that she will not misappropriate his dough. This assumption is explicit in *Sifre Numbers* 110 (ed. Horowitz 115), in which R. Yehudah (commenting on *m. Hallah* 2:7, noted above) asserts that men are more liberal with their dough offering, whereas women are more stingy. However, contrast *t. Hallah* 1:7 (ed. Lieberman 1:276), in which R. Yehudah claims that men are liberal and *male bakers* are stingy.

[33] I thank my colleague Steven Larson for helping me to sharpen this point. As one of the anonymous reviewers pointed out to me, it is also possible to view this threat as

remains uncertain whether these threats were conveyed to women, and if so, in what manner this information was relayed. In general, I understand the regulations and, in fact, the entire conversation surrounding women baking bread in tannaitic literature as an attempt to negotiate and control a situation perceived by these authors to be fraught with danger. This conclusion accords with Anne Allison's observations about the gendered ideology underlying the preparation of nursery school lunch boxes (*obentōs*) by modern Japanese women for their children: namely, that "women are what they are through the products they produce."[34]

Tannaitic texts about women preparing dough and baking bread together generally depict women working together in one of two ways: (1) sharing baking ingredients and equipment for, one would assume, reasons of social and economic necessity and (2) sharing baking tasks and working together in a "sort of domestic production line."[35] Although these texts address a variety of concerns, in every case, the matters at hand are perceived as directly affecting the status of the food itself vis-à-vis male identity. This underscores a paradox that exists within the discursive site of the tannaitic kitchen: the Tannaim attempt to assert control over a domain by limiting, but not removing, the power granted to women via resource control. After all, even though a "sous-chef" may be under (*sous*) the supervision of a chef, she is still a chef. This problem, also encountered in rabbinic menstrual regulations, results in a tension, as the possibility for women undermining this schema is ever present.[36]

---

applying to the male, rabbinic chef, who is unable to control the actions of his female sous-chef, his wife, and hence, to control the tannaitic kitchen. Although this is true, I believe that the threat is mainly intended to ensure that the wife/sous-chef stays in line. After all, it is she who would be divorced, penniless, and quite possibly dead.

[34] "Japanese Mothers," 307.

[35] Weingarten, "'Magiros,'" 293. Weingarten is commenting on *m. Pesahim* 3:4 (ed. Albeck 2:150; cp. *t. Pisha* 3:8 [ed. Lieberman 2:153] and *Mekilta d'Rabbi Shimon b. Yohai* at Exodus 12:17 [ed. Epstein and Melamed 22]), which, for purposes of efficiency on Passover, divides the task of baking among three women: one kneads, one rolls, and one bakes. On the manuscript variants and the relationship between *m. Pesahim* 3:4 and *t. Pisha* 3:8, see Shamma Friedman, *Tosefta Atiqta: Pesaḥ Rishon: Synoptic Parallels of Mishna and Tosefta Analyzed with a Methodological Introduction* (Ramat-Gan, Israel: Bar-Ilan University Press, 2002 [Hebrew]), 289–290.

[36] On this problem in rabbinic menstrual impurity legislation, see Fonrobert, *Menstrual Purity*, 103–127.

Baking ingredients and equipment are often described as being shared among rabbinic and nonrabbinic Jewish women. These references usually appear in the midst of scholastic discourse in a variety of contexts, including tithing,[37] vows,[38] and purity.[39] In each instance, the generative rationale for the scholastic discussion seems to be the theoretical discourse of ascertaining how women lending baking ingredients and equipment to one another ultimately affects the bread that men ingest. A Tanna relies on his wife to provide him with properly tithed and pure food (as well as to act in accordance with his vows); failure to do so affects his identity vis-à-vis the tannaitic community. It is for these reasons that the issue of women sharing baking ingredients and equipment is raised in the tannaitic corpus. The Tannaim are not unique in this endeavor, as cross-cultural studies document the attempt to control women by controlling their actions in and around the kitchen, a domain that nevertheless remains gendered as female (e.g., World War II America and modern Japan).[40] The effect of this trend is to make the domestic actions of women in the kitchen invisible, or at least significantly obscure.[41]

When women are depicted as working side by side in the kitchen, the concern for tannaitic control is even more apparent, as these texts almost always focus on two issues that are perceived to directly affect male

---

[37] For example, according to *m. Shevi'it* 5:9 (ed. Albeck 1:153–154) and *m. Gittin* 5:9 (ed. Albeck 3:289), a woman who suspects her female neighbor of not properly observing the tithing laws associated with the sabbatical year may still lend her a sifter, sieve, millstone, or an oven, but may not actually sift or grind flour with that neighbor.

[38] E.g., *t. Ketubbot* 7:4 (ed. Lieberman 3:79), which explores a case in which a husband prohibits by a vow his wife from lending a sifter, sieve, millstone, or an oven (one would assume to a female neighbor). Purity is never raised as an issue in this text.

[39] E.g., *m. Betzah* 5:4 (ed. Albeck 2:300; = *t. Yom Tov* 4:6 [ed. Lieberman 2:302]), which discusses a woman lending her female friend "spices, water, and salt for her dough."

[40] On World War II America, see the work of Amy Bentley on the role of American women as cooks in World War II propaganda (*Eating for Victory*, 4, which forms part of the epigraph for this chapter). On Japan, see Allison's discussion of the role of Japanese mothers in preparing their children's lunch boxes (*obentōs*), a discursive site wherein she detects the operation of a gendered ideological state apparatus ("Japanese Mothers," especially pp. 305–310). Although women themselves enforce this system in Allison's example, these women do so in compliance with the gendered ideological state apparatus (see pp. 309–310). For this reason, I consider Allison's data to provide a useful analog.

[41] See Baker, *Rebuilding the House*, 42–47, who refers to the relationship between visible extant material cultural and archeological remains and invisible Palestinian Jewish women by the neologism "anopticon."

practice in rabbinic literature: tithing and purity. For example, *m. Hallah* 4:1 (ed. Albeck 1:284) discusses the applicable tithing rules when two women are preparing dough together and their batches of dough touch.[42] Ensuring that one's dough is properly tithed has significant ramifications for women, as we have already seen. Although purity concerns appear in some texts involving the sharing of baking supplies, they come into much sharper relief when the kitchen itself is shared.[43] In these cases, the texts appear to reflect a fear that no matter how careful a "proper" tannaitic wife is, given certain economic necessities, a less-than-careful kitchen partner may affect the purity status of her bread.[44] Once again, it is worth noting that purity concerns in culinary and commensal contexts in tannaitic literature always involve rabbinic or nonrabbinic Jews only. Thus, these (imagined or real) domestic bread-making encounters between women do not involve non-Jews.

With these observations in mind, we turn to the texts involving baking bread and women in the kitchen. In tannaitic literature, the vast majority of discussions about women sharing in the domestic baking of bread appear in the midst of scholastic conversations about the relationship between the wife of a *ḥabēr* (an "associate," who adheres to additional purity regulations, in particular with regard to food production, commerce, and consumption) and the wife of an *'am hā'āreṣ* (literally "a person of the land," who does not partake of these additional purity restrictions – and a term that, over time, takes on pejorative connotations).[45] As such, I treat these texts separately. The fact that these

---

[42] The text reads as follows: "Two women who made two [separate] one-*qab* [portions of dough], and [the portions] touched one another, even if [the portions of dough] are from a single species [of grain] – they are exempt [from dough offering, since they each belong to a different woman]. But when [the portions] belong to the same woman – [if they are] from the same species, [the dough] is subject [to dough offering]; but [if they are] of a different species, [the dough] is exempt [from dough offering]."

[43] Purity is discussed in regard to dough and bread in general on numerous occasions, including: *m. Hallah* 2:3, 7 (ed. Albeck 1:279, 280 [= *Sifre Numbers* 110 (ed. Horowitz 115)]); *m. Ohalot* 5:4 (ed. Albeck 6:139–140); *m. Teharot* 1:7–9; 3:8; 4:1; 8:8 (ed. Albeck 6:302–303; 308–309; 309; 326–327); *m. Tevul Yom* 4:2–3 (ed. Albeck 6:467).

[44] Of course, purity concerns also exist in regard to a woman baking alone (e.g., *m. Niddah* 10:7 [ed. Albeck 6:406–407]; *t. Ahilot* 5:11 [ed. Zuckermandel 602–603]) and to the work of a baker (e.g., *m. Kelim* 15:2 [ed. Albeck 6:69]).

[45] Plurals: *ḥabērîm* and *'ammê hā'āreṣ*. I discuss these categories in more depth in Chapter 4.

pericopae revolve around the interactions between wives further buttresses my argument that these texts are interested in female actions only insofar as they affect male practice directly.

Sharing the Kitchen with the Ḥabēr and the 'Am hā'Āreṣ

Following the order of bread production described in Chapter 1, we first encounter the wives of a *ḥabēr* and an *'am hā'āreṣ* sharing in the process of grinding grain.[46] To offer one example:

> The wife of a *ḥabēr* lends to the wife of an *'am hā'āreṣ* a sifter and a sieve. She sifts, winnows, and grinds with her. But once she pours water [into the flour, to make dough], she may not come near her, because they do not give assistance to idolaters. And all of these [rules] they said only in the interest of peace.[47]

The wife of a *ḥabēr* may lend to the wife of an *'am hā'āreṣ* a sifter or a sieve, as well as engage in the actions associated with those baking implements.[48] However, she must withdraw from the shared process after water is poured onto the flour. The reason given for the leniency allowing these wives to interact in the kitchen at all is "peace." It would seem that the economic necessity of sifting, winnowing, and grinding wheat into flour takes precedence here over the erection of an absolute,

---

[46] In fact, this is the most common scenario in which they are depicted interacting while baking bread. One could offer several possible explanations for this occurrence, including: (1) it is due to the random preservation of data; (2) this situation is perceived to provide a useful example for theoretical discourse; or (3) this to some degree reflects social history, as sharing in the process of milling grain is quite common.

[47] *m. Gittin* 5:9 (ed. Albeck 3:289); cp. *m. Shevi'it* 5:9 (ed. Albeck 1:153–154).

[48] *t. Teharot* 8:4 (ed. Zuckermandel 668–669) limits the applicability of this statement: "The wife of an *'am hā'āreṣ* grinds [grain] with the wife of a *ḥabēr* when she is impure [i.e., menstruating], but when she is pure, she should not grind. R. Shimon says: 'Even when she is impure she should not grind, for even though she does not eat, she gives to other women and they eat.'" For a brief discussion of this pericope, see Aharon Oppenheimer, *The 'Am ha-Aretz: A Study in the Social History of the Jewish People in the Hellenistic–Roman Period*. trans. Israel L. Levine (Leiden, the Netherlands: Brill, 1977), 168. Compare *m. Zabim* 3:2 (ed. Albeck 6:444–445), which allows a *zāb* and a pure person to grind wheat together, except when they do so using a hand mill. Apparently (perhaps for pragmatic reasons?), grinding wheat together on larger mills is allowed, even when one person is impure (so too *m. Zabim* 4:2 [ed. Albeck 6:446]).

nonpermeable boundary.[49] Allowing an *'am hā'āreṣ* neighbor to prepare flour for dough is one thing, but a line is drawn in tannaitic literature after that flour starts to become dough.[50] It would appear that at the stage at which maintaining purity becomes a much more difficult task (i.e., the introduction of water into the flour, as liquids are especially problematic – even more so than solid foods – in tannaitic purity regulations, because wet items are more susceptible to transfers of impurity than dry items), cooking together is no longer permitted.[51] In fact, at that very moment, the wife of an *'am hā'āreṣ* is compared to an idolater. As such, giving any assistance to her after her dry flour becomes wet dough is tantamount to abetting idolatry.[52] The leniency allowing for shared food preparation is thus limited to the stages that are both economically vital and less complicated from a purity standpoint. Further, by applying Lévi-Strauss's observations here, this stage is the cultural moment at which the raw ingredients begin their physical and metaphorical transformation into the cultural cooked entity of bread. In sum, although they allow for leniencies in the initial preparatory stages for reasons of economic necessity, the Tannaim prescribe a practice that separates one social group from another at the vital moment: when flour becomes dough.

Another interesting shared kitchen experience is the case in which a male *ḥabēr* gives food to a female *'am hā'āreṣ* to cook for him. In this

[49] Similarly, see Weingarten, "'Magiros,'" 292 (which aptly references Deuteronomy 24:6, in which one is forbidden from taking another's millstone as a pledge, as doing so is equated with taking one's life as a pledge).

[50] See *m. Teharot* 7:4 (ed. Albeck 6:321–322), where the wife of a *ḥabēr* may leave the wife of an *'am hā'āreṣ* alone in her house, so long as the sound from the millstone never ceases.

[51] Adding water to dough is also a concern in *m. Teharot* 4:10 (ed. Albeck 6:312–313), in which one is unsure whether the water added to flour to make dough came from a jar containing pure or impure water. For an extended exposition of tannaitic purity rules vis-à-vis liquids, see *m. Makhshirin* (ed. Albeck 6:415–434). However, this is not unique to the Tannaim, as the Dead Sea Scrolls, for instance, prescribe a longer interval between a novice's access to the "pure food of the Many" and the "pure drink of the Many" (1QS 6:16-23). For a discussion, see Jacob Licht, *The Rule Scroll: A Scroll from the Wilderness of Judea. 1QS, 1QSa, 1QSb. Text, Introduction, and Commentary* (Jerusalem: The Bialik Institute, 1965 [Hebrew]), 294–303; Lawrence H. Schiffman, *Sectarian Law in the Dead Sea Scrolls: Courts, Testimony and the Penal Code*, BJS 33 (Chico, CA: Scholars Press, 1983), 162–165. In contrast, Mary Douglas suggests that solid food and shared meals are invested with greater social meaning than liquid food and shared drinks in our own culture ("Deciphering a Meal," in *Food and Culture: A Reader*, ed. Carole Counihan and Penny van Esterik, 36–54 [New York: Routledge, 1997], 40–41).

[52] I thank one of the anonymous reviewers for helping me to sharpen this point.

instance, the effect of the woman's actions on male practice is even more explicit. For example, *t. Demai* 4:31 states:

A man gives to his female neighbor a dish [of food] to cook for him, and dough to bake for him, and he does not scruple about the yeast and the spices that are in it with regard to tithes and with regard to Sabbatical-year [produce, to which special tithing laws apply]. Under what circumstances? When he [himself] has put into them yeast and spices. [If] he has not put into them yeast and spices, behold, this one scruples about yeast and spices with regard to tithes and with regard to Sabbatical-year [produce].[53]

This text contains the assumption that the female *'am hā'āreṣ* respects the *ḥabēr*'s wishes and does not add any ingredients to the dough before baking it in an oven.[54] As is the case with similar instances in tannaitic literature, a male *ḥabēr* is permitted to give food to a female *'am hā'āreṣ* to cook for him, as long as he makes assurances that the food is properly tithed.[55] Once again, a leniency allows for the negotiation of a potentially problematic encounter. By supervising the mixing of ingredients, the male *ḥabēr* plays the role of the "chef," controlling the situation and allowing the female *'am hā'āreṣ* to perform the function of the "sous-chef" and to cook for him.

Cumulatively, these texts imagine a shared social and physical environment in which the wives of the *ḥabēr* and the *'am hā'āreṣ* share baking equipment and space, as well as one in which a male *ḥabēr* feels (relatively) comfortable having a female *'am hā'āreṣ* cook or bake his already prepared dish/dough. This observation is buttressed by texts and archaeological remains that evidence shared courtyards with utensils and ovens out in the open.[56] Although certain purity and tithing

---

[53] *t. Demai* 4:31 (ed. Lieberman 1:84). Compare *t. Ma'aserot* 3:13 (ed. Lieberman 1:241), which states: "a man gives to his female neighbor a dish [of food] to cook or dough to bake for him *only* if he knows that she will separate a dough offering for him and will prepare it in purity" (emphasis added).

[54] For a similar conclusion, see Sarason, *Mishnaic Law of Agriculture*, 149.

[55] Elsewhere, a male *ḥabēr* gives food to a female innkeeper (*m. Demai* 3:5 [ed. Albeck 1:79]; *t. Demai* 4:32 [ed. Lieberman 1:84]) and mother-in-law (*m. Demai* 3:6 [ed. Albeck 1:79]).

[56] E.g., *m. Teharot* 8:1 (ed. Albeck 6:32; cp. *t. Teharot* 9:1 [ed. Zuckermandel 670]). On the extant archaeological data for Palestinian dwellings, see Yizhar Hirschfeld, who notes, "In archaeological sites of various periods, courtyards have been found to contain a variety of baking and cooking installations" (*The Palestinian Dwelling in the Roman–Byzantine Period* [Jerusalem: Israel Exploration Society, 1995], 274).

regulations control the culinary and commensal interactions between these groups, as I will discuss further in Chapter 4, tannaitic regulations make allowances for interaction between the ḥabēr and the ʿam hāʾāreṣ in the sphere of domestic baking. In each of these encounters, the actions of women are described and prescribed with direct reference to how they affect male practice. "The woman baking in her own home was not always alone,"[57] as her domestic baking both produces bread and (re)produces male identity. It is for these reasons that the Tannaim seek to exert control over women in the tannaitic kitchen.

Preparing Food as (Re)Producing Male Identity: Conclusions

Throughout this section, we have continually encountered texts in which the actions of female domestic cooks are discussed in direct reference to how they affect male practice. In this textual environment, the baking of bread is invested with cultural significance. Even though women retain the power of resource control in the domain of the domestic kitchen, their power is mitigated by the actions they must take to ensure their husbands' compliance with tannaitic notions of male Jewish identity.[58] In short, women become sous-chefs, whereas their tannaitic husbands become chefs.

Further, the actors in this domestic theater are not only women, but also Jewish women. Whether the wife of a ḥabēr, an ʿam hāʾāreṣ, or a rabbinic Jew, these kitchen encounters involve a cast of characters that does not include non-Jews. In contrast, cooking encounters between Jews and non-Jews in tannaitic literature involve, with one possible exception, men only. This observation is not entirely surprising, as tannaitic commensality regulations between Jews and non-Jews – and, indeed, the tannaitic corpus in general – tend to focus on interactions between

---

[57] Weingarten, "'Magiros,'" 292.
[58] One of my reviewers suggested that the example from *t. Demai* 4:31 (ed. Lieberman 1:84) cited above was an exception, as the man controls the yeast and spices. However, I would argue that the woman still possesses the power of resource control here, because the man must enter into her kitchen and use her equipment and physical labor. If the man had simply taken over the entire cooking process and kitchen domain, then this would be an exception. Once again, therefore, women are ceded (at least a modicum of) power via resource control, although this power is clearly mitigated.

Jewish males and non-Jews (usually male, although sometimes female).[59] Although women appear in prescriptive and descriptive texts concerned with culinary and commensal regulations between rabbinic and nonrabbinic Jews (often in the midst of scholastic discussions about purity), they do not appear in contexts in which the kitchen is shared with a non-Jew. In these interactions, a Jewish male is depicted as participating in the cooking process with a non-Jewish male.

Jews and non-Jews are not completely forbidden from cooking together, as previously demonstrated in Chapter 2. Rather, tannaitic regulations exhibit leniencies that allow for shared food preparation, as long as certain conditions are met. In general, these conditions involve a Jew controlling the situation by supervising the process in the role of the "chef." In this way, a Jew confers his status on the food item produced, so that that culinary item can play an appropriate part in his, or his fellow's, edible identity. It would appear, then, that only men play the role of the tannaitic "chef."

The shared kitchen between a Jew and a non-Jew is gendered as a male domain. When the slaughter of animals is involved, the absence of women may be due to the remnants of biblical sacrificial systems, which almost always – if not, in fact, always – excluded female participation. Perhaps because women either rarely or never participated in animal sacrifice – a cross-cultural phenomenon detected by Nancy Jay – then they do not, at least explicitly in tannaitic literature, participate in

---

[59] In fact, as we saw in Chapter 2, commensal encounters between Jewish men and non-Jewish women were often sexualized. Although the assumption in these texts is that non-Jewish women entice Jewish men into idolatry, they do not presume that non-Jewish men similarly entice Jewish women (e.g., *Sifre Numbers* 131 [ed. Horowitz 171]). However, in at least one non-food-related context, a rabbinical student does entice a woman (in this case, a prostitute) to renounce idolatry and convert to Judaism. See *Sifre Numbers* 115 (ed. Horowitz 128–129). Many scholars have written about this tale, including Shaye J. D. Cohen, *The Beginnings of Jewishness: Boundaries, Varieties, Uncertainties* (Berkeley and Los Angeles: University of California Press, 2000), 162–164; Alon Goshen-Gottstein, "The Commandment of *Tzitzit*, the Prostitute, and the Exegetical Story," in *Mahshevet Hazal*, ed. Tzvi Groner and Menahem Hirschman, 45–58 (Haifa, Israel: University of Haifa, 1990 [Hebrew]); Warren Harvey, "The Pupil, the Harlot, and the Fringe Benefits," *Prooftexts* 6 (1986): 259–271; and Michael L. Satlow, *Tasting the Dish: Rabbinic Rhetorics of Sexuality*, BJS 303 (Atlanta: Society of Biblical Literature, 1995), 164–166.

noncultic animal slaughter.[60] However, this accounts only for the extant evidence about meat. What about the nonmeat food items? The absence of women in this context (and in the previous one, as well) may be a result of the fact that women are often literary foils, appearing only to signify that the law is different in a particular circumstance. Thus, men represent the "normal" scenario.[61] This suggestion accords with the fact that, in tannaitic literature in general, non-Jews are often painted with a rather broad brush, whereas nonrabbinic Jews are painted more finely. Women appear in discussions of rabbinic and nonrabbinic Jews sharing the kitchen because, for the Tannaim, such scenarios require more careful consideration. This leads them to a more refined set of regulations.[62] Finally, the absence of women in both contexts accords with a general trend in tannaitic literature of paying attention to women only at times when they directly affect the lives of men.[63]

[60] See Nancy Jay, *Throughout Your Generations Forever: Sacrifice, Religion, and Paternity* (Chicago: University of Chicago Press, 1992). I return to Jay's gender theory later in this chapter. The two possible exceptions (of which I am aware) in texts from the Hebrew Bible to Jay's theory do not offer definitive counter-evidence. Leviticus 12:6 mentions the purification offering that a new mother must bring. However, even though a woman brings the offering, a male priest is the one who actually sacrifices it. Deuteronomy 16 includes women in lists of those who should celebrate pilgrimage festivals. However, women are never explicitly depicted therein as participating in the applicable sacrifices.

[61] This understanding may explain the one exception to the rule: the *baraita* on b. Avodah Zarah 38a–b.

[62] Chapter 4 details a further series of regulations that help to paint more finely the differences between rabbinic and nonrabbinic Jews. These rules share many commonalities with the ones discussed thus far with regard to women. In each instance, a group of people, who are legally Jewish, is parsed according to its practices. The primary difference between the nonrabbinic Jews discussed in Chapter 4 and the ones encountered here are the fact that the practices of the women treated in the preceding texts directly affect the status of male Tannaim. Nonrabbinic men and women are not necessarily fungible. Thus, for example, when we discuss the tannaitic reinterpretation of Jewish festivals, nonrabbinic men (and perhaps women, but that is a difficult subject, as we shall see later) can choose not to follow tannaitic prescription, and their decision will not necessarily have a direct impact on the identity status of a tannaitic Jew. But if a man's wife decides to ignore tannaitic food prescriptions when preparing his dinner, then the sous-chef has undermined both the chef and the entire system on which the tannaitic kitchen is based.

[63] For a list of tannaitic sources organized by topic, see Satlow, "Fictional Women," 233 n. 45; for a discussion, see Jacob Neusner, *The Mishnaic System of Women*, vol. 5, *A History of the Mishnaic Law of Women* (Leiden, the Netherlands: Brill, 1980). This same statement, *mutatis mutandis*, is probably equally valid with regard to Gentiles. In general, see Gary G. Porton, *Goyim: Gentiles and Israelites in Mishnah-Tosefta*, BJS 155 (Atlanta: Society of Biblical Literature, 1988).

WOMEN AT THE TANNAITIC TABLE?

Except for discussions of cooking, women are almost nowhere to be found in tannaitic discussions of commensality. Does this absence of evidence indicate an evidence of absence of women from the tannaitic table?

To clarify, I use the phrase "tannaitic table" throughout to refer to the discursive, rhetorical table at which the Tannaim depict commensality as occurring. In the social world in which these texts are composed, women and men may very well have eaten at the same table, at a separate table, or in different locations. Although Roman banquet custom indicates an increased allowance for respectable women dining with men, as discussed in Chapter 1, the tannaitic corpus is silent as to whether or not this Roman custom also reflects tannaitic practice. Further, there is no evidence that indicates whether women were included at the tannaitic table to the extent that they were at the early Christian table, where women's presence was "notable but not unique" in comparison to its milieu.[64] My main point in this section is that the Tannaim make no

---

[64] Dennis E. Smith, *From Symposium to Eucharist: The Banquet in the Early Christian World* (Minneapolis: Fortress Press, 2003), 208. However, when women appear at banquets in Greek and Roman texts, they are sometimes depicted as sitting (as opposed to reclining, like the men) or characterized as prostitutes. For references and discussion, see Kathleen E. Corley, *Private Women, Public Meals: Social Conflict in the Synoptic Tradition* (Peabody, MA: Hendrickson, 1993), 26–34; Matthew B. Roller, *Dining Posture in Ancient Rome: Bodies, Values, and Status* (Princeton, NJ: Princeton University Press, 2006), 96–156; Smith, *From Symposium to Eucharist*, 42–44, 208–209. For a careful (though, ultimately, more positivistic than my own) consideration of the nonrabbinic and rabbinic evidence for women at wedding banquets in the ancient Mediterranean, see Susan Marks, "Present and Absent: Women at Greco–Roman Wedding Meals," paper presented at the SBL Meals in the Greco–Roman World Seminar, Washington, DC, November 2006. Available online at www.philipharland.com/meals/2006%20Marks%20Paper.pdf.

Sexual innuendo perhaps underlies tannaitic texts regulating certain commensal interactions between men and women, a trend that may parallel this tradition (e.g., m. Ketubbot 5:9 [ed. Albeck 3:107; discussed previously]; t. Shabbat 1:14 [ed. Lieberman 2:3–4; discussed later]). Further, in the book of Judith, when Judith reclines in the presence of Holofernes, the scene is highly sexualized (12, especially 12:15–20). I leave aside the curious case of Philo's *Therapeutae/Therapeutrides* (*De Vita Contemplativa*), a text that scholars have approached from a variety of perspectives (e.g., Joan E. Taylor, *Jewish Women Philosophers of First-Century Alexandria: Philo's 'Therapeutae' Reconsidered* [New York: Oxford University Press, 2003]; Troels Engberg-Pederson, "Philo's *De Vita Contemplativa* as a Philosopher's Dream," *JSJ* 30 [1999]: 40–64). I also do not discuss the ambiguous evidence found in Paul (see Smith, *From Symposium to Eucharist*, 207–209).

explicit statements concerning the presence or absence of women in their contemporary mealtime reality. Women are not of direct interest to the Tannaim, whose literature is primarily concerned with the commensal practices of other men. Therefore, I understand the "tannaitic table" to be a literary construction – perhaps with some basis in reality.

Although the data are limited, a few texts possibly suggest that if women were present at these (real and imagined) tannaitic meals at all, their ability to participate in any meaningful way is seriously called into question. The important point to remember for the present study is that women are either ignored, exempt, or excluded from commensal encounters in tannaitic literature. In these prescriptive and descriptive texts, the "normative" identity constructed via commensality practices is that of a male Jew.

As we have already seen in Chapter 1, in literary representations the banquet begins by guests entering and being seated. According to *Sifre Deuteronomy* 249, the role of greeter at a tannaitic banquet is gendered as masculine:

"An Ammonite or a Moabite shall not enter into the assembly of Yhwh" [Deuteronomy 23:4]. Concerning men Scripture is speaking, but not women[65] – a male Ammonite but not a female Ammonite; a male Moabite but not a female Moabite, the words of R. Yehudah. The Sages[66] say: "'Because they did not meet you with bread and water' [Deuteronomy 23:5]. *Who goes out to meet [guests]? Men and not women.*"[67]

In the middle of a discussion about the applicability of the prohibition against Ammonites and Moabites entering into the congregation of Yhwh, a small piece of banquet ideology is revealed. Limiting the applicability of Deuteronomy's injunction to men (based on the masculine

---

[65] This line is in smaller print in Finkelstein's edition because it appears in the margin and is repetitive in light of its preceding sentence (R. Yehudah's statement). For a similar opinion regarding the applicability of this verse, see *m. Yevamot* 8:3 (ed. Albeck 3:42–43), which also understands this prohibition as referring only to men and, as such, allows Ammonite and Moabite women to enter into the assembly of Yhwh immediately. The fact that Deuteronomy uses the withholding of commensality as a reason for socially shunning a non-Israelite neighbor highlights the absence of identity-based commensality restrictions in the Hebrew Bible (in general, see David Moshe Freidenreich, Foreign Food: Restrictions on the Food of Members of Other Religions in Jewish, Christian, and Islamic Law [Ph.D. dissertation, Columbia University, 2006], 32–57).
[66] *b. Yevamot* 77a attributes this saying to R. Shimon.
[67] *Sifre Deuteronomy* 249 (ed. Finkelstein 277), emphasis added.

forms of the terms that appear in the Hebrew Bible), the Sages provide a social explanation for this grammar: men greet guests, not women. Although this does not prove the absence of women throughout the banquet, it certainly argues against a woman's ability to host such an event. Further, this passage highlights the fact that, from the very start, tannaitic commensal practices are about male identity.

Another mention in passing about women's presence (or lack thereof) at banquets comes from *t. Yom Tov* 4:10:

His minor son and daughter he brings with him to a house of mourning, a house of banqueting, or a house of rejoicing, in a place in which it is customary [to do so]. A man should not give [a portion] from his present [of food, provided by the host] to the son or daughter of the host, because of enmity.[68]

According to this text, only some places have the custom of allowing minor children (both male and female) to attend banquets.[69] It is most likely in these locales that a Tanna would have the opportunity to interact with, and give extra food to, the host's children. However, it is telling that the guest is told not to feed the children, perhaps assuming that they have not eaten the overabundance of food (after all, there are leftovers) enjoyed by the guest.[70] Either way, this text speaks only of minors; it tells us nothing about adults. Although we know that adult men can attend such events, this text does not indicate whether mature women may do so as well. The failure to address this matter is part of a larger tannaitic trend of primary concern for male practice and male identity.[71]

---

[68] *t. Yom Tov* 4:10 (ed. Lieberman 2:303). I understand this text as assuming a male as normative and hence render *ādām* "man" instead of the more common translation, "person." Lieberman suggests that this enmity refers to the host, who becomes angry due to embarrassment over his guest's diminished gift.

[69] *t. Demai* 3:7 (ed. Lieberman 1:74–75) mentions the presence of the son – but not the daughter – of a *ḥabēr* at a banquet of an *'am hā'āreṣ*. However, this text neither specifies the age of the son nor, most likely, offers a generalizable example, as this is a unique situation.

[70] On the social role of gifts in antiquity, see Paul Veyne, *Bread and Circuses: Historical Sociology and Political Pluralism*, trans. Brian Pearce (New York: Penguin Press, 1990). On the power dynamics of gift giving in tannaitic literature, see Gregg Elliot Gardner, Giving to the Poor in Early Rabbinic Judaism (Ph.D. dissertation, Princeton University, 2009).

[71] The presence of women, as well as children, may be glossed amid a discussion about determining the portions of food that various diners receive at the Sabbath table. *m. Shabbat* 23:2 (ed. Albeck 2:70) makes reference to a host casting his lot (to determine who receives which portion) "with his children and with the members of his household at

Evidence for women's presence at a house of mourning and one of feasting, mentioned in passing in *m. Ketubbot* 7:5, does not specify whether, if at all, they are participating in mixed- or separate-gender meals, simply stating, "He who makes his wife vow not to go to a house of mourning or a house of feasting – he sends her out [i.e., divorces her] and gives her her *kĕtûbbā*, because he locks [the door] before her." Rather, this text focuses on the effect that a husband's prohibitory vow has on the state of their marriage. As such, it does not necessarily provide evidence for the presence of females at the tannaitic table. Could this text refer to separate all-female meals?[72] Or mixed-gender commensality? Although the paucity of evidence allows only for speculation, the fact remains that this text implies that a husband who makes his wife vow not to attend either of these commensal events is making an unreasonable request. It therefore seems a logical conjecture that women at least attended such events. Once again, however, this text reflects more of an interest in reporting how women's actions affect men, rather than in women's practice in and of itself.

Women do not even appear in tannaitic discussions of the commensal encounter in which we usually expect to find them: the wedding banquet.

---

the table." This text clearly suggests the presence of children at the table, an occurrence that we have previously seen. However, does the phrase "members of his household" (*bĕnê bêtô*) imply that women are present at the tannaitic table? This seems to be Albeck's understanding of this passage in his commentary. Yet, the phrase could refer to servants and slaves, and perhaps other kin. Although this is a possibility, the extant evidence is ambiguous and perhaps prescriptive. Similarly, Ben Zoma's statement about the bad guest – who claims that all the food offered at the banquet by its host is "prepared to provide for the needs of his wife and children" (*t. Berakhot* 6:2 [ed. Lieberman 1:34]) – tells us only that a host (literally, "home-owner" or "master of the household") provides food for his dependents; we do not learn whether or not they are present at this meal. Although the presence of wife and children at the table may prompt this remark, which would be in line with symposium literary conventions, I am unconvinced that their presence is in any way necessarily implied in Ben Zoma's statement. On the Greek and Roman parallels to this tradition, see Henry A. Fischel, "The Midrash of Ben Zoma and Ben Zoma in the Midrash," in *Rabbinic Literature and Greco–Roman Philosophy: A Study of Epicurea and Rhetorica in Early Midrashic Writings*, 51–89 (Leiden, the Netherlands: Brill, 1973).

[72] *m. Ketubbot* 7:5 (ed. Albeck 3:111–112). There is at least one Roman tradition of an all-female banquet: the festival of the "Good Goddess" (*Bona Dea*). On this festival, see H. H. J. Brouwer, *Bona Dea: The Sources and a Description of the Cult* (New York: Brill, 1989); Ross Shepard Kraemer, *Her Share of the Blessings: Women's Religions Among Pagans, Jews, and Christians in the Greco–Roman World* (New York: Oxford University Press, 1992), 52–55.

JEWISH MALE IDENTITY 127

The presence of women at the wedding banquet would not be a tannaitic innovation, as Greek and Roman texts attest to a similar phenomenon.[73] Further, John 2:1–5 mentions a wedding feast at which both Jesus and his mother were present.[74] Although women's presence at a wedding banquet is nowhere explicitly mentioned in tannaitic literature,[75] it would not be odd, given the extrarabbinic evidence for this phenomenon in both Jewish and non-Jewish sources. Despite the common tannaitic parlance of a man making "a wedding banquet [*mišteh*] for his son,"[76] I am uncertain here whether the absence of evidence is necessarily evidence of absence.[77] Rather, this seems in line with a trend in tannaitic literature of ignoring the presence (or absence) of women at a meal and focusing instead on how commensal practices construct a specifically male identity.

The remaining evidence for the presence of women at meals is, at best, ambiguous. For example, *m. Ketubbot* 5:9 mentions that a wife may eat with her husband on the night of the Sabbath. However, this passage refers only to one day of the week and only to a peculiar case, in which a husband maintains his wife via a third party.[78] The extent to which one can generalize from this terse comment is uncertain. It is unclear

---

[73] For a discussion, including references, see Smith, *From Symposium to Eucharist*, 39–40.
[74] Women do not explicitly appear in other ancient, nonrabbinic texts that mention wedding banquets (e.g., Tobit 7–10; *Joseph and Aseneth*, 21:6; Josephus, *Jewish Antiquities*, 5:289). On the uncertain religious identity of the author of *Joseph and Aseneth*, see Ross Shepard Kraemer, *When Aseneth Met Joseph: A Late Antique Tale of the Biblical Patriarch and His Egyptian Wife, Reconsidered* (New York: Oxford University Press, 1998), 245–285.
[75] It is possibly implied in *t. Berakhot* 4:19 (ed. Lieberman 1:24–25), which discusses rules about grace after meals for men who leave (presumably) a wedding banquet to escort the bride (presumably) to the banquet. See also the enigmatic reference on *m. Pesahim* 7:13 (ed. Albeck 2:168), in which a bride is described as turning her face away while she eats at Passover.
[76] E.g., *t. Shabbat* 7:9 (ed. Lieberman 2:26); *m. Hallah* 2:7 (ed. Lieberman 2:7; = *Sifre Numbers* 110 [ed. Horowitz 115]). For additional references, see Satlow, *Jewish Marriage*, 339–340 n. 107. An inscription from the synagogue at Ḥorbat Susiya (southern Palestine) mentions a rabbi making a donation vow at the feast (*mišteh*) of his son. This mosaic inscription, which is roughly contemporary to the Tannaitic period, provides extrarabbinic evidence for both this event and this terminology. On this inscription, see Joseph Naveh, *On Stone and Mosaic: The Aramaic and Hebrew Inscriptions from Ancient Synagogues* (Jerusalem: Karta, 1978 [Hebrew]), no. 75 (pp. 115–116); Satlow, *Jewish Marriage*, 179–180.
[77] For a cautious consideration of the evidence for women at wedding banquets in the ancient Mediterranean, see Marks, "Present and Absent."
[78] *m. Ketubbot* 5:9 (ed. Albeck 3:107). See also *m. Ketubbot* 5:8 (ed. Albeck 3:106–107). For a discussion, see Wegner, *Chattel or Person?*, 74–75.

whether this text implies that all husbands and wives eat together only on the Sabbath or if this is simply a sexual innuendo, referring to conjugal relations[79] and not to commensality.

Another ambiguous datum is provided by texts that exclude women from certain commensality regulations. For example, are women assumed to be present at a meal based on the fact that a text speaks of their inability to count toward the prayer quorum necessary for reciting grace after meals?[80] And, does the fact that women (as well as slaves and minors) cannot constitute a table-fellowship association (ḥăbûrāh) for the Passover necessarily dismiss them entirely from the table?[81] The context of the first passage, at least, suggests that women were likely present at such meals. However, the Tannaim are concerned with establishing how their commensal practices construct male Jewish identity, and so the pertinent data (from our perspective) on women are not necessarily provided.

Further evidence for exclusion of women from the Passover ḥăbûrāh is found in *t. Pisha* 8:6, which states, "*They do not make an association [consisting] of women, slaves, and/or minors, so as not to increase indecency.*"[82] Discussing the meaning of this deceptively simple passage, Wegner notes:

The Babylonian rabbis (B. Pes. 91a) and Maimonides (*Mishneh Torah: Laws of Passover Sacrifice*) interprets the Mishnah [*m. Pesachim* 8:7; = *t. Pisha* 8:6] to forbid a fellowship of women and slaves combined or of children and slaves combined (for fear of various kinds of licentious conduct) but to permit a fellowship consisting of women alone. But the mishnaic text is distinctly ambiguous, and we must be circumspect in relying on later interpretations of the original meaning of an earlier text.[83]

---

[79] See Wegner, *Chattel or Person?*, 75. For more references about the innuendo of the Sabbath meal and conjugal relations, see R. Kraemer, *Her Share*, 227 n. 47. The Sabbath table is the setting for another text that possibly implies the presence of women in a mixed-gender commensal context (*m. Shabbat* 23:2 [ed. Albeck 2:70], discussed previously).

[80] *m. Berakhot* 7:2 (ed. Albeck 1:27).

[81] *m. Pesahim* 8:7 (ed. Albeck 2:171). I discuss this passage – and the concept of Passover table-fellowship associations – in more detail in Chapter 4.

[82] *t. Pisha* 8:6 (ed. Lieberman 2:185). The words in italics also appear in *m. Pesahim* 8:7 (ed. Albeck 2:171).

[83] *Chattel or Person?*, 239 n. 217. For an argument that supports the traditional view, albeit through the lens of modern feminist interpretation of rabbinic sources, see Judith Hauptman, "Women in Tractate *Pesahim*," in *Atara L'Haim: Studies in the Talmud*

Although Wegner is correct to point out the ambiguity of this passage, the fact remains that women, slaves, and minors are, in some fashion, excluded from participating in Passover associations. Whether this meant that women could join a Passover fellowship consisting of men or only women, women (as well as slaves and minors) are still somehow categorically excluded. Men, on the other hand, are not subject to an analogous proscription. Although I prefer the reading that these three classes of people are generally excluded from participation, the other possible reading – that this refers to combinations of these categories – still indicates a social exclusion from tannaitic commensal practice. Further, the previously cited texts often group women with minors and slaves. Male minors grow up and become men and male slaves can, potentially, become free men. Women (and female minors and slaves), however, have no chance to cross that boundary. Therefore, women are particularly excluded from the Passover table, the physical location where the Tannaim reenact the Exodus from Egypt.

Passover table customs not only connect the Tannaim to the mythical past, but they also echo Temple sacrifice and establish fictive kinship with those who eat the meal together in "one house."[84] Unrelated males, as we shall see further in Chapter 4, come together at the Passover table and, via prescribed commensal practices, construct a Jewish, male, rabbinic

and *Medieval Rabbinic Literature in Honor of Professor Haim Zalman Dimitrovsky*, ed. Daniel Boyarin, Shamma Friedman, Marc Hirshman, Menahem Schmelzer, and Israel M. Tashma, 63–78 (Jerusalem: Magnes Press, 2000 [Hebrew]), 75–77; Judith Hauptman, "From the Kitchen to the Dining Room: Women and Ritual Activities in Tractate *Pesahim*," in *A Feminist Commentary on the Babylonian Talmud: Introduction and Studies*, ed. Tal Ilan, Tamara Or, Dorothea M. Salzer, Christiane Steuer, and Irina Wandrey, 109–126 (Tübingen, Germany: Mohr Siebeck, 2007), 122–124. In contrast to Hauptman, Marjorie Lehman argues that the ambiguous and seemingly conflicting *halakhic* opinions about women and Passover are indicative of the quandary that the Tannaim found themselves in when they tried to reconcile the domestic ritual aspects of Passover with their desired social order. See Marjorie Lehman, "Women and Passover Observance: Reconsidering Gender in the Study of Rabbinic Texts," in *Women and Judaism: Studies in Jewish Civilization 14*, ed. Leonard J. Greenspoon, Ronald A. Simkins, and Jean Axelrad Cahan, 45–66 (Omaha, NE: Creighton University Press, 2003), 50–53, especially pp. 52–53.

[84] This is interesting in light of Baker's work on how the rabbinic notion of a "house" itself is gendered, becoming "a cultural discourse about (among other things) control, order, and disorder" (*Rebuilding the House*, 42). On the connection between eating the Passover meal in "one association" and in "one house," see *t. Pisha* 6:11 (ed. Lieberman 2:175). In Chapter 4, I comment on this text and discuss further how commensal practices at the tannaitic Passover *seder* construct identity.

identity. If the association is the house, and the house is the family, then perhaps by transitive logic, the association is the family. If this principle is (even unintentionally) in operation, then the work of Nancy Jay sheds light on this pericope. Jay seeks to explain why "[i]t is a common feature of unrelated traditions that only adult males – fathers, real and metaphorical – may perform sacrifice."[85] She concludes that the patrilineal fictive kinship commonly associated with sacrificial cults "remedies having-been-born-of-woman, establishing bonds of intergenerational continuity between males that transcend their absolute dependence on childbearing women."[86] Tannaitic literature, by attempting to replicate biblical sacrificial systems on a one-to-one scale, can also be understood via Jay's methodological framework. In light of this understanding, one could suggest that, by interpreting "one house" to mean "one association," tannaitic literature builds a fictive familial relationship via tablefellowship. The role that women play in this fictive kinship is, at best, uncertain. Much as in sacrifice, then, tannaitic practices at the Passover table exclude women from their emerging identity construction.

Tannaitic discussions about the festival of Sukkot (Tabernacles) provide yet another possible example of the exclusion of women from commensality practices. The Tannaim understand the biblical commandment in Leviticus 23:42 to "dwell" in booths for Sukkot as referring to the manner in which one dwells in a house, which specifically includes eating therein.[87] However, according to *m. Sukkah* 2:8:

Women, slaves, and minors are exempt from [the religious obligation to dwell in] the *sûkkāh* [booth]. A minor who does not need his mother [to take care of him] is obligated with regard to [dwelling in] the *sûkkāh*. It once

---

[85] *Throughout Your Generations Forever*, xxiii.
[86] *Throughout Your Generations Forever*, 147.
[87] *Sifra Emor* 17:5 (ed. Weiss 103a). Compare *t. Sotah* 3:10 (ed. Lieberman 4:161–162), which states, in regard to the people of the Tower of Babel, that "dwelling refers only to eating and drinking." On the connection between eating and Sukkot, see also *Sifra Emor* 12:4 (ed. Weiss 102a), which states, "And with what do you sanctify the day [of Sukkot]? With eating, drinking, and nice [literally, 'clean'] clothes." The same statement is made in regard to sanctifying Passover (*Mekilta d'Rabbi Ishmael Pisha Bo* 9 [ed. Horowitz 30:1–4]; = *Mekilta d'Rabbi Shimon b. Yohai* at Exodus 12:16 [ed. Epstein and Melamed 18:18–20]) and to honoring one's father and mother (*Mekilta d'Rabbi Ishmael Bahodesh Yitro* 8 [ed. Horowitz 231:6–7]). On the history of Sukkot in biblical and rabbinic sources, see Jeffrey L. Rubenstein, *The History of Sukkot in the Second Temple Period and Rabbinic Periods*, BJS 302 (Atlanta: Scholars Press, 1995).

happened that the daughter-in-law of Shammai the Elder gave birth and he broke away some of the plaster [covering the ceiling] and covered [the hole] with *sûkkāh*-roofing [*sīkkēk*][88] over [its] bed on account of the infant.

Exempting women, slaves, and minors from the commandment to dwell in the *sûkkāh* logically also exempts them from participation in Sukkot meals; if dwelling means eating, then an exemption from one is also an exemption from the other. Although an exemption does not necessarily equate to an exclusion, it seems significant to me that the Tannaim exempt women, slaves, and minors from the very obligation that is central to their reinterpretation of the festival of Sukkot itself.[89] Although the story about Shammai the Elder's actions provides some contradiction about the application of this statement to minors,[90] the status of women and slaves is never questioned. Women, unable to switch status as male slaves (under certain circumstances) can, are therefore seemingly excluded by exemption from commensal practice by tannaitic prescription. Although they literally dwell in the house for the duration of the year, they do not "dwell" in the house for the purposes of fulfilling the Sukkot commandment, as interpreted by the Tannaim.[91] As we have seen previously, and we will see again in Chapter 4, the Tannaim use a ritual remembrance of an imagined collective past to negotiate and order their contemporary world via commensal practices.[92]

---

[88] *m. Sukkah* 2:8 (ed. Albeck 2:265). For a discussion of *sûkkāh*-roofing, see Rubenstein, *History of Sukkot*, 203–216.

[89] On the tannaitic reinterpretation of Sukkot, see Chapter 4. Marjorie Lehman has written about the exemption/exclusion of women in the *sûkkāh*, with particular regard to texts from the Babylonian Talmud. See Marjorie Lehman, "The Gendered Rhetoric of Sukkah Observance," *JQR* 96/3 (2006): 309–335, especially pp. 333–335. In the 1970s and 1980s, the Conservative movement in America justified counting women in prayer quorums and ordaining female rabbis based on this passage and others, which exempt – but not prohibit – women from these obligations. For a brief discussion, see Michael L. Satlow, *Creating Judaism: History, Tradition, Practice* (New York: Columbia University Press, 2006), 48–49.

[90] Rubenstein believes that Shammai the Elder's actions – which directly contradict the previous statement in the Mishnah – are historically reliable, "since no motive for fabrication exists" (*History of Sukkot*, 206 n. 92).

[91] For amoraic interpretations of "dwelling" in the *sûkkāh*, see Lehman, "Gendered Rhetoric."

[92] Or, in the words of Lehman, "the experience of sukkah may not only be about remembering an uncertain past. It is also an expression of the rabbis' present-day struggles" ("Gendered Rhetoric," 334).

Finally, as we have already discussed, tannaitic table talk revolves around "words of Torah" – an activity gendered as male.[93] Adding to this identification between masculinity and Torah study is the fact that rabbinically ordained Torah study replaces biblically ordained animal sacrifice. This association further removes women from the picture, as tannaitic literature depicts both the sacrificial (following most, if not all, texts from the Hebrew Bible) and the pedagogical table as the domain of men. Once again, Nancy Jay's gender critique of sacrifice sheds light on this translation from a biblical to a rabbinic context. Women rarely, if ever, sacrifice in the Hebrew Bible; therefore – so it would seem – they are not depicted slaughtering meat, belonging to the "one house" on Passover, or participating in Torah study at the tannaitic table.

The difficulty in locating women at the tannaitic table results from the fact that this corpus reflects an interest primarily in how commensal practices construct a Jewish, male identity. Even when women do appear at the table, their ability to participate in the same manner as Jewish men comes into question. Once again, the table serves as a locus for identity negotiation, an arena in which tannaitic commensal practices demarcate an "Us" and a "Them." As further proof of this claim, I turn now to a specific case: the regulation about male and female *zābîm* eating together.

"It Leads to Transgression": Commensality Among Zābîm

The term *zābîm* (singular: *zāb* [m], *zābâ* [f]) refers to "[g]enital discharges unconnected to seminal emission, menstruation, and parturition."[94]

---

[93] In general, see Michael L. Satlow, "'Try to Be a Man': The Rabbinic Construction of Masculinity," *HTR* 89/1 (1996): 19–40.

[94] Saul M. Olyan, *Rites and Rank: Hierarchy in the Biblical Representations of Cult* (Princeton, NJ: Princeton University Press, 2000), 42. In general, see David P. Wright and Richard N. Jones, "Discharge," in *ABD*, ed. David Noel Freedman, 2:204–207, 6 vols. (New York: Doubleday, 1992), 205–206. Although this term is often translated "gonorrhea," this is not the preferred translation. As Wright and Jones note, "though gonorrhea is a major cause of urethral discharge, it is not the only cause. Consequently translation of Hebrew *zāb* as 'gonorrheic' should be avoided" ("Discharge," 205). According to *t. Megillah* 1:14 (ed. Lieberman 2:346), the only difference between a *zāb* and a *zābâ* is in regard to the purification ritual required to become pure again. Further, some texts suggest that non-Jews defile like *zābîm*. For a discussion, see Christine E. Hayes, *Gentile Impurities and Jewish Identities: Intermarriage and Conversion from the Bible to the Talmud* (New York: Oxford University Press, 2002), 122–131. It should be pointed out, however, that these texts do not explicitly connect this purity

According to several texts in the Hebrew Bible, those suffering from this medical condition are impure and must be separated, to a greater or lesser degree, from the community.[95] Tannaitic literature imagines – perhaps purely scholastically – the possibility of male and female *zābîm*,[96] almost certainly in social isolation from others, eating a meal together:

Said R. Shimon ben Lazar:[97] "Come and see how far [the keeping of cultic] purity has spread. For the ancients did not decree, saying 'a pure man should not eat with a menstruating woman'; for the ancients did not eat with menstruating women. But they did say: '*A* zāb *should not eat with a* zābâ *because it leads to transgression.*'"[98]

A pure man and an impure woman cannot eat together because of purity regulations.[99] Hence, there is no need for an additional regulation specifically prohibiting such an occurrence. *Zābîm*, on the other hand, present a difficulty. Because both are already impure, one could imagine them breaking bread together. Therefore, the Mishnah must explicitly prohibit such a commensal encounter.

The reason given for this prohibition – "because it leads to transgression" – is suggestive. The context implies that the type of "transgression" that this meal leads to is a sexual one. While the very nature of the category of *zāb/zābâ* is sexual, in that it involves discharge from the sexual organs, one could read a bit more into this tannaitic rationale. In line with a cross-cultural trend, commensality between the opposite sexes is often imagined as an erotic event.[100] A commensal encounter between

---

issue to culinary or commensal concerns. This observation supports my argument, discussed further in Chapter 4, that purity issues appear only in tannaitic discussions about commensality between rabbinic and nonrabbinic Jews.

[95] E.g., Leviticus 15; Numbers 5:2–3.

[96] I follow the Hebrew grammatical convention of referring to men and women together by using the masculine form of a noun. The feminine plural is *zābôt*.

[97] Several manuscripts attest the name "Elazar," which also appears in a *baraita* of this tradition (*b. Shabbat* 13a).

[98] *t. Shabbat* 1:14 (ed. Lieberman 2:3–4). The words in italics also appear in *m. Shabbat* 1:3 (ed. Albeck 2:18). According to *Mekilta d'Rabbi Shimon b. Yohai* at Exodus 13:22 (cd. Epstein and Melamed 47–48), the "pillar of cloud by day and the pillar of fire by night" mentioned in Exodus 13:22 make a division between *zābîm* and *zābôt*.

[99] The extent to which a pure man and a pure woman, at least in public, could eat together is up for debate, as I discuss earlier in this chapter.

[100] For example, there is a cross-cultural connection between appropriate meal partners and appropriate marriage partners. As Hasia R. Diner states: "Put bluntly, the person with whom one cannot eat (and whose food cannot be consumed) is often the same

two people – already sexualized because of their medical condition – is thus envisioned as one step too many down the slippery slope that leads to illicit sexuality. The association between intergender commensality and sexual transgression was encountered previously in Chapter 2, in which eating with Gentile women is envisioned as a seductive enterprise, leading down a slippery slope to idolatry.[101] Because non-Jews were the issue in that context, the Tannaim were ultimately concerned there with idolatry, a subject that – although not unprecedented – rarely appears in discussions about interactions with Jews. Here, therefore, the Tannaim are concerned primarily with the issue of sexual transgression.

Further, it is interesting to find a text that understands men and women eating together as a social practice that results in sexual transgression. Does this logic perhaps explain the absence of women from depictions of tannaitic commensality in general? Even if this is an isolated or scholastic event, this connection is another example of a persuasive rhetoric preventing a commensal encounter.

The previous text suggests that even (or perhaps especially) while one is socially isolated due to his or her status as a *zāb/zābâ*, the rules of social decorum at the table remain in place. This logic further underlies the immediately adjoining text in Tosefta: "For the House of Shammai says: 'A *zāb* who is a Pharisee shall not eat with a *zāb* who is an *'am hā'āreṣ.*' But the House of Hillel permits it."[102] Although the House of Hillel is almost always the victor in these debates, this regulation appears to be one of the later additions to a series of laws promulgated at a conclave wherein the rulings of the House of Shammai were preferred to those of the House of Hillel.[103] As such, the context implies that the opinion of

---

person with whom sexual relations must be avoided" (*Hungering for America: Italian, Irish, and Jewish Foodways in the Age of Migration* [Cambridge, MA: Harvard University Press, 2001], 4; see also Douglas, "Deciphering a Meal," 45). This connection plays itself out in a variety of ways: for example, many languages linguistically connect these two appetites, using the same verb for eating and copulating. For a list of various languages, see Jeremy MacClancy, *Consuming Culture: Why You Eat What You Eat* (New York: Henry Holt, 1993), 70–71. See also Goody, *Cooking, Cuisine and Class*, 114.

[101] E.g., *Mekilta d'Rabbi Shimon b. Yohai* at Exodus 34:17 (ed. Epstein and Melamed 222); *Sifre Numbers* 131 (ed. Horowitz 171).

[102] *t. Shabbat* 1:15 (ed. Lieberman 2:4). For a discussion of how this text is understood in the Palestinian Talmud, see Oppenheimer, *'Am ha-Aretz*, 156–157.

[103] These rulings, traditionally known as the "Eighteen Decrees," begin in the immediately following verse in Tosefta (*t. Shabbat* 1:16–23 [ed. Lieberman 2:4–6]; *m. Shabbat* 1:4–11 [ed. Albeck 2:19–21]). For an historical discussion about the Eighteen Decrees, see Freidenreich, *Foreign Food*, 215–223.

the House of Shammai is here preferred. Whether this is the majority or minority opinion, however, we encounter an instance in which the social status quo of separation at the table is assumed to remain in place even while one is a *zāb* or *zābâ*.[104]

Commensality among *zābîm*, although rarely discussed in tannaitic literature, seems to parallel commensality among those who are not *zābîm*. The extant evidence therefore suggests that at least some of the social mechanisms for group identity formation of permitted and prohibited table-fellowship operate on both sides of the purity spectrum.[105] Because *zābîm* are most likely socially isolated only for a limited extent of time, they must conform to commensal norms to maintain their status as "proper" tannaitic Jews; therefore, a *zāb* and a *zābâ* must not engage in commensality. In short, if "you" do not eat together while pure, then "you" do not eat together while impure.

JEWISH MALE IDENTITY: CONCLUSIONS

Tannaitic culinary and commensal practices construct a Jewish, male identity. Although women are excluded from this identity, they sometimes appear in these texts to play a literary role. Thus, even in instances in which women are encountered, their presence is often rhetorical, elucidating the social and legal effects of certain culinary and commensal practices on tannaitic men.[106] When a woman is depicted as grinding

---

[104] *b. Shabbat* 13a also understands this regulation as relating to social separation. I discuss the subject of social separation at the table from an *'am hā'āreṣ* in Chapter 4.

[105] There is a dispute in *m. Berakhot* 3:6 (ed. Albeck 1:20) over whether or not a *zāb* who had a genital discharge requires ritual immersion before reciting the *šěma'* (a central rabbinic prayer that is comprised of biblical quotes; see Deuteronomy 6:4–9). In context, this may also specifically refer to the blessings before and after meals (see the earlier discussion in *m. Berakhot* 3:4 [ed. Albeck 1:19]).

[106] Although it is pure speculation, I wonder whether, in the utopian rabbinic world, men would not engage in commensality with women. A possible analog to this hypothetical question is the manner in which women are removed from participation in the (re)production of Torah scholars. As Howard Eilberg-Schwartz notes, "But in the rabbinic form of reproduction women were altogether dispensable. Males could now reproduce homosexually. If husbands inseminated women, sages disseminated Torah to their male students" (*The Savage in Judaism: An Anthropology of Israelite Religion and Ancient Judaism* [Bloomington and Indianapolis: Indiana University Press, 1990], 233). Further, even though a woman ushers a child into this world, it is only through establishing a fictive kinship with one's teacher (rabbi, from the Hebrew root meaning "to multiply/make many") that one may enter into the World to Come. See Eilberg-Schwartz, *Savage in Judaism*, 231–232.

grain or picking up a rolling pin, we must wonder whether that woman is producing bread or (re)producing male identity (or, most likely, both); when a text contains a discussion about, or alludes to, the presence or absence of women at or from the tannaitic table, we must wonder whether this is descriptive or prescriptive. In short, after surveying the data concerning women preparing food with other (almost always Jewish) women and women at the tannaitic table, I find significant evidence to suggest that women appear in commensal encounters in this corpus only when their actions are of interest, often merely scholastically, to informing how various social practices construct a Jewish, male identity.

Throughout, I argued that the Tannaim used a variety of culinary and commensal regulations to counteract the power of resource control available to women in the tannaitic kitchen. In an analog to rabbinic legislation concerning menstrual purity, as well as to several cross-cultural studies of gender, women must willingly comply with these rules; otherwise, the system collapses on itself.

Even with the imposition of these rules, though, the Tannaim create leniencies allowing for the economic necessity of shared cooking. However, the limits that they set on these processes provide information about how these regulations conform to their notion of edible identity. For example, the *ḥabēr* and the *'am hā'āreṣ* may sift, winnow, and grind grain together. But after water is added to the flour, the cultural transformation of the flour into dough has begun, thus requiring social separation. In this example, purity and food regulations intersect, another trend encountered in this chapter. This chapter has demonstrated that when these two sets of legislation cross paths and women are involved, the women are almost invariably Jews, rabbinic or otherwise.

Finally, after investigating the scant evidence for women's presence at the discursive site of the tannaitic table, the ambiguous nature of these data made it difficult to reach a solid conclusion about the presence or absence of women at or from the tannaitic table. For example, even though many texts exempted women from table-based practices, it is not necessarily clear whether an exemption is tantamount to an exclusion. Although these terms are not exact equivalents, I conclude that the exemption of women from the very commensal practices around which the Tannaim base their reinterpretation of festivals, for example, is not insignificant. Further, using the insights of Nancy Jay, the tannaitic attempt to translate the biblical sacrificial system into a rabbinic table-based one suggests that women's presence at the ideal (if not the real) tannaitic table is, at best, problematic.

4

Jewish Male Rabbinic Identity

> The [European Jews'] encounter with food in America in the context of novelty and abundance also subverted a culture built around food taboos. Food, so central to the Judaic sacred system and the promise of America, got caught up in a complicated set of *internal* Jewish fights about class, immigrant status, religion, generation, and gender. Because they venerated food, and because so much about their food world changed in America, it became a locus of contestations and conflict.[1]

In the epigraph to this chapter, Hasia Diner discusses how various factors contribute to food becoming a "locus of contestations and conflict" between European Jews who immigrated to America. This is by no means a modern phenomenon.[2] Just as the Tannaim use culinary and commensal practices to establish distinct Jewish and male identities, so too did these practices serve to establish a Jewish, male, and rabbinic identity. In fact, the Tannaim devote more attention to parsing how their culinary and commensal practices distinguish themselves from other Jews than they do to any other "Other."

The Tannaim construct their Jewish, male, rabbinic identity in part by way of four food practices. First, they develop the notion that there is a distinctive cuisine that comprises the diet and foodway of (and, thus, marks the socially constructed identity of) a rabbinic Jew.[3] (Throughout

---

[1] Hasia R. Diner, *Hungering for America: Italian, Irish, and Jewish Foodways in the Age of Migration* (Cambridge, MA: Harvard University Press, 2001), 206, emphasis added.

[2] In general, see David Kraemer, *Jewish Eating and Identity Through the Ages* (New York: Routledge, 2007).

[3] I follow Warren Belasco's definition of cuisine: "I define a cuisine as a set of socially situated food behaviors with these components: a limited number of 'edible' foods

this book, the term "rabbinic Jew" refers to a Jew who chooses to follow the prescriptions of rabbinic Judaism, as opposed to a nonrabbinic Jew, who, although unquestionably Jewish even in the eyes of rabbinic Judaism, has chosen not to adhere to rabbinic practice.) Second, they greatly expand the role that purity plays in legislation regulating food consumption. Tannaitic Jewish culinary and commensal practices therefore distinguish rabbinic and nonrabbinic Jews from one another at the table via different purity requirements. Third, they once again draw an analogy between the status of food and the status of its cook. For this reason, food slaughtered or produced by a nonrabbinic Jew is often considered idolatrous simply because a nonrabbinic Jew served as its "chef." Fourth, festival rules are reinterpreted to exclude nonrabbinic Jews from the "proper" observance of these festivals, as defined by the Tannaim.

This chapter explores how these four tannaitic practices construct a Jewish, male, and distinctively rabbinic identity. Throughout, I keep in mind the fact that these texts affect only those who "buy into the system." As Pierre Bourdieu notes, "In accordance with the law that one only preaches to the converted, a critic can only 'influence' his readers insofar as they grant him his power because they are structurally attuned to him in their view of the social world, their tastes and their whole habitus."[4] Therefore, tannaitic prescriptive language is often just that:

(*selectivity*); a preference for particular ways of preparing food (*technique*); a distinctive flavor, textural, and visual characteristics (*aesthetics*); a set of rules for consuming food (*ritual*); and an organized system of producing and distributing the food (*infrastructure*). Embedded in these components are a set of ideas, images, and values (*ideology*) that can be 'read' just like any other cultural 'text'" ("Food and the Counterculture: A Story of Bread and Politics," in *The Cultural Politics of Food and Eating: A Reader*, ed. James L. Watson and Melissa L. Caldwell, 217–234 [Malden, MA: Blackwell Publishing, 2005], 219–220). For a more in-depth anthropological discussion of cuisine, see Peter Farb and George Armelagos, *Consuming Passions: The Anthropology of Eating* (Boston: Houghton Mifflin, 1980), 185–202.

[4] *Distinction: A Social Critique of the Judgment of Taste*, trans. Richard Nice (Cambridge, MA: Harvard University Press, 2002), 240; this quote appears almost verbatim in Pierre Bourdieu, *The Field of Cultural Production: Essays on Art and Literature*, ed. Randal Johnson (New York: Columbia University Press, 1993), 96. Further, see Loïc Wacquant's description of Pierre Bourdieu's concept of a field: "a field is a patterned system of objective forces (much in the manner of a magnetic field), a *relational configuration endowed with a specific gravity* which it imposes on all the objects and agents which enter in it" (Pierre Bourdieu and Loïc J. D. Wacquant, *An Invitation to Reflexive Sociology* [Chicago: University of Chicago Press, 1992], 17, emphasis in

"delineating the *ought* rather than the *is*; the *prescriptive* rather than the *descriptive*."[5] The persuasive and legal rhetorics of the Tannaim may be ineffective if a nonrabbinic Jew were to encounter them.

THE CUISINE OF THE RABBINIC JEW

Non-Jews eat the distinct cuisine of "Them." What happens to the status of Jews, however, when they too eat "Their" food? The Tannaim address this question in *t. Horayot* 1:5, which states:

> One [i.e., a Jew] who eats abominations – behold, this one is an apostate.[6] [This also applies to] the one who ate carrion and/or[7] *ṭerēfāh*, abominations or creeping things; the one who eats pork or drinks libation wine;[8] the one who desecrates the Sabbath; the one who stretches his foreskin [in order to

---

original). Tannaitic Jews are those subject to the tannaitic field's forces – to its proverbial magnetic pull. Nonrabbinic Jews, on the other hand, are outside this magnetic field and, as such, are not subject to the identity construction created via its magnetic attraction.

[5] Michael L. Satlow, *Creating Judaism: History, Tradition, Practice* (New York: Columbia University Press, 2006), 92, emphasis in original. Although Satlow's comment specifically refers to the Hebrew Bible, it applies equally to rabbinic literature.

[6] Both the term in Zuckermandel's manuscript (*mešûmād*) and the variant (*mûmār*) mean "apostate." According to Sacha Stern, "The apostate is called *mumar* (lit. 'converted') or *meshumad* (lit. 'destroyed'); both terms are interchangeable in the various recensions. Curiously, *mumar* and *meshumad* are nowhere mentioned in the *Mishna*. But the *mumar* enjoys a relatively well-defined Halakhic status in subsequent sources" (*Jewish Identity in Early Rabbinic Writings* [New York: Brill, 1994], 106). Perhaps noting the public nature of these – literally and figuratively – nonkosher acts (as they are presented in this and other texts), Marcus Jastrow offers as one possible translation for both terms, "*an open opponent of Jewish law*" (*A Dictionary of the Targumim, the Talmud Babli and Yerushalmi, and the Midrashic Literature* [New York: Judaica Press, 1996], 744 s.v. *mûmār*; 851 s.v. *mešûmād*, emphasis in original). However, the term "apostate" should not be interpreted in the Christian sense (i.e., as no longer in any way Christian or, in this case, Jewish). For example, after surveying the rabbinic attitudes toward the apostate, S. Stern compares the apostate to the convert, concluding: "However, the apostate differs from the convert in that the latter divests himself entirely from his original non-Jewish identity, whereas the apostate retains his basic identity as Israel, even though it is seldom referred to" (*Jewish Identity*, 109; the survey is found on pp. 106–109). The apostate, though not engaging in rabbinically approved practices, nevertheless remains – albeit tenuously – a Jew.

[7] The *waw* here could semantically mean either "and" or "or." As the result is the same if one were to eat either multiple categories of nonkosher food or only one of them, I render the *waw* as "and/or" to indicate that both options apply equally to this case. Each preceding "or" in this translation could equally have been rendered "and/or," but doing so would make this translation a bit too cumbersome.

[8] Several of these foods are equated elsewhere in tannaitic literature. See *m. Nedarim* 2:1 (ed. Albeck 3:149–150).

conceal his circumcision].⁹ R. Yosi b. R. Yehudah says: "Also the one who wears garments of mixed species."¹⁰ R. Shimon ben Elazar says: "Also the one who does something [prohibited] that his impulse does not desire."¹¹

In this text, apostates are explicitly identified based on their diet.¹² Although cuisine is not the only marker of early rabbinic identity, it accounts for the majority of the categories mentioned in this passage. Yet, these practices do not transform a Jew into a non-Jew; they simply mark one as a "bad" rabbinic Jew, but still a Jew nonetheless. I do not think that it is a coincidence that each of these actions can, and most do, occur in public. Whether being naked at the bathhouse or eating pork at a banquet, (male) identity is a visual social performance.¹³ What a Jew – or anyone, for that matter – ingests can therefore be understood as a public statement about one's relationship to a community.

Unlike the examples discussed in Chapter 2, Jews who eat the cuisine of the "Other" are not "Them"; they are still somehow part of "Us." Throughout this chapter, we will encounter rabbinic taxonomies that finely divide Jews into several categories of "internal others."¹⁴ This trend, which is a *leitmotif* of this chapter, perhaps explains the enigmatic rabbinic innovation of separating milk and meat.

Three times in the Hebrew Bible the following injunction appears: "Do not cook a kid in its mother's milk."¹⁵ With the notable exception

---

⁹ It is interesting to note that the pork taboo, the practice of circumcision, and the observance of the Sabbath are often noted as distinctively Jewish praxis (e.g., Petronius, *Fragmenta*, no. 37).

¹⁰ Wearing garments of mixed species (i.e., wool and linen) is prohibited in the Hebrew Bible (e.g., Leviticus 19:19; Deuteronomy 22:11).

¹¹ *t. Horayot* 1:5 (ed. Zuckermandel 474), emphasis added. For a discussion of the Babylonian Talmud's interpretation of this passage, see S. Stern, *Jewish Identity*, 106.

¹² Compare the food-based definition of at what point one becomes a "rebellious and incorrigible son" found in *m. Sanhedrin* 8:2 (ed. Albeck 4:195–196).

¹³ On rabbinic Jews at the bathhouse, see *m. Avodah Zarah* 3:4 (ed. Albeck 4:333). For a discussion, see Seth Schwartz, *Imperialism and Jewish Society 200 B.C.E.–640 C.E.* (Princeton, NJ: Princeton University Press, 2001), 165–174.

¹⁴ I take this phrase from Christine Hayes, "The 'Other' in Rabbinic Literature," in *The Cambridge Companion to the Talmud and Rabbinic Literature*, ed. Charlotte Elisheva Fonrobert and Martin S. Jaffee, 243–269 (New York: Cambridge University Press, 2007), 243, in which she defines "internal others" as "members of [a] group that would contest the group's identity or construct it in a different way." Of course, women also function as "internal others," as discussed in the previous chapter. On the social power of taxonomies in general, see Bourdieu, *Distinction*, 479–481.

¹⁵ Exodus 23:19; 34:26; Deuteronomy 14:21.

of rabbinic literature, all other extant Jewish sources that address this prohibition read it literally: do not cook a kid in milk provided by its mother.[16] In the Mishnah, however, we encounter a radical departure:

All meat is forbidden to be cooked in milk, except for the meat of fish and locusts. And it is forbidden to bring [meat] up on the table with cheese, except for the meat of fish and locusts. One who vows [to abstain] from [eating] meat, is permitted [to eat] the meat of fish and locusts. "Fowl goes up on the table with cheese, but it is not eaten," the words of the House of Shammai. But the House of Hillel says: "It does not go up, and it is not eaten." Said R. Yose: "This is one of the lenient [rulings] of the House of Shammai and the strict [rulings] of the House of Hillel."[17] Concerning what [type of] table did they speak? Concerning a table upon which one eats; but in regard to a table upon which one arranges [i.e., prepares] the cooking, one puts this beside that and does not scruple.[18]

For the first time, the biblical injunction against cooking a kid in its mother's milk is understood as referring not only to cooking *all* meat and milk together, but also to separating the two items at the table itself. The potential social repercussions of this tannaitic innovation are often missed. David Kraemer corrects this common error by clearly articulating the ramifications of the Tannaim's novel interpretation:

On a purely pragmatic level, if the milk-meat prohibition is an innovation, promulgated by the rabbis and accepted only by those who followed them, then this enactment will effectively have separated rabbinic from non-rabbinic Jews on significant occasions [when meat is most likely to have been eaten]. Presumably, non-rabbinic Jews continued to eat like pre-rabbinic Jews. That is, if they respected Jewish custom at all (and the evidence suggests that many did), they will have avoided the animals proscribed by the Torah. But thy [sic] needed have no concern for the mixing of meat and dairy. The small rabbinized population, by contrast, will have distinguished themselves from the general Jewish population by creating separation between meat and dairy. The new rabbinic prohibition, in other words, separated

---

[16] E.g., Philo, *De Virtutibus*, 143–144, in which, as one would expect, Philo offers an allegorical interpretation of this prohibition. For a general discussion, see D. Kraemer, *Jewish Eating*, 35–37.

[17] See *m. Eduyyot* 4:1; 5:2 (ed. Albeck 4:297, 304–305).

[18] *m. Hullin* 8:1 (ed. Albeck 5:137–138). For other tannaitic references to this principle, see *t. Hullin* 8:1–3 (ed. Zuckermandel 509); *t. Terumot* 8:16 (ed. Lieberman 1:153); *t. Makkot* 4:7 (ed. Zuckermandel 442).

Jew from Jew (at least on certain occasions) and set off rabbinic Jews as the keepers of what was then a more esoteric law.[19]

The upshot of this legislation is that an innovative practice serves to construct a distinct rabbinic cuisine, foodway, and identity. Kraemer further observes that this prohibition is a metaphor for rabbinic identity in general. Unlike in the previous example of *t. Horayot* 1:5, which cites carrion and pork among other prohibited foodstuffs, meat and milk are both permitted foods. The issue at hand is the mixing of these permitted foods, which is symbolic of social relations with nonrabbinic Jews. Jews who do not engage in rabbinic practices are nevertheless still Jews. However, by abstaining from these practices, they do not construct for themselves a rabbinic identity. To offer an anachronistic example, Jews who eat cheeseburgers nonetheless remain Jews; they are simply not rabbinic Jews. In this interpretation, rabbinic and nonrabbinic Jews are like milk and meat: best kept separate.[20]

Having established the connection between the consumption of rabbinic cuisine and the construction of rabbinic identity, we now turn to other tannaitic culinary and commensal practices that affect the formation of rabbinic identity.

PURITY AND COMMENSALITY

Recent studies have explored how rabbinic literature in general expands on biblical purity legislation in an attempt to construct a rabbinic identity.[21] The tannaitic data on commensality regulations add much to this discussion. Purity concerns appear in commensal encounters between rabbinic and nonrabbinic Jews, but not in contexts in which Jews and non-Jews interact, a trend also evidenced in Chapter 3.[22] Although

---

[19] *Jewish Eating*, 50.
[20] D. Kraemer, *Jewish Eating*, 51.
[21] E.g., Charlotte Elisheva Fonrobert, *Menstrual Purity: Rabbinic and Christian Reconstructions of Biblical Gender* (Stanford, CA: Stanford University Press, 2000); Christine E. Hayes, *Gentile Impurities and Jewish Identities: Intermarriage and Conversion from the Bible to the Talmud* (New York: Oxford University Press, 2002).
[22] Here I follow Hayes' argument, contra Gedaliah Alon (*Gentile Impurities*, 138–142; Gedaliah Alon, "The Levitical Uncleanliness of Gentiles," in *Jews, Judaism and the Classical World*, trans. I. Abrahams, 146–189 [Jerusalem: Magnes Press, 1977]).

"[t]annaitic sources of the first two centuries c.e. attest to a rabbinic principle of Gentile ritual impurity," this principle does not seem to affect tannaitic regulations concerning commensality with Gentiles.[23] For example, we do not find a purity discussion about commensality with Gentiles analogous to the ones concerning commensal relations between the *ḥabēr* and the *'am hā'āreṣ*.

This point is highly significant for the overarching methodology of this study. I argue that one must consider commensality regulations between first, Jews and non-Jews and second, rabbinic and nonrabbinic Jews separately to understand the role that commensality plays in tannaitic identity construction. By separating these commensality regulations in cross-cultural studies more generally, scholars are able to see whether different social mechanisms are deployed to create an edible identity. This methodological point is reinforced by studies of nationalism and nation building, processes in which purity often is an intrinsic component.[24] In the case of tannaitic literature, one of the most notable differences is that purity, and its concomitant rules and assumptions, affects only Jewish rabbinic identity construction. Purity regulations, another system that affects identity construction, do not govern commensality with Gentiles.

To leave the discussion here would result in a rather shallow analysis. Noting that purity concerns influence tannaitic commensality regulations regarding nonrabbinic Jews – but not Gentiles – is an observation that, if not probed deeper, provides more of an observation than an explanation. The question remains, then, how to account for this difference. For example, Hayes argues that the tensions about purity found in discussions of the *ḥabēr* and the *'am hā'āreṣ* can also be found in

---

[23] Hayes, *Gentile Impurities*, 142. Jonathan Klawans reaches a similar conclusion (*Impurity and Sin in Ancient Judaism* [New York: Oxford University Press, 2000], 134). In this context, S. Stern's notion of solipsism seems to be in operation (see *Jewish Identity*, 200–223). Although purity concerns do not inform tannaitic discussions about commensality with Gentiles, they may appear in Daniel and *Jubilees*, as noted (with caveats) in Chapter 2.

[24] For a synthetic summary with references, see Emiko Ohnuki-Tierney, *Rice as Self: Japanese Identities through Time* (Princeton, NJ: Princeton University Press, 1993), 131–132. For an interesting discussion of the connection between these social processes (including purity) and human biology, see Paul Rozin, Jonathan Haidt, Clark McCauley, and Sumio Imada, "Disgust: Preadaptation and the Cultural Evolution of a Food-Based Emotion," in *Food Preferences and Taste: Continuity and Change*, ed. Helen Macbeth, 65–82 (Providence, RI: Berghahn Books, 1997).

contexts pertaining to interactions with Gentiles, noting, "As was true of the *am ha'arets*, the Gentile's ignorance and/or lack of observance of the rules that govern the ritual and moral observance of a Jew means that the Jew must be on guard against unintentional violations in his interaction with a Gentile."[25] The same tensions therefore exist but are resolved in different manners. Rules concerning Gentiles often focus on idolatry, for example.[26] Concern for idolatry permeates discussions of interactions with Gentiles (social, economic, etc.), yet it is rarely a significant issue in regard to nonrabbinic Jews.[27] Following Hayes, I argue that tannaitic literature evidences concern for commensal interactions with both nonrabbinic Jews and non-Jews. In each case, these concerns connect to larger tensions vis-à-vis the specific group at hand. When the subject is nonrabbinic Jews, then purity is an applicable issue; on the other hand, when non-Jews are the subject, then idolatry is often the most applicable issue.

Further, as noted in Chapter 3, non-Jews are usually painted with a rather broad brush in tannaitic texts, while nonrabbinic Jews are painted with a more fine brush. Non-Jews, often perceived as idolaters and hence the binary opposite of Jewishness, are easier to dismiss than, for example, an *'am hā'āreṣ*. As Sacha Stern states, "But the ability of our sources to ignore the existence of other peoples, even their immediate neighbours, suggests their lack of interest towards non-Jewish ethnic diversity, which may be related to the assumption that all non-Jews are confused and blurred into a single, homogenous collectivity."[28] The broad label of idolatry therefore suffices to designate Gentiles as belonging to the category of the "Other." However, when nonrabbinic Jews – but Jews nonetheless – are the subject at hand, then a more nuanced discussion is seemingly required.

---

[25] Hayes, *Gentile Impurities*, 141.
[26] Hayes points as an example to three motivating reasons from the tractate *Avodah Zarah*: (1) idolatry; (2) concern for violating dietary laws; and (3) danger (*Gentile Impurities*, 141). Hayes' list overlaps somewhat with S. Stern's list of the three motivating factors for Jewish social dissociation with non-Jews in rabbinic literature in general: (1) personal safety; (2) avoidance of scriptural prohibitions; and (3) avoidance of idolatry (*Jewish Identity*, 155–159). I discuss the connection between idolatry and commensality with Gentiles in Chapter 2.
[27] Though rare, it is not unattested. For example, see *m. Gittin* 5:9 (ed. Albeck 3:289; cp. *m. Shevi'it* 5:9 [ed. Albeck 1:153–154]), discussed in Chapter 3.
[28] *Jewish Identity*, 15.

Identity construction, a fluid and constantly negotiated social process, occasionally draws on different blueprints and building materials depending on who is, or is not, involved in the process. Although practice is a key component of identity construction in each case, the specific practice varies depending on the category of people being discussed. To buttress my claim about the prevalence of purity concerns in tannaitic regulations concerning commensality with nonrabbinic Jews, I turn now to the case that I have continually cited: commensal interactions between the ḥabēr and the 'am hā'āreṣ.

Commensality between the Ḥabēr and the 'Am hā'Āreṣ

Like the Essenes, the Qumran sect, and other Second Temple-period Jewish groups mentioned in extant literature, according to tannaitic sources, the ḥabērîm ("associates") mark social separation from 'ammê hā'āreṣ (literally "the people of the land") through food rules.[29] Keeping in mind that "[t]able fellowship is synonymous with fellowship in all aspects of life,"[30] food regulations that either limit or prohibit commensality between ḥabērîm and 'ammê hā'āreṣ inherently create distinct identities, which are then mapped onto social intercourse with nonrabbinic Jews and rabbinic Jewish identity in general in tannaitic literature.[31] Although the subject of commensal relations between the ḥabēr and 'am hā'āreṣ

---

[29] For a brief summary of the Essenes and the Qumran sect, see Albert I. Baumgarten, *The Flourishing of Jewish Sects in the Maccabean Era: An Interpretation* (New York: Brill, 1997), 93–96. Dennis E. Smith compares both the term ḥabērîm and the structure of a ḥabûrāh to Greek and Roman dining clubs (*From Symposium to Eucharist: The Banquet in the Early Christian World* [Minneapolis: Fortress Press, 2003], 152). Further, it is telling that the so-called parting of the ways between Judaism and Christianity is often couched in terms of one's relationship to the food rules, a point also noted by Jean Soler ("The Semiotics of Food in the Bible," in *Food and Culture: A Reader*, ed. Carole Counihan and Penny van Esterik, 55–66 [New York: Routledge, 1997], 65). John Dominic Crossan expands on this point, arguing that Jesus creates a revolutionary social program at the table, which he labels "open commensality" (*The Historical Jesus: The Life of a Mediterranean Jewish Peasant* [San Francisco: Harper Collins, 1991], 341–344). For a critique of Crossan's approach, see Smith, *From Symposium to Eucharist*, 237–239.

[30] Gillian Feeley-Harnik, *The Lord's Table: The Meaning of Food in Early Judaism and Christianity* (Washington: Smithsonian Institution Press, 1994), 86.

[31] For a discussion of the 'am hā'āreṣ in the Palestinian Talmud, see Stuart S. Miller, *Sages and Commoners in Late Antique 'Ereẓ Israel: A Philological Inquiry into Local Traditions in Talmud Yerushalmi* (Tübingen, Germany: Mohr Siebeck, 2006), 301–338.

is in many ways an historical curiosity for the Tannaim, referring to an earlier "association" (*ḥăbûrāh*) tradition to which the Tannaim are to some extent heirs, "[n]evertheless, it contains many rules governing the production of food, preparations for its consumption, and even table etiquette, that seems designed to limit the range of Jews with whom rabbinic families might have common meals."[32] Further, as we have already seen (for example, with regard to "manna eaters"), to associate with a particular history or historical claim is itself a practice of identity construction.[33] As such, discussions on this subject can further elucidate the role that tannaitic commensality regulations play in rabbinic Jewish identity formation.[34]

An excellent example of this phenomenon is encountered in the tannaitic treatment of the categories of *ḥabēr* and *'am hā'āreṣ*. When seeking to define these terms, the Tannaim themselves use commensal actions to "inscribe the border lines":[35]

It once happened that Rabban Gamaliel the Elder married off his daughter to Shimon ben Netanel the priest and made an agreement with him [that this marriage is based] on the condition that she will not prepare food requiring conditions of cleanliness under his supervision.[36] Rabban Shimon

---

[32] Martin S. Jaffee, *Early Judaism: Religious Worlds of the First Judaic Millennium*, Second Edition (Bethesda: University Press of Maryland, 2006), 160. Although the immediate subject of Jaffee's statement is the Mishnah, his comment applies to tannaitic literature in general. I leave aside the issue of the Pharisees, "as doubts concerning the identification of the *haverim* and the Pharisees bedevil the effort to reach firm conclusions" about their commensality regulations (Baumgarten, *Flourishing of Jewish Sects*, 97; see also Jacob Neusner, "The Fellowship [חרובה] in the Second Jewish Commonwealth," *HTR* 53/2 [1960]: 125–142, 125). Further, the Pharisaic data do not add anything significantly different to the discussion at hand. For brief treatments of the Pharisaic data in rabbinic literature vis-à-vis the social ramifications of their food rules, see Baumgarten, *Flourishing of Jewish Sects*, 96–100; E. P. Sanders, *Judaism: Practice and Belief, 63 BCE–66 CE* (Philadelphia: Trinity Press, 1994), 431–437; Smith, *From Symposium to Eucharist*, 150–152. The fact that Pharisaic practice includes purity regulations regarding food is also attested in the New Testament (e.g., Mark 7:3–4; Luke 11:37–41; Matthew 23:25–26). For a concise historical survey of some of the eating scenes between Jesus and the Pharisees in the New Testament (with particular attention to Luke), see Anthony J. Saldarini, *Pharisees, Scribes and Sadducees in Palestinian Society: A Sociological Approach*, Second Edition (Grand Rapids, MI: William B. Eerdmans, 2001), 178–181.

[33] I thank one of the anonymous reviewers for helping me to sharpen this point.

[34] See Chapter 3 for questions relating to the food preparation and cooking process.

[35] Boyarin, *Border Lines*, 2.

[36] According to Aharon Oppenheimer, this passage indicates that "[s]ome Sages, it should be added, were themselves not scrupulous about purity and impurity" (*The 'Am ha-Aretz: A Study in the Social History of the Jewish People in the Hellenistic–Roman Period*,

ben Gamaliel says: "This is not necessary, since they do not force a *ḥabēr*[37] to prepare food requiring conditions of cleanliness under the supervision of an *'am hā'āreṣ*."[38] And who is an *'am hā'āreṣ*? "Anyone who does not eat his unconsecrated food in conditions of cultic cleanliness," the words of R. Meir. And the Sages say, "Anyone who does not properly tithe."[39]

Even though differing food regulations do not prevent this marriage from occurring, it is worth observing that these culinary differences necessitate both stipulation and negotiation prior to Rabban Gamliel the Elder's sanctioning of this union. Rather than getting bogged down in a technical discussion about this particular marriage, I would like to focus our attention on the fact that, according to R. Meir, the difference between a *ḥabēr* and an *'am hā'āreṣ* is in their approach to the importance of purity for food preparation.

It is interesting to note that R. Meir defines an *'am hā'āreṣ* in culinary terms when the pericope to which R. Meir's words are appended seems to suggest, following Aharon Oppenheimer, that not all rabbis adhere to R. Meir's orthopraxy. Since the designation of "*'am hā'āreṣ*" is pejorative in tannaitic literature – generally indicating an uneducated layperson[40] – this datum creates an ambiguity vis-à-vis this category and that of "normative" Tannaim. Perhaps this is because the term, despite the attempts

---

trans. Israel L. Levine [Leiden, the Netherlands: Brill, 1977], 223). For this reason, I do not consider the terms "*ḥabēr*" and "rabbi" to be synonymous.

[37] Neusner inserts here the following: "[who observes the rules of eating unconsecrated food in conditions of cultic cleanliness]" (*The Tosefta*, 6 vols. [New York and Hoboken, NJ: Ktav Publishing House, 1977–1986], 4:320). This reading makes sense in this context and is part of Neusner's larger argument regarding the Pharisees' extensions of purity laws to the ordinary table. For example, see Jacob Neusner, *From Politics to Piety: The Emergence of Pharisaic Judaism* (New York: Ktav Publishing House, 1979); or his more recent, "Mr. Sanders' Pharisees and Mine: A Response to E. P. Sanders, 'Jewish Law from Jesus to the Mishnah,'" *SJT* 44/1 (1991): 73–95, especially pp. 84–92. Also see Hannah K. Harrington, *The Impurity Systems of the Qumran and the Rabbis: Biblical Foundations*, SBLDS 143 (Atlanta: Scholars Press, 1993), 267–281; E. P. Sanders, *Jewish Law from Jesus to the Mishnah: Five Studies* (Philadelphia: Trinity Press International, 1990), 131–254.

[38] In addition to the obvious concerns regarding purity involved in this scenario, it would appear that Rabban Shimon ben Gamaliel (and perhaps Rabban Gamaliel the Elder, as well) takes issue with the possibility of an *'am hā'āreṣ* serving as a "chef," while a *ḥabēr* is a "sous-chef."

[39] *t. Avodah Zarah* 3:10 (ed. Zuckermandel 464), emphasis added. See also the parallel *baraitot* (*b. Berakhot* 47b; *b. Gittin* 61a); but, contrast the noncommensal definition attributed to R. Meir in a *baraita* on *b. Sotah* 22a.

[40] For example, see the *baraita* on *b. Sotah* 22a or *m. Avot* 3:10 (ed. Albeck 4:365–366).

by both R. Meir and the Sages in *t. Avodah Zarah* 3:10 to construct it as a legal category with a precise definition, is rather imprecise, serving as both the binary opposite of the category *ḥabēr* and of the category *talmīd ḥăkām* (the "Torah scholar" that is normative for the Tannaim). As this pericope suggests, although the antitheses of these categories have some similarities, the categories themselves are not always quite the same.[41]

This ambiguity, however, could also result from the fact that the Tannaim are attempting to both create and negotiate the boundaries between themselves and the *'ammê hā'āreṣ*. Between the seams of these texts – where identity is negotiated – the clear distinctions between one entity and another blur, often indicating, "a greater diversity of rabbinic behavior (and opinion?) than the rabbinic sources indicate."[42] Oppenheimer reaches this conclusion with regard to the *'ammê hā'āreṣ*, noting:

Numerous halakhot testify to the shunning of the 'ammei ha-aretz by haverim and to the taking of precautions by haverim in order not to come into contact with them. From these halakhot it might be inferred that there was an unbridgeable gulf between the haverim and the 'ammei ha-aretz. In point of fact, however, these halakhot express the opposite trend. For the desire to create a social gulf had no need of the scores of halakhot which laid down when and how the 'am ha-aretz was to be shunned. *Instead this could have been conveyed by means of a single, unambiguous halakhah proclaiming a general prohibition against all contacts and close relations with the 'ammei ha-aretz.* The many halakhot which set out in detail and minutely examine the problems relating to contacts with 'ammei ha-aretz and which declare when something is permitted and when prohibited in themselves testify that even as the haverim did not wish to separate themselves entirely from the normative community, as we have seen above, so they also did not want to estrange themselves completely from the 'ammei ha-aretz.[43]

Contrary to Oppenheimer, I do not consider the rabbis to represent the "normative community" for Jews, especially in the Tannaitic period. However, his point that the Tannaim did not shelter themselves completely from the outside world, including the *'ammê hā'āreṣ*, is correct. Although the Tannaim attempt to control their social environment, they

---

[41] See Oppenheimer's discussion, which examines the *'am hā'āreṣ* with regard to the *ḥabēr* and the *talmīd ḥăkām* in separate chapters (*'Am ha-Aretz*, 67–117 and 118–199, respectively).

[42] Schwartz, *Imperialism*, 174.

[43] *'Am ha-Aretz*, 161, emphasis added.

do not close themselves off entirely from either their nonrabbinic or non-Jewish neighbors. Similar to the rabbinic rhetoric of accommodation toward idolatry suggested by Seth Schwartz,[44] the tannaitic identity negotiation vis-à-vis the *'ammê hā'āreṣ* seeks ways to accommodate living side by side. The distinctions created are not always as crisp as the Tannaim perhaps would have liked, as the culinary practice-based definition of an *'am hā'āreṣ* indicates. However, they represent a tannaitic endeavor to address what appears to be both the social reality of *'ammê hā'āreṣ* and *ḥabērîm* living in the same environment and the economic necessity of interactions with one another. In short, these prescribed practices are an attempt to separate, while not existing completely separate.

Further evidence for the role that culinary and commensal practice plays in the tannaitic construction of a rabbinic identity is found in a brief summary of the code of conduct for *ḥabērîm* in *m. Demai* 2:3,[45] which includes the following:

He who accepts it upon himself to become a *ḥabēr* does not sell to an *'am hā'āreṣ* wet or dry [produce],[46] and does not purchase from him wet [produce], and does not accept the hospitality [*mit'āreḥ*] of an *'am hā'āreṣ*, and does not receive him as his guest while he [i.e., the *'am hā'āreṣ*] is wearing his own clothes...

Amongst a list of requirement for a *ḥabēr*, we find a statement seemingly proscribing commensality between these two categories of Jews.[47] A *ḥabēr* must not eat at the house of an *'am hā'āreṣ*; should the *'am hā'āreṣ* come over to the home of a *ḥabēr*, the *'am hā'āreṣ* must wear different clothes.[48]

While *m. Demai* 2:3 provides an apparently straightforward statement regarding commensality between *ḥabērîm* and *'ammê hā'āreṣ*,

---

[44] *Imperialism*, 162–176.
[45] *m. Demai* 2:3 (ed. Albeck 1:76).
[46] Richard S. Sarason explains this as referring to "either produce which has been rendered susceptible to uncleanliness or produce which has not been rendered susceptible" (*A History of the Mishnaic Law of Agriculture: A Study of Tractate Demai* [Leiden, the Netherlands: Brill, 1979], 69).
[47] See also *t. Demai* 2:2 (ed. Lieberman 1:68–69). The previous mishnah (*m. Demai* 2:2 [ed. Albeck 1:76]) proscribes against an *'am hā'āreṣ* eating at the home of a *ne'ĕmān* ("trustworthy"). Neusner argues that this category refers to the first membership stage of the *ḥabērîm* ("The Fellowship," 131–134).
[48] This text appears to be concerned with the purity status of the clothing of the *'am hā'āreṣ*. For a discussion, see Sarason, *Mishnaic Law of Agriculture*, 72. Clothing impurity is a concern in regard to novice *ḥabērîm* in *t. Demai* 2:12 (ed. Lieberman 1:71).

t. Demai imagines several scenarios in which commensality can occur, provided that certain purity safeguards are employed.[49] In many ways, this approach parallels *m. Demai* 2:3, which allows for an *'am hā'āreṣ* to eat at the home of a *ḥabēr*, as long as the former wears "clean" attire. However, Tosefta (literally, "The Addition") lives up to its name and "adds" several scenarios that allow for social leniencies. First of all, exceptions are made to allow for commensality among family members (grandchildren, spouses) in "mixed" families (between *ḥabērîm* and *'ammê hā'āreṣ*).[50] The presumption in these texts appears to be that, in these cases, the *'am hā'āreṣ* will respect the purity regulations of the *ḥabēr*.[51] Second, Tosefta allows *ḥabērîm* to both serve and eat at the banquets of *'ammê hā'āreṣ*, provided certain conditions are met. In order for a *ḥabēr* to serve at the banquet of an *'am hā'āreṣ*, the *ḥabēr* must supervise the tithing of all of the food served therein;[52] in order for a *ḥabēr* to eat at the banquet of an *'am hā'āreṣ*, the *ḥabēr* must stipulate that he will later separate tithes for himself and, if his son is present, for his son as well.[53]

---

[49] *t. Teharot* 8:3; 8:7; and 9:2 (ed. Zuckermandel 668; 669; 670) also imagine an *'am hā'āreṣ* in the house of a *ḥabēr*.

[50] Grandfather and grandson: *t. Demai* 2:15; 3:5 (ed. Lieberman 1:71; 74); spouses: *t. Demai* 2:16–17; 3:9 (ed. Lieberman 1:71–72; 75). These texts also indicate that the category of a *ḥabēr* is open to women, children, and slaves, as well as to men (and even to priests, as *t. Demai* 2:2 [ed. Lieberman 1:68–69] suggests). For a brief discussion, see Neusner, "The Fellowship," 127–129.

[51] For a more detailed explanation of this theory, see Sarason, *Mishnaic Law of Agriculture*, 92–94, 102.

[52] *t. Demai* 3:6 (ed. Lieberman 1:74). I am aware that by discussing tithing here, and not just purity, I am somewhat conflating these issues. However, I remind the reader that in *t. Avodah Zarah* 3:10 (ed. Zuckermandel 464), discussed previously, when R. Meir defined an *'am hā'āreṣ* as "Anyone who does not eat his unconsecrated food in conditions of cultic cleanliness," the Sages countered with the following definition: "Anyone who does not properly tithe." It would therefore seem that even the Tannaim had a hard time separating these two discussions. I have decided to include these tithing-related texts here because they build on the same point and, in my opinion, they belong in this discussion. Unfortunately (or, perhaps, fortunately), crisp distinctions between certain categories are sometimes difficult when working with the tannaitic corpus.

[53] *t. Demai* 3:7 (ed. Lieberman 1:74–75). If unable to tithe food at the moment (for example, if the meal occurs on the Sabbath), then one is allowed to stipulate to oneself that, the following day (or, if one knows in advance, the day before), he will offer other food as a fungible exchange for the food that he consumed at that earlier time (see Saul Lieberman, *Tosefta Ki-fshuṭah: A Comprehensive Commentary on the Tosefta*, 10 vols., Second Augmented Edition [New York: Jewish Theological Seminary, 1992 (Hebrew)], 1:225). On orally stipulating the separation of tithes when one is unable to do so, see also *m. Demai* 7:1–2 (ed. Albeck 1:89–90); *t. Demai* 8:4–5 (ed. Lieberman 1:101–102).

These two leniencies permit commensality between *ḥabērîm* and *'ammê hā'āreṣ* under controlled circumstances. In each instance, the *ḥabēr* "controls" the social situation. In the first case, a family member who is an *'am hā'āreṣ* is assumed to accede to the purity concerns of the *ḥabēr*. In the second case, the *ḥabēr* is provided with options to allow for commensality with an *'am hā'āreṣ*. These accommodations – albeit perhaps "merely of historical interest"[54] (though, as noted above, a claim to a particular history is a practice of identity construction) – fit with the general attitude in tannaitic literature toward the *'am hā'āreṣ*: even though the texts display disdain for the *'ammê hā'āreṣ*, they do not contain the outright hatred for this group that one encounters in later rabbinic literature.[55] Lacking this polemic, Tosefta imagines scenarios that, even if they are purely scholastic or refer to a time prior to the text itself, do not erect an impenetrable wall between the table of the *ḥabēr* and the table of the *'am hā'āreṣ*. As *t. Demai* 2:2 wistfully states, "Householders [who were *ḥabērîm* and *'ammê hā'āreṣ*] have never refrained from eating with one another."[56]

According to tannaitic texts, purity regulations establish distinct identities for the *ḥabērîm* and *'ammê hā'āreṣ*. These identities, however, do not prove to be insurmountable obstacles in the path between the table of one and the table of the other.[57] Yet they do create obstacles. Although

[54] Jaffee, *Early Judaism*, 160.
[55] See Shaye J. D. Cohen, "The Place of the Rabbi in Jewish Society of the Second Century," in *The Galilee in Late Antiquity*, ed. Lee I. Levine, 157–173 (New York: Jewish Theological Seminary, 1992). I discuss this subject in more detail later in this chapter.
[56] Ed. Lieberman 1:69. Commenting on this passage, Hayes notes, "The Tosefta's tradition reaffirms the dissenting view that maintaining a high standard for oneself does not mean that one cannot associate closely with others who do not do so" (*Gentile Impurities*, 267 n. 101). Compare this statement to the following *baraita*: "R. Judah said: 'Householders have never refrained from being the guests of householders who were their friends [and were *'ammê hā'āreṣ*]" (*y. Demai* 2, 22d). For a discussion, see Saul Lieberman, *Tosefta Ki-fshuṭah*, 1:211; Oppenheimer, *'Am ha-Aretz*, 164.

One could read the prohibition found in *m. Avot* 3:10 (ed. Albeck 4:365–366) against "sitting in the synagogues of the *'ammê hā'āreṣ*" as including a commensality restriction, because engaging in communal meals in a synagogue is a common practice in antiquity (discussed later in this chapter). However, this argument seems to me to be a bit of a stretch.

[57] Although a *baraita* on *b. Berakhot* 47b precludes an *'am hā'āreṣ* from counting toward the necessary prayer quorum for grace after meals, this text may be post-tannaitic. Even if it is not, this text still imagines a scenario wherein an *'am hā'āreṣ* is at the table.

a *ḥabēr* may engage in commensality with an *'am hā'āreṣ*, this particular social interaction is controlled by a separate set of rules. For this reason, I understand tannaitic commensality regulations to function as social practices that construct distinct identities. As also seen in earlier discussions of the chef/sous-chef principle, the Tannaim articulate a set of rules in an attempt to control a situation perceived to be potentially problematic. Once again, their solution to defuse such a scenario is to create a leniency, allowing that interaction to occur as long as a rabbinic Jew sets the ground rules and controls the situation. Although the *ḥabēr* and the *'am hā'āreṣ* may eat at the same table, the rules surrounding that meal are intended to demarcate and reinforce social differentiation.

Purity and Commensality: Conclusions

Purity practices are another social system that affects identity formation. This connection is, of course, not a rabbinic innovation, as numerous texts from the Biblical and Second Temple periods can attest.[58] However, "[t]he rabbis, elaborating on biblical impurity legislation, developed a vocabulary of degree missing from the biblical text, thereby making explicit what is only implicit in biblical materials."[59] In doing so, the Tannaim use the purity system as another mechanism by which culinary and commensal practices, among others, establish a distinct Jewish, male, and rabbinic identity.

The tannaitic understanding that "you are what you eat" culminates in the Babylonian Talmud, in which numerous passages explicitly link food with identity. For example, a reputed *baraita* on *b. Pesahim* 49b

---

Further, as will soon be discussed, the claim in a *baraita* on *b. Pesahim* 49b that a Torah scholar should not eat with an *'am hā'āreṣ* is almost certainly post-tannaitic. Finally, although *t. Shabbat* 1:15 (ed. Lieberman 2:4) states that a *zāb* who is a Pharisee cannot dine with a *zāb* who is an *'am hā'āreṣ*, this may refer only to a unique situation. For a discussion of how this text is understood in the Palestinian Talmud, see Oppenheimer, *'Am ha-Aretz*, 156–157.

[58] On the subject of purity and impurity in general, see Saul M. Olyan, *Rites and Rank: Hierarchy in the Biblical Representations of Cult* (Princeton, NJ: Princeton University Press, 2000), 38–62 (Hebrew Bible); Klawans, *Impurity and Sin*, 21–42 (Hebrew Bible); 43–60 (Second Temple period); 67–91 (Qumran); and 136–157 (New Testament).

[59] Olyan, *Rites and Rank*, 39. For a more detailed discussion, see Harrington, *The Impurity*.

claims that only a Torah scholar – and not an *'am hā'āreṣ* – should eat meat.[60] In the Tannaitic period, however, this connection is more inchoate and nascent. The early rabbinic movement clearly bundles together identity and diet, yet this earlier corpus preserves merely the beginning of an expanding rhetoric that aims to enact and control social boundaries via commensality regulations. Although the Amoraim make this connection explicit, their tannaitic predecessors often leave it tacit – as an assumption, often employed when defining ambiguous categories.

THE STATUS OF FOOD CORRELATES WITH THE STATUS OF ITS COOK

We turn now to the third means by which tannaitic food practices establish a Jewish, male, and rabbinic identity. In Chapter 2 we encountered the tannaitic principle that the status of a food item directly correlates to the status of its preparer. Now, however, this notion is marshaled for the construction of a Jewish, *rabbinic* identity, not just a Jewish one. To begin, I return to *t. Hullin* 1:1:

All [Jews] are fit to slaughter [an animal], even a Samaritan, even an uncircumcised [Jew], even a Jewish apostate.[61] An animal slaughtered by a heretic

---

[60] On this passage, see Jonathan Brumberg-Kraus, "Meat Eating and Jewish Identity: Ritualization of the Priestly 'Torah of Beast and Fowl' (Lev 11:46) in Rabbinic Judaism and Medieval Kabbalah," *AJSR* 24/2 (1999): 227–262. Although this is reputed to be a *baraita*, I follow Cohen, who considers the series of *baraitot* among which this one is found to be "*allegedly* tannaitic material," on the basis that tannaitic texts reflect disdain for the *'am hā'āreṣ*, but not outright hatred; that hatred, according to Cohen, is found in later rabbinic literature ("The Place of the Rabbi," 173, emphasis added). As Cohen notes, "There is no way to verify the authenticity of this material, but the fact that these statements and the ethos they represent are completely absent from Palestinian texts raises serious doubts" (p. 167). To Cohen's argument, I would add that the tannaitic exposition of Leviticus 14:26 (the proof-text for this "alleged" *baraita*) on *Sifra Shemini pereq* 12:8 (ed. Weiss 57b) mentions neither the *'am hā'āreṣ* nor his required vegetarian diet. Contrast Cohen's view to the approach taken by the majority of previous scholars, who accept the authenticity of this material (e.g., Lee I. Levine, *The Rabbinic Class of Roman Palestine in Late Antiquity* [New York: Jewish Theological Seminary, 1989], 112–117).

[61] As was also the case in *t. Horayot* 1:5, the term for "apostate" in Zuckermandel's manuscript is *mešûmād*, with the variant *mûmār*. I discuss the issues associated with Samaritans later in this chapter.

[*mîn*] is [regarded as an act of] idolatry.[62] An animal slaughtered by a Gentile – behold, this is invalid. And an animal slaughtered by an ape – behold, this is invalid. As it is said: "*you* may slaughter... and *you* may eat."[63] *You* may not [eat] that which a Gentile has slaughtered; *you* may not eat that which an ape has slaughtered; *you* may not eat that which is slaughtered by its own action.[64]

This passage in Tosefta begins by validating animal slaughter by every (male) Jew – "normative" rabbinic, Samaritan, uncircumcised, and apostate – except for the heretic (*mîn*).[65] There seems to be a distinction here between an apostate and a heretic. However, this distinction is not always consistent throughout the tannaitic corpus,[66] perhaps owing to the fact that, as many scholars have pointed out, the *mîn* (plural: *minim*) appears to be a rhetorical construct created for use in discourse on theoretical law;[67] it is not necessarily – nor even likely – a specific historical

---

[62] See also *t. Hullin* 2:20 (ed. Zuckermandel 503). Philip S. Alexander argues that the term *mîn* in *t. Hullin* 2:20 refers to Christ-believing Jews ("'The Parting of the Ways' from the Perspective of Rabbinic Judaism," in *Jews and Christians: The Parting of the Ways, A.D. 70 to 135*, ed. James D. G. Dunn, 1–25 [Tübingen, Germany: Mohr Siebeck, 1992], 15–16).

[63] This is a partial quotation from Deuteronomy 12:21, which states, in regard to valid animal slaughter and meat consumption, "If the place where Yhwh your God has chosen to establish His name is far from you, *you may slaughter* from the cattle or the sheep that Yhwh gives you, as I have commanded you; and *you may eat* to your heart's content in your gates" (emphasis added).

[64] *t. Hullin* 1:1 (ed. Zuckermandel 500), emphasis added.

[65] This opening differs significantly from its parallel version in *m. Hullin* 1:1 (ed. Albeck 5:115), as I discuss in Chapter 2. I leave aside the issue of gender, having already discussed its relevance to animal slaughter in Chapter 3.

[66] E.g., *Mekilta d'Rabbi Ishmael Bo* 15 (ed. Horowitz 53), which, in reference to the biblical exclusion of the foreigner from the Passover in Exodus 12:43, says "All the same are a Jewish apostate (*mešûmād*) and a Gentile" (cp. *Mekilta d'Rabbi Shimon b. Yohai* at Exodus 12:43 [ed. Epstein and Melamed 35], which states, "This [refers to] the Jewish apostate [*mešûmād*] who practices idolatry"). In this case, then, the *mešûmād* does not necessarily belong to the category of "Us." However, a pericope found in the next chapter of *t. Hullin* offers evidence for at least some internal consistency in this tractate. *t. Hullin* 2:20 (ed. Zuckermandel 503) states, "Meat that is found in the possession of the Gentile is permitted for benefit; [but, if meat is found in the possession of] the heretic [*mîn*], it is forbidden for benefit."

[67] E.g., Daniel Boyarin, *Border Lines: The Partition of Judaeo-Christianity* (Philadelphia: University of Pennsylvania Press, 2004), 57; Martin Goodman, "The Function of Minim in Early Rabbinic Judaism," in *Geschichte – Tradition – Reflexion: Festschrift für Martin Hengel zum 70. Geburtstag*, ed. Hubert Cancik, Hermann Lichtenberger, and Peter Schäfer, 1:501–510; 3 vols. (Tübingen, Germany: Mohr Siebeck, 1996), 508.

community. Further, the term may be nuanced to fit different scholastic scenarios. Therefore, the importance of the category of *minim* for our purposes here is, as Stern notes:

The fact that the *minim* are distinguished... from the non-Jews is itself significant, as it indicates that they retain, just as do ordinary apostates, a distinct identity as 'Israel'.... However, that the *minim* are part of Israel is only, at best, implicit. To some extent they have forsaken their identity.[68]

Although the identity of those to whom the term "*mîn*" applies in tannaitic literature is being questioned, the debate remains over a Jewish, rabbinic identity. Even though the *mîn* may forsake some of his identity, as Stern suggests, he is nonetheless not grouped with non-Jews in tannaitic taxonomy.[69] In short, the text still preserves a distinction between Gentile and *mîn*: the former's slaughter is invalid, whereas the latter's slaughter is regarded as an act of idolatry. Therefore, the practices that class a Jew as a *mîn*, from a tannaitic perspective, affect the status of his (seemingly otherwise permissible) animal slaughter.[70]

David Moshe Freidenreich correctly interprets the section of the toseftan passage that refers to Gentiles, stating:

The reference to an animal "which is slaughtered by its own action," a strange phrase found nowhere else in Rabbinic literature, reflects the author's effort to incorporate a reference to carrion into the literary structure of his interpretation of the Biblical verse. The message is that animal slaughter performed by a non-Jew, even if the act of slaughter conforms to all the dictates of Rabbinic law, is prohibited simply because it was performed by a non-Jew. *Slaughter by a gentile is legally equivalent to no slaughter at all, so an animal slaughtered by a gentile is equivalent to carrion*, whose consumption (but not benefit) is prohibited according to *Deuteronomy*.[71]

---

[68] *Jewish Identity*, 111–112.
[69] My usage of the masculine pronoun in this sentence is intentional. As in the case of rabbinic texts in general (as previously noted), "[i]t is characteristic of rabbinic discourse that all minim were treated by the Tannaim as male" (Goodman, "Function of Minim," 508 n. 33).
[70] I insert the phrase "seemingly otherwise permissible" because *t. Hullin* 1:1 does not *specifically* mention a *mîn* slaughtering a nonkosher animal or deviating from any other standard practice.
[71] David Moshe Freidenreich, Foreign Food: Restrictions on the Food of Members of Other Religions in Jewish, Christian, and Islamic Law (Ph.D. dissertation, Columbia University, 2006), 162, emphasis added.

Slaughter by a Gentile, according to the logic of *t. Hullin* 1:1, is equated with carrion.[72] However, slaughter by a *mîn* does count as an act of slaughter – albeit, from the tannaitic perspective, an idolatrous one. The logic here appears to be that a Gentile is incapable of producing valid slaughter.[73] In contrast, the *mîn* is *technically* capable of proper slaughter because he is technically a Jew. As such, slaughter by the *mîn* – unlike that of the Gentile – must "count" for something; hence, it is classified as idolatrous.

In my reading of *t. Hullin* 1:1, therefore, the *mîn* is not categorized as a non-Jew, in contrast to the Gentile, who obviously is classified as such. Rather, the *mîn* remains in an ill-defined status, somewhere on "Our" side, but close to the boundary between "Us" and "Them." Even though the rabbinic Jew cannot consume the meat of a *mîn*, his meat is not treated like that of a Gentile. The *mîn* is, in fact, even described as slaughtering animals differently, in a manner prohibited to a rabbinic Jew: occurring in the middle of the market and collecting blood in a utensil or a hole.[74] In short, the status of the meat of the *mîn* parallels the status of the *mîn* himself: classed with neither Gentile nor rabbinic Jew. Once again, an analogy is made between tannaitic food regulations and desired social relations, whereby the Tannaim use legislation regarding animal slaughter to effect social distance from a category of nonrabbinic Jews. As such, regardless of whether he follows the tenets of tannaitic slaughter practices, animal butchery performed by a *mîn* is prohibited for ingestion by a rabbinic Jew.

The practical implication of differentially classifying slaughter by a *mîn* and slaughter by a Gentile is uncertain. Even though at least one Hebrew Bible text prohibits the consumption of carrion, it explicitly allows this type of meat to be sold to a non-Israelite or given to a *gēr*.[75] Tannaitic literature, on the other hand, prohibits both the consumption and the sale of carrion.[76] In tannaitic legislation, therefore, a Jew can

---

[72] For other tacit examples of this principle, see *t. Hullin* 5:3; 6:4 (ed. Zuckermandel 507; 507–508).
[73] With "appropriate" Jewish participation, a Gentile can partake in valid slaughter. However, as discussed in Chapter 2, this type of slaughter is classed as "Jewish" slaughter.
[74] *m. Hullin* 2:9 (ed. Albeck 5:122; = *t. Hullin* 2:19 [ed. Zuckermandel 503]).
[75] Deuteronomy 14:21.
[76] *m. Shevi'it* 7:3 (ed. Albeck 1:157; cp. *t. Shevi'it* 5:8 [ed. Lieberman 1:187]); *t. Hullin* 7:3 (ed. Zuckermandel 508). There are some texts that suggest that a Jew can benefit

neither consume nor profit from either carrion or idol-meat. Thus, the distinction between an animal slaughtered by a *mîn* or one slaughtered by a Gentile appears to be symbolic. Although in different theoretical categories, animals slaughtered by a *mîn* or a Gentile are both to be completely avoided.[77] Symbolic or not, however, the fact remains that animal butchery is yet another instance in which tannaitic literature evidences the construction of a practice-based Jewish, male, rabbinic identity.

The fact that the status of meat is considered by the Tannaim to be a dependent variable (depending on, for example, whether the one holding the knife is a rabbinic Jew, a *mîn*, or a Gentile) is reinforced in yet another tannaitic text, which requires that "one who slaughters [an animal] must [recite] a separate benediction. He says: 'Blessed [is the One who has sanctified us in His commandments and commanded us][78] regarding slaughter." Thus, the act of valid animal slaughter requires one to recite a blessing formulated for and propagated by rabbinic Jews. This blessing – unique to meat – ensures (in theory) that a Jew versed in rabbinic law is the only one "capable" of tannaitically proper animal slaughter. Without this blessing, which brings the practice of animal slaughter under further rabbinic control, a rabbinic Jew presumably could not eat the otherwise acceptable meat.

Before concluding this subject, it is instructive to examine tannaitic attitudes toward a Samaritan food item, namely bread. The Samaritans are a group who claim direct descent from the northern Israelite tribes of Ephraim and Manasseh, having survived the Assyrian destruction of the kingdom of Israel in 722 B.C.E. Because of this shared (real or imagined) history, Samaritan traditions and texts share many similarities with those of the Judeans, although different interpretations and historical

---

economically from Gentile meat. If this is so, then there is a practical implication for these distinctions.

[77] As we have also seen in Chapter 2, not all meat slaughtered by a Gentile is necessarily considered idolatrous slaughter. Although suspicion of Gentile libations leads the Tannaim to regulate eternal vigilance in regard to wine, for example, the interpretation that Gentile slaughter is tantamount to a natural death and, hence, no slaughter at all, explains why Gentile animal slaughter is not always classified in tannaitic literature as an idolatrous practice.

[78] *t. Berakhot* 6:11 (ed. Lieberman 1:36). I have supplied these words following the reading of the Erfurt manuscript. However, because Lieberman does not include them in his text, I leave these variant words in brackets.

circumstances lead to distinct differences.[79] Tannaitic texts are aware of this shared history but seem unsure of how to taxonomically classify Samaritans in the Jew/non-Jew polarity. As Gary G. Porton observes:

> In several texts, the gentile is contrasted with the Samaritan, while in other passages the two are treated the same. In the rabbinic texts, the Samaritans occupied a middle ground between the gentiles and the Israelites. At times the Samaritans were treated as if they were the Israelites, while in other instances they were seen as non-Israelites. Also, the Israelites, Samaritans, and gentiles were, from the point of view of the authors of our texts, the three major classes of people who dwelt in the Land of Israel, held property within its borders, and were the actors in the events which occurred there. Thus, on a number of issues, the Samaritans would be important people with whom our texts should deal, and they could serve as the "intermediate group" between the Israelites and the non-Israelites.[80]

This taxonomic confusion is occasionally reflected in tannaitic food regulations. For example, although it seems that rabbinic Jews could both eat with a Samaritan[81] and consume meat properly slaughtered by a Samaritan butcher,[82] Samaritan bread is a more complicated issue.

In at least one text, tannaitic literature appears to permit the consumption of Samaritan bread. *t. Pisha* 2:1–3 discusses the regulations concerning access to Samaritan leaven after, and unleavened bread

---

[79] For a brief overview of Samaritan history, see Robert T. Anderson, "Samaritans," in *ABD*, ed. David Noel Freedman, 5:940–947, 6 vols. (New York: Doubleday, 1992). On the Samaritan literary corpus, see Robert T. Anderson and Terry Giles, *Tradition Kept: The Literature of the Samaritans* (Peabody, MA: Hendrickson, 2005). For an extensive bibliography on Samaritan history and literature, see Alan David Crown and Reinhard Pummer, *A Bibliography of the Samaritans: Third Edition, Revised, Expanded, and Annotated*, ATLA Bibliography Series 51 (Lanham, MD: Scarecrow Press, 2005).

[80] *Goyim: Gentiles and Israelites in Mishnah-Tosefta*, BJS 155 (Atlanta: Society of Biblical Literature, 1988), 133 (in general, see pp. 132–144). On the problems associated with distinguishing Jewish from Samaritan material culture, see Leah di Segni, "The Samaritans in Roman–Byzantine Palestine: Some Misapprehensions," in *Religious and Ethnic Communities in Later Roman Palestine*, ed. Hayim Lapin, 51–66 (Bethesda: University Press of Maryland, 1998).

[81] According to *m. Berakhot* 7:1 (ed. Albeck 1:26), a Samaritan can count toward the prayer quorum necessary for reciting grace after meals, implying his presence at the meal itself. *t. Demai* 3:3 (ed. Lieberman 1:73–74) describes the conditions under which an Israelite priest may eat with a Samaritan priest, indicating that such a commensal situation was possible, if only from a purely scholastic perspective.

[82] *t. Hullin* 1:1 (ed. Zuckermandel 500).

during, the festival of Passover,[83] apparently assuming that Samaritan bread is permitted for tannaitic Jews. In other texts, Samaritan bread is prohibited. According to *t. Hullin* 2:20, the bread of the Samaritan is compared to that of the *mîn*, implying that it is prohibited to tannaitic Jews.[84] This prohibition is most explicit in *m. Shevi'it* 8:10, which states that "R. Eliezer used to say: 'One who eats bread [baked by] Samaritans [*cûtîm*] is like one who eats pig-meat.'"[85] In R. Eliezer's opinion, Samaritan bread is equal to pork – the metonymic food of the "culinary Other." Of course, "*cûtîm*" here could be a general term, simply referring to non-Jews, in which case this text is just another explicit example of the chef/sous-chef principle in regard to bread baked by non-Jews.[86] If the term refers to Samaritans, as the phrase *cûtîm* is traditionally understood, then perhaps Samaritan bread is equated with pork because, like the *mîn* whose slaughter is equated with idolatry in *t. Hullin* 1:1,[87] the Samaritan's act of baking is perceived by the Tannaim to be an act of cultural transformation. If this same logic underlies this passage, then pork and idolatry function in similar fashions: namely, to stigmatize the cultural and culinary products of certain nonrabbinic Jews.[88]

Unsure of how to classify Samaritans, the Tannaim therefore appear to be unsure of how to classify their food. Thus, the inconsistencies and contradictions associated with tannaitic regulations concerning Samaritan bread – alternatively allowing and prohibiting it – mirror those concerning the Samaritan in general, indicating that, once again, the status of the preparer directly affects the status of the item being prepared. As in the case of bread baked by a non-Jew, the tannaitic discussions

---

[83] *t. Pisha* 2:1–3 (ed. Lieberman 2:144–145). Leavened bread is forbidden to Jews on Passover (e.g., Exodus 12). Regulations regarding acquiring bread from Samaritans after Passover also appear in the second chapter of the minor tractate *Kutim*. I do not reference this tractate in the main body of my text because it is most likely post-tannaitic.

[84] *t. Hullin* 2:20 (ed. Zuckermandel 503).

[85] *m. Shevi'it* 8:10 (ed. Albeck 1:162). This statement was not wholeheartedly endorsed, as R. Akiva ardently rejects it. Compare R. Eliezer's objection (in some manuscripts) to the anonymous opinion permitting the unleavened bread of Samaritans in *t. Pisha* 2:3 (ed. Lieberman 2:145).

[86] See Chapter 2 for a discussion of the chef/sous-chef principle with regard to bread baked by non-Jews. *Cûtîm*, a term sometimes inserted in manuscripts subject to censorship, is attested in the extant manuscripts for this mishnah.

[87] *t. Hullin* 1:1 (ed. Zuckermandel 500).

[88] Pork and idolatry are also used to stigmatize non-Jews, as discussed in depth in Chapter 2.

about Samaritan bread do not quibble over the recipe; instead, they are concerned with the identity of the baker.

In this section, I have once again argued that tannaitic literature contains a principle that the status of a food item (primarily meat, but in one instance bread) follows the status of its preparer. This principle allows the Tannaim to parse Jewish identity into two categories: rabbinic and nonrabbinic Jews. The bundle of social practices that leads one to be classified, at least by the Tannaim, as a *mîn* or a Samaritan, for example, also affects the classification of the food that the person produces. By correlating the status of food and the status of the preparer, tannaitic legislation connects food practices into the larger matrix of social identity formation. By prohibiting rabbinic Jews from consuming meat from an animal slaughtered by a *mîn*, which is labeled as an idolatrous offering, and by comparing Samaritan bread to pork, the rabbinic Jew is further distanced in social settings (and, by extension, in social-constructed and practice-based identity) from the nonrabbinic Jew. In sum, this principle, like so many others that we have already encountered, indicates that there is a predictable analogy between food regulations and desired social relations, suggesting that the latter generates the former.

REINTERPRETING FESTIVAL OBSERVANCE

Tannaitic culinary and commensal regulations establish practices that form, in part, a distinct Jewish, male, rabbinic identity, and these rules often apply to meals that can occur on any given day. Festivals, however, offer an additional opportunity to set apart rabbinic Jews from nonrabbinic Jews at the same time as one distinguishes between the sacred (festival meals) and the profane (daily meals). Tannaitic interpretations and reinterpretations concerning the culinary and commensal legislation (among others) that regulates particular festivals therefore comprise a system of rituals that divides Jews into two categories: those who celebrate each festival "Our" – and hence the "correct" – way, and those who do not ("Them").[89]

---

[89] Here I am influenced by Catherine Bell, who writes that "ritual systems do not function to regulate or control the systems of social relations, they *are* the system" (*Ritual Theory, Ritual Practice* [Oxford: Oxford University Press, 1992], 130, emphasis in original).

In this section, I examine three case studies to determine how the Tannaim reinterpret culinary and commensal festival regulations to establish a Jewish rabbinic identity: Passover, Sukkot, and the Sabbath. I use the term "(re)interpret" here to call attention to the fact that the Tannaim both draw on earlier precedents and introduce innovative understandings and legislation. Even though I refer to this process as "reinterpretation" throughout, it is important to remember that the Tannaim are sometimes offering completely novel interpretations (a difference of kind, which I understand to be a complete recasting – hence reinterpretation – of earlier traditions), and not simply repackaging an earlier understanding of a festival (a difference of degree, which I understand to be a slightly different reading – hence interpretation – of earlier traditions). I conclude this section with a brief discussion about meals in the synagogue: by all other accounts, a common Jewish practice, with which the Tannaim are uncomfortable.

Passover

Describing a census of Jerusalem taken by Cestius during the festival of Passover, Josephus notes:

Accordingly, on the occasion of the feast called Passover, at which they sacrifice from the ninth to the eleventh hour, and *a little fraternity*,[90] as it were, gathers round each sacrifice, of not fewer than ten persons (feasting alone not being permitted), while the companies often included as many as twenty, the victims were counted and amounted to two hundred and fifty-five thousand six hundred; allowing an average of ten diners to each victim, we obtain a total of two million seven hundred thousand, all pure and holy.[91]

---

[90] This is Thackeray's rendering of *phratria*, following the manuscript variant for the otherwise incomprehensible *phatria*. See H. St. J. Thackeray, R. Marcus, A Wikgren, and L. H. Feldman, eds., *Josephus*, 10 vols., LCL (Cambridge, MA: Harvard University Press, 1926–1965), 3:498 n. 1. In Greek, this term can refer to a brotherhood, clan, or tribe (see H. G. Liddell and R. Scott, *An Intermediate Greek-English Lexicon*, Seventh Edition [New York: American Book Company, 1995], 871 s.v. *phratra*).

[91] *Jewish War*, 6:423–425, emphasis added. On prerabbinic descriptions of Passover in general, see Baruch M. Bokser, *The Origins of the Seder: The Passover Rite and Early Rabbinic Judaism* (Berkeley and Los Angeles: University of California Press, 1984), 14–28.

According to Josephus, the Passover is consumed in a social context that he calls "a little fraternity." Commemorating the mythical Exodus from Egypt in community serves to strengthen group cohesion by reinforcing a shared past by way of a present-day meal ritual.

Tannaitic literature also speaks of "a little fraternity" in regard to the festival of Passover: the table-fellowship association (*ḥăbûrāh*).[92] Although the concept of a *ḥăbûrāh* appears in several commensal contexts in tannaitic literature,[93] it is by far most often associated with consuming the Passover in table-fellowship. As discussed in Chapter 2, the Passover is a metonymic food. If access to the Passover signifies inclusion in the collective body of "Israel," then eating the metonymic food with peers can be understood as a communal ritual of identity enactment and maintenance. Concomitantly, refusal to ingest the Passover can be construed as an act of social separation and group disintegration, as one might read Jesus' abstention from the Passover in Luke 22:15–16.[94]

A good starting point for this discussion is a tannaitic exegesis of Exodus 12:46, which states: "In one house [the Passover] shall be eaten; you shall not take any of the meat outside the house; and as for the bones,

---

[92] The formation of social groups based around commensality in antiquity is not unique to Judaism. For an overview of the Greek and Roman evidence for dining clubs, see Smith, *From Symposium to Eucharist*, 87–125. On the concept of the *ḥăbûrāh* in rabbinic literature in general, see Oppenheimer, *'Am ha-Aretz*, 118–156. On the connection between the rabbinic Passover *seder* and the *ḥăbûrāh*, see Yosef Tabory, *The Passover Ritual Throughout the Generations* (Tel Aviv: Hakibbutz Hameuchad, 1996 [Hebrew]), 48–59. Although Philo and the Tannaim may refer to a different social institution, both practices seem to serve a similar social function. The biblical basis for the Passover table-fellowship appears to be Exodus 12:4, which instructs households that are too small to consume a lamb in one sitting to combine with neighbors for this purpose.

[93] For example, with regard to betrothal and wedding meals (*t. Megillah* 3:15 [ed. Lieberman 2:357]) and associations for unspecified commandments (*ḥăbûrat miṣwāh*) (*m. Sanhedrin* 8:2 [ed. Albeck 4:195]; cp. *t. Sanhedrin* 11:6 [ed. Zuckermandel 431–432], which simply states *ḥăbûrāh*). It should be stated that both of the previously cited cases may not be generalizable because the former refers to a custom in Jerusalem and the latter to an action taken by a "rebellious and incorrigible son."

[94] On the ramifications of Jesus' actions for table-fellowship, see Jonathan Brumberg-Kraus, "'Not By Bread Alone...': The Ritualization of Food and Table Talk in the Passover *Seder* and in the Last Supper," in *Food and Drink in the Biblical Worlds*, ed. Athalya Brenner and Jan Willem van Henten, Semeia 86, 165–191 (Atlanta: Society of Biblical Literature, 1999), especially pp. 178–182; Smith, *From Symposium to Eucharist*, 261–263.

you may not break any of them."⁹⁵ Explicating this pericope, *t. Pisha* 6:11 offers a wealth of information:

What [does Scripture] teach [when] it says: "In one house [the Passover] shall be eaten"? In one association. R. Shimon says: "Behold, [if] they were sitting and eating and saw a snake or a scorpion, these [people] take up their Passover and eat it in another place, as it is said: 'upon the houses in which they will eat [the Passover].'⁹⁶ If so, why does [Scripture] say: 'In one house [the Passover] shall be eaten'? That two associations should not eat [the Passover] facing one another." *When the waiter [who serves two associations but eats with only one of them] stands to mix [wine for the association with which he does not eat], he shuts his mouth and he turns his face away [from them] and he chews [his food] until he reaches his own association* and he swallows [it], in order that he does not appear to eat from two Passovers. If there is only one association there, he eats throughout the entire house and he does not scruple.⁹⁷

First, we learn that the reference in Exodus 12:46 to "one house" refers to "one association."⁹⁸ The biblical "house" is now understood to mean an "association," perhaps suggesting a notion of fictive kinship; if the association is the house, and the house is the family, then perhaps one can infer that the association is the family. As noted in Chapter 3, drawing from the work of Nancy Jay, one could suggest that, by interpreting "one house" to mean "one association," tannaitic literature builds a fictive familial relationship through table-fellowship. Thus, by helping to establish a fictive kinship, this interpretation of Exodus 12:46 can have ramifications for tannaitic social formation. Members of each association are potentially perceived as fictive kin, making this meal an important one for identity construction.

Second, and in a somewhat related point, *t. Pisha* 6:11 (quoting *m. Pesahim* 7:13) mandates that associations should not consume their

---

⁹⁵ The Hebrew text has both "bones" and "them" in the singular, but I render them as collective plurals to provide a more idiomatic English translation.

⁹⁶ This is a partial quote from Exodus 12:7, which discusses placing blood on the houses' doorposts as part of the Passover celebration. The logic here is that the word "houses" is in the plural and, as such, the Passover can be consumed in another house if one's life is in imminent danger due to the presence of a wild animal.

⁹⁷ *t. Pisha* 6:11 (ed. Lieberman 2:175). The italicized text also appears in *m. Pesahim* 7:13 (ed. Albeck 2:168).

⁹⁸ *t. Makkot* 4:1 (ed. Zuckermandel 441) also compares the house and the association in regard to Exodus 12:46; however, unlike *t. Pisha* 6:11, it does not make this one-to-one correlation explicit.

Passover while facing one another. I connect this point to my previous one because I read this text as envisioning each association as a separate "house"; as such, they must separate themselves from one another. In doing so, each association strengthens bonds with those in that association (family?). Despite being eligible to join an association – a status that socially marks one as a closer fictive relative than an ineligible man who is, nonetheless, Jewish – separate tables mean separate houses, which, in turn, mean separate immediate "families." The meal ideology of separate tables, however, does not necessarily limit this commensal act of social formation to the members of each individual association. The fact that multiple associations can share a room (and a waiter) suggests that these fictive kinships are somehow connected. To share the dining room could be understood to bind each "family" unit into a larger fictive family tree.

Third, even if two associations share a waiter, that waiter must choose to dine with one of them and must consume all his food at that association's table (i.e., its "house"). This minor, and possibly merely scholastic, point is interesting not only because it, once again, envisions a more upper-class milieu,[99] but also because it suggests that the waiter himself must be eligible to participate in the association's activities. Although other tannaitic texts mentioning waiters do not necessarily address this issue, *t. Pisha* 6:11 imagines that a waiter is (one would assume, based on this context) a male, rabbinic Jew, as he is part of an association (ergo, a member of the "family").

Building on this final point, it is important to address the fact that the social bonding of the Passover banquet also serves, both literally and figuratively, to exclude several categories of Jews from the table. Even though *m. Pesahim* 10:1 states that everyone in Israel reclines while eating on Passover, that does not mean that all are treated completely equally. For example, *m. Pesahim* 7:3 differentiates between an association of priests and an association of Israelites.[100] One could argue, however, that this distinction occurs in the midst of a theoretical discussion about a specific case in which "one basted [the Passover] in oil in the status of

---

[99] See Chapter 1 for my discussion of class and meals in rabbinic literature.
[100] *m. Pesahim* 10:1 (ed. Albeck 2:176; = *t. Pisha* 10:1 [ed. Lieberman 2:196]); *m. Pesahim* 7:3 (ed. Albeck 2:164–165). *m. Pesahim* 9:8 (ed. Albeck 2:174) implies a similar difference. Because I read both passages with the same caveats in mind and it does not add anything specific to the discussion at hand, I do not devote additional time and space to this passage.

heave offering" and, as such, is, at least, a set of special circumstances and, at most, a purely scholastic discussion. Regardless, I find it interesting that priests are here contrasted with Israelites when, according to at least one passage in Philo, Passover is an occasion where every (male?) Jew becomes, at least metaphorically, a priest and every house transforms into a temple:

On this day [the fourteenth of Nisan][101] *every dwelling-house is invested with the outward semblance and dignity of a temple.* The victim is then slaughtered and dressed for the festal meal which befits the occasion. The guests assembled for the banquet have been cleansed by purificatory lustrations, and are there not as in other festive gatherings, to indulge the belly with wine and viands, but to fulfil [sic] with prayers and hymns the custom handed down by their fathers. The day on which this national festivity occurs may very properly be noted.[102]

Although scholars have debated the meaning of this passage,[103] "[t]he most natural reading of the whole passage, however, is that all Jews, whether in Jerusalem or not, could gather in companies and participate in the Passover sacrifice. The Bible ordains that this is the one time each year laymen may act as priests."[104] Even when "laymen may act as priests," the Mishnah distinguishes, at least scholastically, between priest and layman.[105]

Further, as discussed in Chapter 3, women, slaves, and minors are, in some fashion, excluded from participation in a Passover association.

---

[101] Jews currently observe Passover on the fifteenth day of the month of Nisan. For a discussion about the history of this change in date, including an explication of the Philo passage at hand, see Sanders, *Judaism*, 133.

[102] *De Specialibus Legibus*, 2:148–149, emphasis added (cf. *Quaestiones et Solutiones in Exodum*, 1:10).

[103] For references to these authors, see Bokser, *Origins of the Seder*, 22–23; Sanders, *Judaism*, 133–134, 511 n. 43.

[104] Sanders, *Judaism*, 134. For an argument against Sanders' interpretation of this passage, see Jutta Leonhardt, *Jewish Worship in Philo of Alexandria* (Tübingen, Germany: Mohr Siebeck, 2001), 31–33. I find Leonhardt's argument to be based on the same "ambiguous" evidence on which Leonhardt accuses Sanders of basing his argument (*Jewish Worship*, 31 n. 41).

[105] Elsewhere, those who engage in rabbinic activities (i.e., Torah study) are likened to those who engage in priestly activities (e.g., *Mekilta d'Rabbi Ishmael Beshelah Vayehi* 1 [ed. Horowitz 76], discussed in Chapter 2). According to some later rabbinic texts, those who study Torah deserve to be given tithes by other Jews. For references and a brief discussion, see Levine, *Rabbinic Class*, 71.

According to *t. Pisha* 8:6: "*They do not make an association [consisting] of women, slaves, and/or minors*, so as not to increase indecency."[106] Women, slaves, and minors are proscribed – albeit ambiguously – from participating in tannaitic commensality, marking them as social "Others" to tannaitic men, who lack any analogous regulations regarding participation in the Passover association.

Although there are other laws in regard to Passover associations that address sacrificial concerns (which are, by the time of the third century C.E., scholastic),[107] several more passages contain discussions that provide information about possible social mechanisms (e.g., the *ḥăbûrāh*) for integrating commensal activities into tannaitic identity. Chapter 7 of *t. Pisha* contains a series of data that underscore the role that the association plays in the creation and maintenance of a tannaitic communal identity. Thus, we learn that the association should partake of the Passover only if there is enough food for everyone registered.[108] Each member must get his share.[109] It therefore seems that, once admitted into the *ḥăbûrāh*, the member is entitled to the full benefits of inclusion, namely access to the food and the social status that comes with partaking of the Passover in that particular association. If the *ḥăbûrāh* functions as a Passover practice that reifies inclusion and exclusion, then participation is, ideally, an all-or-nothing proposition.

We also learn that one who takes more than his fair share can be excluded from the association, but not his share in the Passover itself.[110] Gluttony, therefore, does not preclude one's fulfillment of one's personal

---

[106] *t. Pisha* 8:6 (ed. Lieberman 2:185). The words in italics also appear in *m. Pesahim* 8:7 (ed. Albeck 2:171).

[107] E.g., *t. Pisha* 4:7; 9:1 (ed. Lieberman 2:162, 189–190); *t. Terumot* 2:3 (ed. Lieberman 1:112).

[108] *t. Pisha* 7:6 (ed. Lieberman 2:178). Although there is a provision for associations that registered members via a sort of rolling admissions policy, the communal aspect of this first statement remains. *t. Pisha* 7:7–8 (ed. Lieberman 2:178–179) contains further information about how one registers for an association. It seems that the act of registering for an association is socially significant in itself.

[109] See also *t. Pisha* 7:16 (ed. Lieberman 2:182), which states that even a member of an association who is registered out of charity is given a share. Lieberman understands this as referring to one who is given a portion of the Passover free.

[110] *t. Pisha* 7:10 (ed. Lieberman 2:179). In an interesting comparison, according to *m. Pesahim* 8:4 (ed. Albeck 2:169), this social exclusion occurs if one registers someone else in his share, a practice that Tosefta explicitly permits (*t. Pisha* 7:8 [ed. Lieberman 2:178–179]).

biblical obligation to consume the Passover;[111] it does, however, lead to social exclusion, as an overeater is asked to leave the group. Further, this text explicitly states that this principle applies not only to the Passover, but also to any meal in which an association partakes. The fact that manners mark social distinction is not historically surprising. As Massimo Montanari notes, "In collective dining rituals, the meaning of particular gestures resides in the elaboration of rules that serve to delineate the field of action, excluding whoever does not know them and therefore does not respect them."[112] If manners reinforce who "We" are, then how can one who violates "Our" manners be one of "Us"? Therefore, even after one is eligible to join an association, one's actions at the meal itself can distance that person from the commensal group. This is especially so when one's actions are perceived as gluttonous – as gluttony is the opposite of self-restraint, a desired rabbinic (and male) trait.[113]

Although much of the legal discussion surrounding the Passover association may be scholastic, even these possibly theoretical situations suggest the importance of the association as a social unit. As Freidenreich notes, "Legal discourse . . . is not always practically oriented, but even in its more scholastic manifestations it remains a vehicle for defining boundaries and preserving distinct categories."[114] Several of the regulations surrounding the table-fellowship group for Passover – the association – serve to differentiate one from another.[115] At this ritual of social formation and

[111] This is clearly a case of gluttony. *t. Pisha* 7:17 (ed. Lieberman 2:182) explains the rules when one member of a Passover association *mistakenly* eats another's portion. Further, *t. Yom Tov* 4:10 (ed. Lieberman 2:303; cp. *m. Betzah* 5:7 [ed. Albeck 2:301]) regulates the amount of food that a guest can bring home from a Passover banquet house.

[112] *Food Is Culture*, trans. Albert Sonnenfeld (New York: Columbia University Press, 2006), 97. On dining rituals in general, see Margaret Visser, *The Rituals of Dinner: The Origins, Evolution, Eccentricities, and Meaning of Table Manners* (New York: Penguin Books, 1991).

[113] See Michael L. Satlow, "'Try to be a Man': The Rabbinic Construction of Masculinity," *HTR* 89/1 (1996): 19–40.

[114] Foreign Food, abstract p. 1.

[115] Although purity concerns surround the interactions of those associated with associations in tannaitic literature in general (discussed earlier in this chapter), it is interesting to note that they do not play a significant role in the discussion at hand. Although we do learn that an individual's impurity does not affect the rest of the association (*t. Pisha* 7:9 [ed. Lieberman 2:179]), as long as we know which member is impure and can separate him out (*t. Pisha* 7:15 [ed. Lieberman 2:182]), there is not much other discussion about specific additional purity concerns with regard to eating the Passover in association. I assume, however, that the usual purity concerns for associations remain in operation.

maintenance – revolving around the sharing of a metonymic food item – with whom one eats makes a statement that affects more than just one meal; this social identity performance resonates throughout the tannaitic community.

Another example of how the Tannaim reinterpret Passover regulations to establish a rabbinic identity is their usage of table talk in a special kind of banquet: the Passover *seder*. Contrary to Baruch M. Bokser, I view the *seder* as a tannaitic symposium.[116] The tannaitic *locus classicus* is *m. Pesahim* 10, which contains the basic structure of a *seder*. In sum, this entire mishnaic chapter is the stage direction and dialogue for a ritual performance.[117] For example, this dialogue includes a script for a father to teach his son the basic lessons of Passover.[118] The importance of table talk for this particular symposium, however, is best summed up in *m. Pesahim* 10:5:

Rabban Gamaliel said: "Whoever did not say these three things on Passover did not fulfill his ritual obligation: the Passover [*pesaḥ*], unleavened bread [*maṣāh*], and bitter herbs [*mārôr*].[119] The Passover – because God [*māqōm*] passed over [*pāsaḥ*] the houses of our ancestors in Egypt. Unleavened

[116] *Origins of the Seder*, 50–66. Even though Bokser may be correct in arguing against Siegfried Stein, who claimed that the symposium literature was the impetus for the Passover *seder*, Bokser still fails to adequately account for the similarities between the two meal types (Stein, "The Influence of Symposia Literature on the Literary Form of the Pesah Haggadah," *JJS* 7 [1957]: 13–44, 15; Bokser, *Origins of the Seder*, 52–53). For examples of the opposite view, see Jonathan Brumberg-Kraus, "Meals As Midrash: A Survey of Ancient Meals in Jewish Studies Scholarship," in *Food and Judaism: Studies in Jewish Civilization 15*, ed. Leonard J. Greenspoon, Ronald A. Simkins, and Gerald Shapiro, 297–317 (Omaha, NE: Creighton University Press, 2004), 300–302; Smith, *From Symposium to Eucharist*, 149–150; Tabory, *The Passover Ritual*, 367–377.

[117] *m. Pesahim* 10 (ed. Albeck 2:176–180). For a similar analogy, see Brumberg-Kraus, "'Not By Bread Alone...,'" 173. Further, Brumberg-Kraus's article contains a comparison between the ritualized table talk of the rabbinic Passover *seder* and the Christian Eucharist.

[118] *m. Pesahim* 10:4 (ed. Albeck 2:177–178).

[119] For an examination of tannaitic views on woman's obligations to consume the Passover and unleavened bread (as well as lettuce), see Judith Hauptman, "Women in Tractate Pesahim," in *Atara L'Haim: Studies in the Talmud and Medieval Rabbinic Literature in Honor of Professor Haim Zalman Dimitrovsky*, ed. Daniel Boyarin, Shamma Friedman, Marc Hirshman, Menahem Schmelzer, and Israel M. Tashma, 63–78 (Jerusalem: Magnes Press, 2000 [Hebrew]), 66–69; Judith Hauptman, "From the Kitchen to the Dining Room: Women and Ritual Activities in Tractate *Pesahim*," in *A Feminist Commentary on the Babylonian Talmud: Introduction and Studies*, ed. Tal Ilan, Tamara Or, Dorothea M. Salzer, Christiane Steuer, and Irina Wandrey, 109–126 (Tübingen, Germany: Mohr Siebeck, 2007), 115–117.

bread – because our ancestors were redeemed in Egypt. Bitter herbs – because the Egyptians embittered [*mērĕrû*] the lives of our ancestors in Egypt."[120]

The ritual obligation of the Passover changes, "replacing" animal sacrifice with required verbalization.[121] Now, in addition to the biblical prescriptions regarding those who are eligible to observe the commandment to make a Passover, tannaitic literature adds yet another component: "the ritualization of Torah study at the table."[122] From now on, according to Rabban Gamaliel, the only way for a Jew to fulfill his ritual obligation on Passover is to engage in tannaitically approved and ordained table talk: the *seder*.

By establishing rules that govern the "house" in which the Passover is ingested, the Tannaim reinterpret the festival of Passover to establish boundaries between rabbinic and nonrabbinic Jews. Now, Passover is "properly" commemorated by eating together in table-fellowship, which requires specific rabbinically ordained practices (e.g., self-restraint and table talk). This reinterpretation of how a Jew "must" observe a festival becomes a *leitmotif* in tannaitic (and later amoraic) literature, as we shall see throughout this section.

Sukkot

The pilgrimage festival of Sukkot (Tabernacles) is originally a biblically ordained commemoration of the final agricultural harvest, which is later associated with the wandering of the post-Exodus Israelites through the desert.[123] Commanded to "dwell in booths seven days," numerous Second Temple-period sources attest to the fact that various Judeans/Jews adhere to this principle.[124] The celebration of Sukkot is also noted by non-Jewish

---

[120] *m. Pesahim* 10:5 (ed. Albeck 2:178). According to Brumberg-Kraus, "the things said and the things done – namely, the acts of eating – are arranged in such a way as to internalize Torah by in effect *eating it*, at least metaphorically" ("'Not By Bread Alone...,'" 174, emphasis in original). Brumberg-Kraus argues that this is accomplished via the "punning association of the scriptural proof texts with the ritual foods that are eaten" ("'Not By Bread Alone...,'" 174).

[121] See Bokser, *Origins of the Seder*, 42.

[122] Brumberg-Kraus, "Meals as Midrash," 306.

[123] For an overview of this history, see Jeffrey L. Rubenstein, *The History of Sukkot in the Second Temple Period and Rabbinic Periods*, BJS 302 (Atlanta: Scholars Press, 1995), 13–30.

[124] Leviticus 23:42. For an overview of the Second Temple evidence, see Rubenstein, *History of Sukkot*, 31–102. On the history of the terms *Judean* (an ethnic category) and *Jew*

witnesses. In the same passage in which he discusses the Sabbath (cited below), Plutarch notes that:

> ... the time and character of the greatest, most sacred holiday of the Jews clearly befit Dionysus. When they celebrate their so-called Fast, at the height of the vintage, they set out tables of all sorts of fruit under tents and huts plaited for the most part of vines and ivy. They call the first of the days of the feast Tabernacles. A few days later they celebrate another festival, this time identified with Bacchus not through obscure hints but plainly called by his name, a festival that is a sort of "Procession of Branches" or "Thyrsus Procession," in which they enter the temple each carrying a thyrsus. What they do after entering we do not know, but it is probable that the rite is a Bacchic revelry, for in fact they use little trumpets to invoke their god as do the Argives at their Dionysia...[125]

Even though much of Plutarch's statement is problematic historically,[126] it is nevertheless worthy of note that he associates the celebration of Sukkot with consuming food in the *sûkkāh* (booth). The connection between dwelling in a *sûkkāh* and eating therein is thus not to be considered a tannaitic innovation. However, the Tannaim build on this connection, reinterpreting commensality in the *sûkkāh* as a central and essential component of Sukkot observance and, by doing so, establishing Sukkot practices that construct a rabbinic identity.

The tannaitic principle regarding commensality and the *sûkkāh* is explicitly (but, at least for nonrabbinic Jews, most likely prescriptively) stated in *Sifra Emor* 17:5:

> "You shall dwell [in booths]" [Leviticus 23:42]: "dwell" refers only to the manner in which you reside [normally in your house].[127] From this they said: "One eats in the *sûkkāh*; one drinks in the *sûkkāh*; one rejoices[128] in the *sûkkāh*; one brings his utensils up to the *sûkkāh*."[129]

(a religious category), see Shaye J. D. Cohen, *The Beginnings of Jewishness: Boundaries, Varieties, Uncertainties* (Berkeley and Los Angeles: University of California Press, 2000), especially pp. 69–139.

[125] *Quaestiones Convivales*, 6:2.

[126] See Rubenstein, *History of Sukkot*, 94–97; M. Stern, *Greek and Latin Authors on Jews and Judaism*, 3 vols. (Jerusalem: Israel Academy of Sciences and Humanities), 1:56–561.

[127] Similarly, compare *t. Sotah* 3:10 (ed. Lieberman 4:161–162), which states, in regard to the people of the Tower of Babel, that "dwelling refers only to eating and drinking."

[128] On this translation, see Rubenstein, *History of Sukkot*, 226 n. 170.

[129] *Sifra Emor* 17:5 (ed. Weiss 103a). See also *Sifra Emor* 12:4 (ed. Weiss 102a), which states, "And with what do you sanctify the day [of Sukkot]? With eating, drinking, and nice [literally 'clean'] clothes." The same statement is made in regard to sanctifying Passover

To fulfill the biblical injunction, as tannaitic literature understands it, one must engage in everyday activities; one must live in it as one lives in a home, no more and no less.[130] This principle underlies tannaitic statements about consuming meals in the *sûkkāh*. For example, although one cannot eat a meal outside the *sûkkāh* on Sukkot, he may eat or drink "occasional" food (*'ăra'y*; i.e., a snack) elsewhere.[131] The *sûkkāh* is one's home for the duration of Sukkot and one acts therein as one does in one's home. As Rubenstein notes, "Occasional snacking is permitted outside the sukka, just as throughout the year one might snack outside of one's house. Full meals, however, must be consumed in the sukka, since throughout the year meals are eaten at home."[132] Thus, commensal regulations for Sukkot directly parallel those followed on nonfestival days.

The comparison between the home and the *sûkkāh* informs the tannaitic decision to abandon the structure should it rain too hard:

All seven days [of Sukkot] a man[133] makes his *sûkkāh* regular [i.e., dwells in it] and his house occasional. [If] rain falls, when is he permitted to empty [the *sûkkāh*]? From the point at which the porridge will spoil. They made a parable: To what is the matter comparable? To a slave who came to mix a cup [of wine] for his master, and he poured the flagon in his face.[134]

(*Mekilta d'Rabbi Ishmael Pisha Bo* 9 [ed. Horowitz 30:1–4]; = *Mekilta d'Rabbi Shimon b. Yohai* at Exodus 12:16 [ed. Epstein and Melamed 18:18–20]) and to honoring one's father and mother (*Mekilta d'Rabbi Ishmael Bahodesh Yitro* 8 [ed. Horowitz 231:6–7]).

[130] See Rubenstein, *History of Sukkot*, 226–227. In addition to eating in the *sûkkāh*, the Tannaim also assume that one does another activity that primarily occurs in the home: sleeping. For a discussion, see Rubenstein, *History of Sukkot*, 228–229.

[131] *m. Sukkah* 2:4 (ed. Albeck 2:264). In an obvious parallel, according to *m. Sukkah* 2:9 (ed. Albeck 2:265), the *sûkkāh* is the fixed structure and the home is the occasional one (*'ăra'y*) for the duration of Sukkot. Commenting on this, Rubenstein identifies a similar tannaitic logic with regard to meal location and Sabbath regulations, noting that "[t]he place where one plans to eat serves to establish a residence for the Sabbath" (*History of Sukkot*, 228 n. 174). As support for his statement, Rubenstein cites *m. Erubin* 3:1–8; 6:6–7 (ed. Albeck 2:90–95, 108–109). "Occasional" snacks are mentioned in other culinary and commensal contexts (for example, snacking on dough [*m. Hallah* 3:1 (ed. Albeck 1:281)]).

[132] *History of Sukkot*, 228. The amount that constitutes a snack for this legal purpose is debated in tannaitic literature (e.g., *m. Sukkah* 2:5 [ed. Albeck 2:264]; *t. Sukkah* 2:2 [ed. Lieberman 2:260]). Further, the precise number of meals necessary to be consumed in a *sûkkāh* is also debated (see *m. Sukkah* 2:6 [ed. Albeck 2:264]).

[133] Although '*ādām* is often translated as a generic "person," I believe that this text refers only to a male person, as implied by the immediately preceding mishnah (*m. Sukkah* 2:8 [ed. Albeck 2:265], discussed later in this chapter).

[134] *m. Sukkah* 2:9 (ed. Albeck 2:265).

Rain on Sukkot "indicates divine displeasure, that God no longer desires his commandment to be carried out. Since God does not want the sukka to be occupied, one may return to the house."[135] Although personal discomfort is clearly a concern here, it is interesting that the litmus test for leaving a *sûkkāh* relates to one's food being ruined.[136]

The question remains: How does this tannaitic reinterpretation of "proper" Sukkot practice (which is, to reiterate, most likely prescriptive from the perspective of nonrabbinic Jews) function as a social mechanism for enacting and maintaining rabbinic identity?[137] Although a festival occasion could be used to broaden one's communal boundaries, the borders around the tannaitic table remain in place on Sukkot. The *sûkkāh* is governed by the same rules as the tannaitic house. For example, as we have already seen in Chapter 3, women, slaves, and minors are exempt from the central obligation of Sukkot, as reinterpreted by the Tannaim: to dwell (i.e., to eat) in the *sûkkāh*.[138] The treatment of these categories of people therefore accords with tannaitic prescriptions of other commensal encounters. In sum, tannaitic evidence of Sukkot commensality – albeit slender – reinforces the picture drawn from other contexts: the tannaitic table is a locus for the construction of a Jewish, male, and rabbinic identity.

---

[135] Rubenstein, *History of Sukkot*, 232. According to *m. Ta'anit* 1:1 (ed. Albeck 2:331), rain on Sukkot is considered to be a sign of a curse.

[136] According to *t. Sukkah* 2:4 (ed. Lieberman 2:262), one need not return to the *sûkkāh* until after the rain ceases. Further, a *baraita* on *b. Sukkot* 29a states that one need not return to the *sûkkāh* until after he finishes his meal, even if it has already stopped raining. For a discussion, see Rubenstein, *History of Sukkot*, 232.

A curious datum appears in the midst of a discussion of what constitutes a wall for a *sûkkāh*, *t. Sukkah* 1:8 (ed. Lieberman 2:257–258) mentions that "a man may make his fellow [into] a side-wall, so that he may eat, drink, and sleep." As a by-product of a theoretical exploration about the number of walls necessary for a *sûkkāh*, a subject of debate among tannaitic and later sources (see Rubenstein, *History of Sukkot*, 223–225), one is tempted to simply dismiss this text as purely scholastic. Although that may be true, this text also mentions the inclusion of another person in a Sukkot meal. Consuming food with a fellow – who oddly constitutes one "wall" of the *sûkkāh* – is, at the very least, a by-product of this arrangement.

[137] The Amoraim further use the *sûkkāh* to establish a distinct, and privileged, identity. See *b. Avodah Zarah* 2a–3b, in which the *sûkkāh* is used to distinguish between Jews and Gentiles. For a discussion, see Jeffrey L. Rubenstein, *Talmudic Stories: Narrative Art, Composition, and Culture* (Baltimore: Johns Hopkins University Press, 1999), 212–242, especially pp. 233–234.

[138] *m. Sukkah* 2:8 (ed. Albeck 2:265). Contrast Deuteronomy 16:11, which explicitly mentions the inclusion of women in Sukkot celebrations.

The Sabbath

Looking first at non-Jewish evidence, we find that some first- and second-century C.E. Roman texts note the importance of commensality for Sabbath observance.[139] The two most famous of these accounts, by Persius and Plutarch, highlight the role that wine plays in the Sabbath meal. According to Persius:

> But when the day of Herod[140] comes round, when the lamps wreathed with violets and ranged round the greasy window-sills have spat forth their thick clouds of smoke, when the floppy tunnies' tails are curled round the dishes of red ware, and the white jars are swollen with wine, you silently twitch your lips, turning pale at the Sabbath of the circumcised.[141]

Persius understands the Sabbath meal to involve the ingestion of tunny fish (the largest member of the tuna family) and the drinking of wine. Although later rabbinic sources also suggest the suitability of fish as Sabbath food,[142] there is ample tannaitic evidence for the connection between wine and the Sabbath, as we shall see. Aware of this connection, Plutarch states, "I believe that even the feast of the Sabbath is not

---

[139] There are also several Greek and Roman texts that believe the Sabbath to be a fast day. The implications of these "witnesses" for understanding antique social history is debated. For references and discussion, see Robert Goldenberg, "The Jewish Sabbath in the Roman World up to the Time of Constantine the Great," in *ANRW* 19.1, 414–447 (Berlin: Walter de Gruyter, 1979), 424–425 n. 51, 435 n. 81, 439–441; Louis H. Feldman, *Jew and Gentile in the Ancient World* [Princeton, NJ: Princeton University Press, 1993], 162–164; Peter Schäfer, *Judeophobia: Attitudes toward the Jews in the Ancient World* (Cambridge, MA: Harvard University Press, 1997), 89–90. In contrast, even the *Therapeutae/Therapeutrides* mentioned by Philo, who eat only after sunset during the week, are said to eat – albeit simply – on the Sabbath (*De Vita Contemplativa*, 37).

[140] In the LCL edition, Ramsay renders the phrase "*Herodis dies*" as "Herod's birthday." I have changed the text to a more neutral translation in line with several scholars who suggest that this Latin phrase could also refer to the day of Herod's succession or to the Sabbath itself. See Goldenberg, "Jewish Sabbath," 435 n. 83; M. Stern, *Greek and Latin Authors*, 1:436 n. 179f.

[141] *Saturae*, 5:179–184.

[142] For references and a discussion, see Feldman, *Jew and Gentile*, 164; Samuel Krauss, *Talmudische Archäologie*, 3 vols. (Leipzig: Buchhandlung Gustav Fock, 1910), 110–112, 483–484 n. 514; M. Stern, *Greek and Latin Authors*, 1:437 n 183. Feldman also notes that "[t]he prominence of fish is attested by tiles from the ceiling of the Dura Europos synagogue which show pictures of fish as part of the Sabbath meal" (*Jew and Gentile*, 509 n. 99). The only evidence of this connection in the tannaitic corpus that I am aware of is *t. Pe'ah* 4:8 (ed. Lieberman 1:57, discussed in Chapter 1), which lists the Sabbath provisions given to a poor person as consisting of "oil, legumes, fish, and a vegetable."

completely unrelated to Dionysus.... The Jews themselves testify to a connection with Dionysus when they keep the Sabbath by inviting each other to drink and to enjoy wine."[143] The presence of wine at the Sabbath table, which leads Plutarch to connect this practice with the wine god Dionysus,[144] therefore seems to be a Jewish practice already known by first- and second-century non-Jewish authors. Further, "[t]he Latin name for the 'day of preparation' (i.e., Friday) was in fact *cena pura*, after the Jewish Sabbath-meal. Tertullian (ad nationes 1.13) lists the *cena pura* as a distinct Jewish ceremony."[145]

The enjoyment of food and wine in commensal commemoration of the Sabbath is therefore an experience that we expect to encounter in tannaitic literature. Unfortunately, we do not find much specific information. What we do find, however, is significant. Martin Jaffee summarizes the evidence well, stating:

The Torah of Moses, for example, enjoins Jews to "sanctify" the Sabbath. It offers, however, few explicit instructions on how such sanctification is to be achieved. The Mishnah, for its part, assumes this is done by taking a meal. It records a series of disputes – transmitted by the followers of two early–first century Pharisees named Hillel and Shammai – regarding precisely how to sanctify the Sabbath at the Friday evening meal that inaugurates the holy day. It is done by uttering a blessing called the *kiddush* ("sanctification")....

The disputes of the Shammaites and Hillelites regarding mealtime rituals provided generations of rabbinic disciples with food for thought. For our purposes, the interesting thing is not the theory behind each opinion, but the remarkable assumption shared by both parties. Each assumes that the Sabbath must be sanctified with blessings at a Friday night meal that includes wine. You will look in vain throughout the Torah of Moses for any such requirement. But it is assumed as a firm and noncontroversial fulfillment of a divine commandment to sanctify the Sabbath. The conflict concerns only the details of procedure.[146]

---

[143] *Quaestiones Convivales*, 6:2. Plutarch's comments are taken by most authors to be the only positive view of the Sabbath in the extant Greek and Roman corpus (e.g., Feldman, *Jew and Gentile*, 167; Schäfer, *Judeophobia*, 89–90).

[144] On this connection, see Feldman, *Jew and Gentile*, 501–502 n. 16.

[145] Goldenberg, "Jewish Sabbath," 435 n. 80. Unlike on a festival day, no form of cooking is allowed on the Sabbath. In fact, several tannaitic sources note that "the only difference between a festival and the Sabbath is in the preparation of food alone" (*m. Betzah* 5:2 [ed. Albeck 2:299–300]; *m. Megillah* 1:5 [ed. Albeck 2:357]; *t. Megillah* 1:7 [ed. Lieberman 2:345]).

[146] *Early Judaism*, 77. For these disputes, see *m. Berakhot* 8 (ed. Albeck 1:28–30).

In these debates, the Houses of Hillel and Shammai both assume that the Sabbath is marked by a meal that involves a wine blessing and a grace after meals.[147] Encountering another instance of tannaitically ordained table talk, it is once again apparent how words can affect social separation. Those with whom "We" eat are those who know the rules and the script for "Our" table talk.

m. Berakhot 8:8 highlights how tannaitic prescriptions concerning the wine blessing can serve as a social mechanism for inclusion or, possibly, exclusion:

If wine came to [those eating the Sabbath meal] after the meal, and there is only there that [one] cup – the House of Shammai says: "One recites the blessing over the wine, and afterwards recites the blessing over the meal." But the House of Hillel says: "One recites the blessing over the meal, and afterwards recites the blessing over the wine." They respond "Amen" after a Jew recites a blessing, but they do not respond "Amen" after the Samaritan recites a blessing, until one hears the entire blessing.[148]

The blessing of a rabbinic Jew is accepted forthwith; the blessing of a Samaritan – an ambiguous category somewhere between the binary poles of Jew and non-Jew[149] – is considered guilty until proven innocent. Hence, one must hear the entire blessing before deciding whether or not to endorse it by responding "Amen." Presumably, if a rabbinic Jew cannot respond "Amen" to a Samaritan's blessing, then they cannot break bread together. Although (at least scholastically) envisioned at the tannaitic Sabbath table, the tannaitic prescription that reflects initial distrust of Samaritans' blessing mandates caution when interacting commensally with them.

Besides the information about table talk, tannaitic literature does not contain much explicit evidence for understanding the role that Sabbath commensality plays in rabbinic identity construction. These group gatherings – obviously socially significant events – are not actually discussed in much detail. For example, we find only a fleeting hint about tannaitic

---

[147] Wine blessing: *m. Berakhot* 8:1, 8 (ed. Albeck 1:28, 30); grace after meals: *m. Berakhot* 8:7, 8 (ed. Albeck 1:30).
[148] *m. Berakhot* 8:8 (ed. Albeck 1:30).
[149] See my discussion earlier in this chapter about Samaritan bread.

Sabbath commensality in a reference to "five associations who observed the Sabbath in one dining room."[150] This particular text refers to Sabbath cooking issues and might very well be scholastic.[151] However, the reference to a Sabbath association is tantalizing. Does this function similarly to the previous associations that we have seen?[152] Is this a common tannaitic practice? In the end, we are left with more questions than answers.

An interesting contrast to the social separation affected by the table talk surrounding the tannaitic Sabbath table is found in a conversation about tithing food served at the Sabbath meal. If a guest is invited to another's home for the Sabbath and doubts the tithed status of the food and wine that he will eat there, he can decide prior to the Sabbath to separate out some of the food and wine that he will be served on the Sabbath and declare it as a tithe.[153] This legal fiction allows for a leniency, whereby a "proper" tannaitic Jew may eat in the home of one who is, at the very least, less than meticulous about tannaitic law. In this case, the fact that the host is not in complete compliance with tannaitic law does not necessarily prevent social intercourse from occurring. This potentially problematic commensal encounter is mitigated by the recitation of a formula that allows the rabbinic Jew to "control" the situation. As noted earlier in this chapter with regard to commensal relations between ḥabērîm and ʿammê hāʾāreṣ, although these regulations do not amount to insurmountable obstacles, one must neither ignore nor minimize the fact that they are, nevertheless, obstacles.

---

[150] *m. Erubin* 6:6 (ed. Albeck 2:108). The word for "dining room," *ṭrāqlîn*, is clearly related to the Greek *triklinion* and the Latin *triclinium*.

[151] The question at hand is whether each association needs its own separate ʿērûb (a complicated legal fiction that creates a community and extends the boundaries wherein certain acts otherwise forbidden on the Sabbath can occur). For another example of social food preparation that relates to the Sabbath, see the concept of the communal cooking partnership for the Sabbath and festivals (e.g., *m. Erubin* 7:6 [ed. Albeck 2:112–113]).

[152] It might, as the issue at hand is whether each association needs its own ʿērûb. If so (and both houses agree that it does if it occurs in its own room), then the social logic appears to be that each association constitutes its own community, much as each association constitutes one "house" on Passover.

[153] *m. Demai* 7:1–2 (ed. Albeck 1:89–90); *t. Demai* 8:4–5 (ed. Lieberman 1:101–102). These texts assume that the host has, however, separated the heave offering. For a discussion, with references, of this text in the Mishnah, see Sarason, *Mishnaic Law of Agriculture*, 244–246.

The material about the Sabbath is unfortunately too limited to draw significant conclusions.[154] I am struck, however, by the fact that, once again, tannaitic table talk appears in a commensal situation. The transformative power of "proper" words and liturgical formulae seems to function as a controlling mechanism for social inclusion and exclusion. This appears to be true even in the case of Sabbath commensality between a "normative" rabbinic Jewish guest and his host who serves doubtfully tithed food. To allow this meal to occur, the guest must recite the proper formula that conditionally designates tithes from the food in question, which he will separate after the Sabbath.[155] Although this is not necessarily a case of words spoken at a table, it does (at least) concern words spoken to approach a table. It would seem that, once again, tannaitic literature considers words – as well as the joint partaking of a festival meal – to construct rabbinic identity at the table.

Commensality and the Synagogue

The various tannaitic festival meals discussed thus far occur at several locations (e.g., house, *sûkkāh*). Noticeably absent from locative descriptions of tannaitic commensal encounters is the synagogue. Although *t. Ma'aserot* 2:20 (ed. Lieberman 1:236) allows for, under certain circumstances, the eating of a snack (*'arayy*) in a synagogue, a snack does not equal a meal, as we saw earlier with regard to Sukkot, where one was permitted to consume a snack (*'ăra'y*), but not a meal, outside a *sûkkāh*.[156] In fact, *t. Megillah* 2:18 specifically prohibits eating and drinking within a synagogue:

Synagogues – they do not behave in them light-heartedly. One should not enter into them in the heat because of the heat, nor in the cold because of the cold, nor in the rain because of the rain. *And they do not eat in them, nor drink in them,* nor sleep in them, nor stroll in them, nor enjoy themselves

---

[154] For example, see the (perhaps coincidental) fact that the Sabbath table itself is the setting for two texts that imply the presence of women in a mixed-gender commensal context (*m. Ketubbot* 5:9 [ed. Albeck 3:107]; *m. Shabbat* 23:2 [ed. Albeck 2:70], both discussed in Chapter 3). Whether this suggests that the Sabbath table is a more open, or perhaps simply different, commensal setting remains uncertain.

[155] Sarason, *Mishnaic Law of Agriculture*, 244.

[156] See *m. Sukkah* 2:4 (ed. Albeck 2:264). *t. Ma'aserot* 2:20 prohibits snacking in a synagogue with living quarters, but allows snacking in one lacking such accommodations.

in them. But, they read [Scripture] and repeat [Mishnah traditions] and expound [on exegetical traditions] in them.[157]

Eating and drinking appear among a list of tannaitically prohibited synagogue activities. In contrast, learning and discussing Written and Oral Torah are permitted to occur in a synagogue. Interestingly, the role that these "serious" activities play as suitable topics of discussion at the tannaitic dinner table is not considered. It would seem that table talk makes the meal serious, but not serious enough for the synagogue.[158]

However, it is important to keep in mind the apparent prescriptive nature of this toseftan tradition. As Levine notes:

This source is often mistakenly quoted as an indication of what did not take place in the synagogue. In reality, however, it indicates what was actually happening in the synagogue and that to which the rabbis objected; whether or not the sages were effective in influencing this objectionable behavior is another issue. As of the time of the above statement, at least, the objectionable practices were still very much part of synagogue activity and inspired the above apodictic declaration. By focusing on what the rabbis wished to prohibit, we may gain a clearer idea of how, in fact, many synagogues were then functioning.[159]

---

[157] t. Megillah 2:18 (ed. Lieberman 2:353), emphasis added. In the opinion of some scholars, this tradition is contradicted by m. Zabim 3:2 (ed. Albeck 6:444–445), which uses the expression "members of the synagogue" (bĕnê hakĕneset) in reference, "so it seems, to the haverim who ate their secular food in a state of purity, from which some wish to infer that communal meals were eaten in the synagogue" (Oppenheimer, 'Am ha-Aretz, 137; for an example of such a scholar, see Chaim Rabin, Qumran Studies [Oxford: Oxford University Press, 1957], 34). I am reluctant to make this inference for two reasons. First, some manuscripts of the Mishnah simply read "the synagogue" (replacing the word bĕnê with bêt; see Oppenheimer, 'Am ha-Aretz, 137 n. 61). Although Albeck suggests that this variant could also function as a synonym, I am hesitant to speculate on that which is already speculation. Second, even if this text does refer to "haverim who ate their secular food in a state of purity," this action is not explicitly said to occur in the synagogue. Further, one anonymous reader raised the possibility that t. Megillah 2:18 preserves a minority opinion, wherein the synagogue is "holier" than a dinner table. I do not find this suggestion compelling, because the relevant statement – and, in fact, the entire pericope – is presented in an anonymous, authoritative voice; it is not attributed to a single rabbi, as one might expect with a minority opinion.

[158] Apparently, amoraic literature understands the concept of "if you cannot beat them, join them," as several texts clearly allow dining in the synagogue. For references, see Lee I. Levine, The Ancient Synagogue: The First Thousand Years (New Haven, CT: Yale University Press, 2000), 369.

[159] Ancient Synagogue, 179. Similarly, see Matthew J. Martin, "Communal Meals in the Late Antique Synagogue," in Feast, Fast or Famine: Food and Drink in Byzantium, ed. Wendy Mayer and Silke Trzcionka, 135–146 (Brisbane: Byzantina Australiensia, 2005).

It seems that this practice, among others, is proscribed in an attempt to assert authority over a domain of which the Tannaim did not have as much control as they would like (nor as much as they would like us to believe they did).[160] In the ideal synagogue populated by rabbinic Jews, it seems, meals would not occur; unfortunately for the Tannaim, the extant evidence suggests that the majority of synagogues did not adhere to this rabbinic practice.

The evidence in support of meals occurring in the synagogue both prior to and contemporary with the Tannaitic period is suggestive.[161] The Theodotos inscription, which many scholars date to the first century C.E., describes a Jerusalem synagogue built "for the reading of the Law [i.e., Torah] and the study of commandments, and a guesthouse and rooms and water installations for hosting those in need from abroad."[162] The stated role as a hostel certainly suggests the presence of eating and drinking. Further, Josephus refers to an edict by Gaius Caesar that allows Jews

---

[160] Martin suggests that the cultic connotations of synagogue meals might have discomforted the rabbis ("Communal Meals," 142–145).

[161] For an overview of the material and literary evidence, see Martin, "Communal Meals."

[162] Translation by Levine, *Ancient Synagogue*, 55. On the Theodotos inscription in general, see Levine, *Ancient Synagogue*, 54–56; Leah Roth-Gerson, *The Greek Inscriptions from the Synagogues in the Land of Israel* (Jerusalem: Yad Izhak Ben Zvi, 1987 [Hebrew]), 76–86; L. Michael White, *The Social Origins of Christian Architecture, II: Texts and Monuments for the Christian Domus Ecclesiae in its Environment* (Valley Forge, PA: Trinity Press, 1997), 294–295. White problematizes the regnant scholarly view on the first-century C.E. date of the Theodotos inscription (*Social Origins*, 294 n. 32); however, he offers no concrete alternative dating, so I retain the majority opinion here. Further, possible evidence for meals occurring at a synagogue in the first century B.C.E. may be found in two literary documents. First, a Greek papyrus details a series of feasts at Apollinopolis Magna (Victor A. Tcherikover, Alexander Fuks, and Menahem Stern, *Corpus Papyrorum Judaicarum*, 3 vols. [Cambridge, MA: Harvard University Press, 1957–1964], 1, no. 139 [pp. 254–255]). Some scholars argue that this "Jewish dining-club" (as Fuks terms it) probably met in a local synagogue (e.g., Erich S. Gruen, *Diaspora: Jews Amidst Greeks and Romans* [Cambridge, MA: Harvard University Press, 2002], 307 n. 97; Levine, *Ancient Synagogue*, 129; Magnus Z. Zetterholm, *The Formation of Christianity in Antioch: A Social-Scientific Approach to the Separation Between Judaism and Christianity* [New York: Routledge Press, 2005], 40). Because this datum is not explicit in the extant text of this fragmentary papyrus, I am hesitant to cite this as evidence for synagogue-based banquets. Second, 3 Maccabees 7:20 mentions that a place of prayer (*proseuche*) is dedicated on the site of a banquet. This text seems to imply that this banquet is a yearly event. As Gruen notes: "Whatever credence one gives to the story, the inauguration of such a festival to be celebrated in a synagogue would itself have been perfectly logical" (*Diaspora*, 118). Whether this logical conclusion translates to historical reality, however, is not entirely certain.

to assemble (*sunagesthai*) and hold common meals (*sundeipna*), assumed by scholars to imply the presence of communal meals in the synagogue.[163] Comments made by Origen and John Chrysostom also seem to support the prevalence of meals at the synagogue in antiquity.[164] Finally, other archeological remains may indicate the presence of synagogue-based meals, including *triclinia*.[165] However, the dates assigned to various strata are often contested and the recent trend in scholarship seems to be to continually date these finds to later centuries than were previously thought.[166] Thus, although this is certainly the case for Amoraic-period synagogues, their presence in the Tannaitic period is, at this point, hotly debated.[167]

Extant material remains and external literary witnesses suggest (although, admittedly, sometimes circumstantially) that commensality has a place in the Tannaitic-period synagogue. As at least *t. Megillah* 2:18

---

[163] *Jewish Antiquities*, 14:214–216. For examples of scholars who make this assumption, see Gruen, *Diaspora*, 117; Zetterholm, *Formation of Christianity*, 40. Although this connection is not explicit, the use of the verb "assemble" (*sunagesthai*) is quite suggestive. However, as Schwartz is careful to note in regard to *Jewish Antiquities* book 14, "[r]emarkably, the most commonly mentioned ritual activities are neither prayer nor sacrifice but common meals and fund-raising. Torah reading is not mentioned. If these documents are taken seriously, they show that even in places where the Jews constituted ethnic/religious corporations, the corporations were not in every case synagogue- and Torah-centered, though they were in some places" (*Imperialism*, 221). Many scholars point to the similarity between these activities and those said to occur in contemporary "Pagan" temples (e.g, Levine, *Ancient Synagogue*, 131, 179 n. 64; Zetterholm, *Formation of Christianity*, 40). Further, I leave aside the question as to the extent of the presence of non-Jews in synagogues (see Cohen, *Beginnings of Jewishness*, 55 n. 119; Zetterholm, *Formation of Christianity*, 40).

[164] For references to and discussion on the corroborative statements made by these Church Fathers, see Levine, *Ancient Synagogue*, 272–274; Martin, "Communal Meals," 140.

[165] For references, see Levine, *Ancient Synagogue*, 179, 369–370.

[166] As Schwartz notes, "In the last two decades, however, the traditional chronology of the ancient synagogue has collapsed. It seems unlikely that any post-Destruction [i.e., post-70 C.E.] Palestinian synagogue whose remains survive much predates 300 C.E." (*Imperialism*, 135). Jodi Magness, in particular, has argued in favor of later dates for Palestinian synagogues (e.g., "When Were the Galilean-Type Synagogues Built?," *Cathedra* 101 [2001]: 39–70 [Hebrew]; and "The Question of the Synagogue: The Problem of Typology," in *Judaism in Late Antiquity, Part Three, Where We Stand: Issues and Debates in Ancient Judaism. Volume Four: The Special Problem of the Synagogue*, ed. Alan J. Avery-Peck and Jacob Neusner, 1–48 [Leiden, the Netherlands: Brill, 2001]).

[167] For references to commensality in Amoraic-period synagogues, see Ben-Zion Rosenfeld and Joseph Menirav, *Markets and Marketing in Roman Palestine*, trans. Chava Cassel (Boston: Brill, 2005), 225–226.

indicates, this practice is not wholeheartedly endorsed by the Tannaim, who seek to prohibit such meals from occurring as part of a larger attempt to exert control over the synagogue; however, they lack (at this time) the authority to prevent the occurrence of synagogue-based meals.[168] In the midst of a tannaitic attempt to stake an authoritative claim over activities in the synagogue, we once again encounter a situation in which the Tannaim seek to introduce innovative practices in an effort to construct a different identity.

JEWISH MALE RABBINIC IDENTITY: CONCLUSIONS

Jonathan Z. Smith reminds scholars of the history of religion to search out difference, because "[d]ifference is rarely something simply to be noted; it is, most often, something in which one has a stake. Above all, it is a political matter.... [It] most frequently entails a hierarchy of prestige and the concomitant political ranking of super-ordinate and subordinate."[169] Difference makes all the difference.

Although nonrabbinic Jews remain classified as Jews in tannaitic literature, they are distinguished from rabbinic Jews and marked as "Other" in these texts. In this chapter, I have argued that the Tannaim create difference between rabbinic and nonrabbinic Jews in part via four food practices. First, they develop a distinct rabbinic cuisine and foodway and connect the consumption thereof with the construction of a rabbinic identity. Second, the Tannaim expand the biblical purity system to employ it as another mechanism by which culinary and commensal practices establish a distinct Jewish, male, and rabbinic identity. However, even though purity issues – which are concerned solely with interactions between Jews, and not non-Jews, in this context – problematize many social encounters, they do not necessarily prohibit all table-based social intercourse. Although food practices form distinct identities, these need not be completely isolated identities. Third, they once again correlate the status of food and the status of its cook, suggesting a predictable analogy

---

[168] On the limits of rabbinic authority at this time, see Schwartz, *Imperialism*, 103–128.
[169] "What a Difference a Difference Makes," in *"To See Ourselves as Others See Us": Christians, Jews, "Others" in Late Antiquity*, ed. Jacob Neusner and Ernest S. Frerichs, 3–48 (Chico, CA: Scholars Press, 1985), 4, 5.

between tannaitic food regulations and desired social relations. Fourth, the Tannaim reinterpret festival rules to exclude nonrabbinic Jews from the tannaitically defined "proper" observance of these festivals. Unable to "properly" engage in festival practices, these nonrabbinic Jews are thus marked as an "internal Other" vis-à-vis the Tannaim.

By establishing culinary and commensal regulations that require different social practices for rabbinic Jews, the Tannaim create difference. This difference results in a distinctly rabbinic identity; yet these differences are almost certainly prescriptive. For example, we should not assume that every Jew in third-century C.E. Palestine observed – let alone was aware of – the rabbinic prohibition against consuming meat and milk together found in *m. Hullin* 8:1.[170] Although this behavior marks this Jew as different, it does not mark him as a non-Jew. However, he is still different. A meal of meat and cheese, which was once unworthy of comment, is now "hermeneutically marked" for social difference.[171]

Further, it is important to remember that prescriptive discourse is an attempt to control a situation. Thus, even when the Tannaim create leniencies allowing for social and/or economic interactions between *ḥabērîm* and *'ammê hā'āreṣ*, for example, the nature of that intercourse has been recast. These rules ensure that at every moment rabbinic Jews remember with whom they are engaging in culinary and commensal interactions. Often, the Tannaim used specific words and formulae to affect this control, including required blessings for animal slaughter and a formula to conditionally designate tithes for Sabbath commensality. However, as the data concerning commensality in the synagogue suggest, scholars must remember that these attempts to control are often prescriptive; they do not necessarily describe the practices of all Jews in Roman-period Palestine.

Although the emerging difference between rabbinic and nonrabbinic Jews does not inevitably present an insurmountable obstacle in the path between the table of one and the table of the other, it is an obstacle nonetheless. As time elapses and different practices continue to rcify

---

[170] *m. Hullin* 8:1 (ed. Albeck 5:137–138).
[171] On the concept of "hermeneutically marked" data, see Azzan Yadin, *Scripture as Logos: Rabbi Ishmael and the Origins of Midrash* (Philadelphia: University of Pennsylvania Press, 2004), 48–79.

difference, the borders of one table are distanced more and more from the borders of the other. And as the amoraic evidence indicates, this trend of differentiating the rabbinic from the nonrabbinic Jew would continue, expanding greatly over time.[172]

[172] See Freidenreich, Foreign Food, 177–214.

Conclusion

BASSANIO
If it please you to dine with us –

SHYLOCK
Yes, to smell pork, to eat of the habitation which your prophet the Nazarite conjured the devil into.[1] I will buy with you, sell with you, talk with you, walk with you, and so following; but I will not eat with you, drink with you, nor pray with you.[2]

With whom you eat is a powerful statement about your identity, whether you live in 210 C.E. or 2010 C.E.[3] Breaking bread is a social language that operates under the assumption that commensality is a practice that results in social digestion – breaking groups into smaller social units. This presumption is tacit in English vernacular, as the Latin derivation of the word "companion" literally means "one with whom one shares bread." When Shylock declines Bassanio's dinner invitation, his refusal to participate in commensality with Gentiles contains two assumptions that we have encountered throughout this book: (1) commensality leads to social intimacy and identity; and (2) pork is a metonymic food of the "culinary Other."

---

[1] See Mark 5:1–20; Matthew 8:28–34; Luke 8:26–39, discussed in Chapter 2.
[2] William Shakespeare, *The Merchant of Venice*, act 1, scene 3, lines 26–30. I have consulted the following edition: William Shakespeare, *The Merchant of Venice*, ed. M. M. Mahood (Cambridge, UK: Cambridge University Press, 2003), 84.
[3] The Slow Food movement – a group formed in Italy in 1986 as a response to their perception of the deleterious affects on society caused by fast food culture – has revived the ancient Roman concept of convivium. See Simona Malatesta, Sarah Weiner, and Winnie Yang, *The Slow Food Companion* (Bra, Italy: Centro Stampa srl, 2006), 9.

Throughout, I have argued that the Tannaim innovate and manipulate food practices to construct a distinctly Jewish, male, and rabbinic identity. As I argue in Chapter 1, however, what the Tannaim ate, and how they obtained, prepared, and consumed their food, does not differ on the macro level (i.e., in general structure and appearance) from that of their ancient Mediterranean contemporaries. Where it does differ is on the micro level. For example, the presence of table talk is not unique, but the content – "words of Torah" – is. Tannaitic culinary and commensal practices therefore reflect their social environment, at the same time that they reflect a shift in how these practices construct identity.

Chapter 2 marked the beginning of my overall structure, wherein I broke the effects of tannaitic food regulations on identity down into three categories: Jewish, male, and rabbinic. Chapter 2 explored the establishment of a distinctly Jewish identity, in part, via three practices. First, the Tannaim construct a network of culinary and commensal practices that cumulatively constitute a uniquely Jewish foodway by understanding certain foods as metonymic and embodying (i.e., pig, manna, the Passover, and *kashrut* practices in general). Second, the Tannaim make a predictable analogy between food regulations and desired social relations by correlating the status of a food item with the status of its preparer (i.e., meat and the so-called Mediterranean triad). Third, the Tannaim use legal and persuasive rhetoric, such as the slippery slope argument, to stigmatize and marginalize social relations with those with whom they do not wish Jews to interact convivially – in the fullest sense of the word – by connecting commensality between Jews and non-Jews with the binary opposite of Jewishness: idolatry. This chapter also introduced a trend detected in tannaitic, as well as most Second Temple-period, texts: even though these regulations sought to separate, they did not require Jews to live completely separately. The inclusion of accommodations and leniencies that allowed for economic and social interactions between Jews and non-Jews is not unique, as subsequent chapters demonstrated.

Chapter 3 turned attention to gender and the ways in which tannaitic culinary and commensal practices construct a Jewish, male identity. The primary concern with male identity in the tannaitic corpus underscored the literary role that women play therein. Thus, depictions of women at work in the discursive site of the tannaitic kitchen were found to elucidate how women's actions affect male practice; they were not of interest in and of themselves. In short, women both produced bread and (re)produced male identity when they – either descriptively or prescriptively – adhered to tannaitic food regulations. One repercussion of the literary role that women played was the inability to ascertain to what extent women could, and did, participate in tannaitic commensality. Another repercussion was the tension inherent in a system in which women are ceded the "resource control" provided by control over the kitchen, despite the fact that the actions that occur therein have direct consequences on a male, practice-based identity. In an attempt to mitigate this tension, in the tannaitic kitchen, whether present or absent, the male rabbi is understood to be the "chef," whereas a woman (often his wife) plays the subordinate role of the "sous-chef." Once again, though, the Tannaim create leniencies that allow for the economic necessity of shared cookery. However, they impose limits on these interactions, which are almost always depicted as occurring between two Jewish (rabbinic or otherwise) women. For example, the Tannaim mandate at which step in the bread-making process shared cookery can no longer occur (i.e., the introduction of water, which is both more complicated from a purity standpoint and the cultural moment when nature transforms into culture).

Finally, Chapter 4 examined how the Tannaim employ four food practices to construct a Jewish, male, and rabbinic identity. First, they develop the notion of a distinct rabbinic cuisine and foodway and then connect its consumption with the construction of a distinctly rabbinic identity. Second, they adapt and expand the biblical purity system to use it as yet another mechanism by which food practices establish rabbinic identity. In this context, however, purity issues are concerned solely with interactions between Jews, and not between Jews and non-Jews. Third, they correlate the status of food and the status of its cook, suggesting a predictable analogy between tannaitic food regulations and desired social relations, as also discussed in Chapter 2. Fourth, they reinterpret festival rules, effectively excluding nonrabbinic Jews from the "proper" observance of these festivals. Now, according to the Tannaim, to "properly" observe various holidays – including Passover, Sukkot, and the Sabbath – a Jew must conform to tannaitic practices. Failure to do so marks nonrabbinic Jews as "Others" vis-à-vis the Tannaim. In this chapter, as in those preceding it, tannaitic culinary and commensal regulations were found to contain leniencies allowing for economic and social interactions; at the same time, however, the Tannaim controlled these interactions, which they deemed problematic. Thus, for example, although tannaitic purity regulations regarding *ḥabērîm* and *'ammê hā'āreṣ* may make many social encounters problematic, they do not necessarily prohibit all table-based social intercourse. Tannaitic food practices form distinct – though not necessarily isolated – identities. Finally, as the data concerning commensality in the synagogue suggest, scholars must always remember that tannaitic attempts to control Jewish practice are often prescriptive; they do not necessarily describe the practices of all Jews in Roman-period Palestine.

Although this has been a synchronic historical study – focusing on a literary corpus redacted in circa-third-century C.E. Palestine – future work on how the next generation of rabbis, the Amoraim, construct identity via food practices is a desideratum. As I have occasionally noted throughout this book, the Amoraim greatly expand and make more explicit the function that culinary and commensal regulations serve in the construction of particular identities. For example, several foodstuffs are prohibited in the Babylonian Talmud not because of their ingredients, but "on account of intermarriage."[4] In these instances, the Amoraim perceive the ramifications of eating or drinking certain Gentile food items to be so severe that they explicitly exclude these foodstuffs on the grounds that partaking thereof would inevitably lead to a social mixture of which they are quite concerned. Although several tannaitic texts express discomfort about such encounters, even in regard to intermarriage, none are nearly as direct and blunt as these passages from the Babylonian Talmud. A diachronic study of these practices would bring us into a new temporal horizon, as well as a new geographical location (namely, Babylonia). Before such a diachronic study could be undertaken, however, it was first necessary to collect and parse the tannaitic data, a task accomplished in this book. In particular, it was important to bring the tannaitic *midrashim* into the picture, as they are often given short shrift in relation to the Mishnah and Tosefta.

Further, the approach employed in this work is useful for cross-cultural comparisons. To understand how food regulations help to construct socially specific identities, for example, one must consider both

---

[4] See *b. Avodah Zarah* 31b, 35b (also see 36b).

the "external Other" (in this case, non-Jews) and the "internal Other" (nonrabbinic Jews).[5] The precise way in which each author or group employs food practices to construct identity, however, will obviously not always be the same. Thus, although the topic of gender merited an entire chapter in this study, other projects might require significant discussion of race, ethnicity, class, colonialism, and the like. Further, although tannaitic literature discusses a cornucopia of foods and food practices, for some authors or groups a single food item or practice might serve as a unifying metaphor for first- and second-order analysis.[6]

In extending the approach taken in this book to other historical and/or geographical contexts, the cross-cultural utility of two concepts developed herein should be tested: edible identity and the chef/sous-chef principle. "Edible identity" is a term that refers to the matrix of culturally significant practices surrounding the preparation and ingestion of food that allows for diners to make an identity statement by the manner in which they partake of their dinner. In coining this term, I attempted to account for a variety of concepts and theories: from notions that "you are what you eat" to anthropological observations about foodways. At the same time, it is intended to remind readers that identity is, in fact, edible, as various food practices embody both the individual and the communal body. According to the chef/sous-chef principle, kitchen activity is divided into two categories: the role of the "chef" and the subordinate role of the "sous-chef." By creating such a division, shared cooking between binary categories of people (Jew/non-Jew, etc.) is simultaneously allowed and controlled. It is my contention that both "edible identity" and the chef/sous-chef principle have heuristic value when exploring cultures beyond the boundary of the present study. However, I leave it to other scholars to assess the veracity of this claim. The proof shall be in the proverbial pudding.

---

[5] I take the terms "internal Other" and "external Other" from Christine Hayes, "The 'Other' in Rabbinic Literature," in *The Cambridge Companion to the Talmud and Rabbinic Literature*, ed. Charlotte Elisheva Fonrobert and Martin S. Jaffee, 243–269 (New York: Cambridge University Press, 2007), 243.

[6] To cite one example from which I often draw throughout my own work, rice in Japan, about which Emiko Ohnuki-Tierney writes, "In all of these encounters between selves and others, the multivocal rice and rice paddies have served as the vehicle for deliberation about the self-identity as it transforms into selves and as the internal source of purity for the ever-changing self" (*Rice as Self: Japanese Identities through Time* [Princeton, NJ: Princeton University Press, 1993], 136).

Another methodological point that may be useful to apply to the study of rabbinic food regulations, as well as to other contexts, is the fact that, throughout this study, no global (i.e., monothetic or monocausal) explanation was offered for why the Tannaim chose certain food practices over others. Although Chapter 1 did contextualize the food options available to the Tannaim, tannaitic food practices were always discussed on the local level (i.e., third-century C.E. Palestine). For example, one can account for tannaitic leniencies with regard to Gentile olive oil within the context of the diet and economic factors that were specific to this commodity. However, tannaitic prohibitions of Gentile meat were influenced by different circumstances. As such, there is no one global explanation that accounts for every culinary and commensal regulation enacted by the Tannaim. Although this approach might seem comparable to Marvin Harris's attempt to explain the rationale behind various food taboos,[7] I am actually advocating something quite different. Rather than a transhistorical and transgeographical case study akin to Harris's, I would suggest that scholars need to analyze each individual data set to find trends within. Perhaps a global explanation would work for some of these corpora, perhaps not. However, elegant, overarching explanations for disparate food practices should not be a presumed result of these studies, as often this amounts to a mission destined to failure. Offering piecemeal explanations for a cow taboo in India and a pork taboo in ancient Southwest Asia, as Harris attempts to do, also leaves much to be desired. It seems to me that it is worth the time for scholars to conduct more geographically and temporally localized studies aimed at explaining how and why specific food practices are used to create identity.

While offering advice on how to eat out at restaurants with friends and still remain on a diet, Sarah Ferguson, the former Duchess of York, suggests, "You separate the social (joining the party) from the personal (what you ingest)."[8] Ferguson, however, misses a key point, one that we have encountered several times throughout the course of this study of tannaitic texts: *what* one ingests is often a practice that reinforces one's ability to "join the party." The Tannaim, like many people who

---

[7] See *Good to Eat: Riddles of Food and Culture* (Long Grove, IL: Waveland Press, 1998).
[8] Sarah Ferguson, "Dinner with Friends: Sound, Satisfying Advice (for Body *and* Soul) on How to Rethink a Night on the Town," *Weight Watchers Magazine* November/December (2003): 54.

come before and after them, define identity in part by what is on one's plate and in part by who is on one's guest list. When analyzing the food practices of any given culture, one must always remember that the table is an important locus for identity construction – a contested space that provides both food for biological sustenance and food for thought.

Bibliography

PRIMARY SOURCES

Arrian: Oldfather, W.A., ed. *The Discourses as Reported by Arrian, The Manual, and Fragments: Epictetus*. 2 vols. LCL. Cambridge, MA: Harvard University Press, 1978–1979.

Avot d'Rabbi Natan: Schechter, Solomon, ed. *Aboth de Rabbi Nathan: Edited from Manuscripts with an Introduction, Notes and Appendices*. New York: Philipp Feldheim, 1967.

Cato: Hooper, William Davis and Harrison Boyd Ash, eds. *Cato and Varro: On Agriculture*. LCL. Cambridge, MA: Harvard University Press, 1979.

Contra Celsum: Chadwick, Henry. *Contra Celsum*. Cambridge: Cambridge University Press, 1965.

Damascus Document: Baumgarten, Joseph M. *Qumran Cave 4: XIII: The Damascus Document (4Q266–273)*. DJD 18. Oxford: Clarendon Press, 1996.

Diodorus Siculus: Walton, Francis R., ed. *Diodorus Siculus: Library of History, XI, Fragments of Books 21–32*. LCL. Cambridge, MA: Harvard University Press, 1957.

Diodorus Siculus: Walton, Francis R., ed. *Diodorus Siculus: Library of History, XII, Fragments of Books 33–40*. LCL. Cambridge, MA: Harvard University Press, 1967.

Genesis Rabba: Theodor, J. and Ch. Albeck, eds. *Midrash Bereshit Rabba*. 3 vols. Jerusalem: Wahrmann Books, 1965.

Gerim: Kanevski, Shemaryahu Yosef Hayim ben Y. Y, ed. *Baraita Masekhet Sefer Torah*. Bene Barak, Israel: H. Kanevski, 1998.

Gerim: Simon, M., ed. "Gerim." In *Minor Tractates: Translated into English With Notes, Glossary and Indices*, ed. Abraham Cohen, 60a–61b. London: Soncino Press, 1984.

Greek and Latin Authors on Jews and Judaism: Stern, Menahem. *Greek and Latin Authors on Jews and Judaism*. 3 vols. Jerusalem: Israel Academy of Sciences and Humanities, 1976.

Hebrew Bible: *Biblia Hebraica Stuttgartensia*, ed. A. Alt, O. Eißfeldt, and P. Kahle. Stuttgart: Deutsche Bibelgesellschaft, 1997.

Herodotus: Godley, A. D., ed. *Herodotus: The Persian Wars*. 4 vols. LCL. Cambridge, MA: Harvard University Press, 1999.

Josephus: Thackeray, H. St. J., R. Marcus, A. Wikgren, and L. H. Feldman, eds. *Josephus*. 10 vols. LCL. Cambridge, MA: Harvard University Press, 1926–1965.
Juvenal: Ramsay, G. G., ed. *Juvenal and Persius*. LCL. Cambridge, MA: Harvard University Press, 1979.
Letter of Aristeas: Pelletier, André, ed. *Lettre d'Aristée a Philocrate: Introduction, Texte Critique, Traduction et Notes, Index Complet des Mots Grecs*. Sources Chrétiennes: Série Annexe de Textes Non–Chrétiens 89. Paris: Les Éditions du Cerf, 1962.
Mekilta d'Rabbi Ishmael: Horowitz, Hayim Shaul, ed. *Mekilta d'Rabbi Ishmael*. Jerusalem: Bamberger & Wahrmann, 1960.
Mekilta d'Rabbi Shimon b. Yohai: Epstein, J. N. and E. Z. Melamed. *Mekilta d'Rabbi Shimon b. Yohai*. Jerusalem: Meqisei Nirdamim, 1955.
Mekilta d'Rabbi Shimon b. Yohai: Hoffman, David Zvi, ed. *Mekilta d'Rabbi Shimon b. Yohai*. Frankfurt: J. Kauffman, 1905.
Mishnah: Albeck, Hanokh, ed. *Six Books of the Mishnah*. 6 vols. Jerusalem: Bialik Institute, 1952–1958.
New Testament: Aland, Barbara, Kurt Aland, Johannes Karavidopoulos, Carlo M. Martini, and Bruce M. Metzger. *The Greek New Testament*. Stuttgart: Deutsche Bibelgesellschaft, 2005.
Papyri Graecae Magicae: Preisendanz, Karl, ed. *Papyri Graecae Magicae: Die griechischen Zauberpapyri*. 3 vols. Leipzig: Teubner, 1928–1944. Second Improved Edition, ed. Albert Henrichs. 2 vols. Stuttgart: Teubner, 1974.
Persius: Ramsay, G. G., ed. *Juvenal and Persius*. LCL. Cambridge, MA: Harvard University Press, 1979.
Pesikta d'Rav Kahana: Mandelbaum, Bernard. *Pesikta de Rav Kahana*. New York: Jewish Theological Seminary, 1987.
Petronius: Hezeltine, M. and W. H. D. Rouse, eds. *Petronius: Satyricon; Seneca: Apocolocyntosis*. LCL. Cambridge, MA: Harvard University Press, 1913.
Philo: Colson, F. H., trans. *Philo: In Ten Volumes (and Two Supplementary Volumes)*. LCL. Cambridge, MA: Harvard University Press, 1984.
Philostratus: Conybeare, F. C. *Philostratus: The Life of Apollonius of Tyana*. LCL. Cambridge, MA: Harvard University Press, 1912.
Plutarch: Clement, P. A. and H. B. Hoffleit, eds. *Plutarch: Moralia, VII; Table-talk, Books 1–6*. LCL. Cambridge, MA: Harvard University Press, 1969.
Porphyry: Clark, Gillian. *Porphyry: On Abstinence from Killing Animals*. Ithaca, NY: Cornell University Press, 2000.
Sextus Empiricus: Bury, R. G., ed. *Sextus Empiricus*. 4 vols. LCL. Cambridge, MA: Harvard University Press, 1968–1983.
Sifra: Finkelstein, Louis, ed. *Sifra or Torat Kohanim: According to Codex Assemani LXVI*. New York: Jewish Theological Seminary, 1956.
Sifra: Weiss, Isaac Hirsch. *Sifra on Leviticus*. New York: Om, 1947.
Sifre Deuteronomy: Finkelstein, Louis, ed. *Sifre on Deuteronomy*. New York: Jewish Theological Seminary, 1969.
Sifre Numbers: Horowitz, Hayim Shaul, ed. *Siphre d'be Rab: Sifre to Numbers and Sifre Zutta*. Leipzig: Gustav Fock, 1917.
Tacitus: Moore, Clifford H. and John Jackson, eds. *Tacitus: Histories 4–5; Annals 1–3*. LCL. Cambridge, MA: Harvard University Press, 1931.

Tosefta: Lieberman, Saul, ed. *The Tosefta: According to Codex Vienna, with Variants from Codex Erfurt, Genizah Mss. And Editio Princeps (Venice 1521), Together with References to Parallel Passages in Talmudic Literature and a Brief Commentary.* 5 vols. New York: Jewish Theological Seminary, 1955–1988.

Tosefta: Zuckermandel, Moses Samuel, ed. *Tosefta: Based on the Erfurt and Vienna Codices with Parallels and Variants.* Jerusalem: Bamberger and Wahrmann, 1937.

SECONDARY SOURCES

Alexander, Philip S. "'The Parting of the Ways' from the Perspective of Rabbinic Judaism." In *Jews and Christians: The Parting of the Ways, A.D. 70 to 135*, ed. James D. G. Dunn, 1–25. Tübingen, Germany: Mohr Siebeck, 1992.

Allison, Anne. "Japanese Mothers and Obentōs: The Lunch Box as Ideological State Apparatus." In *Food and Culture: A Reader*, ed. Carole Counihan and Penny van Esterik, 296–314. New York: Routledge, 1997.

Alon, Gedaliah. "The Levitical Uncleanliness of Gentiles." In *Jews, Judaism and the Classical World*, trans. I. Abrahams, 146–189. Jerusalem: Magnes Press, 1977.

Anderson, Gary A. "The Status of the Torah before Sinai: The Retelling of the Bible in the Damascus Covenant and the Book of Jubilees." *DSD* 1/1 (1994): 1–29.

Anderson, H. "3 Maccabees." In *OTP*. 2 vols., ed. James H. Charlesworth, 2:509–529. New York: Doubleday, 1985.

———. "4 Maccabees." In *OTP*. 2 vols., ed. James H. Charlesworth, 2:531–564. New York: Doubleday, 1985.

Anderson, Robert T. "Samaritans." In *ABD*. 6 vols., ed. David Noel Freedman, 5:940–947. New York: Doubleday, 1992.

Anderson, Robert T. and Terry Giles. *Tradition Kept: The Literature of the Samaritans.* Peabody, MA: Hendrickson, 2005.

Appadurai, Arjun. "How to Make a National Cuisine: Cookbooks in Contemporary India." *Comparative Studies* 30/1 (1988): 3–24.

Baker, Cynthia M. *Rebuilding the House of Israel: Architectures of Gender in Jewish Antiquity.* Stanford, CA: Stanford University Press, 2002.

Balfet, Hélène. "Bread in Some Regions of the Mediterranean Area: A Contribution to the Studies on Eating Habits." In *Gastronomy: The Anthropology of Food and Food Habits*, ed. Margaret L. Arnott, 305–314. Chicago: Mouton Publishers, 1975.

Barak-Erez, Daphne. *Outlawed Pigs: Law, Religion, and Culture in Israel.* Madison: University of Wisconsin Press, 2007.

Barclay, John M. G. *Jews in the Mediterranean Diaspora: From Alexander to Trajan (323 BCE–117 CE).* Berkeley and Los Angeles: University of California Press, 1996.

Barthes, Roland. "Toward a Psychosociology of Contemporary Food Consumption." In *Food and Culture: A Reader*, ed. Carole Counihan and Penny van Esterik, 20–27. New York: Routledge, 1997.

Baumgarten, Albert I. *The Flourishing of Jewish Sects in the Maccabean Era: An Interpretation.* New York: Brill, 1997.

Beall, Todd S. "Essenes." In *Encyclopedia of the Dead Sea Scrolls*, 2 vols., ed. Lawrence H. Schiffman and James C. VanderKam, 1:262–269. New York: Oxford University Press, 2000.

Beard, Mary. "Re-reading (Vestal) Virginity." In *Women in Antiquity: New Assessments*, ed. Richard Hawley and Barbara Levick, 166–177. New York: Routledge, 1995.
Belasco, Warren. "Food and the Counterculture: A Story of Bread and Politics." In *The Cultural Politics of Food and Eating: A Reader*, ed. James L. Watson and Melissa L. Caldwell, 217–234. Malden, MA: Blackwell Publishing, 2005.
Bell, Catherine. *Ritual Theory, Ritual Practice*. Oxford: Oxford University Press, 1992.
Bentley, Amy. *Eating for Victory: Food Rationing and the Politics of Domesticity*. Urbana and Chicago: University of Illinois Press, 1998.
Betz, Hans Dieter, ed. *The Greek Magical Papyri in Translation, Including the Demotic Spells*. Chicago: University of Chicago Press, 1992.
Bickerman, Elias J. "The Colophon of the Greek Book of Esther." *JBL* 63 (1944): 339–362.
Blenkinsopp, Joseph. *Isaiah 40–55: A New Translation with Introduction and Commentary*. AB, vol. 19a. New York: Doubleday, 2000.
———. *Isaiah 56–66: A New Translation with Introduction and Commentary*. AB, vol. 19b. New York: Doubleday, 2003.
Bokser, Baruch M. *The Origins of the Seder: The Passover Rite and Early Rabbinic Judaism*. Berkeley and Los Angeles: University of California Press, 1984.
Borgen, Peder. *Bread from Heaven: An Exegetical Study of The Concept of Manna in the Gospel of John and the Writings of Philo*. Leiden, the Netherlands: Brill, 1965.
Bourdieu, Pierre. *Language and Symbolic Power*, ed. John B. Thompson; trans. Gino Raymond and Matthew Adamson. Cambridge, MA: Harvard University Press, 1991.
———. *The Field of Cultural Production: Essays on Art and Literature*, ed. Randal Johnson. New York: Columbia University Press, 1993.
———. *Outline of a Theory of Practice*, trans. Richard Nice. New York: Cambridge University Press, 1998 (1977).
———. *Distinction: A Social Critique of the Judgment of Taste*, trans. Richard Nice. Cambridge, MA: Harvard University Press, 2002.
Bourdieu, Pierre and Loïc J. D. Wacquant. *An Invitation to Reflexive Sociology*. Chicago: University of Chicago Press, 1992.
Boyarin, Daniel. *Dying for God: Martyrdom and the Making of Christianity and Judaism*. Stanford, CA: Stanford University Press, 1999.
———. *Border Lines: The Partition of Judaeo-Christianity*. Philadelphia: University of Pennsylvania Press, 2004.
Brillat-Savarin, Jean Anthelme. *The Physiology of Taste, or, Meditations on Transcendental Gastronomy*, trans. M. F. K. Fisher. New York: Heritage Press, 1949.
———. *Physiologie du Goût: Première Édition Mise Ordre et Annotée avec une Lecture de Roland Barthes*. Paris: Hermann, 1975.
Brooks, Roger. *Support for the Poor in the Mishnaic Law: Tractate Peah*. BJS 43. Chico, CA: Scholars Press, 1983.
Broshi, Magen. "The Diet of Palestine in the Roman Period: Introductory Notes." In *Bread, Wine, Walls and Scrolls*, 121–143. New York: Sheffield Academic Press, 2001.
———. "Wine in Ancient Palestine: Introductory Notes." In *Bread, Wine, Walls and Scrolls*, 144–172. New York: Sheffield Academic Press, 2001.

Brouwer, H. H. J. *Bona Dea: The Sources and a Description of the Cult.* New York: Brill, 1989.
Brubaker, Rogers and Frederick Cooper. "Beyond 'Identity.'" *Theory and Society* 29 (2000): 1–47.
Brumberg-Kraus, Jonathan. "Meat-eating and Jewish Identity: Ritualization of the Priestly 'Torah of Beast and Fowl' [Lev. 11:46] in Rabbinic Judaism and in Medieval Kabbalah." *AJSR* 24/2 (1999): 227–262.
———. "'Not By Bread Alone...': The Ritualization of Food and Table Talk in the Passover Seder and in the Last Supper." In *Food and Drink in the Biblical Worlds*, ed. Athalya Brenner and Jan Willem van Henten, 165–191. Semeia 86. Atlanta: Society of Biblical Literature, 1999.
———. "Meals As Midrash: A Survey of Ancient Meals in Jewish Studies Scholarship." In *Food and Judaism: Studies in Jewish Civilization 15*, ed. Leonard J. Greenspoon, Ronald A. Simkins, and Gerald Shapiro, 297–317. Omaha, NE: Creighton University Press, 2004.
Bryan, David. *Cosmos, Chaos and the Kosher Mentality.* Sheffield, UK: Sheffield Academic Press, 1995.
Burchard, Christoph. "Joseph and Aseneth." In *OTP.* 2 vols., ed. James H. Charlesworth, 2:177–247. New York: Doubleday, 1985.
———. *Joseph und Aseneth: Kritisch Herausgegeben.* Boston: Brill, 2003.
Bynum, Caroline Walker. *Holy Feast and Holy Fast: The Religious Significance of Food to Medieval Women.* Berkeley and Los Angeles: University of California Press, 1988.
Cohen, Shaye J. D. "The Place of the Rabbi in Jewish Society of the Second Century." In *The Galilee in Late Antiquity*, ed. Lee I. Levine, 157–173. New York: Jewish Theological Seminary, 1992.
———. *The Beginnings of Jewishness: Boundaries, Varieties, Uncertainties.* Berkeley and Los Angeles: University of California Press, 2000.
———. *Why Aren't Jewish Women Circumcised?: Gender and Covenant in Judaism.* Berkeley and Los Angeles: University of California Press, 2005.
———. "The Judean Legal Tradition and the Halakhah of the Mishnah." In *The Cambridge Companion to the Talmud and Rabbinic Literature*, ed. Charlotte Elisheva Fonrobert and Martin S. Jaffee, 121–143. New York: Cambridge University Press, 2007.
Collins, John J. *Daniel: A Commentary on the Book of Daniel.* Hermeneia. Minneapolis: Fortress Press, 1993.
———. *Between Athens and Jerusalem: Jewish Identity in the Hellenistic Diaspora.* Second Edition. Grand Rapids, MI: Eerdmans, 2000.
Cooper, John. *Eat and Be Satisfied: A Social History of Jewish Food.* Northvale, NJ: Jason Aronson, 1993.
Corley, Kathleen E. *Private Women, Public Meals: Social Conflict in the Synoptic Tradition.* Peabody, MA: Hendrickson, 1993.
Crossan, John Dominic. *The Historical Jesus: The Life of a Mediterranean Jewish Peasant.* San Francisco: Harper Collins, 1991.
Crown, Alan David and Reinhard Pummer. *A Bibliography of the Samaritans: Third Edition, Revised, Expanded, and Annotated.* ATLA Bibliography Series 51. Lanham, MD: Scarecrow Press, 2005.

Cubberley, Anthony. "Bread-Baking in Ancient Italy: Clibanus and Sub Testu in the Roman World: Further Thoughts." In *Food in Antiquity*, ed. John Wilkins, David Harvey, and Mike Dobson, 55–68. Exeter, UK: University of Exeter Press, 1996.

Dalby, Andrew. *Food in the Ancient World from A to Z*. New York: Routledge, 2003.

Dar, Shimon. "Food and Archaeology in Romano-Byzantine Palestine." In *Food and Antiquity*, ed. John Wilkins, David Harvey, and Mike Dobson, 326–335. Exeter, UK: University of Exeter Press, 1996.

Davidson, James N. *Courtesans and Fishcakes: The Consuming Passions of Classical Athens*. London: Harper Collins, 1997.

de Light, L. *Fairs and Markets in the Roman Empire: Economic and Social Aspects of Periodic Trade in a Pre–Industrial Society*. Amsterdam: J. C. Gieben, 1993.

Dickie, John. *Delizia!: The Epic History of the Italians and Their Food*. London: Hodder & Stoughton, 2007.

Diemling, Maria. "'As the Jews Like to Eat Garlick': Garlic in Christian-Jewish Polemical Discourse in Early Modern Germany." In *Food and Judaism: Studies in Jewish Civilization 15*, ed. Leonard J. Greenspoon, Ronald A. Simkins, and Gerald Shapiro, 215–234. Omaha, NE: Creighton University Press, 2004.

Diner, Hasia R. *Hungering for America: Italian, Irish, and Jewish Foodways in the Age of Migration*. Cambridge, MA: Harvard University Press, 2001.

di Segni, Leah. "The Samaritans in Roman–Byzantine Palestine: Some Misapprehensions." In *Religious and Ethnic Communities in Later Roman Palestine*, ed. Hayim Lapin, 51–66. Bethesda: University Press of Maryland, 1998.

Douglas, Mary. "Deciphering a Meal." In *Food and Culture: A Reader*, ed. Carole Counihan and Penny van Esterik, 36–54. New York: Routledge, 1997.

———. *Purity and Danger: An Analysis of the Concepts of Pollution and Taboo*. New York: Routledge, 1999 (1966).

———. *Leviticus as Literature*. New York: Oxford University Press, 2000.

Dunbabin, Katherine M. D. *The Roman Banquet: Images of Conviviality*. New York: Cambridge University Press, 2003.

Eilberg-Schwartz, Howard. *The Savage in Judaism: An Anthropology of Israelite Religion and Ancient Judaism*. Bloomington and Indianapolis: Indiana University Press, 1990.

Eliav, Yaron Z. "Viewing the Sculptural Environment: Shaping the Second Commandment." In *The Talmud Yerushalmi and Graeco-Roman Culture*. Vol. 3., ed. Peter Schäfer, 411–433. Tübingen, Germany: Mohr Siebeck, 2002.

Engberg-Pederson, Troels. "Philo's De Vita Contemplativa as a Philosopher's Dream." *JSJ* 30 (1999), 40–64.

Fabre-Vassas, Claudine. *The Singular Beast: Jews, Christians and the Pig*, trans. Carol Volk. New York: Columbia University Press, 1997.

Farb, Peter and George Armelagos. *Consuming Passions: The Anthropology of Eating*. Boston: Houghton Mifflin, 1980.

Feeley-Harnik, Gillian. *The Lord's Table: The Meaning of Food in Early Judaism and Christianity*. Washington, DC: Smithsonian Institution Press, 1994.

Feldman, Louis H. *Jew and Gentile in the Ancient World*. Princeton, NJ: Princeton University Press, 1993.

Feliks, Jehuda. "Five Species." In *Encyclopaedia Judaica*. 16 vols. Second Printing, 6:1331–1332. Jerusalem: Encyclopaedia Judaica, 1973.

Ferguson, Sarah. "Dinner with Friends: Sound, Satisfying Advice (for Body and Soul) on How to Rethink a Night on the Town." *Weight Watchers Magazine* November/December (2003): 54.

Fessler, Daniel M. T. and Carlos David Navarrete. "Meat is Good to Taboo: Dietary Proscriptions as a Product of the Interaction of Psychological Mechanisms and Social Processes." *Journal of Cognition and Culture* 3/1 (2003): 1–40.

Fischel, Henry A. "The Midrash of Ben Zoma and Ben Zoma in the Midrash." In *Rabbinic Literature and Greco–Roman Philosophy: A Study of Epicurea and Rhetorica in Early Midrashic Writings*, 51–89. Leiden, the Netherlands: Brill, 1973.

Fischler, Claude. "Food, Self and Identity." *Social Science Information* 27/2 (1988): 275–292.

Flandrin, Jean-Louis and Massimo Montanari, eds. *Food: A Culinary History from Antiquity to the Present*, trans. Albert Sonnefeld. New York: Penguin Books, 1999.

Fonrobert, Charlotte Elisheva. *Menstrual Purity: Rabbinic and Christian Reconstructions of Biblical Gender*. Stanford, CA: Stanford University Press, 2000.

Forbes, Hamish and Lin Foxhall. "Ethnoarchaeology and Storage in the Ancient Mediterranean: Beyond Risk and Survival." In *Food and Antiquity*, ed. John Wilkins, David Harvey, and Mike Dobson, 69–86. Exeter, UK: University of Exeter Press, 1996.

Foss, Pedar William. Kitchens and Dining Rooms at Pompeii: The Spatial and Social Relationship of Cooking to Eating in the Roman Household. Ph.D. dissertation, University of Michigan, 1994.

Frankel, Rafael. "Presses for Oil and Wine in the Southern Levant in the Byzantine Period." *Dumbarton Oaks Papers* 51 (1997): 73–84.

Frayn, Joan M. *Subsistence Farming in Roman Italy*. London: Centaur Press, 1979.

Freidenreich, David Moshe. Foreign Food: Restrictions on the Food of Members of Other Religions in Jewish, Christian, and Islamic Law. Ph.D. dissertation, Columbia University, 2006.

Friedman, Shamma Yehudah. "Mishnah and Tosefta Parallels (1): Shabbat 16:1." *Tarbiz* 62 (1993): 313–338. (Hebrew)

———. *Tosefta Atiqta: Pesaḥ Rishon: Synoptic Parallels of Mishna and Tosefta Analyzed with a Methodological Introduction*. Ramat-Gan, Israel: Bar-Ilan University Press, 2002. (Hebrew)

Gardner, Gregg Elliot. Giving to the Poor in Early Rabbinic Judaism. Ph.D. dissertation, Princeton University, 2009.

Garnsey, Peter. *Famine and Food Supply in the Graeco–Roman World: Responses to Risk and Crisis*. New York: Cambridge University Press, 1988.

———. *Food and Society in Classical Antiquity*. New York: Cambridge University Press, 1999.

Gilders, William K. *Blood Ritual in the Hebrew Bible: Meaning and Power*. Baltimore: Johns Hopkins University Press, 2004.

Ginzberg, Louis. *The Legends of the Jews*. 7 vols. Philadelphia: Jewish Publication Society, 1979.

Glezer, Maggie. *A Blessing of Bread: The Many Rich Traditions of Jewish Bread Baking Around the World*. New York: Artisan, 2004.
Goldberg, Abraham. "The Mishnah – A Study Book of Halakha." In *The Literature of the Sages: Part 1: Oral Tora, Halakha, Mishna, Tosefta, External Tractates*, ed. Shmuel Safrai, 211–251. Philadelphia: Fortress Press, 1987.
Goldenberg, Robert. "The Jewish Sabbath in the Roman World up to the Time of Constantine the Great." *ANRW* 19.1, 414–447. Berlin: Walter de Gruyter, 1979.
Goldstein, Jonathan A. *II Maccabees: A New Translation with Introduction and Commentary*. AB, vol. 41a. New York: Doubleday, 1983.
Goodman, Martin. "Kosher Olive Oil in Antiquity." In *A Tribute to Geza Vermes: Essays on Jewish and Christian Literature and History*, ed. Philip R. Davies and Richard T. White, 227–245. Sheffield, UK: Sheffield Academic Press, 1990.
———. "The Function of Minim in Early Rabbinic Judaism." In *Geschichte – Tradition – Reflexion: Festschrift für Martin Hengel zum 70. Geburtstag*, 3 vols., ed. Hubert Cancik, Hermann Lichtenberger, and Peter Schäfer, 1:501–510. Tübingen, Germany: Mohr Siebeck, 1996.
Goody, Jack. *Cooking, Cuisine and Class: A Study in Comparative Sociology*. Cambridge: Cambridge University Press, 1996.
Goshen-Gottstein, Alon. "The Commandment of Tzitzit, the Prostitute, and the Exegetical Story." In *Mahshevet Hazal*, ed. Tzvi Groner and Menahem Hirschman, 45–58. Haifa: University of Haifa, 1990. (Hebrew)
Grantham, Billy. *A Zooarchaeological Model for the Study of Ethnic Complexity at Sepphoris*. Ph.D. dissertation, Northwestern University, 1996.
Gray, Alyssa M. *A Talmud in Exile: The Influence of Yerushalmi Avodah Zarah on the Formation of Bavli Avodah Zarah*. BJS 342. Atlanta: Society of Biblical Literature, 2005.
Grossfeld, Bernard. *The Targum Onqelos to Exodus: Translated, with Apparatus and Notes*. Vol. 7. Wilmington, DE: Michael Glazier, 1988.
Grottanelli, Cristiano. "Avoiding Pork: Egyptians and Jews in Greek and Latin Texts." In *Food and Identity in the Ancient World*, ed. Cristiano Grottanelli and Lucio Milano, 59–93. Padova, Italy: S.A.R.G.O.N. Editrice e Libreria, 2004.
Gruen, Erich S. *Diaspora: Jews Amidst Greeks and Romans*. Cambridge, MA: Harvard University Press, 2002.
Hall, Robert G. "Circumcision." In *ABD*. 6 vols., ed. David Noel Freedman, 1:1025–1031. New York: Doubleday, 1992.
Hamel, Gildas. *Poverty and Charity in Roman Palestine, First Three Centuries C.E.* Berkeley and Los Angeles: University of California Press, 1990.
Hammer, Reuven. *Sifre: A Tannaitic Commentary on the Book of Deuteronomy*. New Haven, CT: Yale University Press, 1986.
Harrington, Hannah K. *The Impurity Systems of the Qumran and the Rabbis: Biblical Foundations*. SBLDS 143. Atlanta: Scholars Press, 1993.
Harris, Marvin. *Good to Eat: Riddles of Food and Culture*. Long Grove, IL: Waveland Press, 1998.
Hartman, Louis F. and Alexander A. Di Lella. *The Book of Daniel: A New Translation with Introduction and Commentary*. AB, vol. 23. New York: Doubleday, 1978.
Hartog, François. *The Mirror of Herodotus: The Representation of the Other in the Writing of History*, trans. Janet Lloyd. Berkeley and Los Angeles: University of California Press, 1988.

Harvey, Warren. "The Pupil, the Harlot, and the Fringe Benefits." *Prooftexts* 6 (1986): 259–271.

Hauptman, Judith. "Women in Tractate Pesahim." In *Atara L'Haim: Studies in the Talmud and Medieval Rabbinic Literature in Honor of Professor Haim Zalman Dimitrovsky*, ed. Daniel Boyarin, Shamma Friedman, Marc Hirshman, Menahem Schmelzer, and Israel M. Tashma, 63–78. Jerusalem: Magnes Press, 2000. (Hebrew)

———. "From the Kitchen to the Dining Room: Women and Ritual Activities in Tractate Pesahim." In *A Feminist Commentary on the Babylonian Talmud: Introduction and Studies*, ed. Tal Ilan, Tamara Or, Dorothea M. Salzer, Christiane Steuer, and Irina Wandrey, 109–126. Tübingen, Germany: Mohr Siebeck, 2007.

Hayes, Christine E. *Between the Babylonian and Palestinian Talmuds: Accounting for Halakhic Difference in Selected Sugyot from Tractate Avodah Zarah.* New York: Oxford University Press, 1997.

———. *Gentile Impurities and Jewish Identities: Intermarriage and Conversion from the Bible to the Talmud.* New York: Oxford University Press, 2002.

———. "Do Converts to Judaism Require Purification?: M. Pes. 8:8 – An Interpretative Crux Solved." *JQR* 9 (2002): 327–352.

———. "The 'Other' in Rabbinic Literature." In *The Cambridge Companion to the Talmud and Rabbinic Literature*, ed. Charlotte Elisheva Fonrobert and Martin S. Jaffee, 243–269. New York: Cambridge University Press, 2007.

Hecker, Joel. *Mystical Bodies, Mystical Meals: Eating and Embodiment in Medieval Kabbalah.* Detroit, MI: Wayne State University Press, 2005.

Henten, Jan Willem van. *The Maccabean Martyrs as Saviours of the Jewish People: A Study of 2 and 4 Maccabees.* New York: Brill, 1997.

Hesse, Brian and Paula Wapnish. "Can Pig Remains Be Used for Ethnic Diagnosis in the Ancient Near East?" In *The Archaeology of Israel: Constructing the Past, Interpreting the Present*, ed. Neil Asher Silberman and David Small, 238–270. Sheffield, UK: Sheffield Academic Press, 1997.

Hezser, Catherine. *Jewish Literacy in Roman Palestine.* Tübingen, Germany: Mohr Siebeck, 2001.

Hirschfeld, Yizhar. *The Palestinian Dwelling in the Roman–Byzantine Period.* Jerusalem: Israel Exploration Society, 1995.

Hoenig, Sidney B. "Oil and Pagan Defilement." *JQR* 61/1 (1970): 63–75.

Huss-Ashmore, Rebecca and Susan L. Johnston. "Wild Plants as Famine Foods: Food Choice Under Conditions of Scarcity." In *Food Preferences and Taste: Continuity and Change*, ed. Helen Macbeth, 83–100. Providence, RI: Berghahn Books, 1997.

Ilan, Tal. *Jewish Women in Greco–Roman Palestine: An Inquiry into Image and Status.* Tübingen, Germany: Mohr Siebeck, 1995.

Jaffee, Martin S. *Torah in the Mouth: Writing and Oral Tradition in Palestinian Judaism 200 BCE–400 CE.* New York: Oxford University Press, 2001.

———. *Early Judaism: Religious Worlds of the First Judaic Millennium.* Second Edition. Bethesda: University Press of Maryland, 2006.

Jastrow, Marcus. *A Dictionary of the Targumim, the Talmud Babli and Yerushalmi, and the Midrashic Literature.* New York: Judaica Press, 1996.

Jay, Nancy. *Throughout Your Generations Forever: Sacrifice, Religion, and Paternity.* Chicago: University of Chicago Press, 1992.

Jewish Study Bible: Featuring the Jewish Publication Society Tanakh Translation, ed. Adele Berlin and Marc Zvi Brettler. New York: Oxford University Press, 2004.

Joselit, Jenna Weissman. "Kitchen Judaism." In *The Wonders of America: Reinventing Jewish Culture, 1880–1950*, 171–218. New York: Henry Holt, 2002.

Kaplan, Marion A. *The Making of the Jewish Middle Class: Women, Family, and Identity in Imperial Germany*. New York: Oxford University Press, 1991.

Kraemer, David. *Jewish Eating and Identity Through the Ages*. New York: Routledge, 2007.

Kraemer, Ross Shepard. *Her Share of the Blessings: Women's Religions Among Pagans, Jews, and Christians in the Greco–Roman World*. New York: Oxford University Press, 1992.

———. "The Other as Woman: An Aspect of Polemic among Pagans, Jews, and Christians in the Greco–Roman World." In *The Other in Jewish Thought and History: Constructions of Jewish Culture and Identity*, ed. Laurence J. Silberstein and Robert L. Cohn, 121–144. New York: New York University Press, 1994.

———. *When Aseneth Met Joseph: A Late Antique Tale of the Biblical Patriarch and His Egyptian Wife, Reconsidered*. New York: Oxford University Press, 1998.

Krauss, Samuel. *Talmudische Archäologie*. 3 vols. Leipzig: Buchhandlung Gustav Fock, 1910.

Lapin, Hayim. *Early Rabbinic Civil Law and the Social History of Roman Galilee: A Study of Mishnah Tractate* Baba' Meṣi'a'. BJS 307. Atlanta: Scholars Press, 1995.

Lauterbach, Jacob Z. *Mekhilta De'Rabbi Ishmael: A Critical Edition, Based on the Manuscripts and Early Editions, with an English Translation, Introduction, and Notes*. 2 vols. Philadelphia: Jewish Publication Society, 2004.

Lehman, Marjorie. "Women and Passover Observance: Reconsidering Gender in the Study of Rabbinic Texts." In *Women and Judaism: Studies in Jewish Civilization* 14, ed. Leonard J. Greenspoon, Ronald A. Simkins, and Jean Axelrad Cahan, 45–66. Omaha, NE: Creighton University Press, 2003.

———. "The Gendered Rhetoric of Sukkah Observance." *JQR* 96/3 (2006): 309–335.

Leonhardt, Jutta. *Jewish Worship in Philo of Alexandria*. Tübingen, Germany: Mohr Siebeck, 2001.

Lev-Tov, Justin. "'Upon What Meat Doth This Our Caesar Feed...?': A Dietary Perspective on Hellenistic and Roman Influence in Palestine." In *Zeichen aus Text und Stein: Studien auf dem Weg zu einer Archaeologie des Neuen Testaments*, ed. S. Alkier and J. Zangenberg, 420–446. Tübingen, Germany: Francke, 2003.

Lévi-Strauss, Claude. *The Raw and the Cooked: Introduction to a Science of Mythology*, trans. John and Doreen Weightman. New York: Harper and Row Publishers, 1975.

———. "The Culinary Triangle." In *Food and Culture: A Reader*, ed. Carole Counihan and Penny van Esterik, 28–35. New York: Routledge, 1997.

Levine, Lee I. *The Rabbinic Class of Roman Palestine in Late Antiquity*. New York: Jewish Theological Seminary, 1989.

———. *The Ancient Synagogue: The First Thousand Years*. New Haven, CT: Yale University Press, 2000.

Levtow, Nathaniel B. *Images of Others: Iconic Politics in Ancient Israel*. Biblical and Judaic Studies. Vol. 11. Winona Lake, IN: Eisenbrauns, 2008.

Licht, Jacob. *The Rule Scroll: A Scroll from the Wilderness of Judea. 1QS, 1QSa, 1QSb. Text, Introduction, and Commentary*. Jerusalem, The Bialik Institute, 1965. (Hebrew)

Liddell, H. G. and R. Scott. *An Intermediate Greek-English Lexicon.* Seventh Edition. New York: American Book Company, 1995.

Lieber, Andrea. "I Set a Table before You: The Jewish Eschatological Character of Aseneth's Conversion Meal." *JSP* 14/1 (2004): 63–77.

Lieberman, Saul. "[Grain] Mills and Those Who Work Them." *Tarbiz* 50 (1980–1981): 128–135. (Hebrew)

———. *Tosefta Ki-fshuṭah: A Comprehensive Commentary on the Tosefta.* 10 vols. Second Augmented Edition. New York: Jewish Theological Seminary, 1992. (Hebrew)

Lieu, Judith M. *Christian Identity in the Jewish and Graeco–Roman World.* New York: Oxford University Press, 2004.

MacClancy, Jeremy. *Consuming Culture: Why You Eat What You Eat.* New York: Henry Holt, 1993.

Magness, Jodi. "When Were the Galilean-Type Synagogues Built?" *Cathedra* 101 (2001): 39–70. (Hebrew)

———. "The Question of the Synagogue: The Problem of Typology." In *Judaism in Late Antiquity, Part Three, Where We Stand: Issues and Debates in Ancient Judaism. Volume Four: The Special Problem of the Synagogue,* ed. Alan J. Avery-Peck and Jacob Neusner, 1–48. Leiden, the Netherlands: Brill, 2001.

Malatesta, Simona, Sarah Weiner, and Winnie Yang. *The Slow Food Companion.* Bra, Italy: Centro Stampa srl, 2006.

Malina, Bruce J. *The Palestinian Manna Tradition.* Leiden, the Netherlands: Brill, 1968.

Marcus, Jacob Rader, ed. *The Jew in the American World: A Source Book.* Detroit, MI: Wayne State University Press, 1996.

Marcus, Joel. *Mark 1–8: A New Translation with Introduction and Commentary.* AB, vol. 27. New York: Doubleday, 2000.

Marks, Susan. "Present and Absent: Women at Greco–Roman Wedding Meals." Paper presented at the SBL Meals in the Greco–Roman World Seminar, Washington, DC, November 2006.

Martin, Matthew J. "Communal Meals in the Late Antique Synagogue." In *Feast, Fast or Famine: Food and Drink in Byzantium,* ed. Wendy Mayer and Silke Trzcionka, 135–146. Brisbane: Byzantina Australiensia, 2005.

Mason, Steve. "Jews, Judaeans, Judaizing, Judaism: Problems of Categorization in Ancient Judaism." *JSJ* 38 (2007): 457–512.

McGowan, Andrew. *Ascetic Eucharists: Food and Drink in Early Christian Ritual Meals.* Oxford: Clarendon Press, 1999.

Milgrom, Jacob. *Leviticus 1–16: A New Translation with Introduction and Commentary.* AB, vol. 3. New York: Doubleday, 1991.

Miliard, Mike. "Thinkin' About Dunkin': How One Little Post–War Doughnut Shop Became Synonymous with Boston's Identity." *The Providence Phoenix* 20/10 (March 9–15, 2007), 6–9.

Miller, Stuart S. *Sages and Commoners in Late Antique 'Ereẓ Israel: A Philological Inquiry into Local Traditions in Talmud Yerushalmi.* Tübingen, Germany: Mohr Siebeck, 2006.

Montanari, Massimo. *Food Is Culture,* trans. Albert Sonnenfeld. New York: Columbia University Press, 2006.

Moore, Carey A. *Daniel, Esther and Jeremiah: The Additions: A New Translation with Introduction and Commentary.* AB, vol. 44. New York: Doubleday, 1977.

———. *Judith: A New Translation with Introduction and Commentary*. AB, vol. 40. New York: Doubleday, 1985.

———. *Tobit: A New Translation with Introduction and Commentary*. AB, vol. 40a. New York: Doubleday, 1996.

Moore, Stephen D. and Janice Capel Anderson. "Taking It Like a Man: Masculinity in 4 Maccabees." *JBL* 117/2 (1998): 249–273.

Murray, Sarah. *Moveable Feasts: From Ancient Rome to the 21st Century, the Incredible Journeys of the Food We Eat*. New York: St. Martin's Press, 2008.

Naguib, Nefissa. "The Fragile Tale of Egyptian Jewish Cuisine: Food Memoirs of Claudia Roden and Colette Rossant." *Food & Foodways* 14 (2006): 35–53.

Nakhimovsky, Alice. "You Are What They Ate: Russian Jews Reclaim Their Foodways." *Shofar: An Interdisciplinary Journal of Jewish Studies* 25/1 (2006): 63–77.

Naveh, Joseph. *On Stone and Mosaic: The Aramaic and Hebrew Inscriptions from Ancient Synagogues*. Jerusalem: Karta, 1978. (Hebrew)

Nelson, W. David. *Mekhilta de-Rabbi Shimon bar Yohai*. Philadelphia: Jewish Publication Society, 2006.

Nemeroff, Carol and Paul Rozin. "'You Are What You Eat': Applying the Demand-Free 'Impressions' Technique to an Unacknowledged Belief." *Ethos* 17/1 (1989): 50–69.

Neusner, Jacob. "The Fellowship (הרובח) in the Second Jewish Commonwealth." *HTR* 53/2 (1960): 125–142.

———. *The Tosefta*. 6 vols. New York and Hoboken, NJ: Ktav Publishing House, 1977–1986.

———. *From Politics to Piety: The Emergence of Pharisaic Judaism*. New York: Ktav Publishing House, 1979.

———. *The Mishnaic System of Women*. Vol. 5. *A History of the Mishnaic Law of Women*. Leiden, the Netherlands: Brill, 1980.

———. *Sifré to Numbers: An American Translation and Explanation*. 2 vols. BJS 118 and 119. Atlanta: Society of Biblical Literature, 1986.

———. *Judaism: The Evidence of the Mishnah*. BJS 129. Second Edition. Atlanta: Scholars Press, 1988.

———. *The Mekhilta According to Rabbi Ishmael: An Analytical Translation*. 2 vols. BJS 148 and 154. Atlanta: Society of Biblical Literature, 1988.

———. *The Mishnah: A New Translation*. New Haven, CT: Yale University Press, 1988.

———. *Sifra: An Analytical Translation*. 3 vols. BJS 138, 139, and 140. Atlanta: Society of Biblical Literature, 1988.

———. "Mr. Sanders' Pharisees and Mine: A Response to E. P. Sanders, 'Jewish Law from Jesus to the Mishnah.'" *SJT* 44/1 (1991): 73–95.

New Oxford Annotated Bible: New Revised Standard Version with the Apocrypha, ed. Michael D. Coogan. New York: Oxford University Press, 2001.

Novak, David. *The Image of the Non–Jew in Judaism: An Historical and Constructive Study of the Noahide Laws*. Toronto Studies in Theology 14. New York: Edwin Mellen Press, 1983.

Ohnuki-Tierney, Emiko. *Rice as Self: Japanese Identities through Time*. Princeton, NJ: Princeton University Press, 1993.

Olyan, Saul M. *Rites and Rank: Hierarchy in Biblical Representations of Cult*. Princeton, NJ: Princeton University Press, 2000.

Oppenheimer, Aharon. *The 'Am ha-Aretz: A Study in the Social History of the Jewish People in the Hellenistic–Roman Period*, trans. Israel L. Levine. Leiden, the Netherlands: Brill, 1977.

Peskowitz, Miriam. "Spinning Tales: On Reading Gender and Otherness in Tannaitic Texts." In *The Other in Jewish Thought and History: Constructions of Jewish Culture and Identity*, ed. Laurence J. Silberstein and Robert L. Cohn, 91–120. New York: New York University Press, 1994.

———. *Spinning Fantasies: Rabbis, Gender, and History*. Berkeley and Los Angeles: University of California Press, 1997.

Pollan, Michael. *The Omnivore's Dilemma: A Natural History of Four Meals*. New York: Penguin Press, 2006.

Porton, Gary G. *Goyim: Gentiles and Israelites in Mishnah-Tosefta*. BJS 155. Atlanta: Society of Biblical Literature, 1988.

Rabin, Chaim. *Qumran Studies*. Oxford: Oxford University Press, 1957.

Roller, Matthew B. *Dining Posture in Ancient Rome: Bodies, Values, and Status*. Princeton, NJ: Princeton University Press, 2006.

Rose, Herbert Jennings and Karim W. Arafat. "Kairos." In *The Oxford Classical Dictionary*. Third Edition, ed. Simon Hornblower and Anthony Spawforth, 806. New York: Oxford University Press, 1996.

Rosenblum, Jordan D. "Kosher Olive Oil in Antiquity Reconsidered." *JSJ* 40/3 (2009): 356–365.

———. "'Why Do You Refuse to Eat Pork?': Jews, Food, and Identity in Roman Palestine." *JQR*: 95–110.

———. "From Their Bread to Their Bed: Commensality, Intermarriage, and Idolatry in Tannaitic Literature." *JJS*: in press.

Rosenfeld, Ben-Zion. "Innkeeping in Jewish Society in Roman Palestine." *JESHO* 41/2 (1998): 133–158.

Rosenfeld, Ben-Zion and Joseph Menirav. *Markets and Marketing in Roman Palestine*, trans. Chava Cassel. Boston: Brill, 2005.

Rosenthal, David. *Mishnah Avodah Zarah: Critical Edition Plus Introduction*. 2 vols. Jerusalem: Hebrew University, 1981. (Hebrew)

Roth-Gerson, Leah. *The Greek Inscriptions from the Synagogues in the Land of Israel*. Jerusalem: Yad Izhak Ben Zvi, 1987. (Hebrew)

Rozin, Paul. "The Selection of Foods by Rats, Humans and Other Animals." *Advances in the Study of Behavior*, ed. J. S. Rosenblatt, R. A. Hinde, E. Shaw, and C. Beer. 6 (1976): 21–76.

Rozin, Paul, Jonathan Haidt, Clark McCauley, and Sumio Imada. "Disgust: Preadaptation and the Cultural Evolution of a Food-Based Emotion." In *Food Preferences and Taste: Continuity and Change*, ed. Helen Macbeth, 65–82. Providence, RI: Berghahn Books, 1997.

Rubenstein, Jeffrey L. *The History of Sukkot in the Second Temple Period and Rabbinic Periods*. BJS 302. Atlanta: Scholars Press, 1995.

———. *Talmudic Stories: Narrative Art, Composition, and Culture*. Baltimore: Johns Hopkins University Press, 1999.

Safrai, Ze'ev. *The Economy of Roman Palestine*. New York: Routledge, 1994.
Saldarini, Anthony J. *Pharisees, Scribes and Sadducees in Palestinian Society: A Sociological Approach*. Second Edition. Grand Rapids, MI: William B. Eerdmans, 2001.
Sanders, E. P. "Jewish Association with Gentiles and Galatians 2:11–14." In *The Conversation Continues: Studies in Paul & John in Honor of J. Louis Martyn*, ed. Robert T. Fortna and Beverly R. Gaventa, 170–188. Nashville, TN: Abingdon Press, 1990.
———. *Judaism: Practice and Belief, 63 BCE–66 CE*. Philadelphia: Trinity Press, 1994.
Sarason, Richard S. *A History of the Mishnaic Law of Agriculture: A Study of Tractate Demai*. Leiden, the Netherlands: Brill, 1979.
Satlow, Michael L. "Reconsidering the Rabbinic *Ketubbah* Payment." In *The Jewish Family in Antiquity*. Ed. Shaye J. D. Cohen, 133–151. BJS 289. Atlanta: Scholars Press, 1993.
———. *Tasting the Dish: Rabbinic Rhetorics of Sexuality*. BJS 303. Atlanta: Society of Biblical Literature, 1995.
———. "'Try to be a Man': The Rabbinic Construction of Masculinity." *HTR* 89/1 (1996): 19–40.
———. *Jewish Marriage in Antiquity*. Princeton, NJ: Princeton University Press, 2001.
———. "Fictional Women: A Study in Stereotypes." In *The Talmud Yerushalmi and Graeco–Roman Culture*. Vol. 3., ed. Peter Schäfer, 225–243. Tübingen, Germany: Mohr Siebeck, 2002.
———. *Creating Judaism: History, Tradition, Practice*. New York: Columbia University Press, 2006.
Schäfer, Peter. *Judeophobia: Attitudes toward the Jews in the Ancient World*. Cambridge, MA: Harvard University Press, 1997.
———. "Jews and Gentiles in Yerushalmi Tractate Avodah Zarah." In *The Talmud Yerushalmi and Graeco–Roman Culture*, ed. Peter Schäfer, 335–352. Tübingen, Germany: Mohr Siebeck, 2002.
Schatzki, Theodore R. *The Site of the Social: A Philosophical Account of the Constitution of Social Life and Change*. University Park: Pennsylvania State University Press, 2002.
Schiffman, Lawrence H. *Sectarian Law in the Dead Sea Scrolls: Courts, Testimony and the Penal Code*. BJS 33. Chico, CA: Scholars Press, 1983.
Schlosser, Eric. *Fast Food Nation: The Dark Side of the All-American Meal*. Boston: Houghton Mifflin, 2001.
Schwartz, Daniel R. *The Second Book of Maccabees: Introduction, Hebrew Translation, and Commentary*. Jerusalem: Yad Ben-Zvi Press, 2004. (Hebrew)
Schwartz, Seth. Review of Gildas Hamel, *Poverty and Charity in Roman Palestine, First Three Centuries C.E. AJSR* 17/2 (1992): 293–296.
———. *Imperialism and Jewish Society, 200 B.C.E.–640 C.E*. Princeton, NJ: Princeton University Press, 2001.
Shakespeare, William. *The Merchant of Venice*, ed. M. M. Mahood. Cambridge: Cambridge University Press, 2003.
Sheerin, Daniel J. *The Eucharist*. Wilmington, DE: Michael Glazier, 1986.
Sheraton, Mimi. *The Bialy Eaters: The Story of a Bread and a Lost World*. New York: Broadway Books, 2000.

Shutt, R. J. H. "Letter of Aristeas." In *OTP*. 2 vols., ed. James H. Charlesworth, 2:7–34. New York: Doubleday, 1985.

Simoons, Frederick J. *Eat Not This Flesh: Food Avoidances in the Old World*. Madison and Milwaukee: University of Wisconsin Press, 1967.

Siporin, Steve. "From Kashrut to Cucina Ebraica: The Recasting of Italian Jewish Foodways." *Journal of American Folklore* 107/424 (1994): 268–281.

Soler, Jean. "The Semiotics of Food in the Bible." *Food and Culture: A Reader*, ed. Carole Counihan and Penny van Esterik, 55–66. New York: Routledge, 1997.

———. "Biblical Reasons: The Dietary Rules of the Ancient Hebrews." In *Food: A Culinary History*, ed. Jean-Louis Flandrin and Massimo Montanari, 46–54. New York: Penguin Books, 2000.

Smith, Dennis E. *From Symposium to Eucharist: The Banquet in the Early Christian World*. Minneapolis: Fortress Press, 2003.

Smith, Jonathan Z. "What a Difference a Difference Makes." In *"To See Ourselves as Others See Us": Christians, Jews, "Others" in Late Antiquity*, ed. Jacob Neusner and Ernest S. Frerichs, 3–48. Chico, CA: Scholars Press, 1985.

Stein, Siegfried. "The Influence of Symposia Literature on the Literary Form of the Pesah Haggadah." *JJS* 7 (1957): 13–44.

Steinfeld, Zvi Aryeh. "Concerning the Prohibition Against Gentile Oil." *Tarbiz* 49 (1980): 264–277. (Hebrew)

———. "Concerning the Prohibition Against Gentile Bread." *Proceedings of the Ninth World Congress of Jewish Studies* 3 (1985): 31–35. (Hebrew)

———. "On the Prohibition of Eating with a Gentile." *Sidra: A Journal for the Study of Rabbinic Literature* 5 (1988): 131–148. (Hebrew)

Stern, Menahem. *Greek and Latin Authors on Jews and Judaism*. 3 vols. Jerusalem: Israel Academy of Sciences and Humanities, 1976.

Stern, Sacha. *Jewish Identity in Early Rabbinic Writings*. New York: Brill, 1994.

Stowers, Stanley. *A Rereading of Romans: Justice, Jews, and Gentiles*. New Haven, CT: Yale University Press, 1994.

———. "Greeks Who Sacrifice and Those Who Do Not: Toward an Anthropology of Greek Religion." In *The Social World of the First Christians: Essays in Honor of Wayne A. Meeks*, ed. L. Michael White and O. Larry Yarbrough, 293–333. Minneapolis: Fortress Press, 1995.

Strack, H. L. and Günter Stemberger. *Introduction to the Talmud and Midrash*, trans. and ed. Markus Bockmuehl. Minneapolis: Fortress Press, 1996.

Sussman, Lance J. "The Myth of the Trefa Banquet: American Culinary Culture and the Radicalization of Food Policy in American Reform Judaism." *American Jewish Archives Journal* 57/1–2 (2005): 29–52.

Tabory, Yosef. *The Passover Ritual Throughout the Generations*. Tel Aviv: Hakibbutz Hameuchad, 1996. (Hebrew)

Taylor, Joan E. *Jewish Women Philosophers of First-Century Alexandria: Philo's 'Therapeutae' Reconsidered*. New York: Oxford University Press, 2003.

Tcherikover, Victor A., Alexander Fuks, and Menahem Stern. *Corpus Papyrorum Judaicarum*. 3 vols. Cambridge, MA: Harvard University Press, 1957–1964.

Tomson, Paul J. *Paul and the Jewish Law: Halakha in the Letters of the Apostle to the Gentiles*. Minneapolis: Fortress Press, 1990.

Urbach, Ephraim E. "The Rabbinical Laws of Idolatry in the Second and Third Centuries in the Light of Archaeological and Historical Facts." In *Collected Writings in Jewish Studies*, ed. Robert Brody and Moshe D. Herr, 151–193. Jerusalem: Magnes Press, 1999.

Ullucci, Daniel. The End of Animal Sacrifice. Ph.D dissertation, Brown University, 2008.

Unnik, W. C. van. "Josephus' Account of the Story of Israel's Sin With Alien Women in the Country of Midian (Num. 25:1ff)." In *Travels in the World of the Old Testament: Studies Presented to Professor M. A. Beek on the Occasion of his 65th Birthday*, ed. M. S. H. G. Heerma van Voss, Ph. H. J. Houwink ten Cate, and N. A. van Uchelen, 241–261. Assen, the Netherlands: Van Gorcum, 1974.

Vaux, Roland de. "Les Sacrifices de Porcs en Palestine et dans l'Ancien Orient." In *Bible et Orient*, 499–516. Paris: Les Éditions du Cerf, 1967.

Vermes, Geza. "'He is the Bread': Targum Neofiti Exodus 16:15." In *Post–Biblical Jewish Studies*, 139–146. Leiden, the Netherlands: Brill, 1975.

Veyne, Paul. *Bread and Circuses: Historical Sociology and Political Pluralism*, trans. Brian Pearce. New York: Penguin Press, 1990.

Visser, Margaret. *The Rituals of Dinner: The Origins, Evolution, Eccentricities, and Meaning of Table Manners*. New York: Penguin Books, 1991.

Wegner, Judith Romney. *Chattel or Person?: The Status of Women in the Mishnah*. New York: Oxford University Press, 1988.

Weinfeld, Moshe. "Grace After Meals in Qumran." *JBL* 111/3 (1992): 427–440.

Weinfeld, Moshe and David Rolph Seely. "4Q434. 4QBarkhi Nafshi." In *Qumran Cave 4. XX, Poetical and Liturgical Texts, Part 2*. DJD 29, 267–286. Oxford: Clarendon Press, 1999.

Weingarten, Susan. "'Magiros,' 'Nahtom' and Women at Home: Cooks in the Talmud." *JJS* 59/2 (2005): 285–297.

White, K. D. "Cereals, Bread and Milling in the Roman World." In *Food and Antiquity*, ed. John Wilkins, David Harvey, and Mike Dobson, 38–43. Exeter, UK: University of Exeter Press, 1996.

White, L. Michael. *The Social Origins of Christian Architecture, II: Texts and Monuments for the Christian Domus Ecclesiae in its Environment*. Valley Forge, PA: Trinity Press, 1997.

Wintermute, O. S. "Jubilees." In *OTP*. 2 vols., ed. James H. Charlesworth, 2:35–142. New York: Doubleday, 1985.

Wright, David P. and Richard N. Jones. "Discharge." In *ABD*. 6 vols., ed. David Noel Freedman, 2:204–207. New York: Doubleday, 1992.

Yadin, Azzan. *Scripture as Logos: Rabbi Ishmael and the Origins of Midrash*. Philadelphia: University of Pennsylvania Press, 2004.

Zahavy, Tzvee. *The Mishnaic Law of Blessings and Prayers: Tractate Berakhot*. BJS 88. Atlanta: Scholars Press, 1987.

Zetterholm, Magnus Z. *The Formation of Christianity in Antioch: A Social-Scientific Approach to the Separation Between Judaism and Christianity*. New York: Routledge Press, 2005.

Selected General Index

agriculture, 23, 55n76. *See also* dairy; fruit; grains; olive
ʿam hāʾāreṣ, 116–120, 134, 136, 144–151, 177, 183, 188
apostate, 57n84, 64n104, 79, 140–141, 154–156

baker, 24, 26nn47, 48, 27n54, 28nn57, 58, 30, 85, 112–113, 161
baking, 25–28, 28n58, 30, 85, 90, 109, 110n22, 112–120, 135–136, 160. *See also* bread
banquets, 1, 9–10, 30–33, 41, 91–94, 98, 123–127, 141, 151, 165–169, 180n162
banquets, funeral. *See note above*
banquets, wedding. *See note above*
blood, 50, 63n103, 66, 70, 77, 108n17, 157 *See also* butchery, animal
bread, 17–19, 24–28, 57n84, 58–59, 81, 83–87, 89–90, 108–109, 110n22, 112–120, 124, 133, 136, 158–161, 169–170, 176, 185, 187. *See also* baking; grains; Mediterranean Triad
butchery, animal, 20n23, 79–81, 84, 90, 104, 157–159. *See also* slaughter, of animals

carrion, 68–70, 73, 78, 79nn159, 160, 80n163, 81, 87–88, 140, 156–158. *See also* metonym, food as; purity, food; sacrifice; slaughter, of animals
cheese, 12, 21, 26n48, 84–85, 87–89, 142–143, 183. *See also* dairy

Chef/sous-chef principle, 11–12, 83–88, 106, 112n28, 113–114, 119–121, 139, 153, 160, 186–187, 189
circumcision, 7, 12, 44n30, 64–68, 79, 141, 154–155, 174
converts, 56–57, 61, 65–73, 139, 140n6
cookbooks, 4
cooking, 11–12, 20, 24, 26n48, 38, 77, 81, 84, 90, 104, 108–112, 119–121, 136, 175n145, 177. *See also* baking

dairy, 12, 21, 26n48, 84–89, 141–143, 183
dough. *See* baking

edible identity, 7–8, 52n66, 60, 90, 110, 121, 136, 144, 189. *See also* embodiment; fat; identity; manna; metonym, food as
eggs, 21
embodiment, 11, 35, 38, 45–47, 53, 59–60, 62–63, 65, 68, 72–74, 96, 101, 104n4, 186. *See also* edible identity; identity; metonym, food as
Essenes, 43, 146. *See also* Qumran sect
Eucharist, 29n63, 63

fat, 70–71. *See also* edible identity; meat
fish, 18, 20, 89n192, 142, 174
flour. *See* baking
fruit, 1, 18, 19, 29–30, 171

grace after meals, 99, 100n232, 128, 152n57, 159n81, 176

SELECTED GENERAL INDEX

grains, 17, 18n13, 24, 26, 30, 109, 117, 136
grinding, grain. *See* baking
grape, 18, 29–30. *See also* wine

ḥabēr. *See* ʿam hāʾāreṣ
ḥăbûrāh. *See* Passover
heretic, 79–80, 154–158, 161
honey, 19, 22, 59
hostels. *See* inns
hunting, 23–24

identity, 1–13, 15, 34, 35–37, 41, 44–51, 53, 55–63, 65–68, 72–77, 83, 86, 89–90, 93, 95, 97–98, 100–101, 103–106, 107n15, 108, 110, 113, 115, 120–121, 122n62, 124–125, 127–128, 130, 132, 135–136, 138–141, 143–147, 149–150, 152–154, 156, 158, 161–164, 167, 169, 171, 173, 176, 178, 182–183, 185–191. *See also* edible identity; embodiment; fat; metonym, food as
idolatry, 11, 36, 40n16, 50, 56, 76, 79–83, 88–89, 91–98, 100–102, 111, 117–118, 134, 139, 145, 150, 155–158, 160–161, 186
inns, 23, 180
insects, 20, 142
intermarriage, 11, 37, 83n174, 91, 93–97, 102, 188

kashrut, 68–72, 83
kĕtûbbā, 109, 113, 126

leaven, 26–27, 159–160, 169. *See also* bread
legumes, 18–19

manna, 47, 58–63, 72, 101, 147, 186. *See also* edible identity
markets, 16, 22–23, 27n54, 104n5, 157
meat, 2n4, 9, 12, 16, 19–21, 23–24, 40–41, 43, 47–58, 60, 66, 69n122, 70–81, 84, 94, 102, 111, 122, 132, 140–143, 154–163, 183, 185–186, 190. *See also* butchery, animal; fat; sacrifice; slaughter, of animals

Mediterranean Triad, 24, 29, 81, 83, 86, 98, 102, 186. *See also* bread; olive oil; wine
merchants, 30, 82n173
metonym, food as, 35, 45–75, 160. *See also* edible identity; manna; pork
mills, 25–26, 117. *See also* grains
milk. *See* dairy
minors, 77–78, 80, 125, 128–131, 166–167, 173

nevēlāh, 67n121, 78
Noahide Laws, 70–71
nuts, 22

olive, 18, 28–30
olive oil, 18, 28–30, 81, 86–89, 190. *See also* Mediterranean Triad
ovens, 28, 112n28, 119. *See also* baking

Passover, 13, 27n55, 47, 61, 63–68, 72, 98, 101, 128–130, 132, 160, 162–170, 186–187. *See also* identity; sacrifice
Pharisees, 42n25, 134, 147n32, 175
pig. *See* pork
pork, 9, 16, 21, 47–58, 72–73, 80, 101, 140–141, 143, 160–161, 190. *See also* edible identity; metonym, food as
purity, food, 2, 12, 37, 40n17, 76n148, 78, 91n201, 109n21, 110–112, 115–119, 135–136, 139, 146–148, 151–153, 179n157, 182, 187–188. *See also* edible identity; metonym, food as
purity, menstrual, 108, 114, 132–133, 136. *See also* zābîm

Qumran sect, 43, 90, 99n229, 146

Sabbath, 13, 18, 19, 23, 32, 78, 112n28, 127–128, 140, 162, 171, 174–178, 183, 187. *See also* identity
sabbatical year, 119
sacrifice, 44, 47, 51–53, 63, 65, 68, 71, 76, 87–88, 92, 94–95, 100, 121, 129–130, 132, 161–162, 166, 170. *See also* carrion; purity, food

salt, 22, 26
Samaritans, 47, 79, 154–155, 158–161, 176
sinew, 71–72. *See also* edible identity; kashrut
slaughter, of animals, 24, 51, 69n122, 75, 77–81, 84, 90–91, 121–122, 132, 139, 154–161, 166, 183. *See also* butchery, animal; carrion; purity, food; sacrifice
slaves, 64, 71, 99, 128–131, 166–167, 172–173
spices, 22, 26, 119
staples, dietary, 17, 24, 74, 81, 88–89, 112. *See also* Mediterranean Triad
Sukkot, 13, 33, 130–131, 162, 170–173, 178, 187
synagogues, 89, 162, 178–183, 188

table talk, 98–105, 132, 169–170, 176–179, 186
ṭerēfāh, 70, 73, 80, 140. *See also* carrion
Terefah banquet, 1. *See also* kashrut
tithes, 112–113, 115–116, 119, 148, 151, 177–178, 183

vegetables, 9, 15, 18–20, 38

wine, 1, 18, 24, 29–31, 39, 81–83, 86, 88–89, 92, 95–96, 140, 164, 166, 172, 174–177. *See also* Mediterranean Triad

Yom Kippur, 78

zābîm, 132–135. *See also* purity, menstrual

Index of Pre-Modern Sources

Hebrew Bible

Daniel 1:5–16, 37n6
Daniel 1:12–16, 19n18, 38n8
Deuteronomy 6:4–9, 135n105
Deuteronomy 12:15–27, 77n152
Deuteronomy 12:21, 79n161, 155n63
Deuteronomy 14:6–8, 48
Deuteronomy 14:8, 49n51
Deuteronomy 14:21, 68n121, 141n15, 157n75
Deuteronomy 14:28–29, 24n40
Deuteronomy 15:23, 77n152
Deuteronomy 16, 122n60, 173n138
Deuteronomy 22:11, 141n10
Deuteronomy 23:4, 124
Deuteronomy 23:5, 124
Deuteronomy 24:6, 118n49
Deuteronomy 24:19–22, 24n40
Exodus 12, 160n83
Exodus 12:4, 163n92
Exodus 12:7, 164n96
Exodus 12:43, 155n66, 64n104
Exodus 12:43–49, 64
Exodus 12:46, 163, 164
Exodus 12:48, 66, 67
Exodus 13:17, 61
Exodus 13:18, 61n95
Exodus 13:22, 133n98
Exodus 16:4, 59, 62n100
Exodus 16:4–5, 58n89
Exodus 16:15, 59, 60n91
Exodus 16:16, 59

Exodus 16:31, 59
Exodus 23:19, 141n15
Exodus 34:15, 79n160, 92, 94
Exodus 34:15–17, 94
Exodus 34:17, 94, 134n101
Exodus 34:26, 141n15
Ezekiel 41:22, 100n234
Ezekiel 44:31, 68n121
Genesis 9:3–4, 38n8
Genesis 32:23–33, 71n131
Genesis 32:33, 71
Isaiah 28:8, 100n233
Isaiah 46:1, 56n82
Isaiah 65:4, 50
Isaiah 66:3, 50
Isaiah 66:17, 50
Judges 14, 91
Leviticus 7:22–27, 70
Leviticus 7:24, 69n122
Leviticus 11:3, 48
Leviticus 11:7, 49n51
Leviticus 11:40, 68n121
Leviticus 12:6, 112n60
Leviticus 15, 133n95
Leviticus 17:10–14, 77n152
Leviticus 17:15–16, 68, 69n122
Leviticus 19:9–19, 24n40
Leviticus 19:19, 141n10
Leviticus 22:8, 69n122
Leviticus 23:22, 24n40

INDEX OF PRE-MODERN SOURCES

Leviticus 23:42, 130, 170n124, 171
Numbers 5:2–3, 133n95
Numbers 9:1–12, 66n113
Numbers 11:7–9, 58n89
Numbers 15:18–20, 27n54
Numbers 21:16–20, 61n96
Numbers 21:18, 61n96
Numbers 25:1–3, 95
Proverbs 31:15, 109n21
Psalm 106:28, 95n213
Song of Songs 1:2, 88
Song of Songs 1:3, 88

Second Temple Literature, Apocrypha, and Pseudepigrapha

1 Enoch 89:12, 56n78
1 Maccabees 1:44–50, 51n58
1 Maccabees 1:47, 52n66
2 Maccabees 6:18–7, 42, 50
2 Maccabees 15:39, 19
3 Maccabees 3:4, 42n23
3 Maccabees 6:30–40, 42n23
3 Maccabees 7:20, 180n162
4 Maccabees 5–18, 50n57
The Acts of Paul and Thecla 25, 38n8
Addition to Esther C 28, 39n10
Dead Sea Scrolls
   1QS 6:16–23, 118n51
   4Q434, 99n229
   CD VI:3–4, 61n96
Joseph and Aseneth 7:1, 39n13
Joseph and Aseneth 10:13, 39n14
Joseph and Aseneth 20:8, 39n14
Joseph and Aseneth, 21:6, 32n78, 127n74
Joseph and Aseneth 21:8, 39n14
Josephus
   Contra Apion 2:137–142, 52n64
   Contra Apion, 2:148, 44n31
   Contra Apion 2:173–174, 43n28
   Contra Apion 2:174, 43n28
   Contra Apion 2:258, 44n31
   Jewish Antiquities 4:126–151, 95n213
   Jewish Antiquities 4:137, 73n139
   Jewish Antiquities 4:137–139, 43n28
   Jewish Antiquities 4:139, 73n139
   Jewish Antiquities 5:289, 32n78, 127n74
   Jewish Antiquities 12:120, 86n184
   Jewish Antiquities 12:160–236, 42n25
   Jewish Antiquities 12:253–256, 51n58, 52n66
   Jewish Antiquities 13:243, 51n58, 52n66
   Jewish Antiquities 13:289, 42n25
   Jewish Antiquities 14:214–216, 181n163
   Jewish War 2:591, 86n185
   Jewish War 3:50, 21n27
   Jewish War 5:269–270, 51n61
   Jewish War, 6:423–425, 162n91
   The Life 74, 86n184
   The Life 279, 30n70
Jubilees 22:16, 40n16
Judith 10:5, 39n11
Judith 12, 123n64
Judith 12:1–4, 39n11
Judith 12:17–20, 39n12
Letter of Aristeas 128, 41
Letter of Aristeas 130, 41
Letter of Aristeas 139, 40
Letter of Aristeas 142, 40
Letter of Aristeas 142–155, 49n48
Letter of Aristeas 153–155, 49n48
Letter of Aristeas 181–202, 41n21
Philo
   De Fuga et Inventione, 137–139, 59
   De Mutatione Nominum, 258–260, 59n90
   De Specialibus Legibus 2:148–149, 166
   De Specialibus Legibus 4:101, 55n77
   De Specialibus Legibus 4:106–108, 49, 55n77, 60
   De Virtutibus 143–144, 142n16
   De Vita Contemplativa, 123n64
   De Vita Contemplativa 37, 174n139
   De Vita Mosis 2:41, 42n21
   In Flaccum 95–96, 51n59
   Legatio ad Gaium 361–363, 55
   Legum Allegoriae III 175–176, 59n90
   Quaestiones et Solutiones in Exodum 1:10, 166n102
Pseudo-Philo 10:7, 61n96
Tobit 1:10–13, 39
Tobit 7–10, 32n78, 127n74

Rabbinic

Avot d'Rabbi Natan A16:13–17, 73n136
Avot d'Rabbi Natan A26:6, 91n201, 92n205
b. Avodah Zarah 2a–3b, 173n137
b. Avodah Zarah 8a, 91n201, 92n205
b. Avodah Zarah 14a, 92n202
b. Avodah Zarah 31b, 188n4
b. Avodah Zarah 35b, 188n4
b. Avodah Zarah 36b, 188n4
b. Avodah Zarah 37a, 87n185
b. Avodah Zarah 38a–b, 111, 122n61
b. Bava Qamma 82b, 55n76
b. Berakhot 35b, 86n183
b. Berakhot 47b, 148n39, 152n57
b. Eruvin 29b, 20n21
b. Gittin 61a, 148n39
b. Hullin 64b, 21n27
b. Ketubbot 7b–8a, 32n78
b. Ketubbot 67b, 19n18, 20n23
b. Megillah 12b, 101n237
b. Pesahim 42a, 20n21
b. Pesahim 49b, 111n26, 152n57, 153
b. Pesahim 91a, 128
b. Qiddushin 66a, 42n25
b. Sanhedrin 104b, 92n203
b. Shabbat 13a, 133n97, 135n104
b. Sotah 22a, 148nn39, 40
b. Sukkot 29a, 173n136
b. Yevamot 63a, 113n32
b. Yevamot 77a, 124n66
Esther Rabba 3:13, 101n237
Genesis Rabba 17:3, 113n32
Genesis Rabba 21:9, 104n5
Genesis Rabba 355, 73n139
Gerim 4:1, 56n82
Kutim, 160n83
m. Avodah Zarah 1:1–3, 23n35
m. Avodah Zarah 1:3, 92n202
m. Avodah Zarah 2, 82n170
m. Avodah Zarah 2:5, 87
m. Avodah Zarah 2:6, 84n175, 86, 87n186, 89n192
m. Avodah Zarah 2:7, 89n192
m. Avodah Zarah 3:4, 141n13
m. Avodah Zarah 4:8–9, 29n66

m. Avodah Zarah 4:8–5:11, 82n170
m. Avodah Zarah 5:3, 82n172
m. Avodah Zarah 5:5, 82
m. Avot 1:1, 3n9, 97n222
m. Avot 3:2, 100n234
m. Avot 3:3, 100
m. Avot 3:10, 148n40, 152n56
m. Bava Batra 2:3, 26n47
m. Bava Batra 4:5, 29n60
m. Bava Batra 9:5, 32n78
m. Bava Metzi'a 2:1, 85n180
m. Bava Metzi'a 3:27, 18n15
m. Bava Metzi'a 4:10, 73n136
m. Bava Metzi'a 4:11–12, 30n69
m. Bava Qamma 7:7, 55n76
m. Berakhot 3:4, 135n105
m. Berakhot 3:6, 135n105
m. Berakhot 6:6, 31nn73, 75
m. Berakhot 7:1, 99n229, 100n232, 159n81
m. Berakhot 7:1–5, 31n73
m. Berakhot 7:2, 128n80
m. Berakhot 8:1, 176n149
m. Berakhot 8:7, 176n147
m. Berakhot 8:8, 176
m. Betzah 3:1–2, 23n39
m. Betzah 5:2, 175n145
m. Betzah 5:4, 26nn49, 51, 27n52, 110n22, 115n39
m. Betzah 5:7, 168n111
m. Bikkurim 1:3, 18n14
m. Demai 2:2, 150n47
m. Demai 2:3, 150–151
m. Demai 3:4, 26n47
m. Demai 3:5, 23n37, 109n21, 119n55
m. Demai 3:6, 109n21, 119n55
m. Demai 7:1–2, 151n53, 177n153
m. Eduyyot 2:4, 21n27
m. Eduyyot 3:10, 28n58
m. Eduyyot 4:1, 142n17
m. Eduyyot 5:2, 66n114, 142n17
m. Erubin 3:1–8, 172n131
m. Erubin 6:6, 177n15
m. Erubin 6:6–7, 172n131
m. Erubin 7:6, 177n151

INDEX OF PRE-MODERN SOURCES

m. Gittin 5:9, 115n37, 117n47, 145n27
m. Gittin 9:10, 113n32
m. Hallah 1:1, 17, 21n54
m. Hallah 1:4, 17n10
m. Hallah 1:6, 17n10
m. Hallah 1:7, 28n58, 112n29
m. Hallah 2:3, 116n43
m. Hallah 2:7, 27n54, 32n78, 104n5, 112nn28–29, 113n32, 127n76
m. Hallah 3:1, 26n49, 28n56, 172n131
m. Hallah 3:5, 85n179
m. Hallah 4:1, 110n22, 116
m. Hullin 1:1, 78n156, 79n160, 155n65
m. Hullin 2:4, 68n121, 69n122, 79n159
m. Hullin 2:9, 77n152, 157n74
m. Hullin 5:3, 20n23
m. Hullin 7:6, 71n130
m. Hullin 8:1, 142n18, 183
m. Hullin 8:5, 79n159, 88n191
m. Kelim 15:2, 28n56, 116n44
m. Kelim 15:3, 26n48
m. Kelim 15:4, 26n48
m. Ketubbot 1:5, 32n78
m. Ketubbot 1:10, 86n181
m. Ketubbot 5:5, 26n47, 109
m. Ketubbot 5:8, 17n6, 127n78
m. Ketubbot 5:9, 17n6, 123n64, 127, 178n154
m. Ketubbot 7:5, 126
m. Ketubbot 7:6, 28n58, 107n15, 109n19, 113
m. Ketubbot 9:4, 113n32
m. Makhshirin, 118n51
m. Makhshirin 2:8, 85n180
m. Makhshirin 2:9, 85n180
m. Makhshirin 5:11, 109n21
m. Makhshirin 6:2, 17n9
m. Megillah 1:5, 175n145
m. Menahot 5:2, 27n53, 28n56
m. Menahot 8:4–5, 28n60
m. Menahot 8:6, 29n65
m. Mo'ed Qatan 3:7, 32n79
m. Nedarim 2:1, 140n8
m. Nedarim 3:10, 47
m. Nedarim 8:6, 47n42
m. Nega'im 2:4, 28n56

m. Nega'im 3:2, 32n78
m. Niddah 9:3, 110n24
m. Niddah 10:7, 27n54, 116n44
m. Ohalot 5:4, 27n53, 116n43
m. Pe'ah 4:1, 22n29
m. Pe'ah 7:1, 18n14
m. Pe'ah 8:7, 18n12
m. Pesahim 3:3, 27n54
m. Pesahim 3:4, 27n53, 55, 114n35
m. Pesahim 3:7, 32n78
m. Pesahim 7:3, 165
m. Pesahim 7:13, 127n75, 164
m. Pesahim 8:4, 167n110
m. Pesachim 8:7, 128nn81, 82, 167n106
m. Pesahim 8:8, 66
m. Pesahim 9:8, 165n100
m. Pesahim 10, 169
m. Pesahim 10:1, 165
m. Pesahim 10:4, 169n118
m. Pesahim 10:5, 169, 170n120
m. Sanhedrin 2:3, 32n79
m. Sanhedrin 8:2, 141n12, 163n93
m. Shabbat 1:3, 133n98
m. Shabbat 1:4–11, 134n103
m. Shabbat 1:6, 23n39
m. Shabbat 2:6, 113
m. Shabbat 23:1, 112n28
m. Shabbat 23:2, 31n74, 125n71, 128n79, 178n154
m. Shevi'it 5:9, 26nn47, 48, 110n22, 115n37, 117n47, 145n27
m. Shevi'it 7:3, 68n121, 157n76
m. Shevi'it 8:6, 28n60, 29n66
m. Shevi'it 8:10, 58n84, 84n176, 160
m. Sukkah 2:4, 172n131, 178n156
m. Sukkah 2:5, 172n132
m. Sukkah 2:6, 172n132
m. Sukkah 2:8, 130, 131n88, 172n133, 173n138
m. Sukkah 2:9, 172nn131, 134
m. Ta'anit 1:1, 173n135
m. Teharot 1:7–9, 116n43
m. Teharot 2:1, 109n21
m. Teharot 3:8, 116n43
m. Teharot 4:1, 116n43
m. Teharot 4:10, 26n49, 118n51

m. *Teharot* 7:4, 118n50
m. *Teharot* 7:9, 108n116
m. *Teharot* 8:1, 119n56
m. *Teharot* 8:8, 17n53, 116n43
m. *Terumot* 1:9, 18nn14, 15
m. *Terumot* 2:6, 18n14
m. *Terumot* 5:1–3, 17n8
m. *Tevul Yom* 2:3, 47n42
m. *Tevul Yom* 4:2, 27nn53, 54
m. *Tevul Yom* 4:2–3, 116n43
m. *Tevul Yom* 4:3, 27nn53, 54
m. *Yevamot* 8:3, 124n35
m. *Zabim* 3:2, 117n48, 179n157
m. *Zabim* 4:2, 117n48
Mekilta d'Rabbi Ishmael Bahodesh Yitro 8, 131n87, 171n129
Mekilta d'Rabbi Ishmael Beshelah Vayassa 2, 62n100
Mekilta d'Rabbi Ishmael Beshelah Vayassa 5, 58n89
Mekilta d'Rabbi Ishmael Beshelah Vayehi 1, 61n97, 166n105
Mekilta d'Rabbi Ishmael Bo 8, 17n7
Mekhilta d'Rabbi Ishmael Bo 10, 27nn52, 55, 112n28
Mekilta d'Rabbi Ishmael Bo 15, 61, 64nn104, 105, 67, 155n66
Mekilta d'Rabbi Ishmael Mishpatim Nezikin 18, 56, 72
Mekilta d'Rabbi Ishmael Pisha Bo 9, 130n87, 171n129
Mekilta d'Rabbi Ishmael Yitro Amalek 1, 33n81
Mekilta d'Rabbi Shimon b. Yohai at Exodus 12:4, 28n59, 64n104, 67n116, 68n120, 155n66
Mekilta d'Rabbi Shimon b. Yohai at Exodus 12:16, 130n87, 171n129
Mekhilta d'Rabbi Shimon b. Yohai at Exodus 12:17, 27nn53, 55
Mekilta d'Rabbi Shimon b. Yohai at Exodus 12:22, 103n2
Mekilta d'Rabbi Shimon b. Yohai at Exodus 12:43, 64n104, 155n66
Mekilta d'Rabbi Shimon b. Yohai at Exodus 12:48, 68n120

Mekilta d'Rabbi Shimon b. Yohai at Exodus 12:49, 67n116
Mekilta d'Rabbi Shimon b. Yohai at Exodus 13:17, 61n97
Mekilta d'Rabbi Shimon b. Yohai at Exodus 13:22, 133n98
Mekilta d'Rabbi Shimon b. Yohai at Exodus 16:4, 62n100
Mekilta d'Rabbi Shimon b. Yohai at Exodus 34:15, 79n160
Mekilta d'Rabbi Shimon b. Yohai at Exodus 34:17, 94, 131n101
Pesiqta d'Rav Kahana 6, 92n204
Sifra Aharei pereq 12:1, 69n124
Sifra Aharei pereq 13, 56
Sifra Behar pereq 7, 30n67
Sifra Behuqotai pereq 5, 32n78
Sifra Emor 12:4, 130n87, 171n129
Sifra Emor 17:5, 130n87, 171
Sifra Emor parasha 13, 28n60
Sifra Emor pereq 4, 28n59
Sifra Mesora parasha 5, 32n78
Sifra Qedoshim pereq 6, 32n79
Sifra Sav pereq 15 *parasha* 10:1, 71n129
Sifra Shemini parasha 1, 18n15
Sifra Shemini pereq 12:8, 154n60
Sifra Tazria pereq 5, 32n78
Sifre Deuteronomy 235, 113n32
Sifre Deuteronomy 249, 124
Sifre Deuteronomy 354, 73–74
Sifre Numbers 71, 61n94, 67n118
Sifre Numbers 87, 58n89
Sifre Numbers 110, 26n49, 28n56, 32n78, 113n32, 116n43, 127n76
Sifre Numbers 115, 121n59
Sifre Numbers 131, 95, 121n59, 134n101
t. *Ahilot* 2:1, 80n164
t. *Ahilot* 5:11, 27n53, 116n44
t. *Avodah Zarah* 1:1–18, 23n35
t. *Avodah Zarah* 3:10, 148n39, 149, 151n52
t. *Avodah Zarah* 4:6, 91, 92n202, 93–94, 98
t. *Avodah Zarah* 4:8–10, 82n170
t. *Avodah Zarah* 4:11, 84, 87n186, 112n28
t. *Avodah Zarah* 4:12, 82n170
t. *Avodah Zarah* 7, 82n170

t. Avodah Zarah 7:1, 29n66
t. Avodah Zarah 7:3–5, 29n66
t. Avodah Zarah 8, 82n170
t. Avodah Zarah 8:4–8:8, 70n126
t. Avodah Zarah 8:6, 70n126
t. Bava Metzi'a 3:25, 73
t. Bava Metzi'a 3:26, 18n15
t. Bava Metzi'a 8:7, 27n53, 28n58
t. Baba Metzi'a 8:28, 32n78
t. Bava Qamma 10:9, 26n47
t. Berakhot 4:8, 31–32
t. Berakhot 4:10, 32n77
t. Berakhot 4:11, 31n72
t. Berakhot 4:19, 127n75
t. Berakhot 5:12, 17n10
t. Berakhot 5:21, 99n230
t. Berakhot 5:28, 28n59
t. Berakhot 6:2, 26n46, 32n77, 125n71
t. Berakhot 6:11, 158n78
t. Demai 2:2, 70n126, 150n47, 151n50, 152
t. Demai 2:12, 150n48
t. Demai 2:15, 151n50
t. Demai 2:16–17, 151n50
t. Demai 2:24, 70n126
t. Demai 3:3, 159n81
t. Demai 3:5, 151n50
t. Demai 3:6, 151n52
t. Demai 3:7, 125n69, 151n53
t. Demai 3:9, 151n50
t. Demai 4:31, 109n21, 119, 120n58
t. Demai 4:32, 23n37, 109n21, 119n55
t. Demai 8:4–5, 151n53, 177n153
t. Eduyyot 2:2, 28n59
t. Hagigah 1:2, 77n154
t. Hallah 1:2, 17n10
t. Hallah 1:7, 113n32
t. Hallah 1:11, 28n56
t. Horayot 1:5, 57n84, 140, 141n11, 143, 154n61
t. Hullin 1:1, 79, 154, 155n64, 156n70, 157, 159n82, 160
t. Hullin 1:2–3, 80
t. Hullin 1:3, 77n154
t. Hullin 2:6, 85n180
t. Hullin 2:9, 69n122
t. Hullin 2:19, 157n73

t. Hullin 2:20, 79n160, 155nn62, 66, 160
t. Hullin 5:3, 157n72
t. Hullin 6:4, 157n72
t. Hullin 7:3, 157n76
t. Hullin 7:8, 71
t. Hullin 7:9, 70n126, 72n132
t. Hullin 8:1–3, 142n18
t. Kelim Bava Qamma 4:17, 109n21
t. Ketubbot 7:4, 26n47, 110n22, 115n38
t. Ma'aserot 2:20, 178
t. Ma'aserot 3:13, 179n53
t. Makhshirin 1:8, 85n180
t. Makkot 4:1, 164n98
t. Makkot 4:7, 142n18
t. Megillah 1:7, 175n145
t. Megillah 1:14, 132n94
t. Megillah 2:18, 178, 179n157, 181
t. Megillah 3:14–15, 32n78
t. Megillah 3:15, 163n93
t. Mo'ed 2:17, 32n79
t. Niddah 6:9, 26n47
t. Parah 10:3, 88n190
t. Pe'ah 4:8, 18–19, 174n142
t. Pesahim 3:5, 27n53
t. Pesahim 3:7, 27n53
t. Pisha 2:1, 26n47, 86n181, 159, 160n83
t. Pisha 2:1–3, 159, 160n83
t. Pisha 2:3, 160n85
t. Pisha 2:15, 86n181
t. Pisha 3:8, 27nn53, 55, 114n35
t. Pisha 3:12, 32n78
t. Pisha 4:7, 167n107
t. Pisha 6:11, 129n84, 164–165
t. Pisha 7:6, 167n108
t. Pisha 7:7–8, 167n108
t. Pisha 7:8, 167n110
t. Pisha 7:9, 168n115
t. Pisha 7:10, 167n110
t. Pisha 7:11–8:1, 67n116
t. Pisha 7:13–14, 66
t. Pisha 7:15, 168n115
t. Pisha 7:16, 167n109
t. Pisha 7:17, 168n111
t. Pisha 8:4, 67n116
t. Pisha 8:6, 128, 167
t. Pisha 9:1, 167n107

218 INDEX OF PRE-MODERN SOURCES

t. *Pisha* 10:1, 165n100
t. *Pisha* 10:4, 29n64
t. *Sanhedrin* 4:2, 32n79
t. *Sanhedrin* 11:6, 163n93
t. *Shabbat* 1:14, 123n64, 133n98
t. *Shabbat* 1:15, 134n102, 152n57
t. *Shabbat* 1:16–23, 134n103
t. *Shabbat* 7:9, 32n78, 127n76
t. *Shabbat* 7:20, 69n122
t. *Sheqalim* 3:20–21, 68n120
t. *Shevi'it* 5:8, 68n121, 157n76
t. *Shevi'it* 5:9, 84n175, 88n189
t. *Shevi'it* 6:28, 29n66
t. *Sotah* 3:10, 130n87, 171n127
t. *Sukkah* 1:8, 173n136
t. *Sukkah* 2:2, 172n132
t. *Sukkah* 2:4, 173n136

t. *Teharot* 8:3, 151n49
t. *Teharot* 8:4, 117n48
t. *Teharot* 8:7, 151n49
t. *Teharot* 8:16, 108n16
t. *Teharot* 9:1, 119n56
t. *Teharot* 9:2, 151n49
t. *Terumot* 8:16, 142n18
t. *Terumot* 9:5, 21n27
t. *Yevamot* 1:11, 110n23
t. *Yom Tov* 2:5, 28n58
t. *Yom Tov* 4:6, 26n51, 27n52, 110n22, 115n39
t. *Yom Tov* 4:10, 125, 168n111
t. *Zavim* 2:5, 21n27
y. *Demai* 2, 22d, 152n56
y. *Pesahim* 8:8, 36b, 66n115
y. *Ta'anit* 4:5, 68c, 55n76

Early Christian Literature

I Corinthians 10:4, 96n61
I Corinthians 10:20–22, 82n170
I Corinthians 10:23–30, 76
Acts 10:28, 43n27
Acts 15:19–20, 70n126
Clement of Alexandria
    Paedagogus 2.19.3, 63n103
Council of Ancyra
    Canon 7, 92n205
Council of Elvira
    Canon 50, 97n224
Galatians 2:11–21, 43n27
John 2:1–5, 32n78, 127
John 6, 63n103
John 6:41–59, 62n98
John 6:56, 63n103
John 6:58, 60n91

Justin Martyr
    First Apology 66, 63n103
Luke 6:1, 17n8
Luke 8:26–39, 55n77, 185n1
Luke 11:12, 21n27
Luke 11:37–41, 147n32
Luke 22:15–16, 163
Mark 2:23, 17n8
Mark 5:1–20, 55n77, 185n1
Mark 7:3–4, 147n32
Matthew 8:28–34, 55n77, 185n1
Matthew 12:1, 17n8
Matthew 23:25–26, 147n32
Romans 14, 77n150
Romans 14:3, 38n8
Tertullian
    Ad Nationes 1.13, 175

Greek and Roman Literature

Arrianus
    Dissertationes I:22:4, 52n64
Celsus Philosophus
    The True Doctrine, 52n64
Damascius
    Vita Isidori 227, 52n64
Diodorus Siculus
    Bibliotheca Historica 34/35.1.2, 44n29

Bibliotheca Historica, 34/35.1:3–4, 51n58, 52n66
Hecataeus
    Aegyptiaca, apud: Diodorus Siculus, *Bibliotheca Historica* 40.3.4, 44n31
Herodotus
    History 2:47, 52n64

INDEX OF PRE-MODERN SOURCES

Juvenal
  Saturae 6:160, 54n73
Macrobius
  Saturnalia 2:4:11, 54n74
Origen
  Contra Celsum 5:41, 52n64
Petronius
  Fragmenta no. 37, 54n72, 141n9
Persius
  Saturae 5:179–184, 174
Philostratus
  Vita Apollonii 5:33, 44
PGM I:105, 52n65
PGM IV:3007–3086, 52n65

Plutarch
  Quaestiones Convivales 4:5:2, 54n71
  Quaestiones Convivales 6:2, 171n125, 175n143
Porphyry
  De Abstinentia I:14, 52n64
Sextus Empiricus
  Hypotyposes 334:222, 52n64
Tacitus
  Historiae 5.5.1, 44n30
  Historiae, 5.5.2, 44n30, 97n221
  Historiae, 5:4:1–2, 54n71
Varo
  On Agriculture, 2:4:3, 55n76

Selected Index of Modern Scholars

Alexander, Philip S., 155n62
Allison, Anne, 46n39, 105n8, 114, 115n40
Alon, Gedaliah, 143n22
Appadurai, Arjun, 4, 50n55, 75n144
Armelagos, George, 138n3

Baker, Cynthia M., 25, 104n5, 115n41
Barclay, John M. G., 42nn22, 23, 43n28, 44nn32, 33, 45n35, 86n184
Barthes, Roland, 6n23, 8, 9n32
Baumgarten, Albert I., 42n25, 43nn27, 28, 44n33, 90n197, 146n29, 147n32
Beard, Mary, 3n6
Belasco, Warren, 138n3
Bell, Catherine, 161n89
Bentley, Amy, 103n1, 119n40
Betz, Hans Dieter, 52n65
Bickerman, Elias J., 39n10
Blenkinsopp, Joseph, 50nn52, 53, 56n82
Bokser, Baruch M., 162n91, 166n103, 169, 170n121
Borgen, Peder, 60n91
Bourdieu, Pierre, 46, 75n146, 78n158, 90, 105n15, 108n17, 139, 141n14
Boyarin, Daniel, 4n10, 50n56, 128n83, 147n35, 155n67, 169n119
Brillat-Savarin, Jean Anthelme, 6n23
Brooks, Roger, 18n13
Broshi, Magen, 17n6, 18n15, 29nn62, 63, 30n67
Brubaker, Rogers, 5n17

Brumberg-Kraus, Jonathan, 62n102, 100n235, 154n60, 163n94, 169nn116, 117, 170nn120, 122
Bryan, David, 56n78
Bynum, Caroline Walker, 63n103, 75n145, 96n219, 105nn6, 8

Cohen, Shaye J. D., 7, 10, 35n1, 36–37, 43nn26, 27, 44nn30, 33, 64n108, 65n109, 91n199, 109n19, 111n26, 121n59, 152n55, 154n60, 170n124, 181n163
Collins, John J., 37–38, 39n10, 42n23
Cooper, Frederick, 5n17
Cooper, John, 16n5, 26n46
Corley, Kathleen E., 33n82, 123n64

Dalby, Andrew, 17n6, 26n50
Dar, Shimon, 17n6, 18n15, 19nn16, 18, 20nn19, 23, 21n24, 26nn46, 47, 50, 28n60
Davidson, James N., 105n8
de Light, L., 22n34
Dickie, John, 24n41
Diemling, Maria, 47n42
Diner, Hasia R., 6n23, 46n29, 75n144, 133n100, 138
Douglas, Mary, 8–9, 38n7, 48n46, 118n51, 133n100
Dunbabin, Katherine M. D., 31n71

Eilberg-Schwartz, Howard, 64n108, 135n106

SELECTED INDEX OF MODERN SCHOLARS 221

Eliav, Yaron Z., 82n173, 90nn196, 197

Fabre-Vassas, Claudine, 58n86
Farb, Peter, 138n3
Feeley-Harnik, Gillian, 146n60
Feldman, Louis H., 53n70, 54n75, 162n90, 174nn139, 142, 175nn143, 144
Fessler, Daniel M. T., 2n4, 76
Fischler, Claude, 15n1, 45nn36, 37, 54n75, 58
Flandrin, Jean-Louis, 9n33, 48n46, 75n144
Fonrobert, Charlotte Elisheva, 65n109, 106n10, 108n17, 114n36, 141n14, 143n21, 189n5
Frankel, Rafael, 28n60, 29nn61, 66
Freidenreich, David Moshe, 4n11, 36n3, 37n5, 38, 40n16, 41n21, 42n24, 43nn26, 27, 44n29, 45n34, 50n56, 76n148, 78n158, 79n159, 80nn163, 165, 166, 82nn170, 173, 87n186, 88nn190, 191, 89n192, 92nn204, 205, 93n207, 97n224, 98n225, 124n65, 134n103, 156, 168, 184n172
Friedman, Shamma Yehudah, 13n40, 114n35, 128n83, 169n119
Fuks, Alexander, 32n79, 180n162

Gardner, Gregg Elliot, 18n12, 23n38, 24n40, 125n70
Garnsey, Peter, 18n11, 19n18, 20n23, 24n41, 25n42, 32n69, 55n76, 105nn6, 7, 112n29
Gilders, William K., 66n112
Ginzberg, Louis, 56n78
Goldberg, Abraham, 13n39
Goldenberg, Robert, 174nn139, 140, 175n145
Goodman, Martin, 86n184, 87, 155n67, 156n69
Goody, Jack, 77n151, 105n8, 112n29, 133n100
Goshen-Gottstein, Alon, 121n39
Grantham, Billy, 21n25, 55n76, 81
Gray, Alyssa M, 3n7

Grossfeld, Bernard, 64n104
Grottanelli, Cristiano, 18n15, 52n65, 53
Gruen, Erich S., 51n59, 54n75, 180n162, 181n163

Hamel, Gildas, 16n5, 17nn6, 9, 18nn11, 13, 99nn16, 17, 18, 20nn19, 20, 21, 23, 21nn24, 27, 22nn28, 30, 32, 33, 23n39, 29n62, 30n67, 47n43
Harrington, Hannah K., 148n37, 153n59
Harris, Marvin, 2n4, 9, 20n23, 48nn45, 46, 190
Hartog, François, 47, 75n146, 76n147
Harvey, Warren, 121n59
Hauptman, Judith., 128n83, 169n119
Hayes, Christine E., 40n17, 41n21, 66nn114, 115, 76n148, 91n201n92, 94n211, 132n94, 141n14, 143nn21, 22, 144, 145, 152n56, 189n5
Hecker, Joel, 62n99, 100n234
Henten, Jan Willem van, 50n56, 163n94
Hesse, Brian, 55n76
Hezser, Catherine, 33n81
Hirschfeld, Yizhar, 25n45, 26n47, 28n58, 119n56
Hoenig, Sidney B., 86n184

Ilan, Tal, 108n16, 128n83, 169n119

Jaffee, Martin S., 49, 60n92, 65n109, 141n14, 147n32, 152n54, 175, 189n5
Jay, Nancy, 62n102, 121–122, 130, 132, 137, 164
Joselit, Jenna Weissman, 4n13

Kaplan, Marion A., 4n13, 35n1
Kraemer, David, 5n14, 21n25, 51, 56nn80, 81, 73n138, 86n183, 98n228, 138n2, 142–143
Kraemer, Ross Shepard, 39nn13, 14, 103n2, 126n72, 127n74, 128n79
Krauss, Samuel, 16n5, 17n7, 19nn16, 18, 20n19, 21nn24, 27, 22nn30, 32, 23n39, 26n47, 48, 50, 27n53, 28nn57, 58, 60, 29nn65, 66, 174n142

SELECTED INDEX OF MODERN SCHOLARS

Lapin, Hayim, 22n34, 33n81, 103n3, 159n80
Lauterbach, Jacob Z., 56n82
Lehman, Marjorie, 128n83, 131nn89, 90, 92
Lev-Tov, Justin, 20nn22, 23, 21n26, 55n76
Levtow, Nathaniel B., 36n2
Lévi-Strauss, Claude, 38, 76n148, 77, 118
Levine, Lee I., 32n79, 33n81, 76n148, 111n26, 117n48, 147n36, 152n55, 154n60, 166n105, 179, 180n162, 181nn163, 164, 165
Lieber, Andrea, 60
Lieberman, Saul, 26n47, 125n68, 158n78
Lieu, Judith M., 41n20, 50n57

MacClancy, Jeremy, 10n35, 25n44, 133n100
Magness, Jodi, 181n166
Malina, Bruce J., 60n91
Marks, Susan, 123n64, 127n77
Martin, Matthew J., 179n159, 180n160, 181n164
Mason, Steve, 7n26, 37n4
McGowan, Andrew, 22n33
Menirav, Joseph, 22n34, 23nn35, 36, 25n43, 26n47, 28nn57, 60, 30n69, 89nn193, 194, 112n28, 181n167
Milgrom, Jacob, 49n51, 68n121, 70n125
Miller, Stuart S., 146n31
Montanari, Massimo, 8, 9n33, 48n46, 77n151, 168
Murray, Sarah, 16n3

Naguib, Nefissa, 4n13
Nakhimovsky, Alice, 4n13
Naveh, Joseph, 32n78, 127n76
Navarrete, Carlos David, 2n4, 76
Nelson, W. David, 62n101, 79n160
Nemeroff, Carol, 45n36
Neusner, Jacob, 13n39, 56n82, 69n123, 71n129, 82n171, 122n63, 147n32, 148n37, 150n47, 151n50, 181n166, 182n169
Novak, David, 70n126

Ohnuki-Tierney, Emiko, 6n23, 17n6, 46, 74, 89n195, 96n219, 144n24, 189n6
Olyan, Saul M., 64nn104, 107, 68n121, 76n148, 93n208, 132n94, 153nn58, 59
Oppenheimer, Aharon, 76n148, 117n48, 134n102, 147n36, 148–149, 152nn56, 57, 163n92, 179n157

Peskowitz, Miriam, 10n37, 103n2, 104n5, 106, 108n18, 109n20
Pollan, Michael, 15n2, 25n44
Porton, Gary G., 82nn172, 173, 90n196, 122n63, 159

Roller, Matthew B., 31n75, 33n82, 123n64
Rosenblum, Jordan D., 36n2, 46n40, 49n50, 56n78, 86n184, 89n195, 91n198
Rosenfeld, Ben-Zion, 22n34, 23nn35, 36, 25n43, 26n47, 28nn57, 60, 30n69, 89nn193, 194, 112n28, 181n167
Rosenthal, David, 87n187, 92n202
Rozin, Paul, 15n2, 45n36, 144n24
Rubenstein, Jeffrey L., 130n87, 131nn88, 90, 170nn123, 124, 171n126, 128, 172, 173nn135, 136, 137

Safrai, Ze'ev, 13n39, 18nn13, 15, 19nn16, 18, 20n19, 21nn24, 25, 22nn30, 31, 32, 34, 23nn38, 39, 28n60, 29nn62, 65, 30n70
Saldarini, Anthony J., 42n25, 147n32
Sanders, E. P., 43n27, 54n71, 147n32, 148n37, 166nn101, 103, 104
Sarason, Richard S., 109n21, 119n54, 150nn46, 48, 151n51, 177n153, 178n155
Satlow, Michael L., 3n7, 32n78, 73n137, 91n200, 95n215, 96n217, 97, 103n3, 104n4, 106–107, 109n19, 121n59, 122n63, 127n76, 131n89, 132n93, 140n5, 168n113
Schäfer, Peter, 52, 56n82, 82n173, 96n217, 103n3, 155n67, 174n139
Schatzki, Theodore R., 5, 6nn21, 22
Schiffman, Lawrence H., 43n27, 118n51
Schlosser, Eric, 25n44, 74n143

SELECTED INDEX OF MODERN SCHOLARS 223

Schwartz, Seth, 16n5, 50n56, 64n108, 82n173, 89, 95n216, 135n106, 141n14, 149n42, 150, 181nn163, 166, 182n168
Sheerin, Daniel J., 63n103
Sheraton, Mimi, 58
Simoons, Frederick J., 46n39
Siporin, Steve, 4n13
Soler, Jean, 9n33, 48n46, 146n29
Smith, Dennis E., 31nn71, 75, 32n79, 33n81, 70n126, 77n150, 98n227, 123n64, 127n73, 146n29, 147n32, 163nn92, 94, 169n116
Smith, Jonathan Z., 182
Stein, Siegfried, 169n116
Steinfeld, Zvi Aryeh, 84n173, 87n186, 91n201, 92nn203, 205,
Stern, Menahem, 32n79, 52nn64, 66, 54n74, 56n78, 171n126, 174nn140, 142, 180n162
Stern, Sacha, 3n5, 5, 7, 57n84, 65n110, 72, 74, 80, 93, 95–96, 98n226, 99n231, 101n236, 106, 107n15, 108n17, 113n31, 140n6, 140n11, 144n23, 145, 156
Stowers, Stanley, 28n8, 52n63, 107n14
Sussman, Lance J., 1nn1, 2, 3

Tabory, Yosef, 163n92, 169n116
Tcherikover, Victor A., 32n79, 180n162
Tomson, Paul J., 82n173, 92n204

Urbach, Ephraim E., 95n216
Ullucci, Daniel, 52n63, 84n178

Vaux, Roland de, 50n54
Vermes, Geza, 60n91, 86n184
Veyne, Paul, 125n70
Visser, Margaret, 168n112

Wapnish, Paula, 55n76
Wegner, Judith Romney, 109n20, 127n78, 128–129
Weingarten, Susan, 25n42, 26n48, 27n54, 28n58, 104n5, 109n20, 112n29, 114n35, 118n49, 120n57

Yadin, Azzan, 107n13, 183n171

Zahavy, Tzvee, 99n229
Zetterholm, Magnus Z., 42, 43nn26, 27, 180n162, 181n163

Printed in Great Britain
by Amazon